To

Auntie Jill & Un

Love

from

Sharon   (age 2 82)

anchorbooks

BRITISH ISLES
POETS 2006
Today's Poets Today

Edited by
Heather Killingray

anchorbooks

First published in Great Britain in 2006 by:
Anchor Books
Remus House
Coltsfoot Drive
Peterborough
PE2 9JX
Telephone: 01733 898102
Website: www.forwardpress.co.uk

HB ISBN 1 84418 423 4

Designed by Tim Christian

Foreword

For over ten years now, we have been producing regional anthologies of the best poetry we receive. This year, once again, we have found the task of selecting the poems for our anthology a difficult but immensely enjoyable one. Out of the thousands of entries received we chose the very best to go into *British Isles Poets 2006*. Our final selection of poems are as diverse as the people who wrote them.

Contained within, you will find the poetic voices inspired by those wonders we hold closest to our hearts: hills and valleys, rivers and streams, architecture and art and the people around us; our beautiful countryside and vibrant cities provide us with a wealth of inspiring and enticing images.

Whether we reside in the calm and picturesque surroundings of the countryside or the hectic and absorbing world of an inner city, we can all find stimulation and ideas that produce our best verse.

Thus, we present to you, a showcase of outstanding poetry, a collection of today's up and coming poets, alongside those more established poets who have shared with us, over the years, the joy that is poetry.

Heather Killingray

Editor

Prize Winning Poem

Congratulations to Dorothy Buyers from Shropshire whose poem, 'Images', has been chosen by our panel of editors as top poem in this collection. She wins the prize of a fantastic, luxury *Lewis & Cooper Deluxe Hamper*.

The *Lewis & Cooper Deluxe Hamper* is a selection of the finest food and drink presented in a lidded wicker picnic basket with leather straps.

The winning poem can be found on page 420.

Contents of Authors

Name	Page	Name	Page
Harry Weinert	219	Eileen Coates	242
Sonya Nikolosina (17)	220	Barbara A Winter	243
Welch Jeyaraj Balasingam	220	Alan Millard	243
L Molisho	221	Pearl Williams	244
Mark Hutchines	221	L A G Butler	244
Kerry-Anne McChlery	222	D G W Garde	245
Lauren Rassam	222	Sheila Cheesman	245
Roger N Taber	223	Patricia Morris	246
Rajeev Bhargava	223	S M Thompson	246
Kenneth Buckley	224	D C Mundell	247
Liza Jones	224	Eric Hart	248
Scholastica Bennin-Sam	225	Marlene Parmenter	249
Greater Manchester	**225**	**Herefordshire**	**249**
Darren Scott	225	Ann Thompson	249
Sean Ian Riley	226	Jim Lawes	250
James Oliver Moon	226	Mike Thorne	251
Pauline Mayoh-Wild	227		
David McConville	227	**Hertfordshire**	**251**
A P Richardson	228	Ruth Berry	251
Anita McErlean	228	Norman C Edwards	252
Allan Ball	229	Neil Mason	252
James Ayrey	229	Joseph T M Nthini	253
Elizabeth Thorpe	230	Pat Murray	253
Vanessa Alvarez	230	Christine Hardemon	254
		A J Barton	254
Gwent	**231**	James McBeath	255
P Hoddinott	231	Robert Henry	255
Simon Jones	231	Jasmeet Sagoo	255
Samuel Edwards	232	Kevin Raymond	256
Gordon Andrews	232	B J Benton	256
John Horton	233		
Matt Powell	233	**Inverness-shire**	**257**
Camille Metcalfe	234	Sarah L Grigor	257
D T Baker	234		
		Isle of Man	**257**
Gwynedd	**235**	Violet M Corlett	257
Wyn Williams	235	Carlos Phillips	258
Chris Barnes	235	B Lockyer	258
Clifford Jones	236	James Stephen Cameron	259
Beryl Elizabeth Moore	236	Shireen Markham	260
Hampshire	**236**	**Isle of Wight**	**260**
Mary Plumb	236	Vera Morrill	260
Jennifer M Trodd	237	Will A Tilyard	261
Rebecca Penfold	237	Julia Perren	261
William G Thomas	238	Barry Jones	262
Claire-Lyse Sylvester	239	T C Hudson	263
Lucy Campbell	240	Charlotte Harris (13)	263
L Warwick	240	Frank Bedford	264
M Reichlin	241		
Martin Selwood	241		
Lisa Read	242		

Aisha Opoku (18)	321	Robert D Hall (12)	348
Mary E Wain	322	Pamela Evans	349
		Willard Griffiths	349
Lincolnshire	**322**		
Nigel Lloyd Maltby	322	**Midlothian**	**350**
Deanna Dixon	323	Norman Bissett	350
Ann Elizabeth Bruce	323	William Lightheart	350
Charlotte Whitehouse (10)	324	E Pomeransky	351
Stephanie Lynn Teasdale	324	Caroline Carson	351
Gilly Jones	325		
Louise Chafer	325	**Morayshire**	**352**
Paul Birkitt	326	John Fraser	352
John W Skepper	326		
Joanna Malone	327	**Norfolk**	**352**
Vera Hankins	328	Kate Ransom	352
Sharon Grimer	328	Anita Richards	353
Len Woodhead	329	Jean Reynolds	353
Jenny Bosworth	329	Wendy Webb	354
Jane Johnson	330	Betty Nevell	354
Iris E Covell	330	Hazel Gladding	355
W J Oliver	331	B Lockwood	355
Harry Cooper	332	Katrina West	356
		Nina Bates	357
Merseyside	**332**	Isabel Pierce	357
Donna Parry	332	Sian Jenkins (16)	358
Tom Roach	333	Dave White	358
Freda Grieve	333	Sarah Evans-Wrench	359
Mark Ainslie	334	Barbara Robinson	359
John Smurthwaite	334	Carrie-Ann Hammond	360
Florence Bullen	335	E S Peaford	361
Frankie Shepherd	335	Emma Jane Lambert	362
Jim Anderton	336	R Claxton	363
Barbara Hampson	336	Maggie Hickinbotham	363
Ann Blair	337	Gary Miller	364
Pauline Scragg	337	Hazel Cooper	364
K Thompson	338	Alan J Morgan	365
David Bridgewater	338	Margaret Jowsey	366
Martine Corrigan	339	Andrea McDermott	367
Vanessa Dineen	340	S J Robinson	368
G R Bell	341	Steve Glason	368
Greeny	341	A G Revill	369
Judy Dix	342	Paul Harris	369
Joan Thompson	342	Shaun Cook	370
Joan Peacock	343	Suzanne Reeves	370
		Chris Preston	371
Mid Glamorgan	**344**	Paulie Pentelow	371
K D Benson	344		
Brian Lamont	344	**Northamptonshire**	**372**
Celia G Thomas	345	Rodney Pope	372
Grahame Garfield Evans	346	Diana R Cockrill	372
Jean Parry	346	Nancy M Harris	373
Mike Hayes	347	Brian Norman	373
A T Williams	348	David Whitney	374

Maureen Margaret Huber	517
Kamini Manivasagam (13)	517
John H Foley	518
Stella Bush-Payne	519
Brenda Dove	519
Susan Guy	520
Elisha Mesquitta	520
P M Stone	521
Gemma Steele	521
Garry Bedford	522
Seeyam Brijmohun	522
John Hiron	523
M Watts	523
Vinothini Manivasagam (14)	524

West Sussex   **524**

Elysee Rafot	524
Ida Petretta	525
Karen Langridge	525
Ivan Sepp	526
Anna Green	526
Mike Wenham	527
Roger Tremethick	527
Dan Sewell	528
June Marshall	528
Veronica Charlwood Ross	529
Idris Woodfield	529
Peter Lacey	530
Paff-Pafford	530
Gordon E Miles	530
Joseph Brough	531
Sophie Bridger	531
Gavin O'Mally-Richardson	532
Vyna Broom	533
C MacNaughton	533
Leslie de la Haye	534

West Yorkshire   **534**

Anthony O'Sullivan	534
Richard Birch	535
Kevin Whittington	535
Frankie Gaynor-Archer	536
Christine Blayney	536
Amanda Simpson-Cleghorn	537
Janet Harrison	537
Barbara Roberts	538
Kauser Parveen	538
Selena Jayne Marsh	539
Alison Dobson	539
Pauline Boncey	540
Christine Stevens	540
Ian Lowery	541
Ruth Markinson	541

Rachel Inhester	542
Pauline Phillimore	542
Eva Harper	543
Sophia Eason (10)	543
Les Luxton	544
Louisa Smyllie	544
Graham Hare	545
Lorna Lea	545
Jay Whittam	546
Daryl Leslie	546
Donna Wyles	547
Kathleen M Scatchard	547
Terence Leslie	548
Anita Cooling	548
Tim Harvey	549
Mary C Clarke	549
John Roberts	550
Pauline Pickin	551
Ramandeep Kaur (17)	551
Angela Bradley	552
Brenda Artingstall	552
Lesley Elaine Greenwood	553
Susan Barker	553
Melissa Muchemwa	554
Taranom Movahedi	554
Andrew Gruberski	555
H H Atkinson	555
Tony Beeby	556

Wiltshire   **556**

Maddie Reade	556
Kathleen Allen	557
John Wiseman	557
Margaret Ward	558
Raymond Barber	558
Martyn Leroy	559
Susan Turner	559
Sarah Langridge	560
Pamela Carder	560
Kathleen C White	561
Deborah Hall	561
Alison Adams	562
Ann Wardlaw	562
Daniel Golby	563

Worcestershire   **563**

Rita Hardiman	563
E M Eagle	564
Tina Garrington	564
Dorothy M Mitchell	565
John Peaston	565
Helen Dalgleish	566
Bryony Freeman	566

THE
POEMS

Paulo Mintio - Superstar

A football manager on a shaky peg
Looking out for newer players.
Sees foreign imports from abroad
As the answer to his Premier prayers.

Plucked from Italia Seria C
A winger of some little skill.
Built up in his agent's mind
As someone who could pay his bills.

So with slicked back hair, designer shades
Paulo Mintio meets the British press.
Who ask about his model wife
His car, his cash and mode of dress.

No mention of his two left feet,
His dodgy knee, and no one wonders
Why he hasn't scored for 16 months
And is sometimes prone to basic blunders.

His lack of pace, poor fitness rate
Doesn't seem to bother them at all
And being Italian, he crosses himself
More than he ever crossed the ball.

The manager justifies the cost
He'll be a credit to our game.
He must be better than home-grown lads
He's got a fancy foreign name!

Russell Adams
Aberdeenshire

Escape The Nothingness

Every moment without you
Is like an ever increasing black hole
And I can't escape the nothingness
Until once again you are home

And in my arms
Holding you so tight
It's moments like these
I wish would last forever

I get sheer joy
Simply from holding your hand
And to see your smile
Sends my heart soaring high above

You comfort so easily
Effortless you never are
With you by my side
I know that all will be right

And it's you only
Who helps me escape the nothingness
The black hole disperses
You light up my life

Elaine Donaldson
Aberdeenshire

Mr Chalk And Mrs Cheese: The Wine-Tasting Party

'Niver his there been sic an unco perr
as the twa o' thaim standin o'er there.
Dinna leuk taewards thaim jist yet
onless ye wunt a leuk as soor as vinaigrette!
As fir him, I'm shuir ei hauled hir oot o' the loch.
Nae gee tae critters o' the watter. Och
weel, we better gang hin afore we chitter
tae daith in 'is cald norlin wither.'

Lik a sleeve oan a bishop's chimere
the cupple niver agane did appear
onless afore a reflecktive surface
stood Mrs Gossipmonger an' Mr Gormless.

Sharon Reaper
Aberdeenshire

Weald

Wild horses danced with sprightly charm
Whilst snowflakes softly fell
Christmas trees and woeful robins
Pheasants and shrubs of myrtle green

Chestnut mares and stallions grey
Mystical, wavering song chorus
Scarlet-red holly berries and festive mistletoes
A scene of whimsical hippodrome whiffle

Whimbrels plaintive calling sounds
Whilst westerly welkins rang
Wizened ferrets and wiry weasels
Wealded weaning holy land

Woodpeckers pecking at wizened trees
Sawdust and wilting wood sorrel
Astonishment, wisdom and wonderment
Woodbine, honeysuckle and fruitless wrangle

Elfin in their peaked orange caps
Pixies in yellow silk dresses
Wooden beads and leather strap bracelets
Lost bridle of parting sorrow

Gina A Miller
Aberdeenshire

Miss Ailidh

M agic moments, laughter and fun
I ndeed all of these, stated above
S unny natured, happy, a delight in our lives
S imply the best is your sunniest smiles

A ilidh your name is, and always will be
I deally your life will be happy and carefree
L oving you always, you light up our days
I n all that you do, such fun in your ways
D aring and adventurous, your whole life ahead
H appy times little one, no more to be said.

Sheila Macdonald
Aberdeenshire

Temperamental Fools

Peril and danger lie within suspicious circumstances
and high-strung temperamental fools are hidden out of sight,
from the smell that often lingers with the rotting vegetation
and the semi-conscious mind of a novelist's imagination.
Whose journey of illusion treads the rocky path to Hell,
to battle with the darkness and Gothic love, as well.
To pierce the soul and drink the blood from Satan's silver bowl,
to rejoice and kiss his parted lips, with religious self-control.

As if a ghost ascending from the vaults, with a cross hung from his chest,
that swung just as the Reaper's scythe, collecting one more guest
to dine and gorge on madness, in the castle drunk on war,
where terror reigned and nightmares were lavished and endured
by sacrificial lovers, whose emotions were bizarre.
Who danced naked under moonlight and the reflection of the stars.
To cast shadows on the wastelands, before the new sun rose
and the sexually charged frustrations of the vampire overflows,

with tired and breathless honour, in a workshop fuelled by lust.
In a cut-throat world where a handshake is never based on trust
or moral obligation, where weakness is exposed,
that's not the kind of loving that a vampire needs or knows.
So woe betide the ancient curse, written by the scholar's hand,
as when the midnight bell doth toll again, the vampire will demand.
The hand of one, the blood of two and a reason to break free
from the temperamental fools who thought . . .
                                    that vampires could not be!

Alan Glendinning
Aberdeenshire

If We Could Rule The Heart

If we could rule the heart
How easy life could be
No more anguish, hurt and longing
Surely then we'd by happy?

We could let the head take charge
We could let it take the lead
Pick the safest path
Choose not what we want but what we need

There'd be no more sleepless nights
No more pillows soaked in tears
No more waiting for the phone to ring
No uncertainties or fears

The nice guy would get the girl
Life could go on being safe
We could stand still for a moment
And step out of life's fast race . . .

But then we wouldn't get that feeling
When your heart misses a beat
When he walks into your life
And sweeps you off your feet

We wouldn't get that feeling
When reason walks out the door
And every day's a good one
'Cause with him nothing matters anymore

We wouldn't again feel giddy
With the mere memory of a kiss
And all the things that come with love
Which we would have to miss

So which is it to be
Listen to the head or to your heart?
I think I'll take my chance in life
And follow my foolish heart.

Kenna Blackhall
Aberdeenshire

Loch Saugh

Paradise is only miles away,
From an intoxicated motorway,
Weaving an aimless concrete scar,
Jam-packed by truck and bus and car,
Across this land.

Tree clad undulating hills,
Conceal conspiring streams who spill,
Their waters to a sculptured glen,
Patiently carved in an ice age time,
Long passed

Loch Saugh, now brimful resides,
In an unblemished countryside
Of heather slope and crag on high,
Touching a summer's azure sky,
This perfect day

Mirror surface is blemished by,
The skim of mating damsel fly,
And wary trout who quietly break,
The meniscus of this solitary lake,
For beetle and midge

Pristine white, the stately swan,
Glides in presidential form,
Proclaiming this haven as his own,
Before a cloth-capped fisherman,
Who stands alone

William McLellan
Aberdeenshire

The Few

They flew;
Like birds into the sun,
Carving a graceful arc across the sky,
Until death,
Speeding from the reeking barrel of a gun,
Tossed the twisted metal,
Back to Earth.

They fought;
Outnumbered by their foe
Seeking freedom in a vast
And restless sky,
For their loved ones far below
And others not yet born -
You and I.

They died;
Because they believed
That life is ours and ours alone to choose,
They live,
In memory, no longer grieved,
For did they not bestow the greatest gift
Any man can give?

Donald Ferguson
Angus

Vacomage Angus

Angus consists of the How of Strathmore, the Angus Glens, and flatlands.
The Sidlaw Hills encircle and protect this rich area of Scotia,
It is a place synonymous with an ancient people and culture - the Celts.
It is a place protected by the Celtic god of love - Dagade,
He is also an emissary to the fairy world.

The Celtic culture was emulsified with Christianity,
Creating a rich belief system - Celtic Christianity.
The Christian monks settled in Angus and developed the farming,
At Arbroath Tironension Grey Monks, Cuper Angus White Monks,
At Restenneth by Forfar Augustinian Black Canons resided.
Reformation brought further agricultural developments.

Nature's supermarket, the glens, and flatlands of Angus.
Soft fruits, cereals, and vegetables grow in abundance,
Meat, fowl, venison does well from the land.
Fish, shellfish and mussels come from the sea on Angus' shores.
Bannocks, Athol brose, chappit tatties, rumbled thumps, biscuits, tarts and jam.
Boiled beef, mutton, venison, hough, haggis Scotch pies, smokies, soused herrings.

The seasons in Angus are conducive to food production.
The winters are long and cold, fields blanketed in frost and snow.
The deep frosts purify the land ready for the next season.
Each winter the bugs, which could rob Angus of its riches are killed.
Hot humid summers ripen the bounty of Angus,
The beasts of burden and food fatten on the super abundance of Angus.

The glens and flatlands of Angus have spawned many great people,
Writers, artists, scientists, military men,
Knowledge, artistry and scientific advancement have been added to the wealth of Angus.
From the colleges and university sprout the next great?
The lifeblood of Angus is its land.
The embodiment of Angus is its people.
The future of Angus lies in both and its multiculturalism.

Ian R Matthews
Angus

Coal Dust Street

And he saw it now and then
the lamplit row of houses that
stretched beyond the eye
houses where men who dug black
slept and drank when they could

ageless cobbles pried on
men who fought in the street
over want, women and work
while little men sons played
foolish games of childhood

daughter women with prams
mothered their plastic dolls
and the wives gossiped about
young Sally who had a belly
by John Stout the butcher boy

the Reverend Ellis knew
all the stories and chapters
of life in this coal dust street
he birthed them, baptised them
married and buried them

and the street was quiet
no vehement voices tonight
as the deed of death
slipped over the cobbles
and gripped a sleeping soul.

George Carle
Argyll

Mull Of The Bens And Sea Caves

Drift of the mist-blue harebell
In the breeze-blown grasses
By the cuckoo woods,
And wild strawberries
Peeping at the track-side.

Tall-masted ships
Anchored in white sand bays,
Curtseying to their reflections
On the turquoise silk of the ocean,
While out at sea
The currents quarrel beneath rocks
Where the grey seals lie.

Peat, and the heady tang of myrtle
Sharp in the evening air.
And rushes,
Charcoal - etched at sunset
Against a lime-green luminosity
That denotes the horizon.

And sea-fire -
That diamond glitter
On flat calm water where no sun is,
That foretells freshening wind.

Mull of the Bens and sea caves,
And thrift on the tideline
Mull of a thousand moods
In a single day.

Frances Reed
Argyll

A Bedtime Prayer

This is the end of another day,
For me it has been good,
But before I close my eyes in sleep,
A prayer of thanks I must include.

First I pray for family,
In their care I have no fears,
So bless each one with health and strength,
Lots of joy, not many tears.

Thanks are due for nature's beauty,
The trees, the birds and flowers,
Eyes to see and ears to hear,
Such pleasures fill our hours.

Then I pray for our troubled world,
Full of desperate need,
For all those souls who are so lost,
Ask God that He should heed.

My final prayer is for myself,
That I be given skill,
To play a much, much bigger part
In the doing of His will.

Margaret Findlay
Argyll

Happiness

hello there universe where have you been
a zillion miles away dying it seems
plenty of starving human beings at our core
pity we do nothing enough to give more
in your empty soul the devil shall rule
now gone is your life you miserable fool
everyone guilty for eternity of greed
so enjoy your inhumane evil deed
show mercy to god from the tree to the weed

Corinna Angelina Jayne Pinniger Rose McNeillie
Ayrshire

Grief Encounter

When he and she walked by
I knew I'd rather die
Than lose my self possession
So I gave my best ostrich impression.

To maintain a cool decorum
It was better to ignore 'em
As I passed them I strode tall
(Eighteen inches high in all!)

I must slash the ties that bind
Make my heart obey my mind
He no longer will exist
I'll strike him from my Christmas list!

If my life's a void, I'll fill it
If my love won't die - I'll kill it.
The inquest has to show
That *I* dealt the mercy blow.

Let the requiem be said
As the dead inter the dead
No mourners please - just me
Send no flowers -
                    RIP

Maureen Dawson
Ayrshire

Yorkshire

Wild, rugged, but beautiful Yorkshire.
Green rolling hills and dales, with
meandering rivers, where heron fish
and bovine drink.
Lonely farms and dry stone walls.

Stream trains chug across purple heathered moors,
dotted with sheep roaming freely.
Cascading waterfalls flow over rocks down to tea-coloured becks.

Coasted and market towns, rural villages and York's great city,
Skeletons of once majestic monasteries and castles,
stand to remind us of our rich history.

Liz Osborne
Bedfordshire

Texting

To celebrate my brand new job
I bought a new mobile phone
A smart bit of kit costing quite a few bob
And much cooler than the old one at home.

A vibrating sensation gave me a pleasant surprise
As the polyphonic tune blared out
With hands-free wires obstructing my eyes
I started to talk, then shout.

'Can you hear me?' I yelled in my dulcet tones
'I'm on hands-free, so my phone isn't near.'
'No need to scream,' my young son groaned
'Mum your voice is perfectly clear.'

When I got home, I found the messages bit
Create message came up on my screen
Then a stupid underlined word appeared on it
Then lots more. I just sat and screamed.

CUL8r M8 was immediately displayed
What was my friend telling me?
Not English at all - I was completely dismayed
I would reply then wait and see.

See you later mate was the message sent back
With *LOL* at the end
This almost gave me a panic attack
As I believed that we were just good friends.

Texting again, I explained very clearly
That *Lots of love* was not my cup of tea
Reply came back, *Laughing out loud*
Bet now she was laughing at me!

Jo Sinfield
Bedfordshire

My Garden

The garden is a tidy mess
all that grows is in distress.
The grass is brown,
the nettles green,
the brambles wild
as e'er you've seen.
A footpath marches past the pond.
It's derelict, the water's gone.
The moss grows fine,
and ever thicker.
I cut the ivy
but it just grows quicker.
I lop the trees with a wobbly saw,
until my arms can take no more.
The shed has a window
that looks like a hole.
The washing line's held
by a right dodgy pole.
My garage is leaking,
so it's money to spend.
I'm off to the bank
to see what he'll lend.
There's a rickety fence
that's buckled and bent.
The wind gently blew,
and over it went.
We've bought some new panels
and posts and cement,
from a DIY store we
too often frequent.

Bill Surman
Bedfordshire

Sick As A Parrot

We have a parrot, his feathers are green,
He's the funniest bird we have ever seen.
Being so fat he cannot walk,
So far we have not heard him talk.
He came to us from across the sky,
With so few feathers he cannot fly.
Perched on the table I watch him feed,
It's grapes and apple, he don't like seed.
In the cold draught he sits and shivers,
I think he once belonged to Long John Silver.

E Fensome
Bedfordshire

Gardening

What is more enthralling
Than nurturing God's plants?
Pricking out the seedlings,
Providing for their wants,
Watering and feeding,
Watching them grow with care,
Planting for colour and fragrance
In the sunshine and fresh air.

We can work together
To make our little plot
A place for us to sit and dream
Or sunbathe when it's hot.
A place for conversation
With family and friends.
A place infused with colour,
Where beauty never ends.

When I think of Heaven,
Wondering how it will be,
I hope it is a garden
With every flower and tree.
I hope it is a haven
Where I'll forever be
With all the pets and loving folk
Who have meant so much to me.

Doreen Lawrence
Bedfordshire

Let Us Reflect

With each season the plants, trees and crops grow
It's a phenomenon we accept and get to know.
What if they did not rotate as we expect nature to perform
Surely we would wonder why this is not the norm?
With all the impurities in the air and soil, do we consider it a shame?
Do we think that somehow Man may be to blame?
We now know what may be causing some of this pollution
We also know we may have a solution.
But, do we dare think we are possibly the reason
As we look for something better season to season?
Our material wealth is not necessarily to the world's gain
Can we go on like this, it must be insane?
So let us reflect not only on our discoveries and gains of the years
But also reflect on the toil of others - on their pain and tears.
So let us stop and also reflect on how far we go
Then offer help to those unfortunates and let it show!

Peter Parbery
Berkshire

Disaster Zone 2005

The bad events we hear about
Make us want to scream and shout
Earthquakes, floods and yet more war
Just what are we all living for?

The gloom and doom surrounding us
Our daily squabbles and silly fuss
Seem unimportant when millions die
And we, mere mortals, wonder why.

The worst will always bring out the best
When we are finally put to the test
Catastrophes may instantly unite
Those people who continually fight.

Could it be ourselves to blame
For global warming, the eternal flame
Our hearts and minds are stubbornly closed
To thoughts of change we are opposed.

Yet change we must for those who follow
Or else our existence is but hollow
We cannot ignore the devastation
To many of the world's great nations.

What will it take to make us see
The need to change our philosophy?
For we are only as particles of sand
On a shifting and ever-subsiding land.

M Payne
Berkshire

My Bad Dream

I'd won the lottery, or so I thought.
On Saturday afternoon, the ticket I'd bought.
The numbers called, matched the ones I'd got.
No one else claimed, I'd won the lot.
And then to my dismay.
My treasured ticket had gone astray.
It must have gone in the rubbish bin.
To lose it there, was such a sin.
I threw my arms up in the air.
Because alas, I could not find it there.
I sat down and cried, I was in despair.
The bottom dropped out of my old armchair.
I panicked, and started to scream,
And then I awoke, it was just a dream.

William G Evans
Berkshire

Twenty-Four The Number

I said goodbye long ago
The person I saw, I didn't know
The change in you was too much to bare
So I locked you away, but I did really care
You weren't someone who I could relate to,
That's how I coped and saw it through
Even now I can't believe you have gone
To the better place up near the one
I prayed for you so much in the past
But time stood still, it didn't last
I got through the service, we said goodbye,
People can't understand why I haven't cried
But inside the water flows, on my own
All alone,
I thought of the number twenty-four
When they closed the curtain and the door
Bingo you enjoyed so much
But you didn't have good luck
I have one last thing to do right now
Look after my father, keep him safe somehow.

Jan Nice
Berkshire

Bracknell In Bloom

I drive to the town centre, and there in the central reservation are cornucopias of flowers.
I park in my habitual slot, and walk past the Bracknell in Bloom advertising towers.
I purchase some cakes, some food and drink from Marks and Sparks,
Check my balance at the cashpoint, and go to Ottakers for a book on local parks.
I sit upstairs in the coffee shop, the balcony dripping in bundles of colour,
Seeing the flower poster on the wall, makes the place seem less duller.
I read the newspaper intently,
I gave up on the book, local parks, not any!
It's time to pick up the kids from school,
I will have to take them to the local pool.
I walk past the huge towers of flowers,
If I had all day, I could stay in town for hours!
'Mummy where have you been today?'
'Oh nowhere special, just around,' I say.

Emma Lockyer
Berkshire

Larks Ascending

Beneath a mass of threatening cloud,
I'm wrapped against the forecast snow
As I stride out across Larkshill.
Below, the streaming vehicles groan
Down Harvest Ride and on to town.
Yet here, above the traffic's drone,
Comes birdsong over tussocked grass -
Too far to carry from the hedge
But clear above the gusting blast.

Casting about this grassy space
I spot them, dots against the sky,
Riding in air too cold for snow,
Braving this February day.
Whilst others shelter in the hedge,
These tiny crested, feathered scraps
Defy the world that winter brings.
Miraculous, daredevil birds
Sing out a challenge and a prayer:
An invocation to the spring.

Patrick Osada
Berkshire

Trust

There is a stillness.
Not the stillness of calm - but tension.
The waters build behind the logs.
To the un-tutored eye they are chaotic.
The jam looks set to last forever.
But 'this too shall pass'
One log will move.
A man steps confidently on the logs
Carrying an implement elegant in its simplicity
Also carrying years of experience.
He looks and listens
Observing small sounds and movements.
Just a tiny shift
A tiny shift of one log: one aspect
One aspect of a tangle of thoughts
And the dammed, damned river of emotion will be free.
Free to roar through canyons under rainbow spray
Free to feel fingertip branches fondle its ripples
Free to linger through reed bed and sun-drenched plain.
Free, at last, to merge with the great sea
In an infinite expansion of unity with nature.

Barrie Singleton
Berkshire

Sane

It starts off with a boxing match,
She throws in the punches first,
I rebuke her in defence,
Throwing fuel into the fire,
I make things worse.
Practically, she called me,
All the names under the sun,
I try to convince myself,
She never meant all the things,
She said and done.
Powerless, unable to swallow my tears,
I search someone to blame,
Father was the one! Who sent us to boarding school,
That must have driven her into sane.
But why am I the opposite?
Immune to all the challenges,
All the challenges in the world except this.

There's a cause for concern,
She refuses to admit,
I go into hibernation,
This grief is tearing me into bits.
A secret I dare to tell,
They'll label her as a loony,
Hospitalise her in a cell,
Drugging her with Prozac,
That will drown her in more confusion,
This I cannot hack!
Her new personality she'd adopted,
It's so hurtful and unkind,
Negative thoughts unskilled in speech,
Destruction has invaded her mind.

Shazia Kausar
Berkshire

Wimbledon 2005

(Phrases used by commentators and the thoughts they provoked)

'His feet were in the wrong place'
(Were they growing on his arms?)

'She has found her legs'
(Where did she leave them?)

'He needs to get his teeth into the match'
(Hope he won't bite the dust)

'Difficult to tell whether they are going to a final or a funeral'
(What will they do with the flowers they were given?)

'It's the battle of the grunters and the squealers'
(Where is the pigsty?)

'It has become a shriek marathon'
(Any noise you can make I can make louder)

'It has developed into a first class system of fidgets'
(Who put itching powder in his cap and shirt?)

'Their chips have been producing splinters'
(What would it be like if they played with axes?)

'They cover every inch of the court'
(Are they competing with the team who cover the court when it rains?)

'They have to fight the weather as well as the tennis'
(Where is the Rain Man?)

'That dreadful phrase 'Play is suspended''
(Hang the play? Surely not!)

'It's not over, till it's over'
(Where is the fat lady? Will Cliff do?)

Margaret Nixon
Berkshire

A Momentary Pleasure

Elbows leaning on the rail, I wait
To hear a gentle scratching on the gate.
A greeting trill, and then my cat arrives.
Balancing carefully, risking many lives,
She treads across my sun-tanned skin
And rubs her head beneath my chin,
Then turns, purring loudly all the while
And I begin to smile
And stroke her back and murmur in her ear,
Knowing as I do that it's all her own idea
To show affection as I wait,
Leaning on the garden gate.

Eileen M Lodge
Berkshire

Royal Ascot

York staged Royal Ascot this year,
It was really missed in Berkshire I fear.
The stands on the racecourse were all pulled down,
Men in hard hats invading the town.

They were busy constructing buildings all new,
Grandstands, restaurants to name but a few.
Ascot shopkeepers have felt the pinch,
Pulling their belts in at least half an inch.

Jobs for the locals were not there,
The bookmakers too missed their share.
The fashions we only saw on our screen,
Included the Royal Drive by the Queen.

The horses raced for various cups,
We missed the cream teas and champagne to sup.
Let's hope the schedule can be fixed,
So it can come home by two thousand and six.

Enid Thomas
Berkshire

Thoughts

I often sit and think of days gone by,
Of the fun we had you and I,
We would play and frolic amongst the flowers,
Having such fun for hours and hours,
We would go to the pictures for a penny a show,
A halfpenny of chocolate was a treat you know,
Fish and chips for six pennies we could get then,
And sit up in the gods at the theatre for ten,
Have a day at the seaside that was a treat,
And to go to the zoo was quite a feat,
There was no telly, or cars or trips abroad,
And I'll tell you this, and this is a vow,
I wouldn't change what we had, for what they have now,
Violence and swearing and drugs they do,
No, give me the old days for me and you.

S Derbyshire
Buckinghamshire

Some Folk Live In Motor Cars

(Thoughts on Milton Keynes)

This is the place where houses grow,
This is not the place I used to know.
This is a place where shoppers shop,
It's not the place I'd want to stop.

This is a place called Milton Keynes,
I wonder what that really means,
Milton's books are hardly funny,
Nor was Keynes on jobs and money.

This is the town they call a city
Where they love concrete, such a pity.
There's concrete cows and cowboys
Gridlock aplenty and other joys.

Here's a town of 300 roundabouts
And a glorious future there's no doubts.
Twice the size in thirty years
All will be well, there's no fears.

This is where the tyres squeal, and
Boy racers spin their steering wheel.
Milton Keynes, with lots of crime
But not a trace of factory grime.

Here's a town of office space
A haven for our human race.
Houses grow and jobs will come,
That's what they say, but are we dumb?

Milton Keynes grows on and on,
Devouring all until it's gone.
House prices have reached the stars,
Some folk live in motor cars.

Robert John Cook
Buckinghamshire

Wind And Rain

Now wildly the wind is blowing
Tossing the branches and leaves,
In crazy abundant frenzy
It threatens the sentient trees.
The boughs are creaking and groaning
Wind's winning - trees crash to the earth,
The wind goes on shrieking and howling
In manic diabolical mirth.

The rain falls down in silver spears
Heaven is shedding many tears,
To soften and heal the barren earth,
To end for all that dreadful dearth
At last comes down the blessed rain
To make the country green again.
Thirsty gardens, rill and river,
Wetlands all with joy now quiver.

Ivy Allpress
Buckinghamshire

Untitled

Flying through time
In my time machine
I fly above the views
So serene and fruitful.
I fly above the ocean
And over the hilly cliffs.

I enter a cloud and
Through to the other side.
I can see blue above
And green below
From the window of this
Wondrous time machine.

Now I see a star
As I fly high
Into galactic space.
I'll land my machine, right here
On the moon.

Laura Sansom
Buckinghamshire

Friends

'Old friends are the best friends,'
An old friend said to me,
I pondered on this saying,
As I made a cup of tea,
And whilst I would not argue,
As she'd truly said a fact,
I think that there are good friends,
Even when time passed is lacked.
I know the ones who know us,
Longer through the years,
Are the ones we turn to,
When we need to share our fears,
And their friendship and their caring,
Never can be bought,
For this is given freely,
By true friendship as it ought.
But I'd like to say that any friend,
Is valued and a treasure,
For like the passing of the years,
Good friends one should not measure.

M Wilcox
Buckinghamshire

Yes

The only word,
She understands is 'yes'
No if, buts or maybe,
No time to reflect.

You must fulfil her wishes,
And there is no time to delay,
Although you have your excuses,
They won't get in her way.

She will twist you around her finger,
By just fluttering her eyes,
Then all the plans she has made,
Will start to materialise.

L Roche
Buckinghamshire

Memoirs Of A Lazy Man

Friday night my work is over
Saturday morning I lie in bed
And open my eyes to shafts of
Sunshine lighting up my sleepy head.

Tea in bed to start the day
A gentle time a lazy time!
Choose a book to read in peace
And then my weekend starts to rhyme.

The day goes by, I look around
To find some gentle jobs to do
And take my time to see them through
With idle breaks to form a queue.

Sunday I don't need excuses
I love to play the same refrain
I even make up lots of time
To pass the day at rest again.

Monday at work the hours go by
I sit and long for what I seek
The calculator in my head
Counts the days till the end of the week.

The time drags by and at last I am
Once more at peace, I now can rest
For I know my break is here
And my house knows me as honoured guest.

Royston E Herbert
Buckinghamshire

Twenty-Six Ten

Chase the wind and ride the night,
keep up pace, dreams into sight.

Numbers kabbalah in my mind
26 is 10, creation of time

I sleep awake, time unfolds
old for new, stories told.

This dark season, thoughts embrace.

April when then began a race.

Time is now and now is then
9 is time
26 is 10.

Alan Hedgecock
Buckinghamshire

Ode To Ballymena

Ballymena, a prosperous town upon the River Braid
Throughout its grand history great progress has been made.
The Tower Centre was opened
And also the Fair Hill,
Sainsburys and Tescos and many a cafe
Once named the town of the Adairs,
Who named it Seven Towers
While strolling near the Grange House
Among the lush green fields
And majestic Slemish Mountain where Patrick often prayed.
The moat rises above the town and overlooks the Braid,
The seats of education where many students go,
The Academy and Cambridge House, Ballee Dunclug also.
Our town's been twinned with Moorehead in Kentucky, USA
Where sons from Ballymena built that great land they say.
Of James McHenry we have heard, George Washington's General
Eaton went to Canada a great name there he earned.
And Arthur from Cullybackey, the president of great fame
Sam Houston the Texas hero, from Racavan his people came.

James McIlhatton
Co Antrim

The Pink Flip-Flops

In the midst of nothing
There is a light that shines.
It pierces through the darkness,
And reveals a love so kind.

The miracle of giving
To a soul who seems so lost,
Is a demonstration of such love
Of which there is no cost.

This love provides more than enough,
And meets more than a need.
It is anchored in our hearts -
This love will never leave.

In the midst of nothing
Our Father provides the way.
He is faithfully by our side,
And will forever stay.

Gil
Co Antrim

The Healer

The pale shades of evening
Gather round the mountainside
Where the sick await
The coming of
The young Galilean.
Hush - He comes -
His white robes and dark wavy hair
Caught in the freshening breeze.
He moves among the sick
And at His touch
They are healed!
Some say, 'Is this not Jesus
The carpenter son of Mary?
How can He do these things?'
And I cry,
'Because He is the Son of God!
All power is given unto Him!
I have known His touch
And have been healed!'

Pearl Reynolds
Co Antrim

Gone With The Wind

I watched a sheet of paper blown to and fro,
Along a windswept street about a year ago,
Past doorways, shuttered windows and a flapping gate,
Not a moment did it wait,
An exile from an upturned bin,
In a race it couldn't win,
Just an abandoned piece of waste,
Skipping the pavement in its haste,
Flicking a lamp post as it sped,
Not a single word was said,
Onward, upward at its height,
Soaring like a bird in flight,
Though the evening was drawing nigh,
Underneath a brooding sky,
Over the chimney tops it flew,
As the stars came into view,
Then it settled on a tree,
As the wind it ceased to be,
The stars they twinkled till the dawn,
And even the Milky Way looked on.

William A Smyth
Co Antrim

If

If I could meet my great-great-gran
Some facts of life I'd give,
She'd really be astounded
Just at the way we live.

I'd say if your purse is empty
Do not worry - do not fret,
For the DHSS will help you
And your needs will all be met.

And if you go out shopping
You'll find the bus is free,
Another help along the way
I'm sure you will agree.

You'll get the weekly pension
And a bonus for some coal,
'Twill keep you warm in winter
Sure that's everybody's goal.

Your home will be so cosy
You won't shiver from the cold,
Automatic heat will warm you
Not like the days of old!

And keep your mobile telephone
Ever by your side,
Talk to friends both far and near
Or across the ocean wide.

And there are lots more benefits
Too numerous to say,
That are available for the asking
And will help you on your way.

With all these many comforts
Granny - this I surely know,
You'll want to stay in this old world
And never from it go.

E Thompson
Co Antrim

Time

All the time in the world,
Was given to us
Why do we hurry?
Why do we fuss?
To break the dawn
The morn takes time
Leaving the stars to shimmer behind
And the blackbird tunes in with his chime

The old beggar down the byway of his life
Knows no trouble
Knows no strife
Killing time with misfitting shoe prints
Leading him to where? Nowhere
The sun and moon are his golden stair
Yet he takes time off
To say his prayers

The walk of life
We all must do
One step at a time
Until we reach our crossroads
Then dimmer is the view

The stepping stones of life are laid
We've made our vows
And we have strayed
Along the way loved ones we've lost
Never count the dice
Till it is tossed

Elizabeth McIntyre
Co Antrim

Katrina: The Merciless

I open my eyes, it was not a dream
I am really here, my mind begins to scream
It's been 3 weeks since it came
No one's fault, no one to blame
The flashbacks are just as frequent, as vivid
Where could he be? Is he dead or living?
We made a promise not to let go
I'm on my own, I have to know
The water got so high, the currents strong and fast
So many bodies just floating on past
We thought we were high enough to be safe
Then it came, the strong, merciless wave
The dead lists have come in, I check every one
Not on today, another chance I have won
This could go on for a very long time
I won't give up the search, for that love of mine
I lend a shoulder to a woman in despair
A child she has lost, it's so unfair
Just then I hear a voice, I dared not wish to hear
He's asking about his wife, she had disappeared
It's like I'm in slow motion as I turn around
There's only him in my view, I have no sound
Every step I think I'm dreaming, it cannot be true
We touch, we embrace, it really is you!
I'll never let go again, I swear it here today
I feel that I am blessed in every single way
For our love will keep us safe when we are apart
I no longer have to fear to close my eyes in the dark.

Natalie Astbury
Co Antrim

Just For You

At this moment things look bad,
There may seem no end in sight
To the troubles that surround you,
Each day and darkest night.
Yet life often has a way, of turning things around,
And the day once more will come,
When happiness you will find.
So no matter how fierce the gales,
Nor however dark the storm,
Please know there lies on the path ahead,
A bright and beautiful new dawn,
To each new day ahead.

Nancy Elliott
Co Antrim

Black Widow

She's not particular what it is,
Not particular in her tastes.
Wrapping victims in her web
To keep for later dates.
A trap of awesome beauty,
A filigree of lace.
She waits to savour love that comes,
From the males that she mates.
She'll take all they have to offer,
All they've come to give.
Maybe all that is inside of them,
For she may not let them live.
Her life's true and only pleasure,
Is to take and reproduce,
And she'll take all they bring up to her,
There's nothing she will lose.
Will she keep them here or let them go?
It depends on the mood she's in.
They might be good or they might be food,
Her heart they have to win.
To have them dance or die is up to her,
For she is twice their size,
And if they're not quick,
They only get what happens to the flies.
True black widows really love their suitors,
With passion and with zeal.
For she can hold them tight to herself,
Or take them for a meal.

Albert Whiteside
Co Antrim

Resolve Be

I've never said a word hello,
Have never said goodbye,
I've never looked, at anyone,
And here's my reason why.
You see with eyes I do not have,
You talk with all your might,
That tongue, you may well make of use,
I cry into the night.
You take for granted all around,
This little home, our Earth,
To see with eye, and talk with word,
I've never had from birth.
I'm just one of nature's mix,
Just didn't get it right,
And tried my best but not one word,
No vision with no sight.
But there the story ends for me,
I've discovered my new gifts,
With mighty push and fearless shove,
The gloom from me, so lifts.
I've learned to read, with my aid, Braille,
And learned to knit and sew,
And if you find that life's unkind,
Resolve must have its show.
I'll not be beat with my two feet,
But strive with all my might,
For if you do not have the will,
Then long will be your fight.

Hugh Campbell
Co Armagh

Land Of My Birth

Late lingers my gaze in the hues of the day
To the hills of my homeland, that in loveliness sleep
So fair is the dream to a wanderer, whose way
Still lies far o'er the fathomless deep.

When the shadows of twilight veil the green shore
And perfume comes floating on the soft evening breeze
My heart will take comfort and waver no more
My courage refreshed to conquer the seas!

Then rise my thoughts to the sounds of my land
The harp and the pipes on the fresh wind are borne
Neither hushed nor forgotten is the welcoming hand
With unforgotten welcome, will greet my return!

My back to the swells, to the stars, I resign
My destiny, to guide me o'er ocean and earth
With my soul on fire, my Ulster I'm thine
Your green hills and valleys, the land of my birth.

Isaac Smith
Co Armagh

The Omagh Bombing

What were you thinking when you planted the bomb?
Did you know in your heart the location was wrong?
Did you not think the courthouse was too far away?
Did your courage forsake you, on that terrible day?

What were you thinking when you phoned with your lie?
Did you watch as the crowds slowly moved down to die?
Did you whisper a prayer and implore God's forgiveness?
Did your conscience condone this cold-blooded business?

What were you thinking when the smoke billowed high?
Did you hear all the screams and the agonised cries?
Did you look at the victims, the dead and the maimed?
Did your leader feel pleased with his patriot game?

What were you thinking that night in your bed?
Did you think of the poor little children now dead?
Did you think that such carnage would set Ireland free?
Did your psychopath bombing satisfy all your needs?

GFB
Co Armagh

Ways To Find

Winding through many roads
Fears, regrets, running scared
Buildings, countless oceans spun
Check just one day that's gone
Hustle, bustle, weeks go by
Wasted, hated, gloating pride
Who dares to talk of the glory?
Trying hard that gold to find
Strange how the new comes in time
Forlorn bright tide hangs in
Worlds apart, just not the same.

M Trainor
Co Armagh

Patrick Kavanagh 1904-1967

Forever he stands,
A giant hacked out in blunt relief
Against the little hills of home.
Rough cord, binding
The pagan-coloured cloths.
Larger than life,
Fragile as a neonate.
Wrapped against the harsh winds
That ever seemed his lot to bear.
His voice, gruff.
His unprotected heart, naked.
His eyes looking through time
To Adam and beyond.
Touching a hairy nettle leaf
Pausing, counts its heartbeat.
Through stone, his gaze
Isolates the zygote grain.
His third eye
Reading each soul's deep pain.

A man, who life dishonoured, with disdain.
A poet whose like, will never come again.

Mary Buckley-Clarke
Co Cork

7 Deadlies - Lust

A swishing skirt against bare legs,
a tight and swelling jumper -
that musky scent which sits up and begs
for him to strip, caress and hump her.

Taut T-shirts tracing solid pecs,
trousered outline of his buns,
make her dream about a frenzied feck,
drool over the ways she could be done.

Yet they both have ones who love them -
with whom they yearn to share life.
She has her ideal husband, not him;
he likes her thighs, but he's picked a wife.

That night they lie sweaty and drained -
their loyalty is only dust.
Difference 'twixt Man and beast is brain -
free will to curb the hunger they call lust!

Perry McDaid
Co Derry

Capturing Emotion

Anticipating pleasure
Mind begins to wander
Sweet musk of our love's vapour
Like a shadow in my own life
The real me comes forth
Capturing your emotions
Torturing you mentally
Exciting you physically
Draining your immortal soul
Dying briefly
Till the rushes pass
Grounded
Mind, body, soul, heart.

Jeannie Anderson
Co Derry

Friends Forever

You lift me up when I am down
You are the reason I can smile
Where there is doubt, you give me hope
A friendship for all time
I cherish the day you entered
And came into my life
I thank the angels also
Our friendship is sublime
Never let it be said
That we could hurt each other
I feel a bond so strong
Just like a son and mother
You're very special to me that's true
In oh so many ways
And I hope this goes from strength to strength
And stands the test of time
I will never let you down at all
Or ever let you fall
And you know I'm always here for you
All you have to do is call

N Carruthers
Co Down

Sparkling Illusions

Falling pills in a snowy blizzard,
A frosty mind from the winter's chill,
Looking through the eyes of a lizard,
In the breeze, all is still,
The sweeping flood through my veins,
Turns to a trickling stream of violence,
A torrent of confusion overrulingly sustains,
Flowing into the sea of silence,
Dancing pupils by the double,
A world of promise truly hollow,
Foaming smiles over the rubble,
Water, capsule, open, swallow,
Practicing doctors prescribing addiction,
Empty jars sailing the oceans,
On mesmerising journeys without restriction,
Rubbed up genies with magic potions,
Seeing is no longer believing,
Beyond the recommended dose,
The future is cunningly deceiving,
But no longer very close.

Ian McNamara
Co Down

The Mountains Of Mourne

I see no cloud but blue in high
Reflecting on this beautiful tide
A summer's sky harvest warm
Above yon Mournes spread wide

The Mournes touch the heart of Man
As she guards old County Down
Forest woods beneath her grow
Her peak a golden crown

Her colours ever-changing amaze
Beneath the summer's gleam
Standing tall and glorious
Her fringe an emerald green

Watching over our old town lands
Standing proud each day and night
Quenching forests and heathery hills
Rivers forming from her huge height

In winter like an angel white
She enfolds us with her wings
To protect us from the stormy night
A tranquil lullaby she gently sings

She is the majestic of County Down
Such a beautiful sight to see
Her cloak of many colours sweep down
To the dear old Irish Sea.

Geraldine McMullan Doherty
Co Down

God Bless, Sweet Dreams, Goodnight

My dearest, darling gran,
As I wish you goodbye,
I know the place you're going to,
Is way beyond the sky,
I know you will be happy there,
With love and peace each day,
But I will miss you more
Than words could ever say,
You taught me all that's good,
You showed me what was right,
I love you darling Gran,
God bless, sweet dreams, goodnight.

Janet Hagen
Co Down

The Viaduct At Dromore

On the Dromore side of Banbridge leading to the M1 motorway,
that extends from Belfast to Dublin in this modern day.
The ancient viaduct near Dromore is a fine specimen of its kind
when it is lit up on a darker night it's not too hard to find,
this beauty spot on the carriageway will surely catch the eye
and the significant sight that you will see no one can deny.

The seven arches are an architectural splendour,
to which any architect would love to render,
it was designed for the Banbridge, Lisburn and Belfast railway,
by a gentleman named Thomas Jackson in his day.

Later on it was absorbed by the Great Northern Railway (Ireland),
in 1863 the railway was enabled to reach Banbridge land,
it was then further extended to Newcastle at the seaside,
locals paid 1/3d for a return fare for their train ride.

The railway closed in 1956, it was feared it would be demolished,
fortunately the council paid the sum of £15 for the purchase,
the factory chimney that you can see in my former days' picture,
was further down the river, but in modern times it did not endure.

This fine constructed viaduct still stands in all its splendour,
enhanced by modern architects and their design enhancer.
In my modern days' picture of the viaduct of Dromore,
you can see the challenge we all have in store.

Maureen Dawson
Co Down

The World Is Getting Smaller

The world is getting smaller all the time.

I am the sun that circles the world
giving the heat and making the life
in the fish in the waters, and birds in the air,
and the people who live on the land.

I am the moon that shines all the time
reflecting the light of the sun in dark places
making mystery and romance and pulses of wonder
in the minds of the life that the sun has created.

I am the life that the sun has created
and the moon makes me wonder at the magic and mystery
as fish, birds and people reach out from their birthplace
to venture afar and experience living.

The world is getting smaller all the time.

Gerry Miller
Co Down

It All Starts Here

Hello, my name is Allyson, I'm sitting here at home
Surfing on the internet, until I read this poem
'Continuous poem' it said so bold, 'send your entries here'
4 lines later I was hooked, the evidence was clear

It took me just a minute to work out what to write
I never thought I had a talent, I thought I'd have a fight
To find the words to follow such a long and complex poem
It really was not difficult, my mind had far to roam

Soon my mouse was clicking, frantic for some more
Challenges to write a poem were knocking on my door
Fingers tapping merrily, ideas flowing fast
'Have to get the words out quick, this passion will not last!'

I've found a brand new hobby, I never thought I would
Writing poems and stories, I didn't think I could
But then again it's all good fun, a chance to air your views
Have a go! You never know, you might get on the news.

'Brand new poet comes to light, controversial but polite'
But then again if that's not you, let me tell you what to do.
Do anything your heart desires, follow all those burning fires cos
Words are magic, let them be a comfort for both you and me.

Allyson Baker
Co Durham

Well Wouldn't It?

Well wouldn't it be nice
If love could conquer all?
And wouldn't it be nice
If we could have our all?

Well wouldn't it be great
If we could bring good news?
And wouldn't it be great
If we didn't feel so blue?

Well wouldn't it be nice
If we could fill the hole?
Yes, wouldn't it be great
If we could heal our soul?

Helen-Elaine Oliver (18)
Co Durham

Picturing

The living room
Can be the most isolated
Though comforting
Place to be
On your own,
As I sit motionless
Walking upon the road
Between the shade
Of the open trees
All adorned by autumn's witness,
Where not even
A breeze
Stirred,
Or even
A word
Heard
From the silence
Within the picture
Upon the wall,
And then a call
Upon myself
Brings me back
To the present and abound
As all my family were around
In portraits
Framed by past memories
Upon the mantelpiece
Of my mind.

Anthony John Ward
Co Durham

My Dream

Reality or fantasy
How will I know?
This beauty before me
Moving so slow.
So graceful yet powerful
White waves frothing, stumbling
Drape veil-like over seaweed-covered rocks
Crashing, hissing, mumbling
Then, silent as the grave
The scene is sent tumbling
Into a bottomless pit, not a sound
And I know I am dreaming when I see
Phantoms leap from the clouds
And mingle . . . sparkling . . . free.
With the ever-changing birds of prey
Multicoloured life from the sea
And now in soundless splendour
Purple lightning streaks across my dream
Followed by silver showers
And bright crimson moonbeams
What a magic world it would be
If our dreams were reality.

M Armstrong
Co Durham

Scotland

When you're in the Highlands amongst the heather
It won't matter too much about the weather
Around every corner there's something new
Around every bend a panoramic view.

I've passed many a loch along the way
All shapes and sizes I have to say
Some go on for miles, never seeming to end
Then it's gone around the next bend.

The hills and the mountains are all around
Some covered with trees from top to the ground
Some are so barren nothing grows there at all
Just a dull, bluey-grey like a massive stone wall.

When the gale winds are blowing you don't want to be
Catching fish on a trawler on the rough North Sea
When the sea hits your boat round the rugged north coast
You dream of being home by the fire, warm as toast.

Once 'God' looked down, and said, 'I'll give birth
To a brand new place, and call it Earth
And everything beautiful, and everything grand
I'll put in one place, and call it Scotland.'

Patrick J Horrell
Co Durham

Alice's Poem

Alice Woods said she could manage,
Two tots of gin without much damage.
Then she said she could manage more,
Maybe three or maybe four.
Eventually it became eight or nine,
And Alice would claim that she felt fine.
One night her car failed to come home,
Which brings to an end, poor Alice's poem.

David White
Co Durham

Questions Without Answers

'May I ask you some questions?' said the woman in the street.
'About your town centre, is it complete?'
'Of course it's not,' said the passer-by,
'It hasn't a car park that reaches the sky!'

'May I ask you some questions?' said the woman in the street.
'About your local park, is it laid out neat?'
'Of course it's not,' said the woman with a child.
'All its beds and paths are overgrown and wild!'

'May I ask you some questions?' said the woman in the street.
'About your bus service, your needs, does it meet?'
'Of course it doesn't,' said the young man in his prime.
'There aren't enough buses and they're never on time!'

'May I ask you some questions?' said the woman in the street.
'About your police force, are there many on the beat?'
'Of course there aren't,' said the old man with a stick.
'I've been robbed three times, and a criminal they've yet to pick!'

Now these questions that I ask, thought the woman in the street,
Must be laid out on paper all tidy and neat.
For the council to discuss, peruse and explore,
But when the money's not forthcoming, it will be lost in a bottom drawer!

Joan Lister
Co Durham

The Old Oak Tree

Taste autumn in the crispy dark woods,
The dead, colourful leaves,
Falling off the old oak tree,
The wind blowing the rusty and crispy leaves away.

The birds fluttering across the cold autumn sky,
The birds flying off to foreign lands,
But the robin redbreast stays behind,
For the season of Christmas.

The hedgehog rolling up for a winter sleep,
Collects all the food it can find,
Then goes off for a long winter sleep.

Michael McGrath
Co Fermanagh

Humankind

Upon the exquisite glittering beaches;
Under the serene heavenly sky;
Rendering tranquillity infamous merit;
Inspiring an enchanting knot within time to tie.

To the elegant crests upon each wave;
Many hearts can be inspired to sigh;
Witnessing as they serenely grow;
To romantically; gently pass by;

The tenderness which they impressively impel;
To view the luscious waters so blue;
The placid emotions which they cordially provoke;
So immaculate; can they be true?

Yet so provocative, how can it be:
The infinitely baneful sight now brought before me?
Abysmally caused by the infamously candid gluttony;
Of the tsunami; asserting its utter tyranny.

Fathomless indiscrimination;
To both the young and the old;
To the priceless value of all lives;
Causing catastrophic destruction,
To over one hundred thousand tenfold.

Can there be a God?
If so I appealingly pray why;
Allow such tender blue, luscious waters,
Render the previous lives of so many; to devastatingly pass by?

It has brought to light though the compassion and care;
Which for each other throughout our world we share;
Emitting our hearts to the insatiably bare;
Donating for the better of the countless victims;
Our deeds, thoughts, and a prayer.

Patrick Folan
Co Galway

God Spilled The Paint
(On Co Kerry - Republic of Ireland)

God spilled the paint on this beautiful place,
Far away from the stress of human race,
With colours so vivid, the greens and the blues,
Violets and yellows, such wonderful hues,
Colours that blind you, down valleys they spill,
To gaze on this place, what a wonderful thrill.
An artist could never paint such a scene,
God in His wonder - the flora serene,
All the leftover colours He sprinkled so fine,
Such abundance in Kerry our county sublime.

Winifred Curran
Co Kerry

64

Happy Days

Another birthday ruined
What can I say?
You all let your feelings
Get in the way.

Only one more drawn out
Happy birthday to go
You could have made an effort
I'm human, you know.

Presents, gifts useless
Bright cards all lie
Greetings were forced
All I could do was cry.

Dad doesn't care
Mum is upset
Who notices me?
Nobody I've met.

Michelle Clancy
Co Mayo

Bluebells

Chunky leek-like stems
Thrust from the darkness.
Fluorescent-green starlets
Illuminate the bare spring ground.

Skyward longing brings height.
A unison of growth
Driven by an encroaching canopy,
Fuelled by a bulbous reserve.

Brilliant blue washes over green.
A magical floral ocean between the trees.
Form is lost in the vivid colour,
Intoxicating perfume heavy in the air.

Overshadowed, brief dominance slips by.
Green washes over blue,
Energy drains to the warmed soil,
Dormancy approaches.

Lynn Greer
Co Tyrone

Ode To The Sperrins

You stand in the distance so tall and so proud -
Your highest peak blocked by a passing rain cloud.

Since time first began you have stood on that spot,
You've seen transformations that have long since been forgot!

A thing of great beauty, you stand tall by our shore -
All your legends and stories recalled by folklore.

A world constantly changing - the climate as well -
But still you reign over each hill and each dell.

How many feet have trampled your path
Or trying to conquer you has appeared on their epitaph?

How many eyes have scanned your great height,
Yet been overawed by your powerful might?

I know you have secrets that we all long to hear,
But you still keep your silence year after long year.

So long you will stand there - so proud by our shore
Where you'll bring mystery and beauty to our land evermore!

Cora E Barras
Co Tyrone

Giant's Causeway

Let's go for a drive today.
Along the country way.
The little girl and her dad
Hurried along to see the sights.
Beautiful skies and views to see.
They were as happy as could be.
Up the coast they came to a beauty spot.
'Dad, please stop! Look what I can see.'
'Yes,' he said, 'it's the Giant's Causeway.'
'What is this?' said the little girl.
'It's a very special place, where everyone can see
Different shapes of rocks falling into the sea.'
'Oh Dad, please let us have a look.'
'OK my darling, wait until I buy this book.'
It told the story of Finn MacCool and all about the giant fool.
The little girl laughed so loud.
Her dad felt very proud.
To take her on a journey to a superb place.
It was the best day ever, the little girl can remember.
Now when she is older, she paints
The Giant's Causeway for pleasure.

Bernie McGinty
Co Tyrone

The Yorkshire Moors

(Edited by Clarance Whelan)

I walk along the shadow way, alert for any sound
Aware of my soft footfalls upon the soggy ground

Toward a path of hushing leaves and bogs all verdant-crowned
My spirit alive with imaginings of history all around

So let the art of silence penetrate the clouded mind
Live your walk through Mother Nature and answers you will find

As sun and cloud change places, and shadow turns to light
You understand the answers, because you get the questions right

Revealing landscapes that appear like laid-out inner dreams
The healing sound of water, in busy rushing streams

Time to count your blessings, diminish your extremes
Stand still on Yorkshire Moors and remember what life means

Enshrouded by such vastness, you humbly find your pride
Each step you take gets stronger upon a goodwill tide

A new reality rises as you walk the moor at dawn
Of light and air and hope renewed, ongoing not withdrawn

Rochelle Moore
Co Wicklow

Heart's Repose

I've packed my heart up in my case
I'm taking it to a holiday place
It's just not feeling at its best
It's really tired and needs a rest.
When always taken off its guard
It keeps on working much too hard.
Sometimes it's tender, and sometimes tough
But now it's saying, enough's enough!
So I've packed it up and put it in my case
Yes I'm taking it to a holiday place
With a comfy armchair and a velvet seat
Where it can rest its gentle beat
On a cushion soft so it won't break
And there it can dream
'Til it's time to awake
There it can rest and dream away
Until the end of its holiday
Then when it awakes
And the dreaming's all through
With a stronger heart
I'll return it to you.

Constance I Roper
Cambridgeshire

The Eclipse Of The Moon 12/9/97

Great golden orb in your fullness
Reflecting the light from the sun,
Tonight our old Earth came between you
And your light for a time was done.

Your mountains showed up darkly
Before clouds obscured you from view.
You control our tides and our feelings
And shed light on our darkness too.

Where astronauts have landed,
'One small step, one great leap for mankind',
You are still an influence and mystery
For those of us left behind.

Pauline Anderson
Cambridgeshire

At Waterside In Ely

How many miles to Babylon?

From here it is about a hundred yards
Through the iron gate, across the concrete bridge,
Past where the cruisers and narrowboats are moored,
Across the River Ouse to Babylon.

Three score and ten

Not nearly as far as that;
A signpost points out the distances in yards
From here to the Maltings, from here to the Babylon Gallery,
From here to all the visitor attractions.

Can I get there by candlelight?

The setting sun casts a roseate glow
On the water where an angler in a boat
Ships his oars in order to spin for pike and perch
Or even the occasional pike-perch.

There and back again

I start to walk. From where I have been standing
It is, as I have said, about a hundred yards,
Past where the ducks have been all day shilly-shallying,
Across the bridge to the green place known as Babylon.

Stan Downing
Cambridgeshire

What A Prize

A hamper from Harrods!
Oh what a prize.
A few tasty goodies
And pounds on the thighs.

What will be in it?
Wine and chocolates I hope.
Oh horror of horrors
Not bath salts and soap.

Will it be here soon,
Before the end of the year?
With Christmas looming
It might have brandy or beer.

There's only one snag,
I've just had a thought,
I have to pen a poem
And now I'm distraught!

Margaret Rowe
Cambridgeshire

Death Of A Village

Papworth Everard was a unique place
Until they decided to change its face
Now they pull houses down for a plot of land
Now three houses where one used to stand
Yes the old settlement buildings are coming down
A death of a village, a birth of a town
Progress so they say
Somebody making loads of money along the way
But that is something I can't prove
Now the hospital is about to move
The old villagers don't have a say anymore
If you don't like it there's the door
It's all for the better we're told
Maybe for the young not the old.

Richard Trowbridge
Cambridgeshire

A Lover's Poem

A lover's dream is one of which you do not dream, but comes to you when you have found true love.

When you close your eyes and see the shining light, it's a wonder of what you will dream tonight.

Once you have passed the shining light, there you will see your lover tonight.
Standing by the ocean sky, where lovers fly, holding hands and making love upon the golden sand.
Knowing that true love has just begun.

Once you have found your lover's soul, you hope for time to just stand still.

Upon the blue sky, you see the light, shimmering and shining.
Time has run out.

When you look upon your lover's eyes, and he says 'I love you' you wish this feeling would never fade away.

As you wake upon the day, with a cry and a sigh.
This is a lover's cry.

But once you see the shimmering light, you know that you will see one another again tonight.

A lover's dream is only for true lovers.

Daianna Pinto
Cambridgeshire

Cages Within Cages

I watch helpless flutterings of caged birds with bright feathers,
Their innocent eyes shrouded by bars
Confining their beating wings for our fascination,
Song and beauty dulled by stolen liberty.

A downy feather falls to the floor of the prison
As I reach out my hand,
Lift the cage and lift myself from a spectator's lethargy,
Walk into the garden of springtime greens,
Covered by grey clouds beneath which wild birds wheel and turn.

Without hesitation I open the birdcage door,
Hold my breath expectantly,
The birds regaining their beauty as they take flight,
Brightening the day as their wings beat
To the rhythm of freedom's song.

I watch for exhilarating moments; a jailer
Finding redemption in the release of innocent captives,
Then turn back and walk into the confines of the house,
Longing to find my own wings.

Edwin Page
Cambridgeshire

Friend Of The Night

I sit in peace, survey the calm,
The calm that comes at the end of the day.
A toiler has toiled, now makes his way
Thro' twilight shadows that now hold sway.

Gone, now the bustle of daylight's roar,
When, mankind all, rich or poor
Will fight to keep what they have won,
With the madness that comes with the daytime sun.

Am I alone to think like this?
To feel the evening's shadows' bliss,
And know no more, for a short span of time,
The frantic haste, that is day's crime.

To sit beneath a star-kissed sky,
And watch the world as tho' from high
Enveloped, cornered in a velvet sheen,
No more the turbulent toil is seen.

I'll share the dark's most godly charm
With creatures that live with pious calm,
And gaze at the world, and know I'm right,
To be at peace, with my friend, the night.

Len Baynes
Cambridgeshire

Peas In An (i)Pod

Where would we be without technology,
Could we cope without mobile phones?
In my day you either liked The Beatles
Or The Rolling Stones.

Now on my iPod, there's thousands of songs
That I'll never listen to.
Now all alone, I go online
To a chatroom to talk to 'You'.

The whole world at my fingertips,
I've got no time to eat.
Oh if it wasn't for technology,
My life would be incomplete.

And I dream of the time when we are born
With a socket in our thigh!
Just plug us in and we begin
To soar into the sky.

Part of the machine, perchance to dream
Ten billion hearts, with one great soul
And we never get sick and we never grow old
And we never laugh or cry
And we never get scared and we never feel fear,
Because we never die.

That was a dream that I had last night,
But I hope it doesn't come true.
Because what makes life so precious,
Is knowing one day it will be through.

If people didn't die
We'd be like songs on an iPod,
That no one ever listens to,
With no more need of God.

Roger Carpenter
Cambridgeshire

Backstage

Beyond the sparkling footlights, the tinsel and the show,
Behind the throbbing music and lightly dancing feet,
Beyond the velvet curtains, the silver and the gold,
Are struggling lives, disappointments, heartache and defeat.

Behind the laughing faces and sickly forcèd smiles,
Are anxious thoughts and wearing fears, tired hearts and aching heads;
Behind the paint and polish, and boring, practised charms,
Are souls that long for freedom, tired of being human marionettes.

Daphne Foreman
Cambridgeshire

Her Own Place

She's on her own at last.
She's as a bird whose nest
Becomes the focal fact
Of life, forever sees
The need for piece of stick
Or moss to plug a gap.
It's thus she adds a chair,
A table lamp, a vase
On shelf at side, a piece
Of wood in twisted shape,
A picture framed in gold.
And yet I feel she's not
At home. She's all alone,
And free to be herself
Without constraint, except
She needs the interplay
With friends to make herself
Begin to shine, ignite
Her inner fire, release
Her dormant laughter's joy
That lights her face with life.
Without such intercourse
She's flotsam left by tide
At dead of frosty night.

Henry Disney
Cambridgeshire

Wooden Feature

Why did she buy that collapsible thing?
Why was I the donkey she had to bring?
It was right at the start of our shopping marathon trip
That I slowly began losing my grip.

It's wood, made of slats and it weighs a ton,
Cuddling it for hours is really no fun.
She knows just the place at home she wants it to go.
It just slipped from my grip and crushed my left toe.

Why can't I leave it somewhere out of the way?
This box of timber has ruined my day.
I hate this collapsible thing that once was a tree.
The next thing to happen will be a collapsible me!

T A Napper
Cambridgeshire

Pagan Sky

(For Geoff, thanks for everything)

Pagan sky
Clouds on clouds
Wonder why
The sun has gone
Clash in Heaven
The power of the passion
Touch of heathen
Where is compassion
Warmth has left
Gone far away
Should it come back
Another day
Throbbing sky
Heavy with rain
Will the sun
Come back again
Splashes fall fast
Drops multiplying
And then the blast
From a wind, icy cold
Trees bend and groan
Longing only
To be left alone
By this storm-tossed day
Pagan sky

Teresa Whaley
Cambridgeshire

Morning

Morning mist
slowly rising
over dark treetops.

Tiny dewdrops
shining brightly
with rainbow tints.

As sun mounts
the sky in glorious
reds and purples

only forest creatures
stirring and rustling
amongst dead leaves.

Soon bright sun
warming the Earth
wakens the humans.

Silence now broken
by their sounds
echoing everywhere

missing the delights
of silent dawn
bar gentle breeze . . .

J K Branson
Cambridgeshire

My Simple Self

I'm waiting for my pain to go,
dwelling in my own sorrow.
Never happy, always sad,
unable to miss what I never had.

Counting the walls, the lines on the floor,
and how many pine marks reside on the door.
Feeling a cold and miserable air,
with no one to love you - and no one that cares.

No one to tell you, where life begins,
baring no memories, holding no sins.
No one to tell you where life ends,
no one to class you as their friend.

This is me, and I shall remain,
a person that shall never lose or gain.
Locked in a room, kept high on a shelf,
this is the story of my simple self.

Emma Buckingham
Cambridgeshire

Bushes

All day the bin, overthrown with nature's ends and entrails,
rotted in the sun.
It lay rotting and heaving in a crawling bush,
sucking out the green.
Lifeless waste. Frothing swamp that nursed and oozed
a score of poisons.
Above, an electric current
flickered, charged. Died. Rotted my nose.

Now though, as before, it stands as an oil drum - full of awe -
the *keep away* of youthful conscience,
laying waste to all of my existence.
Rainwater spilled out and drowned my throbbing shoe
and I - berry-framed - was carried away by the flood.

On my pane, water begins to fall and have its marathon.
It has been before, but unlike me,
it can return.

John Howlett
Cambridgeshire

What If?

What if I choose left instead of right?
What if I were black instead of white?
What if there were no rich/poor divide?
What if I seek instead of hide?

What if there was peace instead of war?
What if I found what I was looking for?
What if you were me and I was you?
What if the sky wasn't blue?

What if I was old instead of young?
What if the birds never sang their song?
What if we lived forever and did not die?
What if we tell the truth and never lie?

What if we could turn back time?
What if this poem didn't rhyme?
What if tomorrow was today?
What if is what we like to say
What if . . . ?

Sharon Brehaut
Channel Islands

Thee Who Hath Roses Within Thy Cheeks

Wilt thou join thy hand in mine,
Choose me for thy fireside companion?
For I long to see the roses within thy cheeks,
That glow only in response to heat.
Indeed, it pleaseth me to observe one so fair,
Flame-kissed when flames mock love's true glow.
I wonder, wouldst thou dare to sit so bold
If thou couldst know of all who gaze?
So whereupon our eyes feast hence,
I entreat thee not to move an inch,
Unless thine eyes be blackened coals,
And unlike my heart thy speakest in jest.
Hadst I not a pilgrim's soul,
I would take the ashes whereon the hearth they lay,
And throw them 'mongst those in my grate,
In hope that - in ash - thy shadow's robbed,
And if thus, let it forever be,
That mine own shadow ne'er stray from thee.

Samantha Crossley
Channel Islands

My Island Home

Azure-blue to turquoise-green
The bluest sea you've ever seen
The sky above cloudless, but with a morning haze
Quiet - heat to come - just sit and gaze
Not a breath of wind - no foliage stirs
The view of small islands - slightly blurs.

A gem of an island in the sea
Is where I was born and want to be
Some come - some go
But often they return and know
Having toured the world they will agree
It's hard to beat *Sarnia Cherie*.

Jacqueline Bartlett
Channel Islands

Tabletop Sale

There's a tabletop sale this Sunday
Thank God it's not on Monday
Rid the loft out, scrounge for toys
Some for girls and some for boys

Fill the boot up in the car
It won't matter, it's not far
Round the corner, down the road
I'm glad because there's quite a load

Tables cost just five pounds cash
Mum can't go, she's got a rash
All the kids are coming too
Because they've nothing else to do

There's puzzles, jigsaws, lamps and books
Some folks smiling, some black looks
All are welcome, it's for everyone
You may spend a few pounds or even a ton

Everything's numbered you can be sure
If you need direction there's someone on the door
It starts at eleven but if you are late
You may miss the bargains so don't create

There's hot dogs and tea if you feel like a bite
And the raffle is optional but it might feel right
The cause is deserving, there's only one rule
All of the proceeds go to the school.

Esmond Simcock
Cheshire

Ventura Highway

Every night
On Ventura Highway
They're breathing in
Pure gasoline

A crazy stampede
Of red-eyed and weary
Survey the
American dream

It's hard nose to tail
On Ventura Highway
The screamers are
Out of control!

As they watch the big wheel
Chase a brave imbecile
Throwing rocks at
The highway patrol

Then everyone
On Ventura Highway
Flies home on a
Wing and a prayer.

Rod Trott
Cheshire

A Moment In Time

I don't believe that people can't lie
I don't think the desert is dry
I try to imagine how they felt
when their final fate
was swift dealt

Where was hope
where was the lifeline?
How would they cope
would they have time?

I do believe that we all share
I do believe that we all care
Why is it when disaster happens
we think of only gain?
I wish for respect in our fellow Man
and to stop him feeling pain.

Sandra Roberts
Cheshire

St Issey, Cornwall

To bygone moments I reflect
memories dancing in my mind,
ripples of good times spent
sunk below the surface of life,
happy places and faces
made cloudy in aged memories,
sucked into a whirlpool of life
I was carried afar to another realm,
thoughts of my village make me weep
a body too old for travel slumps in a chair.

Amy Culpepper
Cheshire

A Spring Morn

A walk in the wood, into a glade
under trees in the shade.
Snowdrops appear and nod their heads
wild violets and crocus blown in buds.
Squirrels wake from their winter sleep
and robins with chests of red
do sit on the branch and tweet.
Fawns scamper in the glade
but soon run off once again.
Down in the wood on this
new spring day.

Elizabeth A Wilkinson
Cheshire

Beautiful Innocence

Tell me the story of life of old,
When ladies were princesses and knights were bold.
Whisper the words of a bedtime tale,
Of fierce green dragons and giants who would wail.
Show me the land where goblins did roam,
Where fairies danced free within the clouds they called home.
Recreate the forgotten lands upon where the sun would beam,
As I slip gently, deep into my childhood dream.

Kate Boud
Cheshire

Different Light

I saw you on TV
I didn't like what I could see
I read about you
In a magazine
You were not for me
Then I saw you
In a different light
A picture in the paper
Just caught my eye
I'm intrigued by you
And wish to know more
To lay beside you
And simply talk
I want to know you
Now I've seen
Yourself in a different light.

Matthew Holloway
Cheshire

Clean

Radiation, consternation, perspiration, hesitation
All affect this once great nation.
One night whilst asleep in my bed
The nuclear reactor glowed bright red.
After some time, not a lot
It reached the point of white-hot.
The safety limit it did exceed
And coolant water they did need.
Water was inducted from an incoming tide
So a disaster they could override.
The water was pumped back into the bay
But radiation remains till this day.
It will not go away
How long it lasts no one will say.
So while you're asleep in your bed
Think of the reactor glowing bright red.
Then put all thought of safe energy
Clean out of your head.

S Glover
Cheshire

Scenes Of Cheshire

The ever-changing greens of the fields and glades of Cheshire,
Surely in all abundance, did the Lord bless her.
Of all England's fair and beautiful counties,
It is she, above all others, who has all the bounties.

Softly falling rain makes sparkling lakes and meres,
Round millponds and streams running, whirling, gurgling near;
Glorious, glowing sunsets - red, pale green and gold;
Ancient soil trod by Roman legionnaires of old.

In its gentle countryside, leafy lanes abound,
And there, quaint, picturesque magpie cottages are found.
Most of its people are homely but very proud:
They came from kingly men so will not be cowed.

Amidst the pastoral scenes of Cheshire, relax,
Feast your eyes on waving fields of corn, wheat and flax.
One of England's jewels, this county palatine:
It is our heritage, part of an ancient line.

J Millington
Cheshire

My England

A green and quiet country lane
A village pub, good food, but plain
A hotel with a wider choice
A church with choir in full voice
A village green where children play
A little cove, a sandy bay
A dog that barks when you pass by
A plane up high across the sky
A market square where stalls abound
A bargain there must just be found
A silver birch, an oak tree stout
A cricket match, a cry, 'Not out!'
A quiet stream, an angler sat
A welcome shown on every mat
An ice cream van with bells that chime
A lawnmower's noise in summertime
Men out in fields, stock and crops to tend
And everyone greeted as a friend
All this and more it seems to me
My England, as it used to be.

H Banks
Cheshire

Take My Hand

Take my hand, make a wish,
Wish me away from you.
I don't deserve all of this.
I've been bad, oh so bad,
Take me to the highway,
Leave me to my fate,
I'll catch a ride to the discarded lovers' bar,
Buy and drink and let the tears fill my glass.
Take my hand, make a wish,
Wish me away from you.
I've had my chances, and some more,
I'm no good for you.
I'll take my last chance in the discarded lovers' bar
And probably end up with somebody just like me.
You deserve better, you'll meet someone just like you
And be happier than ever before.
You'll see the light and won't make the same mistake twice.
Better go now, catch the night before it runs away from me,
Get to the highway before it has its fill,
It won't wait, after gobbling up all those discarded lovers.
Hope I get a seat in the discarded lovers' bar.

Terry Ramanouski
Cheshire

Angel Of Mons

Sheathed in the flames of God's love,
The soldiers watched,
Eyes distended with fear,
Thunder crashed, gunfire faded.
A figure advanced,
Brandishing a sword wreathed in flame,
Out of the tumult, peace.
Fighting ceased,
Men fled in fear.
Death receded; wonder took its place,
Who was this figure?
Had it appeared by God's grace?
Appeared just to save them,
The Angel of Mons,
Protector of freedom and love.

Jane Dyson
Cheshire

From The Heart

The hands we hold
Entwined with gold
A solemn promise kept.

We've shared so many treasures,
I can't begin to count the pleasures,
That you, my husband, have given to me.

My husband, lover, and most of all, friend,
These qualities are you, on that I depend.
Upstanding, caring, a gift from the heart,
To know you is to love you,
Right from the start.

A companion who shares the joy of living,
A friend to laugh with,
Both loving and forgiving.

Soulmates forever, never to stray,
Sharing togetherness, each waking day.

Carole Umpleby
Cheshire

Twilight

So summertime ends once more,
Twilight shadows creep round the door.
The year itself in its own twilight,
Months ahead, a perpetual night.

No one wants to talk outside,
Even dogs will hurry their stride.
Yellow street lamps light the way,
By them we can see the rain's spray.

Hallowe'en, bonfires and Christmas time
Can even make dark days shine
And welcome firesides, warm invites,
Give us all a winter respite.

In midnight time of year once more,
In warm, light homes we feel secure.
And dream for the days when
Springtime daybreak comes once again.

S Morris
Cheshire

Rejoice

Here we are, we made it through,
Another year over and just look at you!
Peace and goodwill I send your way,
Precious friend, I have to say . . .
You're in my thoughts this festive time,
New resolutions made for Auld Lang Syne.
Each day, may it bring happiness for you,
With all your wishes coming true.
Yesterday's trouble banished into the night,
Every day you face, may the sun shine bright.
All my love sent your way,
Really hope you have the best day!

Annette Smith
Cheshire

Melbourne

In my dreams you hold me close
And place your soft lips upon mine;

My heart is filled with more love
Than could ever be imagined.

You tell me I am yours forever,
Till the breath is taken from our fragile bodies.

Can love be the strength that holds my world together?
For I awake and find you are gone; no longer a part of me.

I struggle to breathe in the life that now awaits me.

Katherine Rosati
Cheshire

The Loneliness Of The Long-Distance Slimmer

It seems so far to go
And I'm only human you know.
All those foods I have to resist
All those cakes so sorely missed,
But it will be worth it in the end
With salad and water my new-found friends.
And every day I endeavour to grow
Into that person I used to know.

Christine Rowley
Cheshire

Davenham

Every Tuesday practice I never tire
Of the village church spire
Echoing with the peal of bells ringing
And angelic voices singing.

The weary rambler can quench his thirst
The question is which to savour first
The Oddfellows' Arms or the Bull's Head
Either way he is greeted with a tasty spread.

The organic farm shop sells its produce
Fruit, vegetables, meat or home-made juice
Take your car to carry the heavy load
One mile down the old church road.

Summer brings out our crowned Rose Queen
Though we may not have a village green
The cricket pitch replaces that
Hear the leather on willow as villagers bat.

The antique shop bursts with treasure
Is that Tim Wonnacott getting the measure
Of our bargains as he hunts for more TV tales
Gleaned from house clearances and local sales?

The garage sells the lotto where a million can be made
The post office does a roaring trade
With stamps, cards, papers and the like
Driver, watch that tot on his trike!

This is the village of Davenham
Away from the bustle and the traffic jam
To love this place is not too hard
Pretty as a picture postcard.

Theresa M Carrier
Cheshire

The Cappuccino Moment

The cappuccino moment
Is a precious one to me
It's my escape from the chains
Of housework, you see.

And when I'm sat with my big white cup
In the smart coffee shop,
I'm in a different reality.

Mary Elizabeth Haigh
Cheshire

Meant To Be

Your life was only meant for you
This world was made for others
Don't get mixed up with the past or future
Only with the present
For even as I speak, time is passing oh so swiftly

Hang your heart out
Hang your heart out to dry
When all around you cry, don't worry
Their tears cannot dissolve you
Their fears cannot destroy you
You are one, you were meant to be

Let love pass slowly
Let love caress your lonely spirit
And when your leaves fall from their branches don't despair
Hang your tears out to dry
They cannot absorb you
Nor your fears destroy you
You were meant to be here

Don't let your mind chase yesterday's sorrow
Think of today, forget tomorrow
For time does not belong to us
It's something we all borrow

You didn't invent this world
You only live in it
At times you may not like it
Sometimes you'll wish you'd faked it
But don't despair
Your life was meant to be
Your love was made for others to share
Everyday things shouldn't wait for special days
Don't soil yourself with someone else
Release your grief to me
We are all meant to be

Mike Hynde
Cheshire

You With Me So Far?

Are you with me so far?
With glasses in hand
So far, do you understand?
Well let's explore
A little bit more

Are you with me so far?
We all stare back with blank masks
I'll continue my lecture
You're right, it's not all conjecture

Are you with me so far?
Glasses off, a little cough
A student rustles a page
Our lecturer, a wonderful old sage

Are you with me so far?
Don't leave your minds ajar
Well if you understood
Hiding expressions of wood
Fold your books and walk away

Have you been with me?
I hope you learnt by the end of the day

Andy Jones
Cheshire

At The Breaking Of Dawn

At the breaking of dawn
I lie wide awake,
Thinking of the times
We all used to take.

Our lives aren't the same
As there's a hole now,
Where our much loved one
Isn't with us anymore.

I feel very sad
About the time without Dad.
I can only remember
The lovely times that we had.

Wendy Wilkinson
Cheshire

A Little Girl So Young

A little girl so young,
Innocent,
Pure.

Just like any other child,
Play, eat,
Sleep.

Happy, just like always,
Smiling, laughing,
Singing.

A little girl so young,
Tortured,
Abused.

What could she do?
Cry?
Scream for help?

Nothing.
She was made to keep quiet.
The little girl so young.

Vicky Tam
Cheshire

Teal Sneer

Cradling,
Combating,
Caressing,
An inflamed curse.

Red, red!
For the love of crimson, scarlet and ruby;
Amend the quicklime scar,
Condemn the allusion to Lucifer
And his teal sneer.

Falling! Falling
Through jet cobwebs
Of scorched desire.

Tangled! Tangled
Amongst mandarin spider eggs;
Fresh but ultimately futile.

Jenny Hill
Cheshire

Friends

Good friends are hard to find,
Tell them your problems
And they don't mind.
You share everything,
From good times to bad,
They're a shoulder to cry on
When you feel sad.
From secrets to pain,
Joy and sorrow,
They are there every day,
Including tomorrow.
They might not live close,
But they are in your heart,
A quick walk away,
Or miles apart.
'Cause friends like these
Are hard to find,
And friends like these
I definitely don't mind.

Paula Massey
Cleveland

I Wish

I wish I could cleanse my mind
remove the pictures I don't want to find
The face I still see, haunts me so
the love I lost, not so long ago

I wish I were blind and never saw your face
never found love, that irrational place
My once fearless heart, now cries alone
the lonely leaf on the cobblestone

I wish my love wasn't a revolving door
I want to close it, for evermore
Lock love's suitcase and never unpack
throw away the key and never look back

I wish I were young and innocent again
never met you, and felt the love of pain
I wanted that feeling, whatever the cost
I did not understand I had already lost

I wish, I were back in the womb and reborn
grow again wiser, and not lovelorn
Rebirth would let me, be me
I wish, I wish, you would let me break free.

John Hoyland
Cleveland

My Happiest Days

Do you remember years ago
Of things you often did
The greatest days of your life
When you were just a kid?

Just an old piece of wood
And a little bit of string
And of course your little 'top'
It gave you everything

Lads and lasses had different games
And on a sunny day
Out would come the coloured chalks
To make your 'itchy bay'
Leapfrog was a favourite
Monakitty too
A rope around the gas lamp
Gave you a bump or two

And what a day we always had
When Mother baked her bread
There was nowt like a chip butty
Before we went to bed

Sea coal fires all aglow
Our 'fender' with its seats
Mam's black-leaded oven
It really looked a treat

Big patches in your trousers
No socks on your feet
The toilet in the backyard
With the hardest and wobbliest seat.

Ted Bage
Cleveland

Thank You

And as I wander this empty street
With golden leaves laying at my feet
I think of those words you said to me
'If you won't love, then seize every opportunity
For who knows when what would make you smile
If you don't walk that extra mile.'

And now I hear your voice in the wind
So energetic, like you could not have sinned
Echoing every word you have spoken
Both morning and night - every day I've woken
The voice of an angel so sweet and tender
'If you love me, then please surrender.'

We shared so much - each laugh, each tear
For together we had nothing to fear
Now times have changed and we're not the same
Yet no one knows quite who's to blame
I write what I feel and I feel what I write
Yet I hide it till the day becomes night.

Now I'm alone and you're no longer around
To help me up whenever I'm down
Each day seems the same as the one before
What I would give to see you once more
But I must move on with a distant memory
Of you teaching me how to be free.

Graham Connor
Cleveland

Victims Of Prejudice

Who creates it and maintains it?
Kinship and age-old influences that are prevalent
From father to son, mother to daughter
Attitudes send those targeted to vulnerable slaughter

I look at the world as a citizen still
Even though doctors say I'm mentally ill
I must confess I've had periods of distress
But I have no criminal record or anything else to confess

They say we are stigmatised
Yet I say that we are mentalised
We are the victims perceived as problems
Due to bad kinship that perceives us without tolerance

Kinship and conflict marginalises tolerance
A balance of things in common of reality and ideology
Ideally kinship would possess no friction
Yet in my vision I seek to reduce the social friction

Social status may maintain us in our cause of concern
Victims have suffered so let the perpetrators learn
I yearn for justice for the victims of prejudices
But I'll learn just on the basis as you perceive
I need to learn from my own prejudices

We all hold inconsistencies with realities in certain vanities
Yet if we learn and don't dwell in anger of life's tragedies
We can overcome our inconsistencies of realities
More aware of distress we can learn to manage our own tragedies or vanities

The victims of prejudice are not only the receivers of prejudice
Those that stereotype are the victims of intolerance
Enriched lives are spiced up by knowing diversity
Once you listen to the victims of prejudices you will see prejudice shouldn't
rule by insistence.

Robert Cowley
Cleveland

Rhyme And Reason

Time was when I took fish and chips for granted,
I could have them when I wanted.
But now, after six years banged up, they're a reward
For making a significant step, me moving forward.

Compared to what I'd become accustomed to in the slammer;
Newspaper, soaked in seawater, covered in brick dust, I needed a hammer!
Or the reconstituted mush from the dorsal fins and tails,
This tasty morsel is something you just don't get in jails.

I nearly fainted at the price like,
Three pound fifty! Hey man, this is cod, not salmon, trout or pike!
When I get home I think I'd better lie down
And try not to think too much about the money I've blown.

I used to eat fish and chips like a miner shovelling spoil.
Today, I'm more like a chimp picking fleas from his mate's back,
Inspecting each fingerful like the Astronomer Royal
Or a jeweller cutting a piece of rough jet-black.

This may not be the greatest rhyme I've ever written,
But I'll tell you what 'the reason tasted fantastic'.

Optimystic
Cleveland

A Childhood Memory

As a child, 10 years of age and very much alone,
During happy wanderings, not very far from home.
They came along the cinder path, past the meadow green,
Gypsies, horse-drawn caravans, the best I've ever seen.
The children made flowers to sell in our small town,
Fed and watered animals before they settled down.
The gypsies also whittled wood, pegs to make and sell,
A wonderful life, campfires at night, interesting tales to tell.
We lived close by the railway in a bungalow made of wood,
Oh to live in a caravan, how I wished I could.
My imagination running riot, a gypsy I would be,
When I was older have a life that always would be free.
I loved their horses and that love has stayed with me to this day,
Visiting gypsies, my favourite pastime when I went out to play.
The gypsies always stayed a while, before they all moved on,
But running down the cinder path, I found that they had gone.
I wondered where they would go next, along a different track,
Hoping to see them the following year, I wandered slowly back.

Leanne Rider
Clwyd

Captive

I heard the screech
A thud of rusty iron gates
A click of shutters
Shutting my sanity
In the shadows of locked doors.

I am now eternal
Captive of your glow -
Maybe you are also
Of my obdurate desire to burn
Of some love lost but held dear
Of a dream never to come true.

You know -
I cannot escape
Nor can you. I know -
I died a thousand deaths
Yet denied, kept thirsty.

I will keep dying
Though your glow
I can only see
And touch, maybe
For a split second
Only to die another death
And remain captive
For evermore.

A Jamil
Conwy

A Mother's Soliloquy (On Valentine's Day)

A tiny bundle of joy, held firmly in my arms.
When I gave you life, you made mine complete;
Your angelic little face, blue eyes, staring into mine;
Love before was good, but never this divine.
Hunger is your forte, night-time, daytime, oft repeat;
Sleepless nights, extra washing, all part of your charms.

The years speed by at an alarming rate,
So what's new? Excessive washing, sleepless nights!
While I wait, as you disco, arriving home late,
Time has eroded a mother's passage of rites.

But these arms are still open to encompass your troubles,
For no matter how old, you are still mine,
When life's in turmoil and bursts your bubbles,
These arms have the strength, to enfold all love divine.

Carole McKee
Conwy

Retirement

He said to me, 'A lawyer I'll be!'
I replied, 'What a grand waste of time!
To feed for a living from hands that are reaching -
For justice struck blind in both eyes.'

He then said to me, 'A tailor I'll be -
Stitching clothes for the gentry refined.'
I said, 'Don't be silly, let them walk chilly -
As brass hanging balls 'neath the pawnbroker's sign.'

At length he declared, 'I will sell stocks and shares -
To the chairmen of firms in the city.'
'O! What a shame to bother one's brain,'
Said I, 'with the pointless and pithy.'

With a sign of regret - 'A salesman I bet -
You think is more suited to me?'
'O! By all means feel free! But if left up to me -
'Tis a job more designed for a circus-trained flea!'

'I'll try one last time - I've a banker in mind,'
He said with a look of despair.
'A minder of cash?' said I in a flash -
'Needs not acumen, talent or flair.'

For nearly an hour he ran through his list -
Each page I rejected he screwed in his fist,
Bouncing each ball in the flames of the fire,
Watching as ash piled higher and higher.

'It seems,' he said, 'I know not the answer.
A fireman? A soldier? A male ballet dancer?'
'Grandfather!' said I. 'Please may I be bold?
At seventy-three you are really too old.
You always tell me the world loves a trier -
You've given your best. Now it's time to retire!'

Philip G Mee
Conwy

Panic-King!

There was a king, during whose reign
No subject dared go out in rain;
But if one did, the king would shout
A warning cry: 'Look out! Look out!
The sky is falling down!' he said.
'Stay in, or it will harm your head!
Repeat - the sky is falling down.
One bit of it dissolved my crown!
A good job that it missed my brain -
That bit was full of acid rain!'
His fear was driving him quite manic -
No king was ever in such panic!

Roger Williams
Conwy

There Must Be A Carrot

There must be a 'carrot' to help us along -
to turn things to right when they all go wrong,
something to help when the going gets tough,
to give us a push when we've had enough.

The first race you run - you've not done it before,
your opponents all seem as tall as a door,
though you're giving your best, you want to give up -
then you think of your name on the base of the cup.

A wet Monday morning when nothing goes right,
you are running around and it's not yet daylight,
is it worth all the effort - still so much to do,
then the rain disappears - and you look at the view.

The shopping is done, you arrive home quite late,
today was the end of the 'two for one bait',
with a bag in each hand - how you wish you had three,
you are greeted by family - no need for a key.

A journey to make when the weather is bad,
maybe visit a grandparent, mother or dad,
you get up and go, though your pet 'soap' you'll miss
cos you know you'll be met with a hug and a kiss.

The 'carrot' can be just whatever you please,
there are no sets of rules for things such as these,
so think of the saying when nothing goes right -

*'Above the cloud with its shadow
is the sun with its light'.*

Jim Pritchard
Cornwall

What Is Life?

What is life? Is it pain and strife?
A struggle to overcome will happen to some
To find their place in the human race
To live their lives with no disgrace.

What is life? Why are we here?
Life is a boat that we all steer on an unknown sea
To find a land that is called free.

What is life? Do we give or take?
Is what we see, a reality or fake?
Truth or lie we don't know why
What do you give so others can live?
What do you take to make a heart break?

What is life? In a world of confusion
A chance to escape the prison of illusion
Hope gives you a reason to know what to do
To know your reality and know it is true.

What is life? Is it love or hate?
Love is a feeling, the choice is your fate
Hate can destroy and love can create
A mistake in time turns the clocks back to crime.

What is life? Child to woman or man
You learn then you earn, anyway that you can
The world is your school, who ends up the fool?
A blackboard sky, a chalk-word eye
Every story ends with a dot
You always want what you haven't got.

James B Woods
Cornwall

Addled Aspirations

In my youth, I'm sure I must have wished a hundred times a day
For things I knew deep down inside would never come my way
All those luxuries that at some time most people would desire
Without the faintest hope that what they covet would transpire
To wish, and not take action to make that wish come true
Is to wish your life away and miss the chances all are due
Just drifting through the years, I yearned, but learned this basic truth
To rely on wishing doesn't work for fate remains aloof
Now, a wasted lifetime later, I realise too late
That to live on naught but hopes and dreams is inappropriate
So every morning when I wake, with nothing to wake for
My fervent wish is but to sleep, for just five minutes more.

Ron Beaumont
Cornwall

The Guardian Angel

The night was cold, the child was two
His feet and hands were turning blue
'A heap of misery' tightly 'coiled'
Rags, he lay on, damp and soiled
His only company was a mouse
Left to die in an empty house
He sobbed and cried in despair
'Is there anybody there?
Please send someone to guide me
Where safe and loved I can be.'

Tears ran down his ghostly face
Lost in a dark and lonely space
Then an angel appeared to him
She said, 'Life's about to begin!
There's no one here, you cannot stay
To Heaven let me lead the way
Feel love's touch, look into His face
And fall into His warm embrace
Follow the path to Heaven above
That's where you find eternal love!'

Sheila Walters
Cornwall

Solitary

They stand unkempt with awkward grace
On haunted Cornish moors.
For this desolation is theirs to face,
Rain whips their souls so sore.

These handsome ponies obscured from view,
Preferring a lonesome existence,
With wisdom, oh my Lord you know,
Cruel moors need intense persistence.

The newborn reared so strong of hoof,
Learn to ignore bad weather.
These beauties survive with pride - aloof,
No need for these to tether.

Permit these hermits this barren abode,
Their haunted cries conveying,
That the good Lord sent them in this mode,
As they stand so strong, just praying!

Lucy Bloxham
Cornwall

Secret Hideaway

Wild and mysterious with tranquil calm
A place of beauty, peace and charm
A haven, from life's desperate chase
An island in a stream, a magical place

A sense of freedom where troubles fade to sleep
Campfire burning with flames that speak
Blue and green sparkle of dragonfly's glow
The sound of birds as fresh waters flow

A beam of sunlight shining through trees
Flowing and dancing in the light gentle breeze
Screech of the buzzard, circles high in the sky
As the wren feeds its chicks in a nest nearby

Beans are bubbling, cork off the wine
Sizzling sausages, the steaks divine
Just the two of us, in our secret hideaway
No phone calls or driving, the dog's gone off to play

Light starts to fade, the long track back
Stump out the fire, on with the haversack
Across the stream of rocks and slippery stones
Through woods, meadows, to cars, people, mobile phones

R S W Hughes
Cornwall

Charity Shops

Charity shops,
you can't keep me away,
that whiff of decay and brief browse
through the fashion of time.
Going for a song vinyl albums
label their decade, rub covers with
wear-worn novels, among the jumble
of everyday stuff.

Life's outcasts
clearly displayed, items that gave joy,
a toy, a necklace, now rejected for
untold reason, long out of season;
owners moved on to other belongings.
For some, there's fresh hope of being
a bargain; a few pence tendered, a life
extension: another chance to find home.

Josie M Hodges
Cornwall

Revival 2005

August anniversary of the Boscastle flood,
The media turn up in force,
North Cornwall is thus back in the news,
Planning had taken its course.

A year on from disastrous conditions,
When the rain had continued to fall
On Crackington Haven and Boscastle,
They need no reminders at all.

Hotels, guest houses, craft shops and supplies
Had been flooded or destroyed in four hours,
These poor people must wonder if it's happening again
With any outbreak of occasional showers.

A hundred-plus vehicles had swept through the village
By swollen springs and three rivers,
Emergency services came out to save lives,
A day when nobody dithered.

That no one was lost was a miracle,
Holidaymakers went home safe and sound,
Leaving behind local residents,
For whom much help must be found.

Cats, dogs and caged birds also survived,
But belongings and mud were piled high,
The local vicar, well known *(seaside parish)*,
Must have prayed to someone on high.

By the power of God or unblocking rods,
They'd get it put straight by and by,
The community have been quite remarkable,
Workers have toiled day and night,
It's the sixth time it's happened since 1827,
But Boscastle is back 'sparkling bright'.

Alan J Nunn
Cornwall

My Main Delight

Upon a freshly foliaged bough,
A thrush with throat aquiver,
To all those astir at dawn,
Such a sweet song does deliver.

Every joyous note I hear
In proclamation of the spring,
To my winter-weary heart,
A much lighter beat does bring.

On and on he gaily sings
Without any sign of tire.
Opening my eyes anew,
To many things to admire.

A sky afresh with colour.
The glow back in the sun.
Dewdrops, spangling bright,
On lacy cobwebs spun.

Snowdrops with dainty faces,
So fairy-like in their allure,
On slender limbs blithely dance,
As if to the thrush's score.

Without doubt - a princess,
Of serenity, dignity and grace,
Is the beautiful primrose,
With her sunny, smiley face.

Daisy buttons, crocus cups,
Golden daffodils all a-sway.
How enlivened I do feel
To be witnessing them today.

My main delight of the day
And perhaps for all of spring?
The thrush with throat aquiver,
And the sweet song he does bring!

Donna June Clift
Cornwall

My Cornwall

Home of myths and legends,
My county in the west.
There is no doubt in my mind,
It simply is the best.

The fresh green fields, the golden sands,
The cottages 'mid farming lands.
The river creeks that hide away,
Concealing smugglers in their day.

Small churches and chapels nestling there,
To help the poor, preachers did their share
To beat the cutters fast and sleek,
To hide the shipwreck's spoil to keep,
                    to sell again another day.

Near hills and woods and rocky bays,
Primroses and bluebells in the spring,
To me this land has everything,
The sunsets in the summertime, each day different, so sublime.

The cliff tops with their flowers so rare
That do not grow everywhere,
The country lanes and honeysuckle's scent,
Surely this place was heaven-sent?

The winds will wail and storms will come
But all the seasons blend into one.
We must have winter to enjoy the spring.
It still, to me, is everything.

Cassandra May Poultney
Cornwall

My Wish

My wish would be
To have been born
Privileged
The apple of my
Parents' eye
To be loved
In abundance
My potential
To be realised
Encouraged and nurtured
So that I too
May live as the
Privileged do.

Penny Kirby
Cornwall

How Long?

We do not know 'what's round the corner';
in this existence we call 'life'.
Rich or poor - or neither,
can foretell luck, chance or strife.

That we are born, one certainty,
is only that of death.
All that happens in-between,
is just perpetual breath!

How long the strand, the piece of string;
from birth 'til end of time,
and would it benefit us at all,
if this knowledge, we might find?

'Life', is like a lottery,
a complex game of chance;
or could it be, terpsichore,
some music-less ritual, 'dance'.

I don't know - and nor do you;
for we rarely give it thought,
but, my friends, I wonder,
perhaps we really ought?

Peter Mahoney
Cornwall

Harbour Life

(In loving memory of 'Ganymede' 1995-2004)

The emerald line of trees pierces through the sky
Boats clank in the harbour as the birds sail on by
Dogs bark from the distance, ringing bells in my ears
The church tower silent now after all these years

The cloudy white shadows scroll across the waves
Surf and tide burst alight in the sun's heated haze
Stony castles point and twist around the sandy bend
Lined by ropes and floating buoys, helping hands to lend

The fishermen's loud laughter hails the daily catch
Fresh gills flapping as rum slips down the hatch
A solitary swan drifts on, outward bound for sea
From the bank of the river where the ducks so often flee . . .

Helen Forsythe
Cornwall

Will Your Ship Return?

As I walk along the river
That flows down to the sea,
I hear your voice in the breeze
That whispers to me.

And I see your vision
Where Land's End meets the sky,
And will your ship return
With the seagull's cry?

Your shadow glides silently
In the surge of tidal sway,
And I feel your fleeting breath
In the salty spray.

And you reach out to me
Across cascading brine
Breaking in icy showers,
Your hand touching mine.

Where waters on granite reef
Are swirling restlessly,
Your words are in the drifting song
Of the scend of the sea.

And your call haunts the night
With the wind and falling rain,
As I wait for you
To return again

And I see your vision
Where Land's End meets the sky,
And will your ship return
With the seagull's cry?

Esme Francis
Cornwall

A Solitary Sunflower

By a sunlit craggy stone wall,
A solitary sunflower slender and tall,
Gold sunray petals flutter in a breeze,
By overhanging trees,
Sunflower, happy to be at one,
With the glowing red setting sun.

M J Harris
Cornwall

Home

Land of meadow,
Copse and stream,
Mossy dells, where bluebells gleam,
Land of hill and moor and vale,
Of sunlit waters
Flecked with sails;
Rugged cliffs
Where seabirds call,
Stormy skies -
And sudden squall . . .
Small boats on their moorings
Swinging gently, side to side,
Rocky pools along the shore -
Left . . . by the outgoing tide.
There's a sense of enchantment
Abroad in the air -
A feel as of something unseen . . .
Giving wings to the spirit,
A lift to the heart
And setting a dulled mind a-dream . . .
Though I've seen many wonders
And travelled afar,
Till my life shall be spent
I'll abide
In the home of my heart -
Here in Cornwall,
My solace, my hope . . . and
My pride.

Elizabeth Amy Johns
Cornwall

Hands

Come hold my hand that I may know,
That you will mean to me,
The friend you are true to life,
As I hope you will also be.

But none is there to take my hand,
To do this simple task,
Oh Heaven do this for me,
This is all I will ever ask.

One day my love I will find,
To take me here and there,
With all this knowledge to be passed,
Means everything I do, I can bear.

Dawn Graham
Cumbria

Parables

Parables are little Bible stories
Which Jesus told to illustrate His teaching,
And their lessons, though some are hard to see,
Are mostly very clear and out-reaching.

'The Good Samaritan' would be the first
That I heard at Sunday School as a child,
And though I want to be a good Samaritan,
I've often passed by on the other side.

For it is easy to not want to be involved,
To hope someone else will help those in need,
But if someone else holds to that same view,
The needy die; their plight we will not heed.

'The Prodigal Son' was an early lesson
Of a son who wished to taste life's charms,
But having squandered his lot, and barely alive,
Is welcomed back by his father with open arms.

For he was his son, his well-beloved son,
Whom he'd lost and thought never again to see,
And the joy at this tender reunion
Far outweighed any animosity.

Now everyone loves a jolly good yarn,
A story, a tale, call it what you will,
And the parables are second to none;
Their messages are very relevant still.

Marlene Allen
Cumbria

My Wish

If I could have one wish
I think it would have to be
the silver lining to my dreams
that match up heavenly

A tall dark stranger
that would whisk me off
to a land of sunshine rays
treat me like a precious gift
and give me happy days

I long for love and true romance
my knight would love me true
but nothing as it really seems
so you will have to do

Margery Rayson
Cumbria

Blue Man In The Moss - Standing Stone

'The imagery of a meeting'

Does he walk?
At a distance, strengthened by forces
A defying outline implying solid grace emerges out of the dark
Immediate silence in the immovable blackness, that profound innocence of passing time
A strangely delicate character, your trance-like state embedded in the mosses
Silently being washed away, ever patient, yet growing thinner as layer of self
And memory stone, circles in the wind and falls far
To touch your vast edges, to feel an eternal tremor, your density so cold, no disorder
Consuming strength being restored by sight and contact
Comforted in your presence, you have endlessly listened to whisperings
Asking guidance through generations
Just talking has transformed and eased their hearts and their voices are
Silently taken away by varying winds
The answers being contained in their souls
Understanding - belonging to no one yet to the friend of the soulless to lost generations
No betrayal, just stored memories
Scared by age, the listening stone stargazes like all sentinels on moonlit nights
Must turn and leave you now
Blue Man in the moss

Hilary Jean Clark
Cumbria

Blue Whale

Looking on the sea, so blue and calm
Why do we cause the blue whale harm?
This mighty creature belongs in the sea
It has more right than you or me.

They glide along and show such grace
And would you like to take its place?
Yes, take its place, try see the moon
And look out for that deadly harpoon.

Yes, mammals, fish, even crustaceans
They all make up the great sea nation
Don't harm the ones we don't have to
Just let them live like me and you.

Now God made mankind, birds and the bees
He gave us flowers, plants and trees
He made the oceans for the fish
So please respect the good Lord's wish.

David Thompson
Cumbria

Hurricane Katrina

Here in a place called New Orleans
Terrible pictures can be seen
Of thousands of people in distress;
O Lord what a disastrous mess!

With all the damage we can see,
Dear Lord, how could you let this be?
There on the rooftops people stand
With no help or aid near at hand.

This awful storm with its strong wind
Blew houses down, killing all within;
Thousands of people left with no home
Were in desperate need and all alone.

Days and nights there in that mess
Put on those people a lot of stress;
Mothers with children in dire straits
In their terrible plight sit and wait.

Seeing men and women who are crying
For their dead and for their dying,
We pray things will be better tomorrow
So they can put behind them this sorrow.

From all of us who see their plight
Go pray for them, day and night,
That Jesus be there by their side
And then to safety be their guide.

When it's all over and things put right
And better times are back in sight,
They'll be in our thoughts every day;
God bless them all, from the heart we say.

Francis Allen
Cumbria

Feelings

Throughout life one experiences many kinds of emotions,
That can fill the mind with the wildest of notions.
They may affect the heart, which then rules the head
And one can say things that are best left unsaid.

Harsh words cause ill feeling when spoken in haste,
Causing long friendships to falter and sometimes waste.
Is life not too short to have strife and conflict?
Compatibility is the road we all depict.

Kindness, a trait that's sometimes missing today,
Is a word expressed in so many different ways.
A little goodwill shared is a path to fulfilment
Bringing a peaceful, relaxed mood of contentment.

Happiness spread around in its simplest form,
Brings people together, willing them to conform.
Building trust and prosperity for the whole community
And providing everyone with complete impunity.

Many people crave that which others have conceived,
Feeling green-eyed with envy, at all they've achieved.
But success is there for everyone to share
Who takes up the challenge and faces the dare.

Of all the emotions we will sometimes feel,
There's one that has the most to reveal.
For love, a small word, carries the tome of the heart
That brings everyone together, though we are worlds apart.

These sections of verse, which are not meant to preach,
May traverse bridges that we finally reach.
With luck, and good fortune, we may all travel
The enigma of life, which we have to unravel.

D T Pendit
Cumbria

Winding Time

The coldness of thought holds this pen to paper
The ink flows as the mind races
Each time I wind the clock
I freeze the memories of you, in Grasmere

My feelings are the logs sitting on a fire
Embracing the embers striking the hearts of dancing flames
I be the mouse, cold at night in the Lamb Inn
Whispering words warming my lips by a blazing fire

Crying, lost my weight
I be this tired mouse
Rushing to carry logs
To the dancing flames

If sorry was a word
I could package and send
With ribbons I now do
Tied parcels of sorrowful tales
I beg be thrown on my fire

Christmas cheer
I wish you were here, resting with Wordsworth
Perhaps the envelopes stashed for a rainy day
Will hold the words I threw your way

Go forth to the bells of joy
Another year has clocked us by.

Anton Nicholas
Cumbria

Theology Beware!

Old *narrative* theology, its gaze
Sharp-focused on an ancient world now lost,
An age of epic deeds and glories past,
Stands guardian to a tale of bygone days,
A tale of Abrahamic faiths ablaze
With fierce prophetic zeal whose scorching blast
Razed pagan gods and creeds to smouldering dust.
But where the lure of cultures past outweighs
The needs of present day, we fail to see
Theology must liberate the mind,
Engage with modern challenges and doubt,
Or else it desiccates and dies, its plea
For deity quite lost on humankind.
Self-centredness creeps in: and God is out!

John Beazley
Cumbria

One Wish

One wish I have is to provide,
Love to the world, with God by my side,
Help to help those who are alone,
Because to these people life may have been overgrown.

Overgrown in bitterness of maybe a lost family,
Who have maybe forgotten a mum or dad, you see,
We don't need you now they say, we have our own lives to lead,
But oh the lonely would love their company and would try to succeed.

Succeed in being part of life again I say,
Please Lord bring them back together I pray,
When you have a mum and dad,
Think back to all the good times you have had.

Parents will not last forever,
So don't leave them alone, try to be a family together,
And if the time comes when they die and both fade away,
You'll know in your heart you did your best for them both every day.

But oh how sad they seem,
When they are all alone, and only memories of you are a dream,
Just remember they gave you life years ago,
When they are alone and old please care and let it show.

Show that you really care,
Please help them if they are in despair,
I looked after my late parents, that's true,
And I've nothing to reproach myself for, now how about you?

Barbara Holme
Cumbria

Unpredictable

Like the bully in the bus queue
Like the cut on jagged tin.
Like the ladder in the stocking
Like the pimple on the chin.
Like the fool who overtakes you
Like the thorn that pricks the thumb.
Like the pain that eats into you
Like the shock that strikes you dumb.
Life is so unpredictable
Each moment a surprise.
Each day is an eternity
Live it well,
        Time is short
           Open your eyes.

Judy Rochester
Cumbria

Just For You

M is for the memories you have given me
Y is for yes I will love you all for eternity

S is for the silly jokes you tell from time to time
I is for I wonder when we'll get to the punchline
X is for Xmas when Santa leaves your toys around the tree

G is for goodie there is even one for me
R is for reading, you have more books than I can tell
A is for actually I love reading them as well
N is for now and then you stay over at my house
D is for dare I hope you will be quiet as a mouse
D is for dancing classes which you go to every week
A is for alas when I dance my bones begin to creak
U is for unconditional the love you give to me
G is for your gentleness which is there for all to see
H is for the happiness you spread throughout the day
T is for the thoughtful things you all do and say
E is for excitement when the six of you are together
R is for the rapport we have which will last for ever and ever
S is for special thanks Amy, Katie, Lucy, Chloe, Sophie and Hannah
    this little poem is just for you with lots of love from Nana

Jackie Richardson
Cumbria

Hero

I enlisted for my country,
Signed my life away,
I thought that I would see the world
And help keep war at bay.

I travelled far and journeyed wide
To many a foreign region,
I witnessed things best left unseen
In the company of my legion.

I hoped I'd make a difference
By doing things that mattered,
But soon my body bore the scars,
Emotions torn and battered.

They sent me home a hero
And I wore the badge with pride,
But no one knows the heartache
I feel for those who died.

K E Evans
Cumbria

The Passing Of A Genius

He was the idol, of millions of boys
They all wanted, his magical feet
Girls were enamoured by his charm and poise
With a ball, he just couldn't be beat.

From Ireland he travelled, across the sea
Intent on seeking his fortune, and fame
What an absolute genius, he turned out to be
Displaying his talent, in our national game.

His name was synonymous, with pure skill
Many a defender, tried to, chop him down
Many a stadium, his name would fill
When George Best, the maestro, was in town.

He was a young man, headed for the top
Sadly his country, found no World Cup glory
Supporters' heads, would begin to drop
He led a life, which was a remarkable story.

He weaved his way, past many defenders
His intention, to place the ball, in the net
Skilled opponents, were just merely pretenders
The football world, is very much, in his debt.

Matt Busby had found, his prodigal son
And he nurtured him, every step of the way
Championship titles and cups, he then won
It was an honour, to watch this lad play.

And in sixty-eight, came his greatest night
The glittering triumph, of a magnificent career
From a disaster, he helped put things right
An evening which loyal fans, still hold dear.

He had abilities which cannot be taught, and which, we will see no more
Excitement to the game he brought, born to bewitch us and born to score.

B W Ballard
Cumbria

Pictures

'I'll paint you a picture,'
He said with a smile.
'No surrealist painting
Cos that's not my style.

I'll make the eyes,
Show the beauty inside
Of men and women
And things they can't hide.

The lines on the face
Of the man who's worked hard
His character there!
And pride in his race.

A woman with child
And spirit within
The happiness there,
So gentle and mild.

Then there's the dawn
As it breaks in the sky.
Stretching out its fingers
'Til the new day is born.

Shade and sunshine
As it filters through trees,
Bluebells in carpets
Against leaves of green.

Yes! I'll paint many pictures,'
He said with a sigh.
'But can you understand
The urge and reason why!'

Joan May Wills
Cumbria

My Dawn

I love you more than words can ever explain.
You have such amazing strength and grace your hand always steadies me,
To me you are the blue sky and white clouds within.
The clear blue shows to the world all your light and love that you give.
You are so fine like the Earth.
You take away badness from this place and bring goodness, love, warmth and light,
If I don't have you, then I have nothing.

Michael Graham
Cumbria

The Heavenly Lark

As I lay on the grass looking up to the sky,
In search of the skylark with its keenest of eye.
I can hear its sweet love song so clear and loud,
He's somewhere above me in that silver-white cloud.

At last I have spied him, this magical bird,
Whose trill on the wing is the sweetest I've heard.
Now up to my feet, I'll go ambling along,
And leave in the distance the skylark's love song.

Down through the meadow, up over the hill,
I'll never forget the sweet sound of its trill.
It's strange but true he maketh no sound,
When the skylark from Heaven, alights on the ground.

Leslie Hogarth
Cumbria

Ethiopia, Somalia Or Anywhere

Bright and toiling in the sun,
I wish your hard day's work was done.
But, when I am dead and gone
I hope this weary world lives on.

O men and women of the land
how I long to make rain for you
but envy your simplicity.

Jennifer H Fox
Cumbria

Autumn's Here

Summer's gone and now autumn's here
Leaves are falling here and there
The trees are now quite bare
As we walk through the leafy ground

Goose Fair come and gone
Then Hallowe'en with trick and treat
Then it's pennies for the guy
And fireworks that go with a bang.

Fog and frost and mist come every morning
And the frost begins to bite
So wrap up warm before you go out
And soon it will be Christmas once again.

Ella Wright
Derbyshire

Greedy Or What?

Do you want a computer?
Do you want a new phone?
Do you want a big telly?
Do you want a new home?
Do you want a new body?
Do you want a new car?
Do you want a new kitchen?
Do you want caviar?
Do you want a new partner?
Do you want flashy clothes?
Do you want a makeover?
Do you want a new nose?
Do you want to be clever?
Do you want to be first?
Do you want what-so-ever?
What you need's a nurse.
What you need's a doctor.
What you need's a priest.
You need know, how to want least.
You need to be happy.
You need to ensure
That you get some help mate
And that is for *sure*.

Sue Comery
Derbyshire

A New Year

This January is in the year two thousand and six!
The weather can leave us in quite a fix!
The roads are slippy with snow and ice,
As people with cars will know - not at all nice!
The shops are busy with goods on show,
With notices saying, 'Everything must go'.
We start booking holidays this time of year,
Looking forward to some sunshine in places far and near.
Older people do not like the January weather,
Most stay indoors and do things together.
Children do not mind the wind, snow and rain,
Wellingtons and raincoats a must each time they go out again.
January is a long, cold month we have to endure each year,
Let's face things with a smile to bring some cheer!

Joyce Hallifield
Derbyshire

Last Night - I Had A Dream

Last night I had a dream,
And you were there;
Last night you smiled a smile,
With wisps of hair;
The road was long and wet
When you were there;
And leaves tripped over leaves,
Forming clumps and sheaves;
I did not care;
When you were there;

Last night I heard your voice,
When you were there;
Last night as if by choice,
And you were there;
For you they had not taken yet -
They did not dare!
Last night I had a dream;
You standing there . . .
There was no scar,
Behind your ear;

Last night I felt so weak,
When you were there;
Last night I heard you speak,
When you were there;
But they took you with no regret,
Their darkest lair;
Last night a purple star
You did not wear;
Last night I had a dream;
And you were there . . .

T Ritchie
Derbyshire

Museum

Ceramics so beautiful,
As they sit in the
Museum, with the
Past coming forward,
To buy or not
To buy, the temptation
Is great, before
It is too late,
And they shut
The door, no more.

B Brown
Derbyshire

Lelanya

The days drift into years,
still I'm lacking the tears,
to mourn what since has passed,
yet self-pity I crave perhaps.

Maybe years wandering this dark bower,
by chance finding my sweet flower,
who shone with a light from her soul,
who warmed this heart through the cold.

Each day we tender for hours,
each night you danced like the breeze,
the world forgotten seemed distant,
we swore together forever and ever.

In time, colour and sparkle seemed faded,
we said to give it some space,
finding fault where once there was none,
never knowing it's so good 'til it's gone.

Days drift into years;
I loved you and lost you it seems,
except in dreams,
swaying to a sad song
you look into these old eyes,
and smile as you cry.

Pause as you read:
remember a treasured face,
be it sweetheart or loved one,
stolen so soon,
do not regret or let spirits fall low,
recall one happy moment, never let it go.

T J Shaw
Derbyshire

Flying

Here we are up in the sky,
Just like birds we are flying high.
Clouds are soft, white and smooth
As they drift high above.
Things below are tiny and small,
Some you cannot see at all.
Cars that look like toys.
Men even look like boys.
Buildings large and tall
Now look so tiny and small.
In this big plane we fly,
Just like floating in the sky.

E Riggott
Derbyshire

No Doubts

Cars, suicides,
trips to the darker sides,
there's no way out
for the tripper's doubt.

Notes left behind
in the hope that they will find,
before the journey starts,
before the crossroads part.

The car will not stall,
before the last post's call,
ironic trap,
of the car-priced scrap.

A tragic end,
they only needed a friend,
only wanted a hand
to hold their gold band.

Clouded vision,
like their life's mission,
there's no way out
for the tripper's doubt!

D E Buck
Derbyshire

Mystery And Fear

Mystery is my dream come true
Dreams of whales killing in the deep sea blue
Dreams of men whipping animals in a zoo
Dreams of Rottweilers coming to eat you
Dreams of demons taking prisoners too

Fear is my dream come true
Dreams which tell me when a ghost is near
Dreams which give me shock and fear
Dreams saying things I don't want to hear
Dreams which say when I'll disappear

Fear is as horrific as a monster coming for your blood
Fear is a house no one comes out of alive
Mystery is as mysterious as a life taken by an unknown murderer
Mystery and *fear* is someone falling, dying on the carpet
They are both filled with murder and wonder

Kiran Kaur Rana
Derbyshire

The Pebble, The Ripple, The Wave

There is a saying about the Pacific which says
you must never turn your back on the ocean,
a quake which wounded the Earth, enraged, its blood
set a trail of death in motion.
As we in the western world slept off the excesses of our Christian festivals and beliefs,
far, far away on another continent,
somewhere a world away from our own, our planet sought relief.

Not from the darkness, but in the morning,
as a new day was in its infancy, we awoke with a start,
a monstrous wall of death sought to vent its anger,
upon the unwary, and water was at its heart.
Cautiously it draped itself over the coastline,
nought could resist, creeping silently as it stole ashore,
the unsuspecting and unprepared eagerly and voraciously consumed,
leaving scenes of the aftermath of a war.

Such was its ferocity sailing vessels, trains and cars were lifted bodily
and deposited a mile or more inland,
people's livelihoods, and houses devastated,
and with the wreckage they lay, with the bodies in the mud and the sand.
The panic-stricken survivors fled with only the clothing they stood up in,
but at least they were alive,
the orphaned were not so fortunate,
the womenfolk deprived of their husbands and the men of their wives.

God had seen fit to shake the world,
the pebble hit the water and the ripples sought out their goals,
eerily the torrent once more becalmed,
and in its wake all that was left was an empty sea of souls.
Countless tens of thousands we are told perished,
many never to be found, unidentified, sent to their grave,
I have told of a saying about the ocean,
now I will tell you of the pebble, the ripple, and the wave.

Michael Hartshorne
Derbyshire

Epitaph

Unto my memory there so kind
To read of that I leave behind
Forgotten I may never be
Though most who read I shall not see

Forget me not, forget me not
These lines to better minds be taught
A melody of spoken word
Of not too plain to be absurd

William Stuart Robertson
Derbyshire

Mystery Tour Through Derbyshire

With blue sky and sunshine over our heads we set out for a pleasant drive,
Only the driver knows where we will go, we others will just 'arrive'.
Refreshments laid on at some point, we are told, we are just to sit back and relax
And enjoy all we see of the countryside - we shan't go back on our tracks,
But a while later a dark cloud is spotted, now what is that going to mean?
'We will go that way,' says the driver, 'where there's hardly a cloud to be seen.'
Oh how lovely it all looks around us, the fresh green of the trees in May,
Every village looking so different as through them we wend our way
Down lanes, by fields, across bridges, horses, cows and sheep we do view,
Round bends, by high hills and then a dale - there is always something new.
Cottages appear by the roadside, churches, inns, farmhouses between,
Flowers and everything lovely, so many joys to be seen,
But now the sky is greying over - oh here comes that torrential rain,
Fork lightning zigzagging down the sky, water everywhere and no road drain.
Everything's black now around us, thunder crashes high up above,
Driver watches the 'catseyes' on the road and we think of their inventor with love.
Oh how wonderful is this county of Derbyshire, with changing moods of weather each hour
Enhancing those beauties of nature, which God, for our joy, did endow.

Muriel I Tate
Derbyshire

Go On, Make His Day

A normal day for me and mine, is up with the larks come rain or shine
But not for our dog, he'd sleep all day, open one eye and growl *go away*
The only thing that will stimulate is when he sees his dinner plate
And as he's too fat to waddle and eat we have to put it down at his feet

A cute little puppy when he was given, we weren't told he was a Heinz fifty-seven
Won't sleep on the floor, needs his own chair, if he sees you on it you'd better beware
Doesn't like postmen or paper boys, his only passion is his squeaky toy
But tickle his belly and he's soft as grease, he almost grins saying *more of that please*

Slobbers and pants and snores like a man, just why we love him we can't understand
Lays about everywhere with no care at all, fat lazy dog never runs for a ball
He's the size of a horse but likes to sit on my lap, tries to get comfy, fancies a nap
He looks so happy then slides onto the floor, he'll have to realise he's no pup anymore

We love him dearly even when he smells bad, he's the scruffiest softy we've ever had
Curled up with me on a cold winter's night, with him on my bed everything is alright
We'd never change him we're sure of that and we'd never dare share him with a cat
So when you meet him don't run away, he just wants to lick you, go on, make his day

Elizabeth McNeil
Derbyshire

Christ Alone

Unto us a child is born
a morning star and brighter dawn
a child who's more than Christmas cheer
a child whose seasons span the year.

A child who did His Father's will
a child who healed the hurt and ill
a child who made the world complete
a child who's sold on shopping streets.

A child who's wrapped in tinsel foil
a child whose head wore holy oil
a child who raised the living dead
a child whose crown of thorns ran red.

A child who fed the hungry crowds
a child who cried in pain aloud
a child who died upon a cross
a child whose care was never cost.

A child whose house was once for sale
a child whose sorrows told a tale
a child who came to bring the light
a child who conquered darkest night.

Sean Kinsella
Derbyshire

A Mother's Love

A mother's love will never die
no matter how you hurt her
she'll stick by you
through thick and thin
you'll never have to doubt her

She's always there to care for you
through good times and bad
she'll make you happy
make you sad
but she'll always help you lad

So treat her gentle
love her true
she'll always have
some love for you
a mother's love is always true

C Davies
Derbyshire

See For Yourself

I live in the beautiful county of Derbyshire
Which has everything for you to see and desire,
We have stately homes and wonderful scenery to view
All waiting to be visited and viewed by someone like you.

We have Chatsworth House with the wonderful paintings to see
Also Chesterfield's 'Crooked Spire' which always amazes me,
In how it stands so high and proud against the skyline blue
Whichever way you approach it from it's a magnificent view.

Derbyshire has such breathtaking scenes
With wonderful hills and dales of bright greens,
We also have Chesterfield's four market days
Which have been going for 800 years so it says.

There is also Bolsover Castle and Hardwick Hall
Hardwick Hall they say 'is more glass than wall',
Built by good Queen Bess so it is said
In the brochures that I have seen and read.

But don't just take my word for what is there
Come and see for yourself and get your share
Of all that Derbyshire has to offer you
We also have Ladybower Lake and Derwent dam too.

George Reed
Derbyshire

Haggs Farm

The crowing of the cockerel,
The prating of the hen,
'O happy we were then'.

My granny's somnolent voice,
My mother's word of choice,
'O happy we were then'.

My grandad's deep yet quiet manner,
My father's voice without a stammer,
'O happy we were then'.

Aunt Maud's raucous laughter,
Uncle Albert's quiet banter,
'O happy we were then'.

Aunt Grace's gracious manner,
Uncle Ken's little stammer,
'O happy we were then'.

Robert Walker
Derbyshire

Loved And Lost

It plainly seems
that the girl of my dreams
won't come while I am alive,
I've sat here and waited
and anticipated
but still she hasn't arrived.

I've had this love long
and it's growing quite strong
I have no one to give it to,
I have searched high and low
and one thing I know
I am sure this love's not for you.

I am charmed by your charms
but you won't come into my arms
and I've found my dreams, are just dreams,
you have planned and you've plotted
but still I'm besotted
still I don't fit into your schemes.

My tears have been flowing
but still you are going
I have nothing left to say,
I'm too weak
you're going out with another
alas, it's my brother
you've been seeing for almost a week.

John J Axon
Denbighshire

Playing Crafty!

Do you really want to eat me when you've fed and reared me?
Can you bear to catch your faithful, feathered friend?
You can't really want me for your Christmas dinner!
I'll starve and starve to make me that much thinner.
I patrol the garden, keeping hens in check,
You'll all miss me if you wring my neck!
It worked. The crafty bird was saved.
They couldn't do the evil deed and send him to the oven door.
Each year he's tougher and older,
They love him more and more.
They bought him a girlfriend, they called them Onion and Sage
And to this day they live happily - a grand, grand old age!

J W Whiteacre
Denbighshire

Deepest Dreams

When the cold light of day fades
and the evening dawn casts its shades.
There is a safe place where I return,
to find my soul, to crash and burn.
Into the fire I shall walk, holding you tight,
as we talk, guarding me is what it seems.
Finding you in my deepest dreams.

Gazing at the burning light,
my mind released and holding you tight,
you share your word of solemn calm,
a frightened child from any harm.
In my realm I will wake,
and wait for the dark, your light to break,
I fall asleep into the arms of sake.
Wishing on undying thought,
I once was found but now I'm lost.
Smiling as you quiet my screams,
embracing me in my deepest dreams.

Patrick Mullen
Devon

Green Grass

How
sweet the sap
to Man his power,
so sweet his fill
of any fruits he gaineth
as yet he ponders, still,
upon the greenness of the meadow spread
in all shades of light, seducing he to visions ever bright
where pastures, rich in wistful greens, would rare a dream sustaineth.
Ah!
but,
among those visions laying wide to view
fresh fields invite, where grow the grasslands ever greener
in images of emerald tread
that bind his thoughts with velvet thread; more than his head containeth.
Those
enticing slopes that beckon he, into
where Man's sighs and deep desires leadeth, and,
wish will he, as dreamers do,
but the grasses grow no greener than
the fate that fate ordaineth.

Diana Mudd
Devon

Fowey/Polperro

Rippling stream o'er cobbles green,
Smoke-haze sky at eventide,
Angel's hair, on branch of fir,
Lure the insects to their fate,
Where the lurking spiders wait.

Trees are shedding summer foliage,
Change of dress to autumn gold,
Summer greens are wrapped away,
Amber, copper, rust and red, so bold,
Berries in profusion here,
Nut brown fungi clustering there,
Help enhance the atmosphere.

Blackberries ripen in the hedgerows,
Sloes are in abundance too,
Harvest-ripe figs in St John's precinct,
Whilst the church clock chimes at two,
The year is on the wane, but timeless is the churchyard's story,
Infants buried yesteryear, who lived so short a time on Earth,
To smell, see, taste and hear and feel,
The treasure of the autumn's glory,
And we, who have been spared to live,
And see the diamonds shimmer on the bough, the rainbow's myriad hue,
Reflect, we too must shed our earthen cloak,
Put on a mantle of the heavenliest blue.

Beryl Moorehead
Devon

February In Devon

How I wish that dull winter was over,
    And that leaden grey skies would all go,
But from what I've just seen on the telly,
    It seems that we're in for some snow!

The wind's howling loud round the rooftop,
    The rain's lashing hard on the pane,
They say it may clear by the pm,
    But I shan't take a stroll down the lane.

I shall stay snug and warm by the fireside,
    Till the spring makes a welcome return,
And while I wait, order some suncream,
    So that when summer comes, I won't burn!

All this is because a fine Candlemas,
    Means winter will not haste away,
This year's was bright sun, you see what it's done,
    But with luck, it may settle by May!

Michael Mayne
Devon

My Little Piece Of Heaven

My county is just wonderful, with such diversity
From country lanes to rolling hills, and an ever-changing sea
Villages that would look lovely on a chocolate box
And fields that stretch for miles and miles, the home of Mr Fox

Country fayre to suit all tastes, the choice could not be wider
From pasties, rock and cream teas too, and not forgetting cider
Enjoy the harvest from the sea, with freshness hard to beat
Or farmhouse honey on your toast, so sumptuous and sweet

Medieval castles that beckon you to call
Museums, zoos, art galleries, we really have it all
West End shows in theatres, a concert or a play
And clubs for all the young and old, to dance the night away

You could try fishing off the pier, horseriding on the moor
Every sport is offered here, on land or out offshore
Or simply take it easy and hire the old deckchair
And snooze away an afternoon, while taking in the air

This place I love in all its splendour, whether rain or shine
No money could tempt me away, this offer I'd decline
Where is this county I refer to as my piece of Heaven?
There's only one place it could be, the place I live is *Devon.*

George Wilford
Devon

Rural Life

Although Devon isn't my county of birth,
I've found it's a restful place here on Earth.
Amongst countryside and sea,
Where else would I want to be?

With the gentle air and sea breezes,
Winter rain that gives me the sneezes.
Warm sun on my face as I doze,
I'm glad this is the space that I chose.

Hedgehogs, squirrels and foxes,
Blue tits in nesting boxes.
Meandering streams,
Alive with hopes and dreams.

A lovely region to retire,
Poetic verses to inspire.
I adore this rural life,
Far away from noise and strife.

Rosemary Davies
Devon

A Steady Stream Of Words

Today, a lone fisherman stood in the embrace
of his beloved river, all her green wings and towers
folding him in the shawl of her watery hem
as he silently probed in the pools of a dream -
bluebells behind him as though sky had fallen
to the ground. *Ah,* I thought, *the ways*
of Earth are very knowing, and the flowing
without parallel in any human scheme.

The rocks lying on the bottom like drowned furniture,
granite dishes rocking slowly in the wet push,
rugs laid down on sand, liquid chairs
and seats preserved under the lissom glide,
water duvets pulled over stony beds
lulling them to sleep in gurglings and eddies.

The sibilant whispers against
barriers, like dialogues of what is and why this,
what design puts down in iron putty
mineral mud, the dark basement of certain depths
where all the rooms and stairs and hidden
crannies are purled over -
where acorns splash like tiny meteors
diving into depthless heaven.

All those elements swirl and deepen,
widen to a flat calm, then ripple white-crowned
in ceaseless murmurs past
faces blurred and bodies promised
to the steady mind of River brought down
to the entry mouth of sea, the very world
opening to receive what began as tiny trickles born
on Dartmoor land where ponies wade and dribble.

Karen Eberhardt Shelton
Devon

Smiles Forged, Emotions Masked

I smile at you
Force myself to believe it's genuine
My energy fades as does my smile
Was it real?

You tell me to let people in
But who can I let in?
Who would want to know?
It hurts that there's no one

You say you'll be there for me
But I've upset you enough already
Can't stand hurting anyone else
Hurting me is different

Crying releases so much
Angst, blame, worry
But it's not enough
And leaves me a wreck

Sometimes I want to reach out
Something always draws me back
Fear grips me
Coldness chokes me

All the names called, remembered
Repetitive, so I label myself
You don't have to ruin me
You've already laid the foundations

I'm not who you want me to be
I've tried to be that person
It's ripping me apart
Knowing you deserve better

Will you hurt me
Like so many others?
I don't want you to
Please don't hurt me

Vicki Thompson
Devon

Autumn

The apples fall and the leaves like winter snow
Gently float down to earth and disappear
Where do they go?
This is the time of rest
For animal and winter guests
A time for flora and fauna to withdraw
Making ready for the hoar
Nuts and berries taken off and hid
And rose heads from the stem got rid
Summer breezes change their temper
Always do in mid November
And we whomever we may be
Put on the fleece and sock up to the knee
Show our colours to the wintry sky
Look at me I hear us cry
Our heads put on all shapes and sizes
Some put on for disguises
Some to keep the hair in place
What a strange human race
Scarves, gloves, muffs, boots
Then the foghorn toot, toot, toots
How the autumn fills my heart with joy
Summer's not for me no matter how hard I try
But wind and lashing rain
That fills my pulsing vein
And chills my blood to stone.

Janet Vessey
Devon

Weather Blues

What a day I had today
You won't believe what people say
About the weather, wet or shine
It seems the blame is always mine
You may wonder why this is so
Well I'm the sky above you know
And when I'm clear the sun shines bright
Then the clouds come billowing white
Shutting out the glowing sun
So then I'm blamed by everyone.

Terry Rowberry
Devon

Spring Colours

First everything is mostly green
Grass grows taller than we've ever seen
Little birds fly up and pass
A multitude of life down in the grass

Then we look and all is white:
Snowy blossom shining bright
On each hawthorn branch up high
As white clouds sail across the sky

Now we see there's lots of gold -
Nature's story once more told -
Drifts of golden gorse smell sweet
As winter storms beat their retreat

All the spring colours showing through
Against a clear bright sky of blue -
Spring's new colour out again
Helped by light and sun and rain.

Diana Price
Devon

Winter Sun

Out of clouds dark and grey
Winter's sun comes out to play
Turns her eyes from black to blue
Works its magic deep and true

A Wiccan spirit sure and strong
Light streams from the ancient ones
Thawing the frost upon the earth
Warming deep within my heart

The rain is mist among the streams
Heated by the vibrant beams
A minutiae of nature's dance
In light that shines on sky-high chance

Shine on winter's sun
Shine upon that certain one
Turn her black eyes deeper blue
Work your magic deep and true.

Andrew Blundell
Devon

Memories Are Such Sweet Bliss
(The magic of Fred Astaire and Ginger Rogers)

They're in a dancing mood,
A gay, romancing mood,
Whenever they draw near;
She floats like a feather -
When they dance together - cheer!

To music soft and sweet,
Or smoothly so upbeat,
They'd pirouette with grace;
Fred in tails, and white tie -
Ginger in eye-catching lace.

There's 'Swing Time' and 'Top Hat'
And other great films that
Had style and rich romance;
With scores by Berlin and Kern -
New steps they must learn then dance.

In gorgeous 'Cheek To Cheek',
He sang; then they did seek
To synchronise each move;
Face-to-face, with verve and grace,
At brisk pace - right in the groove!

'Twas really heavenly
The way these two could be
So dazzling on the floor;
Debonair, suave Astaire -
And her flair - who'd ask for more?

In sunshine or in rain
I feel quite young again,
Whenever they're in view;
My heart rends, when it ends,
And these friends - must say adieu!

Roy Perry Court
Devon

Give Thanks

Give thanks, for all who gave their lives
Give thanks, for all that did survive
Give thanks, to all the folk, that came and helped
While many of us in prayer, knelt
Amidst the toil and sweat and tears
We will remember them in after years
The sacrifice of most of mankind
Those, in the Blitz, who put their lives on the line
Give thanks to all the unknown heroes
Their life was unexpectedly zero
Who gave their lives in the toil of war
Give thanks, for these brave warriors all
For without them, we nearly did fall
This anniversary, we will never forget
Though time moves on, and yet, and yet
And for the right to be free, it was lend to defend
Give thanks for all who went about their daily lives
When sirens wailed and some who cried,
For every day we were tested and tried
To survive, we were told it would be toil and tears
As we keep our tears for them in after years
And hope that it will never happen again
Give thanks to those on the Home Front
Who also bore the brunt
Of air raids, those in the factory
And the ARP mums and the WVS who somehow
Helped make victory
This anniversary we'll never forget
D Day, 60 years on,
Lest, lest, lest we *forget*.

Rosemary Peach
Devon

Estuary

drop anchor on the dying tide
day colour drains to dimpsy time
lull-lullabies in lap of waves
to cradle ease at set of sun
watch gulls gild grace on laundered sands
deft dunlins forage wakes of waves
and plovers pee-wit to the moon

Alan Chesterfield
Devon

A Pathway To God

A notion, a feeling, a glimpse of the soul,
A moment when time has no place;
Stilling the mind to events of the day,
Clearing the debris and turmoil away;
Permitting a pathway to God.

A thought, a reflection, a shimmering light,
An upliftment of beauty and peace,
Igniting the splendour of spirit within,
Renewing our love and commitment to Him;
Designing a pathway to God.

A scene, an impression, a vision of love,
A wisdom as souls reunite,
Opening doors we might not have seen,
Progressing our lives on a spiritual theme;
Creating a pathway to God.

A passion, a purpose, a strength thus renewed,
A sense of direction at last,
Armed with commitment, endurance and trust,
Driven by spirit to do what we must;
Walking our pathway to God.

An insight, a blessing, a secret revealed;
A knowledge of freedom and joy,
Expanding our vision beyond what we see,
Releasing our shackles, setting us free;
Lighting our pathway to God.

J M Redfern-Hayes
Devon

Inside Me

As I am learning . . .
learning to love myself,
I am willing . . .
willing to accept myself.
I am learning to respect myself.
And willing . . .
I am willing to see
a new world through myself . . .

Laura Jennings
Devon

The Feeling Of Love

It's better to love and lose
Than not to love at all
Tomorrow is another day
See what fate will do.

Your life is very precious
Tomorrow is too late
Make the most of what life can bring
And leave the rest to fate.

Your eyes are like diamonds
They sparkle when you smile
I live within my dreams of you
If for a little while.

A kiss will tell you everything
How you feel inside
Don't let this feeling pass you by
If love will grow or die.

The greatest thing that life can bring
Is when a newborn baby cries
Everybody lives with dreams
And hopes they never die.

I live within my magical world
That I've found eternal love
But only time will let us know
If our love will die or grow.

M B Tucker
Devon

The Earthworm

'Dear old boy' they call me cos I don't sting or bite.
In fact I do a lot of good, though mostly out of sight.
I don't have legs to crawl around,
But I can wriggle and squirm.
I love the dark, the fertile earth,
I'm a happy little worm!
I've got a secret clever trick
I fear not spade not trowel,
For if you cut a worm in half
He'll never shout nor howl -
Instead two worms go wriggling on in happy concentration,
We carry on and multiply the wormy population!

Mary Graves
Dorset

Harvest Moon

I awaited your arrival,
Standing in the harvest-shorn field
Which rustled round my feet
As if little people were playing hide-and-seek.
At first it seemed you did not want attention,
A pale image of yourself
As you glided from the horizon,
No lustre in your face as yet.
Wind blew a wisp of gauze,
Perhaps summoned by you,
As a screen to complete your ensemble
Before bursting on Earth's stage.
Then! there you blazed . . .
Shining disc with shadowed hills and valleys,
Those you touched gave a sigh of wonder.
There is no soft light from a full moon,
You brightened objects here below,
Highlighting, but emphasising darkness,
Reflected by some in monthly homage.
Fat, proud, beneficent,
The special moon of harvest.
And I too feel pagan awe,
Running an ear of corn through my fingers.

Di Bagshawe
Dorset

A Mother

I hold my child in the night,
how can I put this right?
His eyes so wide like an open sea,
how my heart warms when he looks at me.

My tears cannot save me now,
I need to be strong but I don't know how.
I fall to the ground and hit my head,
the wooden floor has changed to red.

So I close my eyes and start to pray,
but I do not know what to say!

Oh angels who watch over me,
I pray with my heart and soul to thee,
please watch over my baby.

I kiss his gentle hands and he looks at me,
we will meet again my son . . . you will see . . .

Hasina Rahman
Dorset

The Snowman

There sat the snowman
His deckchair was his throne
He sat oh so proudly
If he'd only known!
He sat there through the evening
While snow was on the ground
He sat on in the morning
Never making a sound!
The early morning traffic
Whizzed by at such a rate
No one even saw him
In this blissful state!
At lunchtime a lady
Camera in hand
Went walking down the seafront
To see snow upon the sand
She saw this lovely snowman
All happy in repose
Just managed to snap a picture
Before he lost his nose!

Rowena
Dorset

The Buzzard

Perched on a pole by the side of a hill.
I saw a buzzard, so majestic and still.
I lay on my back flat on the ground.
Watching the bird look slowly around.
Then without any effort or even a care,
It spread out its wings and took to the air.
Circling around, it soared into the sky,
Then uttered its call, a shrill, piercing cry.
It was answered at once from across the lake.
Another bird flew, it was obviously its mate.
Calling each other, they met high above.
Swooping and diving, showing their love.
They circled together high into the sky.
How wonderful it must be to be able to fly.
For almost an hour they entertained me.
Then circling down lower, they perched in a tree.
'Oh thank you great birds for that wonderful show,'
I shouted as I stiffly, got up to go.

Alan Deane
Dorset

Bullycide

Why do you punch and kick me so,
As I cower from every blow?
I am no different, from you or kin,
Yet you continue your boy bully sin.
You bruise my skin, I do not move,
I am human, I need not prove.

You fiercely flick as you are fleeing,
I've no self-worth as a human being.
As you terrorise, my body will quake,
Is my blood, really yours to take?
Your violent world, in front of peers,
I try to hide all of my tears.

If I wish, to quietly pass,
You entice others, to attack in mass.
I can't speak out because of my fear,
You hiss and spit, when you are near.
I try to hide, my time is spent,
My only torture, as you torment.

I lay awake with tears at night,
I am less a person, I cannot fight!
I tie this rope around my neck,
My feet will dangle, not touch the deck.
Sixteen youths will die each year,
They take their lives, because of fear.

Anthay
Dorset

The Gap Of Rocks

The Dorset famous secret, Golden Gap,
is always being pounded
by the restless sea,
and to scramble upwards
on slippery rocky paths.
Weary of wearing your mac,
to arrive on a flat table
rock feeling free of time.

Then, look along the lonely,
shiny moonlit bay of Lyme,
under an alluring galaxy of stars.
Watching curving coastline
dwindling afar
and to walk on this golden floor!
The adoring beauty
is to draw you back once more.

Sammy Michael Davis
Dorset

A Special Star

As you listen to the radio,
and you hear a familiar song,
of joy and life, and happy times,
your thoughts turn to someone.

Who was so loved by everyone,
with never an unkind word,
who could melt your heart, like the summer sun,
and charm like a sweet singing bird.

You're remembering now that kind, smiling face,
and those wicked twinkly eyes,
tho' closed and peaceful as he slept,
on the day that you kissed him goodbye.

Well this evening, just as night falls,
glance up into the sky,
God didn't say why he took him from you,
could it be that he's showing you why?

A star that you've never seen before,
that could light up the darkest of nights,
with a wicked twinkle, that whispers to you,
hey kid, I'm right here . . . it's alright!

Trudie Squires
Dorset

One Life

One life is all I have,
to create happy memories to lift me when I feel sad,
to make a difference to someone's day,
helping to take another's pain away.

One life is all I have,
to laugh and smile and feel glad,
to see the smallest flower blossom and grow,
watch the ducks on the pond with their little ones in tow.

One life is all I have,
to recognise life is too short for futile rifts and lovers' tiffs,
to really love those special people who make me feel alive,
and let go of the hurt I feel inside.

One life is all I have,
to cope with both the good and bad,
to try not to dwell too much and become sad,
for life is for living and I don't care if others think I'm mad.

Julie Marie Laura Shearing
Dorset

Grandad, I Love This Place

Let's get up early, pack some food, load car and boat with gear,
Add swimsuits, buckets, spades and towels, blue skies are bright and clear!
The tides are right and so we're sure that we won't go aground.
The engine starts, and off we go; it's such a lovely sound.

Young coots and moorhens hide in reeds along the winding river.
Our boat sends ripples all around; it makes the small craft quiver.
Once in the harbour, engine revs; quite soon we'll see our isle.
Surrounded by the seas so blue, on George's face a smile!

Our landing beach comes into view, there're prints of gulls' webbed feet.
The only mark along the shore, till Bob Dog leaps off seat!
He's off, away like lightning streaks; the birds just disappear,
And Bob looks on, he's quite bemused, what *have* they got to fear?

He's never caught one yet because he only wants to play;
A compromise - he'll just chase waves, so up and down all day!
Now George alights with pail and spade, plus favourite plastic digger,
And castle ramparts, moats, appear, the sand pile getting bigger.

Isabel just watches, she adores her strong big brother,
He means the entire world to her, protects her like no other.
We're heading off now to explore, the saltings look inviting,
But wait, a small craft comes in sight, a sailor is alighting.

We pour him out a cup of tea and share a sandwich snack.
'Are you the owners here?' he says; - 'I've soon to head right back.'
A cormorant standing on a buoy swoops down to spear a fish.
With his long beak - he'll rarely miss an appetising dish!

Now wandering up among the firs, we find a spot to camp.
Groundsheets and rugs, our box of food, warm clothes and tilley lamp.
The sun sinks low - it's almost set, George says, smile on his face!
'Oh Nana, Grandad - do you know - I really love this place?'

Gillian Humphries
Dorset

The Beaufort Monument, Wimborne Minster

Still resting sedately side by side
After so many bell-rung centuries
And gazing at a glittering star-filled ceiling
They lie close to the high altar
Watched over by stained glass saints
A courtly middle-aged couple
Formally holding hands
Lying in an alabaster peace
Their facial features perfectly preserved
A medieval union meticulously displayed.

An imposing aristocratic warrior
Dressed in ceremonial armour
Fashionable buckles adorn his shoes
With a decorative neck-chain confirming his rank
His massive sword is broken at the hilt
And he carries no martial shield.

Her slim figure gracefully carved
She wears a sophisticated gown
The elegant folds carefully arranged
And a veil reaches down to her slender waist
All the fingers on her left hand are broken
Her only recognisable flaw.

Guarded by a pair of smiling angels
Cherub-like with delicate, outspread wings
Each feather carefully chiselled
The original colours still visible
This regal couple recline at ease
As sunlight shimmers all around
And curious visitors marvel at their polished composure.

A feudal marriage set in stone, majestically.

Christopher J Korta
Dorset

The Nursing Home

I look around me
All I see is
Vacant eyes
Lost in other worlds
Of time gone by

Does anyone care
For these lost souls
Sitting waiting as the clock ticks on

Faces look with no expression
As I walk by
Lines of time etched on their faces
Slumped in chairs
With heads bowed low
Reality is emptiness
To these lost souls

Outside mayhem as traffic builds up
Pollution makes it hard to breathe
But in this place time stands still
Quiet is all around
Except for a sigh or cough
Rainbows out of reach
As they sit and stare with glazed eyes
Dribbling, hands reach out for the yesterdays
For what's not there anymore

And life goes on

Lynne Whitehouse
Dorset

A Walk In February

Down leafy lanes and rustic tracks,
Walking without a care,
Past thatched cottages, barking dogs,
And signs, that say, *beware!*
Through boggy fields, past twinkling streams,
The farms looked far beyond,
We came to hamlets, an ancient church,
Ducks on the village pond.
Ponies gazed and cattle grazed,
We waved a cheery, 'Hi!'
The coal-tits in the hedgerows chirped,
A pig came ambling by.
We scrambled over gates and stiles,
Our feet were very sore,
The wind grew chilly; the sky was grey,
Remote out on the moor.
Cold and bitter, the air was fresh,
Perfect peace so rare,
The views across the countryside,
Nothing can compare.
We came upon a woodman's hut,
As we stumbled through the mire,
He welcomed us to have a rest
Beside a roaring fire.
We turned up our collars, round our faces,
Farewell and off we went,
Through the valleys and woodland glens,
Exhilarated and content.

June Melbourn
Dorset

A Dream Of Perfection

Last night I had a dream -
A precious dream
For in it
Everything was wonderful,
The kind of vision I had never experienced
Before.
All was perfection -
No wars, no hating
Just joy, peace, and a
Blissful happiness.
Love was shown like it had never
Been shown before.
It seemed to shine
In a darkened world
Brightening its gloomy misery.
There were no tears, no sadness,
Just perfect
Contentment.
There was a veil of satisfaction
Spread over the entire world.
No more jealousy or bitterness.
People were happy . . .
Suddenly, I awoke!
What bitter tragedy!
My dream was completely
Shattered.
Could this dream ever turn into reality?
I pray that some day it will.
What a day that will be!
When all is perfection.

Janet Kerntiff
Dorset

Partnership

How fanciful of nature
   occasionally to bequeath
   Pan's inheritance.
Master of ferned forests
   and green glades.
Ever mischievous,
   how delicate still
   his sense of humour.
A jagged brown-thrust of bark
   spikes soil, hewn knee-high;
Its ugliness made dainty
   with tumultuous laughter.
A small frivolity; frilled flutes
   that trill a wayward tune
Cloven hooves can dance too.

How she survives, this Earth.
No enmity between the spores,
   but close enchantment
As they drink moisture
   from Pan's eternal spring.
Alive the stump plays throbbing beat
   upon an intimate drum
Known only to the undefeated.
And so, they grow together,
   a paradoxical partnership.
As like wild rose to ammonite
   affixed.
Yet both will outgrow the time
   we take to marvel at the way
   a life is shaped.

Janine Vallor
Dorset

Whisper A Wish

If one wish,
Were granted me,
Spoilt for choice,
Would I be,
I'd ponder a while,
Weighing up the pros and cons,
Then make my wish,
With a smile,
Then all across,
This magical globe,
The children,
Would walk free,
From poverty and illness,
From suffering and adversity,
To come together,
As equals and friends,
A force so strong,
They'd push to one side,
The older generations,
Who have blindly,
Led us to,
This teetering brink,
The children would,
Change our course,
Save us all,
And this planet,
We're living on,
Better get onto,
The department of hopes and wishes,
Before it's too late,
Because for some sanity,
To the order of things,
The world can't wait.

P J Littlefield
Dorset

One Wish

I have but one wish for the human race,
That love be law, and war erased.
Our lovely world is under threat,
From chemicals, we must not let,
Industrial waste pollute our air,
Water supplies, and animals' lairs.
We need all people worldwide
To give more love and be wide-eyed,
To banish hatred, and religious slant,
There is one God, we take no chance.
If we submit to a common cause,
For peace on Earth, and no more wars,
Banish lethal weapons and dynamite,
Let's fight for peace, we have the right
To enjoy our lives, on limited time.
This is not a 'trial', our world's sublime,
We need to care, respect and love
Our families, children, as our God's love.
Millions wish for peace on Earth,
They pray, they die, where there's no mirth.
Let's open our hearts, compromise, rejoice,
Because very soon we will have no choice.
The world will perish, from lack of care,
This is a fact, we should beware,
It's not too late, to change the trend,
Bring back love, let our gods attend
To our normal needs, feed and clothe
Millions, who suffer where war is loathed.
Fight for the rights, without blood and tears,
Walk the streets without any fears,
We all desire to live in an ideal land
Let conflicts cease, and kindness be grand.
Treat others as you would your wife,
We're only human, we have but one life,
We were not born to be abused,
The world needs love, and some good news.
Let's grant our wish to one another,
And be kind to someone else's mother.

Brian M Hurll
Dorset

Read Me A Bedtime Story

You were supposed to be there,
Walk me down the aisle on my wedding day.
You were supposed to be there,
On my 18th, 21st too, blow out my candles and pray.
Read me a bedtime story: while I drift off to sleep

Dancing around the living room, glancing at the clock,
One second has passed, a blink of the eye.
Lying in a white bed, looking at your face,
It tells me a story, but your eyes tell me no lies.

You were supposed to be there,
First passenger in my new car.
You were supposed to be there,
On my 8th, 11th, 13th too, telling me I'm your little star.
Read me a bedtime story: while I drift off to sleep

Gripping my smaller hand, you tell me you love me,
I grin and nod, I already know you do.
You point to my heart, 'That's where I'll always be,' I am told,
But none of this makes sense to a humble six-year-old.

You were supposed to be there,
When I receive my results and on my graduation day.
You were supposed to be there,
At the birth of your first grandchild in the month of May.
Read me a bedtime story: while I drift off to sleep

'Daddy,' I giggle at your corny jokes,
Your laugh that sounded round the room. Stopped.
Pulling out our favourite bedtime story,
I read your bedtime story: while you drift off to sleep.

Laura Ford
Dorset

Newbiggin Ladies (1940)

Haul away! Haul away! Keep the carriage running free,
Get the *'Augustus'* and *'Laura'* down to the sea,
Haul away! Ladies, with a resolute smile,
Haul along *Pant Road*, then nearly a mile
O'er heathland and moor, and doon the 'Ashy Gutter'.
With quickening heart, giving many a flutter.
Haul away! Ladies, haul handsomely
To the White Hole Skears, then we'll see
The *'Augustus'* and *'Laura'* floating free.
Saving the *'Eminent'* crew from a cruel sea.
So haul away! Ladies, a-launching we'll see
By the launching ladies, of Newbiggin-by-the-Sea.

There's Val, Irenie, Susan and Jane,
Catherine and Jeannie, June and Elaine,
There's Bella and Betty, Helen and Claire,
Liza and Lizzie, and the Robinson pair.
There's Dora and Doreen, Maggie and May,
Christine and Chrissie, Ruby and Fay,
There's Margaret and Maureen, Alice and Dot,
Melissa and Ivy, Jennifer and Tot.
There's Ina O'Brien and her daughter Annie,
Kitty and Janet, Louisa and Nannie.

So haul away! Haul away! Keep the carriage running free,
Haul away! Ladies, now handsomely,
Haul away! Ladies, haul resolutely,
Slip the *'Augustus'* and *'Laura'*, float her free,
Launched by the ladies of Newbiggin-by-the-Sea.
So haul away! Haul away! A-launching we'll see,
By the haul away! Ladies of Newbiggin-by-the-Sea.

A Quinn
Dorset

My Dorset

The rolling hills of Dorset, in history abound.
In every church and castle, and every hill fort mound.
Its hillsides and its valleys. The shipwrecks on its shore.
The giant at Cerne Abbas, and still there's many more.

'Whitchurch Canonicorum', this name may seem quite quaint.
The only church in England whose shrine will hold its saint.
A place to where our ancestors, a pilgrimage would make.
While modern man just drives on by and leaves it in his wake.

Lyme Regis down to Bournemouth, there's coves and beaches fair.
The headlands and the heathlands are there for all to share.
The monument to Hardy, hill fort at Pilsden Pen,
Lulworth Cove and Durdle Door, will call you back again.

Swanage. This pretty village enjoys a sandy bay.
The gardens and the Esplanade will make your holiday.
One mile south, at Durlston Head the 'Great Globe' can be found,
Weighing over forty tons and thirty-odd feet round.

From Boscombe Chine to Christchurch, or the beach at Weymouth Bay.
View Chesil Bank from Portland Bill, you'll really want to stay.
Monkey World near Wareham, is where the 'Cronin' family
Have rescued apes around the world and once more set them free.

There's Bridport and Bockhampton. There's Wool and Cranbourne Chase.
You'll need a 'month of Sundays' to visit every place.
Life here is so relaxing, it sets your spirit free.
Like me you'll find that Dorset is the only place to be.

Tony Fuller
Dorset

Toby The Sausage Bandit

(For my three young friends Heather and Abby Nichol and Heather MacLean)

I rose up with the lark one day, and set off down the street
I hummed myself a little tune, the air was clean and sweet
I heard the sound of children's voices, having a good time
And this is how my tale begins, come listen to my rhyme.

Two Heathers and wee Abby, played on a trampoline
Daniel played there with them, upon the Nichols' green
Abby was an acrobat she bounced up in the air
Somersaulted coming down, without a bit of care

Soon they finished playing, and ran off down the street
To try and find wee Toby, and feed him a nice treat
The children couldn'y find him, he'd vanished from the place
They asked me if I'd seen him, I hadn't spied his face

A butcher's van was standing just outside the children's house
Angry shouts came from within, the man had cause to grouse
Mister Gilmour stomped outside wi' Toby on his lead
He'd wired into his sausages, and had a stolen feed

He banged the door where Heather stayed, her mum came to the door
'Here is your sausage bandit!' the poor man he did roar.
'You owe me one pound eighty, for sausages,' he said.
Toby wagged his tail and barked, 'I've not been so well fed!'

Her mother paid the butcher, and Toby barked goodbye
The children all did laugh so much, the tears ran from their eyes
I had great entertainment the truth to you I tell
The little sausage bandit had cheered me up so well.

Roy A Millar
Dunbartonshire

Granda

You stopped eating,
But bad things don't happen to me.

You kept forgetting,
But bad things don't happen to me.

You stopped walking,
But bad things don't happen to me.

You kept needing more and more help,
But bad things don't happen to me.

You kept sleeping,
Your heart stopped beating.

You stopped breathing.

Something bad just happened to me.

You have drenched me in love, pulled me in.
Soaked through the bone, seeped through the skin.

Love pulsed through me like a second blood.
All because of you.

Thank you for being you: for helping me to become me.

Thank you for loving me: for helping me to love you,
And others as I do.

I'm so glad I made your life happier.
Too bad I couldn't make it longer.

I'll never forget you,
Your soul, your smile, your face.

It's hard to imagine life without you,
I guess I'll just have to do my best.

I love you.

Goodbye.

Emma Ritchie
Dunbartonshire

Another Saturday

The drunk staggers,
Shouting and whispering,
Regaling any with tales of war.
He holds the rank of taxi,
Trying to get home.
The most action he ever saw,
Was a knee trembler
With a lady of the night.
A couple of minutes fumbling,
Thirty quid for her next hit.
He echoes into the distance,
To the accompaniment of sirens,
Like screeching owls
Flushing out victims.
Another Saturday,
Rolling with the punches,
As the bars call time,
And the brawls pour out.
Groups of mini-skirted giggles
Link arms
Clip-clopping headlong into oblivion.
As the clocks hit five,
The sweepers push down Detritus Avenue,
Clearing the way,
For Sunday's Bible thumpers.
No blood today,
Just fire and brimstone
Repent all ye sinners.

R Reid
Dunbartonshire

A Grey Afternoon In Aberystwyth

It's a grey Sunday afternoon in Aberystwyth
The sky is slate, the sea is grey and I am grey
Foam flecks fly in the high wind
Without ever escaping the shoreline
A grey-haired lady walking with her arm tight within her partner's catches my eyes
We hold eye contact, she breaks first
Is she afraid I will want her grey-haired man?
It is January, always a grey month
The shiny silver of December has passed
We are left with a grey afternoon in Aberystwyth.

Melanie M Burgess
Dyfed

Autumn Child

She is the child of the rain and the wind and the storm.
With her skirt of fallen autumn leaves whipping around her legs,
Barefoot she dances and skips along with the wind.
She dances with the storm in a quiver of a thousand raindrops.
With her long tangled hair flying behind her
And her small feet light as the wind through the drifting grass,
She skips between the raindrops, never a drop falling upon her.
The dark grey clouds move furiously in the whitewashed blue sky.
Trees, like dancers' hands, twist and turn, contorting into shapes in the wind.
The few damp leaves, which were a moment ago scattered across the ground,
Are now whipped up and dance and dive like fairies across the sky.
The red-brown colours turn the sky red like fire dancing on the wind.
Then with a vast hurricane of wind-blown leaves, she has gone.
The wind stops its roaring and howling and goes back,
Lightly stroking the trees and rustling the leaves on the grass.
The rain ceases its battering and slowly water runs
Trickling along the creases of the leaves, running into the earth.
The angry clouds in the sky slowly dissolve and around the corner follows the sun.

Amber Bruce
Dyfed

My Definition Of Love For You

When you just see darkness
I'll help you see the light
Whenever you feel scared
I'll help you stand and fight.
If ever you feel pulled down
I'll help you stand up tall
If ever you may stumble
I'll catch you if you fall.
If ever you may need me
Just whisper and I'm there
To hold you tight, protect you
To show you that I care.
So we will stand together
Two halves that make a whole,
I pledge to you my spirit
My love, my heart, my soul.

Kelly Morris
Dyfed

The Absent Guest

'Sit up straight!' my mother admonished
Best china and cutlery, table polished.
My feet so barely touched the mat and
Swung idly to and fro like that in time with ticking clock.

I knew, as ever, he wouldn't come
It was always thus, just me and Mum.
And I was dressed in Sunday best with
Clean white socks all neatly pressed, just like my frock.

I cared not much for the absent guest
Making *her* clutch pendant to her breast
And shoulders droop in heavy sigh that
Communicated in her eye, today there'd be no knock.

There would be no steaming rabbit pie
As aromas changed to burnt and dry,
So I'd retreat with empty tum without
A backwards glance at Mum whose pain I couldn't block.

I don't know what came over me,
This empty void grew angrily.
I marched up to the photograph then
Jumped on it with all my wrath 'til sepia eyes could no more mock.

Sharon Copsey
Dyfed

Mouse Trip

Mustn't forget the mouse!
Can't leave it in the house,
Put it in the car -
A trip to town's not far.

Humane traps are in -
Old-fashioned ones a sin!
Now it's catch and take away,
To live another day!

Take the mouse for a ride -
A quick car trip; inside
Now it plans its future life -
No cats, no traps, no strife!

Jo Brookes
Dyfed

Peacefulness

Walking through the hillside
up the hills, and down,
so much more peaceful
than being in town.
A rabbit or a hare
or a squirrel up a tree,
fields and fields of grass
and so many plants to see.
Following the coastal paths
maybe climb a stile,
so much beauty to endure
each and every mile.
The sound of flowing water
a stream or a small river,
all the countryside movement
of the animals who all live there.
Many people having picnics
with respect to take their litter,
so that all the picnickers around
have no reason to feel bitter.
A nice cool breeze a-blowing
cooling your sun-warmed face,
as you gaze around the hillside
with so much eye-viewing space.
A day in the countryside
unspoilt beauty all around,
watching for any animals
in the trees, or on the ground.

Susan Miller
Dyfed

Cymru

The sea has come to kiss the land,
With unseen hand caress the hills.
Sheets that hang, they hold their line,
Spinning time, release the rhyme.

Betrayed emotions, shades of green,
Gleam and glisten, fill the eye.
Reflecting sky, milk strained tears,
Move swiftly on, to blind cold fear.

The love that beats begins to speed,
A need for leaps of faith unknown,
To gentle souls, this helping hand,
A mother's gift, for those who can.

R A Savory
Dyfed

Jenny Goodwich

Opening my door to him tonight, I saw heavy, uncut grass
In my garden, glistening wet, a thick clouded, obscure sky.
No and goodbye, I had told him twice, loyal to you.
The phone rang a third time, melting the bottom of my spine,
My hand undecided, wet from washing dishes.
'I just want to be wanted tonight,' he said, 'can I see you?'
And in a long outward breath I said yes into the distance.

Yes, I've never been cured of that deadly excitement
In my spine at the sight of him, the sound of his voice.
If you ever find out, you'll say what the world has said for years:
Jenny has no elastic in her underwear, she has a habit
Of finding it around her ankles and then she falls down.
But it wasn't the excitement, or him, or his little smile of triumph
As he looked down at my face, my head on the pillow,
It was knowing that I was a sanctuary, a soft and calm place,
Not an object, but his refuge, just as I am yours.
He fell asleep briefly in my arms, twitching in bad dreams,
By 10pm he was gone but my body would not register regret,
Instead his sleep still clung to my breasts as I changed the sheets.
I took a shower, his contentment still there in my hips,
I drove to the airport, at midnight I was smiling at you cloudlessly.

It is 2.30am and you sleep in my arms, your dreams seem good ones.
Jenny the sleep giver, the same body, same bed for you both . . .
The world judges my actions harshly, proud of its own values,
Jenny has no elastic in her underwear and so on.
But not so long ago you could not sleep, my darling lawyer,
Could not sleep for three weeks because of the world's values,
You could not believe the sentences, a year for the rapist,
Seven years for the car thief because his brother owned a gun.
And my visitor tonight? I can still feel his sleep cling to my breasts.
They are sending his nineteen-year-old soldier son
To fight against terror in the desert.
Outside in my garden is heavy, uncut grass, glistening wet,
The wind leaning on it, a thick clouded, obscure sky.

Anthony James
Dyfed

Passing Me By

Life is passing me by,
I feel I'm living a lie,
I should be out there dancing,
For old age is advancing,
And soon it will be too late,
I haven't got time to wait.

A Cooper
East Sussex

Cambridge Revisited

The plaintive floorboards creak as I remember;
The view from the window's the same.
The college court gleams soft as once it did
At evening forty years ago.

Across my gaze two figures stroll and break the screen
Of memory that I have built.
They wear the dress and manners of today,
So shattering my reverie.

An aching to be young again is what remains,
The recollection of those years
When hope and thought and love distilled the prospects
Of a life that's come between.

Ought I to stay and bear more pain or exit now
And leave the haunting days behind?
Renounce the sad hypothesis of what else might
Or should have been their consequence?

The chapel clock at five displays the paradox
Of growing old against the quiet
Permanence of learning, lawn and ancient stone,
And striking, soothes away the pain.

Rex Baker
East Sussex

Hope Comes At Christmas

At the end of a year of destruction and death
Through tsunami, flood, earthquake and bomb
The message of Christ rings out through the Earth
Proclaiming our Saviour has come.

If only the world His commandments would heed
Irrespective of colour or creed
To love one another and help those in need
For 'twas for all He did suffer and bleed.

In every disaster God stands by the side
Of all those who will let Him come near
Through all the trauma He will gently guide
Our sorrows He'll help us endure.

Hope comes at Christmas as we listen and learn
God's way of obedience and love
That leads to the peace for which we all yearn
And assures us of Heaven above.

Beryl R Daintree
East Sussex

Mother Earth Is Not Well

Looking back over the years, how fares Earth?
Apart from natural causes with little worth,
The human factor must bear its responsibility,
Often one wonders at its credibility.

The threat to the ozone continues unabated,
Any chance of control on this is now dated,
So nations carry thundering on, uncaring,
When, with a little sense, there would be worldwide caring.

Now we have the terrorists' threat round about us,
No one could have visualised its effectiveness,
At one time nature could control the land,
Now with so much upheaval, it's out of hand.

So how can we save our Mother Earth?
Surely the most important task is research,
Failure to stem the present rush on oil,
Can only result in nature's lack for all.

Since time began, Earth has always coped,
However, despite the present threat, it's hoped,
Only cooperation between nations will win,
Thus may climate change be free from sin.

W R Burkitt
East Sussex

The Art Of News

Red sky, November afternoon
Trees, dark, shimmering
Squeal, child nearby
Freshness of air, exhilarating
Seems strange -
Red sky this time of year
Must be global warming
It's cold, so cold
We are in for a very cold Siberian winter
Snow already in parts of the country
Today, the Express News let me know
George Best, the footballer died today
No more suffering
He lived his life
But left a message what drink can do
The red sky is now dimming
As his secret emerges -
His organs he hopes will be donated to help others
Winter, so cold
Just history revolving like a spinning wheel.

Josie Lawson
East Sussex

In Country Calm
(For Mum and Dad - 20/9/05)

Still moment
Aware of leaves dancing
In autumn light.
Sitting here
Shadow of this tree
Gathers me
In quietness, allows
Space for me
To find myself.
Coming here
In country calm
I, like a tree
Reach upward for
Truth, I think
Of a country path
Where now
You still walk
Dad, not turned
The corner
Finding Mum
Waiting, gathering.
You both
Stand again, free as
The breeze, end of
All loneliness
End of all pain.
Memories touch gentle
As glowing autumnal light
Singing, sprinkling
Of birdsong
Even here, now, in
Creation there is
A sense of joy, of
Love in truth that
Shall never pass away.

George Coombs
East Sussex

We Are So Damn Lucky To Have You As Our Dad

(Happy Birthday Dad . . . 70)

I hope today is so very special
You enjoy all that you do
Because birthdays like these are for special people
Dad, this day is for you
Seventy is a milestone
Of life and love and happiness
We are so damn lucky to have you as our dad
Guess we were truly blessed

Friends and family will get together
For a party that we have planned
Secretly behind your back
Sorry Dad, but you do understand
Can't wait to see you smile
See the look on your face
A special moment to last forever
Happy people in a happy place

All of my life
I have wanted to tell you how much I care
Now I think is the time
I won't embarrass you Dad, I swear
But I am glad
To have known you, that is true
You are also my friend, George
That's all I want to say to you

So let's raise a toast
To you and me mum
It's your anniversary too
And the night has only just begun
Family all together
Friends around you two
Happy seventieth, Dad
Our best wishes go out to you.

Stephen A Owen
East Sussex

Terror Time

There you are
The shadow in the dark
Conscience less, lost, lying
Lest we see your weakness,

> Making war on me

I do not know you
Yet I fear your gun-metal cold hand
Frozen, iced, spliced
To the trigger of stoic rage.

I am ice too
When you blacken the TV
With reeling rhetoric
Zealously darkening my life

> Making war on me

I wait for you
To kiss me with hate
Sucking my breath effortlessly
Triumphantly
In showers of explosive sparks
Full of direst cruelty

> Making war on me.

E D Darling
East Sussex

The Skirmish

A halt is signalled where the trees
Stop and meet a tufted mead
Magnolia blossoms scent the breeze
In haste are shallow trenches dug
And barricades of trunk and log
Are hunkered in or hid behind
High summer insects buzz and whine
Unshaven faces streaked with sweat
Watch for foes unseen as yet
And four-score apprehensive eyes
Are glued to silver birch-topped rise
Shrilling flute and pounding drum
Announce the enemy to come
As ragged grey forms break the crest
A nightjar flies for quietness
Down the gentle grassy slope
A whooping, yelling horde now lope
And as guns report and crack
The motley force is driven back
In certainty, concealed emerge
In a final battle surge
With thrust of sword and bayonet
Ambushed sons in crimson set.

Andrew Carey
East Sussex

Fantasy

There is a 'beneath world' of childhood
I must try and find for you
Where kings and giants play amongst the velvet tents
Where you can roll and twist and turn
But there are dangers in this mural
Of knives and clawed giant feet that smell of sweat
And splintered wood that turns you inside out.

Is it the springboard of dreams?
Can you find this embroidered world of 'under'?
You can slip in easily, through the crack
And although the journey may be sticky
You need to wriggle carefully in
You will find, over the years, that pillows become smoother
And more comfortable and quilted
And all the lumps and rust have gone.

Fill up a bed with flowers and the smell of grass
Then the wheels of life turn smooth
And you will float like lemonade bubbles
When life slopes away, as it will, depend on that
Remember the story, push against splinters
And clear a path through the paperwork
You and your carved life will babble
With birdsong in the breeze
Now the iron spokes will be as music for sleep.

J Williams
East Sussex

Terror In London 2005

What a terrible, terrible crime
In London, 7th July, around nine
Controlled explosions ripping apart
Trains in the underground's heart
A terrible, terrible loss of life
Causing relatives and loved ones stress and strife
Not knowing if their dear ones had lost their lives
Mothers, fathers, husbands, wives
Horrendous injuries maiming many
Innocent victims unsuspectingly
Leaving their homes on their normal grind
At the end of the day, only to find
Life would never be the same
Scarred for life, agony, pain
Shattered completely, bodily, mentally
Dear God, what has become of our way of life
That folk live in fear on the edge of a knife?
When folk do unto others as they would like to be done by
There will be no conflicts along the way
Dear God, speak to the hearts and minds of Thy people
That life will be precious for one and all
That evil will cease and the world can have *peace.*

Evelyn A Evans
East Sussex

Nurses Are Angels

What would we do without you?
You are angels in disguise

You help us when we are poorly
And tell us to wipe our eyes
Your patience is never-ending
Though tried too far at times

We don't forget and won't forget
How much it pleases us
To know you are there
And know that you care
Thanks from all of us.

Audrey Allott
East Yorkshire

Naught So Queer As Folk

I am not a Yorkshire person
I am from the Isle of Wight
Some treat me like a stranger
Some think I'm quite all right.

It doesn't really matter though
What people think of me
Cos I have lived in Yorkshire
Since nineteen seventy-three.

People often stop and ask me
So where do you come from?
You've got a funny accent
Like Last Night At The Prom.

I tell them God's own country
My accent's southern … true
But my pronunciation
Is naught to do with you.

After all, you speak Hull
You flatten all your vowels
Not particularly attractive
Unless you are an owl.

Only joking really
The Yorkshire folk I know
Speak with lovely accents
Like alreet ducks, mind ya nowa.

Where would we be without them
They are what we're all about
It would be really boring
If we all spoke 'just like that'.

Liane Bell
East Yorkshire

Aurora

I love to see you.
Lighting heavens below cloud
Sweeping arcs of silken light
Feathered flakes of floating gold, with
Colours: subtle, deep and striking
Swaying, arching, swooping, caressing stars
Like rainbows' tears of delight.
Slinking across a holy night
Something sacred
Something so beautiful
A phenomena of nature's creation.
Behind and above, on a horizon of fir
Reflected voluptuously upon lakes
Of teardrops from Heaven
That joy in the display
And weep, weep, weep
At your joy
And hope you never
Fade to grey.

Stephen Tuffnell
East Yorkshire

Sweet Perfection

Eyes as green as summer meadows,
Lips the softest touch,
Skin as smooth as woven silk,
Perfection's infinite clutch.

To love him more than love itself,
To drain that past reflection,
To destroy heart's memory chained secure,
It can only be perfection.

Hand in hand upon the breeze,
Drifting far away,
And if apart, they're never there,
Together every day.

Through the wind and through the rain,
Entwined in sunshine just the same,
For the wind it blows them far away,
Raindrops wash away the pain.

And perfection flows throughout his soul,
Cleansing all perception,
For no single soul shall ever know,
How there could be such sweet perfection.

Sarah Heptinstall
East Yorkshire

Hallowe'en

The doorbell rang - gave me a fright
As the ghost stood on my step tonight
White sheets billowing in the air
Weird wailing sounding everywhere
I shivered in the cold lamplight
As the creature clutched my coins so tight
Down my step he went with a mighty bound
His trainers hardly touched the ground.

The doorbell rang - oh what a scare
A skeleton was standing there
Fluorescent bones shone in moonlight
It was a truly awesome sight
Loudly he rattled a rusty chain
I parted with money yet again
And then the apparition fled
With baseball hat upon his head.

The door bell rang - it's Hallowe'en
There stood a witch with face of green
Long straggly hair 'neath pointed hat
She even managed to scare the cat
I trembled - she held out her hand
Taking the coins from my shaking hand
And with a cackle away she rode
On her skateboard she flew down the road.

These modern things from ancient time
The witch, the ghost, the skeleton
Went on their way. I closed the door,
I'd never laughed so much before

Barbara Dunning
East Yorkshire

Christmas Fayre

I've just finished my dinner
and I'm not any thinner.
I'm hiding my tum,
please don't look at my bum.
I've had six mince pies,
I don't think that was wise,
and the crumbs on the plate,
are the remains of the cake.
I've had lots of sweets
and chocolate treats.
Drank loads of wine,
but I feel just fine.
I'm full to the brim,
so I just sit and grin.
Can't move anywhere,
so I'll stay in my chair.
I look such a fright,
as my dress is too tight.
Yes, I do know I'm fat,
when is Weight Watchers back?
Oh just pass me a sweet,
I'll diet next week.
After all
It is Christmas!

Doreen Hampshire
East Yorkshire

The Bond

Lying in my cot, alone.
Walls of white, like icy stone.
Voices echo in the air,
Coming from I know not where.
Then a face I almost know
Comes and looks, and smiles and goes.
So here I am, alone again.
Perhaps that face could ease my pain.
I hear crying, but cannot see.
There's no one else, it must be me.
But there's the face, the face I know!
Please come to me - you must not go!
I remember voice and face,
Cradle me in love's embrace.
Hold me warmly while I cry.
Only you can pacify.
The mother and baby bond is strong.
You left me here for far too long.

Bill Eden
Essex

House Politics On A Saturday Morning

It began on the coffee table
with your stale mug of my Earl Grey.

Then as you showered,
fragrancing your curls with my shampoo,
I ran the hot tap in the kitchen.
Then when you'd dressed,
in a brown jumper snatched from my drawer
I hung my dressing gown on the sofa.
Then you usurped the TV,
changed the channel when the news came on,
I lost the remote when you left the room.

Then you became bored,
you pondered my choice of outfit aloud
I smiled saying, 'I learnt from you.'
Then you glared,
you made fresh Earl Grey as your getaway
I silently dared you to leave the mug.
But then you caught my eye,
an apology half reached your lips,
but I looked away.

Carly Bareham
Essex

Return Journey On The M4

Unending glorious green we passed,
With here and there a cottage
Tucked in like pocket handkerchief,
And far on the horizon
Bare brown trees
Like wisps of autumnal smoke
Puffed by the wind.
Hedges trimmed erratically
By unseen hand with gargantuan shears,
And canopied above a clear blue sky
That travelled with us eastwards,
Oh cars there were, and lorries too,
But what cared we for them,
For in the fields were newborn lambs
And patient cows awaiting the call
To milking time, while rooks and gulls
Circled the Earth with beating wings,
Screeching as they wheeled,
And it was good to be alive
As we passed each living thing.

Gwen Place
Essex

Warfare Of The Mind

A still autumn day, she is rushing and racing,
No other move against hush but imminent bipolar mayday.
Physically running, mentally gunning
For you, for me, for anyone who dares to stand in her way.
The compulsion to dash
Coiling mind before crash
She's becoming unfurled
Acts as queen ruling the land, no, the world,
Buys presents en masse for those in her midst,
Value of money does not exist,
Owns credit card
Lengthening by the yard,
Caution thrown to the wind
Finances destined
To gush down the drain
Together with rain;
Drawing much needed breath
Weeps into her pillow in hideaway,
Sleep comes to nought,
She's restless, distraught,
Begins whirling to vortex core
Expels raging roar, exhausted from ordeal
Tranquillity of silent graves appeal,
Solitude, perhaps sleep to heal?
On her knees entreats,
'Where are you Dad? I need you Dad!'
Thinks, *I'll lie next to him,*
'Would you like me to sing you a hymn?'
Someone clamps her, screaming she struggles to free,
Injected she quietens
Taken to convalesce
From warfare of the mind to peacefulness.

There but for the grace of Thee any one of us may be.

Hilary Jill Robson
Essex

The End Of The Stars

The stars saunter idly in their trajectories,
whispering quietly in lissome manoeuvres
over the moon and back for midnight tea
for it's said 'starlight is derived from the shining lunar'.

Their spangling diamond-white costumes
cover their skins, so they can dance or act
in the theatre of the ancient black universe
to shout 'love may be fiction, but stars are fact'.

'Long live the stars!' bellow the sequinned stars
but the skies defend: 'Not on your nelly!
we've known you come and go you stars
you've been watchin' too much late night telly!'

'Hah!' say the stars, 'you'd be nothing
without us and the moon to fill your space,
to fill your empty black-night ether
with the galaxy's pride and Jupiter's grace.'

In the end, their tiny burning electric lustre
fade and singe smoky in the cool dark night
falling from the black galactic shallow skies
that shed the stars and wake the dawning light.

James McConalogue
Essex

Essex Village

Did you see them when they came
In their steady marching ranks
Fighting men from far-off Rome?
Did you see them on their way?

Did you see them when they came
In their ragged ill-clad band
With Wat Tyler at their head?
Did you see them on their way?

Did you see them when they came
With the splendid pomp of court
Gloriana at their head?
Did you see them on their way?

Did you see them when they came
High up in the clear blue sky
Modern soldier on the wing?
Did you see them on their way?

Heather Brackley
Essex

To My Soul

Yesterday I wrote a poem, which sang so sweet a tune,
with words so wise and knowing -
t'would make the saddest flower bloom.

My poem was to you my soul, words for only you to hear.
The creation, strong and purposeful -
their meaning loud and clear.

I told you I was taking you to a safe and beautiful place,
where we could huddle behind the dunes -
feel the wind sweep over our face.

I explained the things we would surely keep
in order to be creative and strong
and we would toss the rest into the belly of the sea where they all belong.

The magnificence of the creation I worded for you my soul -
we gave birth to on our journey and when we reached our goal -
my pen lay lifeless in my hand - you had devoured every word -
every single strand!

We shared the pain, we cried, we sighed together -
we reached the anger for the heartache through the years.
We trod the sands, I felt your quickening, as we threw -
the 'offal' to the gulls and the sea washed away our tears.

Much calmer now we retraced our steps -
together heart and soul met with uplifted spirit.
No 'if onlys' nor 'ah buts' - just thankful and much lighter -
for digging to the guts and setting our imprisoned selves free!

Tomboy
Essex

Reflections

(Composed after reading the poem 'Mosquito' by D H Lawrence)

'What sight is this on which to feast my eyes?
A silken gossamer thread intricately woven
Throughout the night.
Who taught you, gardener's friend, your design?
And which unsuspecting prey will meet their plight
In your tangled web?'

As through the mists I gaze and dimly see
The tangled web of life so intricately woven
Throughout the years;
I ponder, and reflect the pattern of life revealed,
And, 'seeing through the glass darkly' now,
Reject my fear of what the future holds.

R A Kemp
Essex

One Last Time

Turn back the shroud just one more time
And let me see this child of mine
The child we'd planned for so sincere
I'll hold here in my arms so near

The future now will hold no laughter
Just broken dreams forever after
The child with plans all laid out clear
Is now so far but once was near

We both avoid all talk of him
To try and hide the pain within
Each one wondering alone
Yearly how much he'd have grown

Those schooldays that will be missed
His first steps, his first kiss
All not to be, no future plan
Not to grow from boy to man

No wife or children will he hold
In loving arms when he is old
All of this he will not see
It stopped right here, his destiny.

So let me see just one more time
The child I'm not to have as mine
Then seal the lid so I can't see
The child for us that's not to be

Daniel Moore
Essex

A Country Girl

I'm just a country girl at heart
I like the simple things, like sunshine
In the mornings, moonshine in the night
I like to hear the birds in my garden
And see the stars that shine at night
I like the simple things in life
I'm just a country girl at heart
I like the simple things, the birds, the bees
The trees, the sunshine, and even pouring rain,
A gentle breeze, a baby's smile
All of these things, are ours for the asking
To all of us for 'free'.

Georgette Poole
Essex

The Porpoise

A sudden movement 'neath the waves
The murky shape - now black - now white
Rolls, as tho' attention craves
Of all who view.
A flash, and through the water's foam
Leaps high, and then, so briefly, quits
The coolness of his watery home
For stifling air.
With arched and rounded back once more
Cleanly breaks the swelling sea.
Dives deeply and obeys the law
Made for his kind.
Then rejoins his fellows all,
This show of freedom now expired,
Speeds onward to that inbred call
Which ever bids.
Go safely 'cross your friendly sea,
On, always on, to where you will,
For you have shown a freedom we
Can never know.

P W Pidgeon
Essex

Goodnight My Love

Goodnight, my love, my angel, I whisper from afar,
sweet dreams, pleasant dreams, beautiful dreams.

For, we are apart, I am here, and you are there miles away.
Two souls drifting on the ocean of life,
destined to be one but not sure when.

Oh, how I wish we were together now, no more time apart.
I would turn to you, next to me,
kiss you and whisper goodnight my love.
Feel your warm body next to mine
as we drift off to blissful sleep in each other's arms.

Your love is all I need to make me complete,
make me smile, make me feel alive, wanted.
It is the only cure for my unhappiness, sadness and despair.

For now, we remain just friends,
staying in touch but meeting only occasionally.
Maybe, one day soon, we will move our relationship onto another level.
I live in hope.

Until then, goodnight, my love, my angel, I whisper from afar,
sweet dreams, pleasant dreams, beautiful dreams . . .

Nash
Essex

The Ballad Of Grays (Essex)

All day and all night the A13 growls;
Beneath the full moon a sprightly fox howls.
Grey is the aura, and Grays is the noun;
Just your regular south-eastern town.

A local masseuse sullies marriage vows.
Private lives broadcast in full public rows.
The Thames is the favoured method to drown;
Just your regular south-eastern town.

The local field hosts both circus and fair.
Industrial smokestacks taint the night air.
Some children roam until well past sundown;
Just your regular south-eastern town.

The centre's the hub for shopping and trains;
Takeaways galore and national chains.
Home to all colours, pink through to brown;
Just your regular south-eastern town.

There's contrasting homes for contrasting lives:
Council flat struggles, and six bedroom thrives.
The north side rejects the rest with a frown;
Just your regular south-eastern town.

Neil Outram
Essex

She Means Nothing To Me

She means nothing to me

She's taken my home, but left me the house
And on her way out, she called me a louse
She settled for cash, and the family car
Ten years later I still bear the scar
She's broken my heart and stolen my soul
Anguish and pain have taken their toll

She means nothing to me

After all this time I still love her so
But why this should be I'll never know

She means nothing to me
For I have nothing left
Except emptiness.

S Friede
Essex

The Collection

I have started many collections
But this is the one that grew
United they sit upon their shelf
Teddy bears, of varied shapes and size and hue
There's Beccles, he's from Suffolk
Hunt, for at that time I was a motor racing fan
Snowy, that's self explanatory, and Jock of Scottish clan
Others dressed as mountaineer and butler
A bride complete with silken dress and ring
One Beanie modelled on an angel
With fine transparent glistening wings
My favourite, he's called Marcus
Cuddly, like a bear should be
Named after someone special
Who showed kindness unto me
I am sure that they're my protectors
For often into them I cry
And when I've regained my self-esteem
I'll gently pat them dry
When the evening is drawing to a close
And I retire to bed
Lay my head upon my pillow
Feel my eyelids turn to lead
I reach my arm towards the cabinet
To turn off the bedside light
And I can just imagine them whispering
Goodnight my child, sleep tight.

Lynda Fordham
Essex

The Furious Dance

The water meadows that in spring
Lay low and sultry
This morning are swollen
Thick and brown by the floodwaters of autumn.
The plaintive call of a moorhen
Cuts the sudden cold air
And life itself seems to rush towards the sea
In the furious dance of the murky waters
Beneath the old iron bridge
As the spirit of summer sinks
So the wind and waters rise.

Clive Cornwall
Essex

Whispers From The Sea

Shh, shh, I hear his whispers, softly lap the shore
Wait for me, 'tis you I love
And will for evermore

The sea, the sea, I wait, but waiting is in vain
I listen, longing for his voice
To one day ease the pain

Ebbs the tide or flows the tide, I walk along the beach
Sometimes I think I see his face
But always out of reach

A shell, a shell, in absent mind I put it to my ear
But salt from tears and salt from sea
My cries are all I hear

I remember, I remember, blue sea and distant shore
We danced, we laughed and love we made
As no one has before

And love we made and love we made in sheltered coves and bays
Our simple dreams fulfilled our needs
And so we passed our days

But time and tide, the seas of life, change with every moon
And dreams they come and dreams they go
And he was gone - too soon.

Christine Bassett
Essex

Sad Eyes Of A Father
(Mr Mohammed Al Fayed)

Watching you on television, the sad look in your eyes,
Took me back to your son's death, it made me realise.
How fate, has so many tricks and turns in life,
Some lead us to happiness, some to utter strife.

Your son and our Diana, spent their last days in utter joy,
When it was so tragic! Death and then no more.
They are together now, no one can separate,
Hands held together, they went through the Golden Gate.

Never ever to be parted, together evermore,
Their hearts entwined, never to part, what joy.
It is those that are left behind, to suffer and to grieve,
But knowing they are together, this you must believe.

Violet Foulger
Essex

Flying Over Clacton

With a wave of a hand and a smile,
She is gone,
The one I love,
In a tiny tin crate, which,
Because it has an engine and wings,
Is called an aeroplane.
One minute she is taxiing down a bumpy grass runway,
And suddenly she is away and
Flying over Clacton.

With a wave of a hand and a smile
They are gone,
The ones we love,
To adventures and new chances, which,
Because they are exciting and a little risky,
Are called growing up.
One minute they are bumping along at home
And suddenly they are away and
Flying over Clacton.

With a wave of our hand and a tear,
We watch them go,
The ones we love,
To dangers and outrageous gambles, which,
Because they represent the untried step,
Are called growing up.
One minute they are over-filling the house
And suddenly they are away and
We are left staring down an empty runway.

David W Lankshear
Essex

Heavens

Petals fall
through a world of
curves and lines
lights that collect
so bright at night
yet fade
when it comes
they rise to meet her
then collapse away
so lovely then
must be our days.

George Jones
Essex

The Old Tree

We thought it was dead
The old tree
As it stood out there
All bent and brittle boned
And then some ivy came
To dress the old tree
With green and shining leaves
It stands there now
Does the old tree
In all its finery
Dressed for whatever the seasons may bring
Even the birds come to settle
And sing their appreciation

We thought it was dead
The old tree
But it revived
Came alive
Became bold
With green and shining leaves
That ivied about its being
It welcomes the silent sowing spiders
The occasional squirrel
Welcomes the mice that run
Oh so quickly about its feet
Mice that squeak their mouse gratitude
On being allowed into its woody rooms
We presumed the old tree was dead
Long dead
How pleased we are to be wrong

John Jones
Essex

Autumn Leaves

Today the leaves
Are blowing in the wind.
It's only October
And you can smell the smoke
From the bonfires, filling the air.
My eyes are cloudy
With tears of sadness
And tears of joy.
In the smoke I see your spirit
Drifting free.

Brian Ross
Essex

Peaceful

It's peaceful here.
On the bank below the weir.
Sun burnt of the morning haze,
In the warmth sit and laze
Up high flecks of clouds
Check blue of the skies.
Beauty of an Essex river
Easy on the eyes.
No hint of wind,
Nothing blowing the river's vegetation fringe.

Nothing dampens the beauty of growing things.
Aromatic fragrance of river mint,
Waters reflect the blaze
Of purple loosestrife,
The pinks of Indian balsams
Are somewhat awesome,
Brown velvets, reedmacs, bulrush
White fluffy seed down
Mix colours on nature's brush.
Rosy purple willow herbs attract colourful birds

That feed on the herbs' fluffy seeds,
Wildflowers are not just weeds.
Picturesque river running under willow leaves.
Near one's feet,
Blending into the riverscape,
A heron watches and waits
On the tiny fish,
For me to go the birds no wish.
On the bank below the weir,
It's peaceful here.

Bryan Clarke
Essex

Me

It's hard to be a single mum and a lover too,
I feel like a piece of rubber being stretched and pulled in two.
I have the kiddies calling, 'Mummy', and my man calling, 'Come to bed.'
It makes me feel dizzy and mixed emotions swirl round in my head.
Sometimes I just want to be left alone
And soak in the bath full of foam.
But I wouldn't change a thing,
Cos this isn't just a fling,
I enjoy being a lover,
And kids, well, I wouldn't mind another.

Nikki Jackson
Essex

Reflections

A babe is born
And from that moment on,
Begins his destined journey
To the grave.
A journey sometimes long
And sometimes short.
The end alone
Is known,
If end and death are one,
But is that so?
How can we know?
Reflections in the deepest pools
Of truth can sometimes
Mirror other unseen truths.
If, from the start of life
We tread the road to death.
Reverse this truth,
And when truth does this give?
Maybe, that from the moment of our death
We truly start to live!

Geoff O'Neil
Essex

Baby Views

A new baby, due any day
In Mummy's tummy, quite cosy
Tiny feet, tiny hands, stretch and punch
My play area becoming firm.

Daddy's voice I recognise
A punch and kick, in response
Playing fun and games, before daylight comes
Daddy cuddles me, even when I'm in Mummy's tummy.

Like a trampoline all around, I like to bounce
Probing about, searching for a way out
A bigger play area, is what I'm looking for
Exploring the world around, playing football

Then the moment arrives, a false alarm
I've decided to stay cosy, a moment's thought
Resting away, until I'm ready
Patience is what I'm teaching you now.

For when I'm born, you will hear my demands
You will serve me, in a pleasing, loving way.

George Petrie
Fife

The Witness

The days were long, long and hard
As we marched our way to war
And in the distance battles roar, hungry for blood,
Put fear into the hearts of many men, with its brutal beckoning call.
And now and then, a flash of light would brighten up the darkened skies ahead
Which seemed like a guiding light for many to meet their deaths,
For we found ourselves upon a road that was long and bitter at its end.

By day we marched, by night we rested,
Huddled together in stinking trenches
Filled with mud, and rat infested,
Exposed to the heavens and freezing cold
Which bit the flesh and chilled the bone,
And we'd think of home and our loved ones there
And the love we share across the miles and for a while at least,
Our thoughts could drift from war - but not for long.

Caught unawares by an enemy flare
We quickly scrambled for cover, at least for some the war was over,
As shell after shell that night did pound us - they'd found us
And I have witnessed grown men weep as comrades lay in a crumpled heap
Face down in the mud - covered in blood.

And in my deep and dark despair, from all that I did witness there
I too did weep in a heartfelt prayer
At the eleventh hour just before the dawn
As I waited patiently for peace to wake from slumbers long
And take her rightful place within the hearts of men.

Judith Ardell
Fife

Our World

You only have to watch the news to see the devastation,
Wars and famine, people dying, children crying in desperation.
The leaders of each nation surely have to take more action,
It is their basic duty to help ease the situation.
Some countries have too much food, others not enough,
It truly is an unjust world, for many life is tough.
We've all been guilty at some point of not doing enough to save our planet,
All that glass, plastic and paper, we really should recycle it.
But some of us say, 'What's the point?' We just like to live for today,
We're not thinking of the future or the price we're going to pay.
Were neglecting our responsibilities, also our children's future,
And if we don't do something now their lives could be unsure.
So let's all change our ways right now and do something positive,
Our children deserve a better world, the best that we can give!

Helen McIntyre
Fife

Prisoners

Down the long winding hall
Light ever so small
The floorboards creak
And the creepy walls speak

Shadows so big
Light so small
Rats so wide
Prisoners so thin

The ghosts groan
The prisoners cry
It's so dark and cold
Their lives go by

The walls crumble
The floorboards crack
The ghosts mumble
And the windows creak like a train track

The mansion drops
The prisoners die
What a disaster!
Now their lives have gone by

Louise Smith
Fife

All In A Day . . .

White fluffy clouds
Drifting slowly in the silent, pale blue skies
Golden sunshine
Giving warmth and light to every living thing on Mother Earth . . .
Crystal-clear rain
Quenching thirst for all that grows
Plush trees
Swaying gently in the whispering breeze . . .
Rippling waters
Winding down the crooked stream
But what is this scent I smell?
The aroma from the rainbow of blossoming flowers . . .
So serene on a summer's evening
As the sunset draws to a close
To reveille the ebony skies
Layered with silver speckles of starlight
Time for bed my little sweetheart . . .

Janet Brook
Fife

Autumn On The Ochils

Your guise is many shades of green
Found in your glens and vales
Brown and gold, red and bronze
Are the colours of the leaves on trees
Nestling in the dales
Streams are flowing faster now
With the rains that have now come
But only to enhance your riches
You share with everyone

Walking along your many paths
Each step, and a change takes place
Showing more of your beauty
That ne'er can be replaced
Clouds passing across the sun
Cast shadows on your glen
And when it is clear once more
Your beauty shines again

You are a credit to God's nature
Time is always on your side
For each year the ugliness beneath
Nature chose to hide
With a covering of fern and heather
A wild flower here and there
Gives you a beauty
Which with the world you share

To walk you is a joy
That gives me quite a thrill
And I find it all on view
On the lovely Ochil hills.

Peter P Gear
Fife

What I Saw

I did not see what I saw
I didn't even see it
But if I saw what I'd seen
I'd tell you, but would you believe it?

If you saw what I'd seen
Would you tell me that you saw it?
Then you know that what I saw
Was both what we saw, because we have seen it.

Niall McManus
Fife

A Trip We All Take

(Dedicated to Pete Nairn)

What reason do you give to explain life
All my years I've lived in Fife
Well travelled, maybe not
Years I wish that I could blot
Through them all I've had my share
Health, happiness, troubles to bear
Some things I know could not be changed
Moments I wish I'd rearranged
What I have learnt can't be taught
Excitement, adventure when young, was sought
Thoughts now otherwise are engaged
Peace and contentment, now I am aged
Life is and will always be one big gamble
Although each day we will have to ramble
Thinking of tomorrow, I might not see
Whatever may happen, let it be
Because in the end I have no say
So I live like it is my last day.

Margaret Nairn
Fife

A Gentleman

It's a year to the day, since my husband passed away
We were a long time together him and I
It seems all these years have swiftly gone by
I'm so grateful for all the good times we had
When I look through his photos I try not to get sad
His pleasures were simple, he was easy to please
He could be funny at times and be quite a tease

We met and we married a long time ago
He worked hard for his family when wages were low
They had their little pencil cases with all the stuff they'd use
And he always made sure they had a shine on their shoes
He was a good father, the children knew they had his love
And often told them of their Heavenly Father above

He was well respected and liked by everyone
Truly loved by his three daughters and also his dear son
Life journeys on, I will do the best I can
And my treasured memories of him will be that he was a good,
                    kind, warm, wonderful gentleman.

Rosina Forward
Fife

A Winter's Day In Spring

Traffic chaos as always first thing
Why's it always got to snow in spring?
By mid afternoon it'll be melting away
Glad I took the easy option, the train

As always, tried to get a window seat
So, along the shore I could gaze
At the splendour of the bay
Over the river behind the capital city
The distant hills are covered again
But no more beautiful a sight to see
As the smoke rises in a bleak outline
Dark against the whiteness of snow behind

As we go through a tunnel my mind drifts back
To the meeting, another tense affair
Like a fly in the spider's lair
Trapped at the mercy of the foe
So desperate to escape but doomed to fail
Such a feeling of despair you cannot know
But it's expected, happens every time
As sure as the track has parallel lines

Oh! To be a gull floating on the cool sea breeze
So high the estuary looks like a stream
To drift away and fulfil a dream
If it was so easy what good life would be.

David McDonald
Fife

My Welsh Childhood Lane

This daydream lane,
With hooded trees that reach the sky,
Celandines, violets
And daisies for my mayoral chain,
When I would be Queen of the May.

Spangled leaves,
With intermittent bluebells,
Ringing for my skipping feet,
The laughter
That made my childhood complete.

This lane was my fairyland,
Where white owls hid in mystery,
The cuckoo sang a greeting
And goblins retreated,
Weaving spells
To the sound of magic . . .

Margarette Phillips
Flintshire

What A Wonderful Thought

Wouldn't it be wonderful
If all the world were at peace
And all fighting, killing and hatred
Did really and truly cease.

Wouldn't it be wonderful
If no more children died
From starvation and diseases
Because no one really tried

To help and teach their parents
The best way how to live
And how to prevent diseases
Just a little time to give.

Wouldn't it be wonderful
If every child could go to school
And learn about each other
That hate is out and friendship is the rule.

Wouldn't it be wonderful
If famine was no more
And bombing and destruction
Were gone for evermore.

Wouldn't it be wonderful
If our grandchildren and their children too
Were able to spend their lives in peace
Which we have failed to do.

I cannot see the world at peace
As time is fleeing by
For I am getting on in years
Having reached the age of ninety-five.

But wouldn't it be wonderful
If every nation got together
And began to learn and understand
The ways of one another.

Phyllis Ing
Flintshire

Framed

Thinking all the time,
How to put these words into rhyme.
No rhyme or reason to the fore.

But then I look through my window,
I see the trees,
Swaying and blowing with the cool autumn breeze.

Cows and sheep grazing, on faraway hills,
What pleasure it gives.

The sun is now shining, a walk would be nice.
Cares and worries, could blow away, wow,
Some fresh air, will suffice.

But I'm here tapping away,
Thinking.
It's so quiet, here in my room.

Looking through my window,
The autumn trees, of reds and golds,
Glowing in the sun, glorious colours.
The red berries on holly,
Just waiting to be picked, Christmas soon.

Now there's a thought,
Presents to buy, and all that.

But for now,
I'm here, quiet, but how the window,
Frames, an ideal picture,
Of peace, tranquillity, and shows,
Nature's way to soothe,
The savage brow.

Elaine Marshall
Flintshire

See Me

See beyond the wife, the mother,
Look into my eyes that reflect
The essential spark, burning brightly,
Illuminating my soul, the *me* bit of me.

See beyond the artist, writer, poet,
Reach out to the elemental forces
That control the quirks and quarks
Of my consciousness, the *me* bit of me.

See beyond the words, the gestures,
Be sensitive to the subtle nuances
Which indicate my own femininity.
See me, hear me, value the *me* bit of me.

Rose-Mary Gower
Flintshire

Am I The One?

Am I the one who echoes sin?
When you lie in death do I tuck you in?
When you blink your eyes do you always find,
The weight of the world weighs down your eyes?
Lying in the destruction of a sacrifice,
When resurrection comes will you be enticed?
Losing your mind I have lost the key,
But the one that you fear most is me.

Like an angel that has descended,
And its broken wings cannot be mended
Like the plague that is finally dead,
I creep into your hollow head,

Am I the one who offers warmth?
When the silence comes, I come to haunt,
The foul twisting creature in your eye,
Tells me when it is time for you to die
When the morning comes and you awake
You are in an unfamiliar place
The devils cry and the fire laughs,
Embrace despair, the Devil's craft.

Like an angel that has descended,
And its broken wings cannot be mended
Like the plague that is finally dead,
I creep into your hollow head.

Lawrence Donohoe
Gloucestershire

Letting Go

I tugged the rooted nettle clumps.
They held. I held.
No thoughts, no reasoning beyond the act.
With each bound truss I wrestled from its fastness
came great followings of matted trails,
nerves jerked from their tenacious grip
backlashing weals across my skin.

The knots had blindly grown, a chaos
gramping down and round and through.
The nettles' arteries had darkly meshed their life
as had my multiplying mind ensnared all thoughts
around one task these recent, striving months.

Yet now, that work complete, I battled still,
compelled unknowing by a deeper need.
It came upon me then, a dawning sense
on shaking out the soil, that both
the earth and I fell free with every loosening braid.

We opened to the summer sky,
an unbound space to breathe, inhale at last.
Through this enactment of release I found
a quiet, sifted warmth, a simple place
from which a transformation can emerge,
a truer, new-gold life unfold.

Maxine Relton
Gloucestershire

Roman Glevum

Glevum they called Gloucester in days gone by
town wall and fort they built of Cotswold stone,
they marched and ruled with spear and shield
laid Ermin Way o'er Crickley on through Birdlip.
At Witcombe built a villa now all but gone
Roman camp at top of old Cold Slad is but a field,
but still those who, curious of the past, search and slip
to ask of what they find, was this Roman life and why?
Hereabout 'tis said, there is at a certain time of year
a ghostly scene of Roman soldiers on the hill,
seen by some but who would not venture near
to ask the spectres, 'Are you here to guard it still?'

John Clarke
Gloucestershire

Single Mum

A single mum with little ones
The pressure is immense
There must be times when it gets hard
And things become intense

She's struggled all her adult life
Trying to make ends meet
By the time she's paid the bills
There's nothing left for treats

She worries about her children
In this world in which we live
She's the only one they've got
And she hasn't much to give

She suffers from depression
She's down and in despair
Anxious to find a better life
For her kids this isn't fair

She really needs some respite
Some time to sort things out
She knows that that's impossible
To her kids she is devout

She needs to find some extra strength
The strength to carry on
Things are looking really bad
All her hopes are gone

She sits down with her head in hands
To contemplate her plight
A little face appears and says,
'Don't cry Mummy, we'll be alright.'

Neil Warren
Gloucestershire

White Tulips

Freshly cut, still secretively closed,
proud and erect in the table vase.
Later, in the room's womb warmth,
ten tulips reflect in polished mahogany,
curving their swan necks downwards.

In pecking order each bloom awaits
its time to thrive then fade.
One by one pale petals drop,
baring the pistil's mystery,
such brief yet lasting history.

Malcolm Williams
Gloucestershire

Paradise Lost

If Man thinks he can control and rule the world
He can't match the power Mother Nature can unfurl
The east is spawning terrorism and making war
And earthquakes are erupting deep within Asia's core

America is again and again hit by strong hurricanes
Seeing the likes of New Orleans eradicated by the rains
Is a power greater than us saying enough is enough
Make peace in your world or nature really will get rough?

Our ice caps are melting and the seas are beginning to swell
And ignorant Man the rainforests continue to fell
We stupidly blame our wildlife for the diseases it brings
And murderously cull anything remotely with wings

Instead of plundering this planet for capitalist gain
We need to work with Mother Nature not create acid rain
She's flexing her muscles but will we listen to her call?
For surely if we ignore her the people of this planet will fall

Jeannie Ashplant
Gloucestershire

Finality

In the twilight of my years,
I dance to the melodies of life.
Pure fantasy of course, but smile
To generate goodwill and friendship.
Memory is not what it was,
But remember tomorrow, awaken
And yesterday is gone!
Celebrate another day, each precious
As the light grows dim.
Who knocks and calls my name,
Unaware, the pleasure that they bring.
The world today, not as it was,
We know the solutions,
But who listens? - No one!
Sadly in this mad merry-go-round,
There is little time to spare.
The elderly become invisible,
Rest homes with waiting lists,
Residents waiting for paradise!

T G Bloodworth
Gloucestershire

The Lonely Night

The night is long,
I toss and turn,
For loving moments
My heart yearns.
But since you left
My bed is cold,
No reassuring
Hand to hold.
No one to tell
About my day
Or listen to
What you might say,
And lay aside
The stress and strife
In peaceful sleep
As man and wife.

Jackie Barker-Smith
Gloucestershire

Seasons

Now that summer's had its fling
And birds are busy on the wing,
The little ones are fully fledged
And come to meet me from the hedge.

Soon the summer starts to fade,
The trees take on a golden shade,
Before the winter settles in,
With the north wind's bitter sting.

Betty Mason
Gloucestershire

The Crocodile

In silent wait,
His eyes bob above the water,
Watching for weary antelope,
That come for a drink.
His rough brown skin makes
Him easy to mistake for a log.
He skulks in the shallows,
Till it comes closer,
Then snap! His jaws close,
Tightly shut around his prey,
The antelope's fate was ineluctable.

Eleanor Garrett (9)
Greater London

Miss You

Nothing like that is coming
Suddenly
As rain, as freedom, as warm feelings
As sea, as honey

All people are sticking!
What happened?
Nobody knows
What happened?
Only your, your eyes
Told me, the secret of life
Without hurt, without money

Nobody knows
What happened?
My lucky daisy
I miss you, my inspiring
I miss you, my hot funny
Speaks to me
I am tired, I am upset, and I am exhausted
Life is not easy, I am in eddy, I dazzle!
Nobody noticed what happened
I'm dead . . . I'm dead
Only your heart sees
Only your ecstasy
Make the life, universe
More healthy and moonlit

I am dead . . . I am dead
Nobody knows what happened

For me all things are not sunny
I'm unduly, I am undated
I want to die

Mekhled Al-zaza
Greater London

Friendship

Friendship is like a butterfly's wing
Quite exquisite and special - a delicate thing
You know it exists, and no proof do you need
For it shows itself in its kindly deed.
Friendship of this kind is a gift
To feel the bond strengthen
Is to feel the heart lift.

B Batchen
Greater London

Cheek To Cheek

Part damaged glitterball rotates overhead
cheek to cheek as slow jazz plays out live
on a makeshift stage.
Feet firmly on the floor as heels
lift in time with the music.
We tiptoe into new songs
raspy vocals become our thoughts.
Minds blank, lost to the realisation of falling in love
that moment when insides flutter
and sighs tumble from mouths.
Years of pent up emotions are exhaled
blended with a heavy dose of cynicism.
released into dank basement air, for
some other lonely fool to suck in.
New lives inhaled deeply
thick with smoky air, slow beats
and an intimacy found only with
dancing and making love.
Nicotine less damaging than
the poisons and pestilent disease
it replaces, feasting on
slices of broken heart.
Our lips meet as the
healing process begins.

Jo Copsey
Greater London

Uncertain Sands

Self-doubt rushes in
as sure as sweeping tides,
softening and swirling
sands of uncertainty.
Rocks of achievement
struggle in simmering seas;
sinuous seaweed strangles
eddies of self-esteem.
The tatters of some talents -
cork floats, shells and driftwood -
swish and bob about
without cohesion or intent.

This seashore of a life's
exposed - a flat and
vulnerable beach,
unresisting to the searching swell's
remorseless questioning.

Wes Ashwell
Greater London

Chelsea - My Town!

Chelsea is the home for me,
The only place I want to be
Where all the citizens can live -
With a view that is superlative.

The Albert Bridge is there to see
We photograph it all with glee.
We even have a football team -
Although that might be just a dream!

The power station stands there still,
Across the water, if you will.
Parks and gardens where we roam
With our lovers in the gloam.

And Battersea's not just for dogs -
(They also have a yen for 'mogs').
Our town hall is a joy to see -
Though marriages are not for free.

Down river we can spy the Eye -
A ride will take us to the sky.
The annual flower show's a must -
I'll live in Chelsea till I rust.

Mary Baird Hammond
Greater London

Bright Red Boots

Bright red boots
sit on my small four-year-old feet.
They click on the playground, a sharp beat,
as I strut over my territory. *Bossyboots.*

Tufts of grey fake fur sprout proudly
around my ankles. I am the Alpha Kid.
They clash deliciously with my pink outfit,
as I giggle, and beguile in nursery.

Then the world turned upside down
in my stomach, as I spewed orange carrots
onto leather, hurled into the bin. Tears
tracked down my crumpled face. Ragamuffin.

Reign over. Fast forward sixteen years -
past powerless heels, Uggs, and Caterpillars -
in the silence that swallowed clicks,
my small size four feet and I burn

for my bright red boots.

Ria Maya Bhatta
Greater London

Sister Dear

Oh well, oh dear, it's not that time
Not sixty years, yes sister dear
It will not hurt, you will see
I promise it as it should be.

Done your bit
You played your part
The sister, the wife
The mum of hearts.

If you think of it
Your arms are of rubber
All the hugs you have given
Your lips must be smooth as glass.

For the kisses you've given to mend that broken heart
Or for all the grazed knees
For the pain you cannot heal
Yes it's all yours in those sixty years.

Your mark is there
You left your print
With those you met
And those that left.

It's worth all the love
So do not fear
Smile and say 'thank you
I loved every year'.

R Mills
Greater London

Sports In London

Olympic Games in two thousand and twelve,
The third time that London medals shall shelve,
Nineteen eighteen and nineteen forty-eight,
Again Britain's hopeful athletes must wait.

Wimbledon tennis in June and July,
It's fun in summer with sun in the sky,
Avid fans go to see cricket at Lords,
And other sport that the city affords.

The Oxford and Cambridge Boat Race in March,
Is seen on the Thames beyond Marble Arch,
Football teams hold their matches and World Cup,
Wembley Stadium and clubs on the up.

Swimming, ice skating and games in the park,
There's plenty of sports to do for a lark.

Susan Mary Robertson
Greater London

Motorway Madness

To get from A to B as fast as he can
Appears to be the prime concern of modern man.
In his haste to pursue his social goal
He seems to have forgotten nature's role.

Our land has been raped and gutted in Man's race
To maintain the ever increasing momentum of life's pace.
Concrete streams criss-cross the land
Until all our countries have been spanned.

Three, four or five speed lanes side by side
As lorries, coaches and sporty cars use the speed limit only as a guide,
Until the sheer volume of traffic slows down the pack
Whilst Man's patience and tolerance begins to crack.

Are our motorways a blessing or a curse
Or would life without them be made worse?
To save time was one of their aims
And to bypass the cities, a laudable claim.

However, strangulation of the centre was never mentioned
By the host of experts, however well intentioned.
In London we are ringed by a belt of traffic
And our motorway users' language is eloquently graphic.

Allen Jessop
Greater London

Waltham Forest

We are the home of William Morris
There is plenty of history in Waltham Forest.
We had the Bremer, the first motor car
From here John Dankworth became a star.
Once we were the butt of all the jokes
Now we're the home to the most clever folks.
We were the idea for EastEnders
Are home now to all the big spenders.
The home of Blue Peter's Christopher Trace
Fred Pontin's schooling here took place.
The mosquito aeroplane we did make
You, your morning fresh bread here is baked.
We're visited by the odd old UFO
The Beatles here put on their show.
From here the start of the Victoria Line
We made dress shirts Real Brook sign.
Had the Ford factory but nowhere to park it
You spend good money at our street market.

Colin Allsop
Greater London

A Christmas Wish

Dear Mr Blair
Please answer my prayer
And send our boys back home
It's Christmas time
And parents want their families together
Not on the phone

Their hearts do ache around the cake
While their youngest child is far away
In a place where they can't pronounce the name
That is in full darkness' fray

We know it's their job to sort out this mess
But the rest would do them good
Let them see their new child on Christmas Day
As a father really should

Then when, sent back
To that land of dust and sand
At least they'll be renewed
And their lives will mean more
They'll have something to fight for
Even if they never come back again

Please hear my prayer at this time of year
When families should be together
Let the love of the angels fill up your heart
And allow the boys home together.

Ann-Marie Spittle
Greater London

Anniversary

That special date has come around,
It happens once in a lifetime.
What a chance for us budding poets,
To put our feelings into rhyme.
The joy of putting emotions into poetic form,
Certainly knows no bounds,
Though most pleasurable it's not as easy as it sounds.
So don't look askance as we take the chance
To put our thoughts and feelings, into prose or verse.
The great bard of long ago, certainly wouldn't be averse,
To penning our humble offering.
For better or for worse.

Edward Hill
Greater London

What Price Progress?

It's hard to imagine that long ago,
most of England was covered in green.
Lush green grass and rolling hills,
no hard surfaced roads to be seen.

Travelling around was easy then,
leather saddles on horses grand.
Wooden carriages in all their splendour,
clip-clopping across the land.

The air then was clean and breathable,
but progress has taken its toll.
Giving us cars, trains and aeroplanes,
and the ozone a gaping hole.

Chimneys from factories spewing fumes,
toxic clouds bellow in the air.
Rivers polluted with chemicals,
with nobody seeming to care.

Our once green world may yet return,
with laws followed strictly to letter.
Universally practised by everyone,
to help make our world so much better.

Elaine Fearn
Greater London

Chin Up

If life starts to get you down,
Wipe away that saddening frown.
Lift your face into the air,
As if you didn't have a care.

Keep your pain deep down inside,
Learn which feelings you need to hide.
People won't know how sad you are,
For no one can see an inner scar.

Do as I say, not as I do,
It will work, you'll see it's true.
Wipe away those unhappy tears,
Hide away those inner fears.

Take all pains in your stride,
For life is a very bumpy ride.
Try to smile and always be nice,
And you'll get by on this advice!

Jennifer Smith
Greater London

I Wish Reality Would End!

If I was granted just one wish,
Can you guess what it would be?
For an end to the hours on the box,
Of reality TV!

No more housemates caged up for days on end,
Playing silly games for food,
A nation gripped night after night,
In case they do anything rude.

No more D-list celebs going into the jungle,
Tempted to scream 'Get me out of here!'
Waiting to be crowned king or queen,
Walking out to a very loud cheer.

No more deluded fools thinking they can sing,
Ruining our favourite songs,
Waiting for someone like Mr Simon Cowell,
To tell them they're doing it wrong.

But the real reason I want it off my TV,
The one that I think beats the rest,
Is strangely I find that I'm glued to them all,
I'm reality TV obsessed!

Julie Gray
Greater London

Daydreaming

He knows that I truly love him, he knows that I really care
I worship the ground he walks upon whenever I am there and aware
Friends say that I am foolish and have a child's simple mind
I adore and am in love with this someone who is so gentle and kind.

So shy when I have to approach him, he smiles and offers his hand
This was not a planned affair but with him life is so grand
His kisses are so tender I just melt as he cuddles me so warm
Enveloped our compatible auras all adoring as in love we abound.

What a fantasy, what a dream if my lovely treasure still persists
Searching upon wakening as I clear that of slumber's mists
This now is reality as those dreams stray and fade
Gone but still remembered this supports me throughout the day.

Daydreaming again as I am continually observed by the supervisor's glare
'Your output of work is non existent, you had better say your prayers'
One last chance is given or I shall be dismissed
But I long for you at bedtime darling and that ever-loving kiss.

R D Hiscoke
Greater London

'Rose' My Baby

I planted it with loving care
And watched it grow, that rose so fair
I carefully tended it each day
Let no one harm it, I used to pray
In early May I watched a bud form
When days were long and nights were warm
Then suddenly that bud burst open
Like magic in my little garden
It was my life, my pride and joy
I was a child with a special toy
I could hardly tear myself away
To go to bed at the end of the day
Up in the morning at first crack of light
After spending such a restless night
That rose whose petals are beyond compare
Was still in full bloom growing there
The perfume from this unblemished flower
Made it stand apart in its final hour
Next day when I did my usual round
Heavens above - what have I found
Jack Frost had come early in all his might
My lovely rose had died in the night
I stood by the bush and shed a tear
My beautiful rose had bloomed and died here.

Gladys Baillie
Greater London

Adoration

Dear Father, I will love You
My whole life and beyond -
For I still feel the greater faith
Of those who've been and gone.
A vision stood before my eyes
When I was only two,
And I have never lost the image
That I saw of You.
You uttered not a word aloud
But delved into my mind,
The meaning of humanity,
To be honest, true and kind.
I never felt a need for church,
Just silence - and a prayer -
For church is but a meeting place,
Whilst You are everywhere.

P Samuels
Greater London

Bucks Fizz

(For Rhona)

From Maidenhead to dreamy Marlow go
The winding roads that trace the river's course
Through dappled meadow-lands or wild hedgerow.
And here, in golden days, by coach and horse,

Came motley bands of literary men:
Bluff Izaak Walton with his angling rod,
Or Percy Shelley, with ecstatic pen
Contending some high argument with God;

While his poor Mary, cooped in Albion House,
Proof-read the galleys of her 'Frankenstein',
Then set decanters for a mad carouse,
As Leigh Hunt brought Lord Byron down to dine

(Or so we're told) with Peacock; whose renown
Sprang from his 'Nightmare Abbey', here composed;
When all their table-talk was jotted down
To ginger up the next book he proposed.

Perhaps they laughed about how, long before,
'Twas rumoured good King Charles with romping Nell -
The Merry Monarch with his merrier whore -
Turned Marlow Place to love's sweet citadel;

While unaware that, in some later year,
When their bright lives were wasted to the bone,
The town would host a poet held their peer -
Tom Eliot in a wasteland all his own . . .

So, fired: 'How glorious to discard one's load,
And settle here, a troubadour, instead!'
I mused awhile . . . then shrugged . . . and took the road
From dreamy Marlow back to Maidenhead.

Adrian Brown
Greater London

London

Let's go down now to my dear London Town today,
You won't get lost, as I will show you all the way.

The home of our great monarch, pearly queens and kings,
The home of so many of the world's greatest things.

The home of the British Museum, V&A and the Tate,
Take care with your actions or The Tower may be your fate.

The home of the Docklands and of Canary Wharf,
With high buildings so tall, imagine being a dwarf.

Covent Garden, the Cutty Sark and Gypsy Moth,
St Paul's, Westminster Abbey and men of the cloth.

River Thames, Nelson's Column in Trafalgar Square,
The Olympics are coming - will you, too, be there?

Tower Bridge has opened for my John (and me) twice,
It's such a privilege, but it's also very nice.

Theatre, wining, dining, and Buckingham Palace
I've been to St James', but with my John, not Alice.

If you're a Lilly 'n' Skinner with cockney rhyming slang
Let us Scapa Flow and learn it with a bang.

The home of the Eye, the Square Mile and Number 10,
And our famous Dickory Dock - yes, our Big Ben.

It's my home too, but with lots of apples and pears,
Madame Tussaud's folk too, with no apparent cares.

You get apple fritters, tiddlywinks in a jar,
In a good rub-a-dub-dub or a jazzy Jack tar.

Chalk Farm and Barnet Fair and even Bushey Park,
And Hampstead Heath are not places, events nor Noah's Ark.

In London are more accents that you've ever heard,
So if you like my verse, please say a Dicky Bird.

Mary M Robertson
Greater London

Metaphors

The cat needs feeding
the witch casts her spell
your close proximity
is making her purr.

The key opens the door
a guitar vibrates the air
don't try to speak
with ice cubes in your mouth.

Each moment melts
in the palm of your hand
close your fingers tight
- stop it slipping through.

This water's drowning-deep
filling up my lungs
weighted by your strokes
sinking in the dark.

The cat stretches out
belly full of food
time to lick her paws
she curls up close and sleeps.

The warlock watches
dark eyes half closed
chanting soft words
his warding charm is here.

As the grey light brightens
and the music fades away
the door that was opened
softly closes again.

Anna Meryt
Greater London

Gone But Not Forgotten

I walked outside my house and there stood my horse,
My stallion, my steed,
Stuck firmly in mortar, mud and weed.
Eyes firmly closed I ride
With my friend close by my side,
On our garden wall of course!

At the end of my road, the swing rope tied to a tree,
Floating high above the sea,
My long blonde hair hangs freely.
Reaching mountains 'cross the ocean,
Swinging rope that's now in motion.
Along the shallow River Lea.

I'd built many a den out of blankets, cushions and chairs,
Rowing boats from airing stands;
Drawing up some sketchy plans.
Held together with clothes pegs,
Draped over table legs,
Hideaways at the bottom of my stairs.

I've created little people with beating hearts, alive with feeling
Out of paper clips,
Moving limbs with Mum's hair grips.
Papier mâché made their beds
And at dusk they lay their heads,
Shadows dancing on the ceiling.

In bygone days when caterpillars were my pets,
Stroked their fur and watched them curl
Until it was time; a tiger moth no longer mine,
Flying unknown into pastures new
Left behind the safety that she knew.
Like a woman from the little girl.

Linda Lawrence
Greater London

If I Were A Celebrity

If I were a celebrity
I wouldn't need to act,
It wouldn't even matter
If my voice was somewhat flat.

I'd pump my breasts and plump my lips
With extract from bovine,
With chemicals I'd peel my face
And Botox every line.

I'd clad myself in Burberry
My bags would be Vuiton,
Well shod my feet with Jimmy Choo
My bling will cost a bomb.

I'd drink champagne in late night bars
With lots of famous geezers,
And then exclaim how really I
Prefer Bacardi Breezers.

A footballer will be my man
To Manchester I'll go,
And we shall wed in splendid taste
Then sell it to Hello.

I would endorse new products
For astronomic fees,
TV ads and billboards
It's all the same to me.

And how I would deserve it!
I'd worked hard for all I'd got,
(Well it takes a lot of time
To sleep your way up to the top)

So I'll enter competitions,
Will you vote for me?
Ant and Dec will sing aloud,
'You're a true celebrity.'

Catherine Noel
Greater London

On The Farm

He stands crest unfurled
Picking daintily at the weeds below
Red crest illuminating under the trees
The not-so-proud wings occasionally flapping
With the frantic gobble-gobble
The turkey searches out the weeds
Surrounded by the pecking order of hens
Pecking and clucking their way across the land
In this order of creatures. Their only defence is to run from any offence
They wait expectantly on the two-legged animals to feed them and nurture them
To give them their daily concentrate

Their trust is complete
In these animals
Who tend them
Offering them biscuits and hay at every turn
Across the way the billy goat stands
Looking for that human presence

To stroke his flanks
And give him food

Yet will come the day when that trust is broken
When animal is moved to a van
Past the uncharted miles
To be stunned and slaughtered
To begin anew the cycle
Yet why are these animals so docile
Going obligingly to their fates
On supermarket shelves
Through the knacker's yard

Is it the vegetable foresight lacking in these beasts
That leads them to accept their fate so meekly?
That stops any resistance against their former friends
Or is it the way of the world to eat or be eaten? Or is it yet some plan for all?

Alasdair Sclater
Greater London

One Wish

Living in this big old world
I feel so small and weak
Like a drop in the ocean
My worth, I seek

And

I wished

Walking in the moonlight
Under the glittering tiny stars
I wished I could fly high
High in the heavens to places far

And in the night I jogged on
With swaying trees by my side
With wind in my hair, playing
I went on without a guide

To get lost in some mist
Or just out of the world's eye
I wanted to run away
From some reason that I never figured out why

Walking into the clouds
Feeling alive, feeling fine
With no limits, no restrictions
I wanted to cross each and every line

Or perhaps like the running water
That flows down into the sea
So vast, so beautiful
I just wanted to be free

In a little hut, in the mid of a forest
With flowers all around
Or someplace words can't explain
I wished for such a place to be found

Or just in some land
Where I could find mountains green
With grassy flowers and singing gales
I wished for this place unseen

And in search for such a place
I went on a voyage so rough
Though worn out I was, I went on
With my road long, my journey tough.

Abeera Wali (17)
Greater London

Traces Of You

And your ghostly touch
Shivered up my spine
You flashed behind my eyes
In an oil-slick-shiny daze
You transcend, do you not?
We should never had ended that way - or did we?
From the metallic shine of everyday streets
Back then and now
Time is stoppable
Encapsulating itself in its ever-moving shell

The cornfields seem to sway
In the wind of yesteryear
The wind is your presence tomorrow
It seems that wherever I go
Whomever I meet
Whatever I say
Whatever I think
There are traces of you
Like a broken shell
On a beach of a thousand dreams

In this continual spiritual timer
Sands of your mind
Pass through the line (time)
On the inner looking glass
See the stains and the smears
That blur the sight
To the inner rights
There is sweet warmth
When I feel traces of you

To accept, to understand
Whichever way you go
The concrete substance of belief
Brings a smile
Across the bright blue skies
Between the sparkle of a distant dewdrop
And the cut of the highest mountain ridge
The big plain-faced clown smile
There is a trickle of sadness
As I realise
When I touch your lace glove
That the hand inside
Belongs to traces of you

Leon Oxenham
Greater London

My Thoughts After 85 Years

Laugh and the world laughs with you,
Weep and you weep alone.
These words my mother taught me
Long, long ago.

And now that I've reached the 'eighties'
I know it's true.
Life gets increasingly difficult
And it's easy to become very 'blue'.

I laugh at my failures and problems,
I forget things I've known all my life.
I laugh as I'm searching for something
I've recently put in a safe place.

I forget the names of my old friends
And sometimes don't recognise them.
I make mistakes and forget it and
I can't believe that it's 'me'.

It's more of a struggle to stand up,
It's easier to lie on the bed.
I need food that is soft and can swallow -
Your teeth fail you in the end.

I need phone calls and certainly letters
To give me an interest and lift,
And if someone comes to see me
I hang on to them like grim death.

I have wonderful friends and children
Who do all that they can to help.
I could never manage without them.
If I lose any of them I'll yelp.

So for 85 years I've been lucky.
I hope it continues to last.
I thank God every day for His blessings
And for each day I've had in the past.

Some day you may read this epistle
And if you do, hear what I say.
Remember the words of my mother,
'A smile frightens terror away'.

Doris E Pullen
Greater London

Her Tiny Busy Hands

She will look at
Her tiny hands,
The back first,
Then the palms,
So tiny,
Then look up and smile
To herself.

She will
Clap her tiny hands
Just to hear the
Sweet sound it makes
Then look up and
Smile to herself again.

She will pull a pole
From her surroundings
Just to see how
Strong she has become
Then look inside of her
Palms, then
Smile again at herself.

She will hold herself
Up by the arm of a chair
And pat her tiny palms
Gently as she
Moves around the room
Then look up and smile
Again to herself
In triumph.

Joana Efua Sam-Avor
Greater London

The One Wish

When I was younger, how I longed and longed to be older!
I'm older.

When I was younger, how I aspired to write and to publish!
I do.

When I was younger, how I pined for a choice of the women!
They're mine.

When I was younger, an innocent wish could charm the future;
alas,

when I was younger, I was too young to desire time
to rhyme.

Thomas Orszag-Land
Greater London

Drooping Melons

They are as heavy as cannonballs,
As soft as marshmallows,
As round as the sun,
And as big as my head,
They droop to my belly button,
They almost break my shoulders
Because they are huge boulders;
The cups of my bra are the size of dinner plates,
That's if I can get one to fit,
Which is rarely the case;
Strapless bras don't support me at all,
So I can't wear tops off the shoulder
Or low-back dresses or jumpers
Because my breasts would fall;
I can't wear fitted blouses
Because the buttons would fall off,
I can't go swimming because few costumes have cups;
If I jump in the air
They will crash down like rocks,
Why does life have to be so unfair?
I think I'll have an operation,
This will solve my problems,
They will be changed from sagging balloons
To firm, pretty peaches,
I will be able to wear
What I would stare at in shop windows;
My shoulders won't have to cope with a nightmare weight
And when I look in the mirror I will feel great.

Sarah Sidibeh
Greater London

Newborn!

Gift-wrapped boxes,
Silver and gold,
Newborn baby cries,
What does life hold
For this little child?

With bated breath,
Her life begins.
She sucks her thumb,
She learns to walk,
She starts to talk.

As time unfolds,
Her story is told!

Cathy Mearman
Greater London

Corpses' Mounds

Soaring bombs on the horizon
Veiled the dazzling stars,
Sweet streams that turned to poison
Quelled the thirst of war.

What else remains to be altered?
Save our beating hearts
Everything has come to halt.
Now we can see the eclipsed moon
Through our broken vault
All is left, to cure these wounds,
A pit of bitter salt.

Though roar of guns has deafened us
We still can hear a song
Song that begins with the growl
Ends up in the moan
When siren sings some magic chants
We get astounded
We sing along all night long
To amuse the flock of hounds.

What peasant mourned? A field of corn
That shone like golden crown,
Hungry fire consumed it all
Left ashes on the ground.

What tyrant found? Corpses' mounds
Lying on the ground
Wild guns devoured these folks
And strewed them all around.

Syed Farhan Ahmed
Greater London

A Rhyme In Time

I have no time to make words rhyme,
To polish them and make them shine.
It's in my haste they get misplaced.
My words jumble, then I grumble.

Rhymes I've written need more rhythm.
The thing to do is see this through.
Forget the tears and write what cheers.
The path I'll take permits mistakes.

I'll slow things down, firm feet on ground.
It's new to me like therapy.
I hope to find with steadfast mind . . .
A rhyme in time, will soon be mine.

M C Barnes
Greater London

Thank You

Just as I thought things were starting to fade
You answered my plea and came to my aid
Although I kept looking, my faith was depleted
Just devastated to see so many ill-treated

Desperately seeking for more than I know
With little to bring me up from my low
Then suddenly you alter my view
I truly believe our dream can come true

You gave me more than I asked, and showed me equality
So I'll fulfil my task according to your policy
Then again today, there was fantastic news
We're on a winning streak, we can't lose

Thank you for showing me that good is there
It's so nice to see that some people care
As for the others, we'll make them see
That it's so much better when all can be free

This is just the beginning there's more to come
I can't wait to see when our job has been done
So you keep watching, and you'll see the change
There's no way I'll let Earth go up in flames.

Andrea Crome
Greater London

Angie - Echo Verse

My darling Angie, I will always love you.
Love you.
We danced till dawn, you became my lover.
I love her.
You gave so much; your heart became a door.
Adore.
Your gifts of love without condition. Trust.
On trust.
Breaking up, torn apart, my heart's for you.
For you.
Every memory golden, joyous too.
Us two.
Now each day my heart remembers glow.
Embers glow.
Do I still miss you? My Angie, never more.
Evermore.

Des Beirne
Greater London

The Budgie's Story

He said to the bird,
'It's really absurd
But you are an incredible size.
If we go to the show
You surely must know
We stand a good chance of a prize.'

But the budgie just sat,
She thought she was fat,
And stared at the bars of her cage.
She was bored with her bell,
Her mirror as well -
It just showed her how much she had aged.

She was fed up with seed,
Yes, even chickweed
And longed for a change in her food.
She'd always been 'Miss',
Never even a kiss
And secretly yearned to be wooed.

If she had her way
She'd be off the next day;
Trees, fields and hedges to roam.
But to the cage she was tied
Till the day that she died.
And that is the end of my poem.

Bridget Pearson
Greater London

Mount Everest

The roof of the world
is usually very cold.
It looks best in white snow
when the sun rises over the hills,
over the most dangerous mountains.
You never know if the massive
power of nature
will let you come back to your home safe.
The snow coat which covers
every hill is most suitable.
Everest is for me special.
I saw something more on top of
the hill, when it once let me
come in and see the panoramic view.

Martha Angelica
Greater London

Gone

Last night I fell asleep with
one hand touching her pink and purple
shredded blanket and the other
resting on the telephone.

I would say like being a child again.
Little securities making
the world go soft -
but I was never that child.

Sometimes it is just as simple
as saying: yes, there are times
when I hurt so much -
physically, mentally, both -

that all it takes is the feel
of her blanket to bring back
a slight scent, a slight pressure
(she could be lying against me)

and the feel of the telephone,
recalling a kind of connection
to you that almost makes
you there if I shut my eyes.

Sometimes these things
can lull me to sleep.

Morney Wilson
Greater London

Late Night Caller

Banging against my door at this time of night,
You have given me such a fright,
But, you won't worm your way into my heart,
Let's get that straight, right from the start,
I have been hurt by your kind before,
But it won't happen to me anymore,
All the stress and the pain,
Oh no, my friend, never again,
No good pleading, using those big brown eyes,
And your nice ways are probably a big disguise,
So go on, go, walk out of the door,
I can't take this anymore,
Oh, I didn't mean it, you can stay,
I have always been a sucker for dogs anyway.

Maureen Arnold
Greater London

The Enfield Beast

There's something lurking in Tenniswood
Some beastly thing it's understood
A beast of prey some people say
Their stories vary from day to day.

A young girl walking home from school
Heard a rustle in bushes; but kept her cool
Spotting a creature black as the night
Panther-like appearance; eyes fiery bright.

A massive black cat with a four foot tail
That prowls through the night; yet leaves no trail
Awakening the locals with a wild cat roar
Leaping at windows; never leaving a spoor.

Sometimes it's brown; larger than a fox
Sneaking through fences; swimming canals and locks
This creature now holds my borough in awe
From Edmonton Green to far Bullsmoor.

No one can catch it; with either camera or net
Is it reality or phantom? Don't call yet for a vet
For I spot it daily from springtime through winter
It's the emblem of Enfield; that dastardly old cur.

Clive Goldsmith
Greater London

The Gym

Do you really know what it's like
riding around town on your bike,
now what if both the wheels fell off
it wouldn't take you long to get off,
but then when I hear the shout for gym
oh! I rush can't wait to get in,
then I head straight for those bikes
and off I go on the little bike hike,
close my eyes and country air I smell
here I am lost in my little spell,
grass, trees, parks all to be found
cars, people, birds, just all around,
reminding me of my days with glee
how I was once so very, very free,
but then to make me cringe and cower
a shout, 'Last chance for the shower.'
Then my dreams just all but disappear
I then start to realise that I am here.

Harry Weinert
Greater London

This Nameless Feeling

Oppression is in store
Waiting till the first tear falls
Waiting till the nails of it break
Gripping onto a mountain of pain.

This touch that makes the skin recoil
Sends hairs screaming in deeper
Deeper to a black void
Of a throbbing heart.

Hands of pain which wrap the soul
Create rings around the neck
The neck of a newborn
Scared and numb.

Brazen shoulders lie heavy with weight
Blinding the sun and its rays
Engulfing the touch
Of any hope.

This feeling that drives the madness wild
Brings an unusual feeling of an unborn child.

The final humiliation is in store
Waiting till the last tear falls
Waiting till the nails of it break
Gripping onto a mountain of pain.

Sonya Nikolosina (17)
Greater London

Far Beyond Compare!

Have you beheld this masterpiece - the spider web,
   Skilfully shuttled in splendour sans any help?
His abode cum snare - spun with gossamer silk threads radiating
   In contrast to the 'concrete monstrosities' humans are building?
Have you beheld a mass of hexagonal waxy cells - the beehive,
   Fashioned with symmetrical precision without tools or knife?
A castle for their queen, nursery for their progeny,
   Quarters for their workers, and storehouse for their honey?
Have you been privileged to espy, a weaver bird at work?
   The Asian warbler sewing twigs together, and hey presto, a nest doth emerge!
Hanging aloft a tree like a gourd, spherical at its end,
   With the entrance below, to ward off predators that threaten them!
Whence acquireth they these skills, intrinsically perfect?
   It's their inherent instinct, endowed by God, the architect!

Welch Jeyaraj Balasingam
Greater London

Song-Like Prose
(For my soulmate, Hani)

I see the effect of your
sombre rose
Beauty flower
touch my soul
Dull-like sky
lay flame my heart
Liar wind,
hold me close
Vibrant red on
black and white
Heavy odour;
stench that grows
Ugly life
conceal the truth
Cloud-light smiles
and overdose
I hear the effect of your
painted prose
Captured beauty;
Heaven's foe
Blue-like lie,
hold me close
Darker eyes
and comatose.

L Molisho
Greater London

The Little People

When I was a lad maybe seven or eight
I used to play in my grandad's garden
Down at the bottom by a rusty old gate
And you wouldn't believe me
You would say that I'd fibbed
But beyond that gate was where the little people lived
Fairies, elves, folk of lore
Pixies, goblins and a whole host more
Dancing around singing their happy song
All day through and all night long
It really was a sight to behold
To see these little people dancing around their crock of gold
I went back to my grandad's the other day
But sadly the little people had all gone away.

Mark Hutchines
Greater London

Karen

You came into my life so suddenly
someone I never knew
but with the beauty of your heart
I couldn't help but love you.

Such an amazing woman you are
an inspiration to all
the Creator's brightest star.

As life would have it
she threw a spanner in the works
turned our lives into turmoil
created so much hurt
but survivors we are
faced greater adversities by far.

Every step of the way I'm with you
when you feel alone at night
remember to embrace this life
think of the great things you've done
how you brought us all together
and created a bond so strong
I love you, Karen,
I know you have the strength to hold on . . .

Kerry-Anne McChlery
Greater London

The Full Picture

I look around at the floral abundance,
Which you view too in a state of ignorance.
Nature's pastiched a veritable palette of colours,
But for you it's all black and white; no others.
Monotone, monochrome, ebony and ivory,
At least your visual spectrum suffers no rivalry.
But you're blind; mind you you've already lost sight,
Of inimitable beauty, so gorgeous and bright.
Imagine though, no more colour,
The world would become so much duller.
What would a grey sky resemble?
What colour's the lava from a volcanic tremble?
Jimi Hendrix's Purple Haze,
Now at what colour can I gaze?
An eternal old-fashioned picture show,
No sun through a black and white rainbow.

Lauren Rassam
Greater London

Living With Ghosts

I glimpsed a ghost
in spring leaves,
a fragile thing, flickering
with loss and pain
till joy, its brighter light
burst through - winter
woods, alive again

I glimpsed a ghost
in summer leaves
a bold thing, enjoying
no finer freedom
than hope, a brighter light
bursting through - green
woods, strong again

I glimpsed a ghost
in autumn leaves,
such a pretty thing, high
on colourful passions
like home fires acting out
our lives like mummers
in a play

I glimpsed a ghost
in winter snow,
a sad thing, its sorrow
shining through . . .
yet love, a brighter light
watching over
our grave

Roger N Taber
Greater London

Travelling In The Air With Munna

You know, Munna darling,
I could never have imagined
that one day I would be flying
high above the clouds . . .
Just the two of us alone.
It's a beautiful feeling to
know you are accompanying me.
So comforting, so lovely
to travel to India with you.
Munna, I don't feel sad anymore
because I know you are watching over me
and waiting to come back to me.

Rajeev Bhargava
Greater London

The Pain Of Love

Please stop me
Stop me now
I'm starting to love you again
But I don't know how
I will end up just hurting you
And making you cry
So please stop me
Stop me now
The path we are choosing
Will only end up in dismay
But your eyes are so beautiful
O please stop me now
The way you walk
Is the only temptation to me
The way you talk
Is so addictive, I need to be free
We have been here before
Another déjà vu
You cried the last time
And it killed me you see
So stop me now
Stop me please
I need to be alone
You need to be free

Kenneth Buckley
Greater London

Fall Of Man

Dusk falls in damnation's wake:
An angel of fragrant desire will I make,
The dowry of her image,
    Make man slave to her imploring lust,
Mock him, in homage,
    Bid him to untimely death - crumble into dust!
Intrepid warrior, heed her power to provoke;
Rouse primordial forces;
Be confounded in her awe, agog!
Elysian fields of vision, beguile the mortal -
Imprisoned in twilight portal,
Infuscate his mind with incensed thoughts, base, animalistic,
Writhing in rhapsody of his vexed corse,
Push him to the brink; whispers will hasten his decent
Flay expirant soul, silent
 - Snuffed out with the morning star.

Liza Jones
Greater London

The Rat And The Lion Of Walford

The rat is sitting on the table,
Bold as brass,
A meal is already on,
Finest glass and cutlery and all,
And Ratty is enjoying the meal
Like the country gentleman that he is.
Mind you, it's somebody's meal
And Ratty has never been invited.

And the cat? The Lion of Walford . . .
He has been relegated to
The floor beneath the table.
He happily laps up the remains
Of someone's fish and chips.
Well, I ask you!

What's this world coming to?
Times have changed, haven't they?
Everything is topsy-turvy.
The rat lords it over the cat,
Twenty-first century, ba!
Give me the last century any day.

Scholastica Bennin-Sam
Greater London

Broken Flowers

You wind a path that's straight and true,
You had everything, but you never knew.
So you kept on walking.

Imagine what we could have seen,
If windows were where doors had been.
And we just kept on talking.

All the things I've ever read,
Are spinning round inside my head.
But words don't form easy.

I take a leaf from a different book,
I start to read, but I just can't look.
The paper cuts right through me.

I am on the edge of sanity,
I've lost all my humanity.
So absorbed am I by sorrow.

My world is over, my dreams are dead,
They're dancing on my flower bed.
And I sit there just watching.

Darren Scott
Greater Manchester

Twice Undone

Undone.
He taught them all of what he knew.
But would they leap to learn?
They grasp a laugh, they grasp a laugh.
Then the lesson goes askew.

Undone.
Torn, roped in, across the ages.
Chased that heart across the pages.
Why, oh why you thrilled,
By the by, you killed.

Undone.
He said their troubles he would know.
Only if they dared to help themselves.
They cried again, they cried again.
Then left with nowhere else to go.

Undone.
Defeated, deleted.
Disgruntled, mistreated.
Crumbled now, that pillar of trust,
Bitch, heartbreaker, you do disgust.

Undone.
So two separate stories are one.
Yet his situation indifferent.
Who was that man, who was that man
Who had surely become undone?

Sean Ian Riley
Greater Manchester

Melissa's Heart Of Gold

Made to perfection
Every man can have his dream
Light shines upon thee
In the wake of her morning stream
Some search the ocean, whilst you soar the skies
Some say that beauty is written way up high
And in the end, if we don't find
Bring a clock and stop my time
Ring a bell and count your hearts
And make a note as they part
Never give in till beauty has laid to rest, a
Never-ending goddess, the queen of all the rest
And in the end a sun will shine
Nectar sweet and as white as wine

James Oliver Moon
Greater Manchester

Home, Sweet Home

Our house was a very old house, as old as it could be
It holds a lot of memories for my little brother and me
Like the freezing winter mornings the tap was frozen up
There wasn't a drop of water to fill my empty cup.

And oh, the outside toilet at the end of our backyard
Using it through the winter months was sometimes kinda hard
Emptying the ashes from the old cast iron grate
Wishing we had a gas fire cos ours was in a state.

I hated washing the pots with only a candle for light
With a kettle of water or two, every single night
We never had a washer, electricity or a phone,
My mother worked in the evening, so I was left alone.

Our stairs didn't have a carpet, just the wood scrubbed white
The floorboards felt so very hard when I said my prayers at night
We used to have a knocker-up who got us out of bed
When she rattled her great big stick she almost woke the dead.

I have a lot of memories, some happy and some sad
When I think of how I weathered the storm, it makes me feel quite glad
But now I have a better house with everything to hand
All the things I want and more, life feels *oh so grand.*

Pauline Mayoh-Wild
Greater Manchester

The Last Time

When was the last time
He told you that he loved you?

Held your hand and smiled;
Told you that you're beautiful
And didn't treat you like a child?

When was the last time
That he hugged you close
To feel your beating heart,
Spun some verses into rhyme
And didn't treat you like a tart?

When was the last time
He just loved you as a fact
And didn't try to block
Your reclamation act?

When was the last time . . . ?

David McConville
Greater Manchester

Goodbye Dream Town

They're watching me die
Laughing with satanic eyes
It's a cruel, cruel world
My mind has been raped
There are tears in my eyes
Can't remember how to laugh
Just remember how to cry
Still don't know how to live
But I know how to die
The reason they all hate me
Still lingers in my mind
They won't give up till they've knocked me down
And taken my dreams away
'Revenge' is the word on their lips
I have to go, I can't stay
Goodbye Dream Town
I have to run, but I swear
I'll be back someday
To change the minds of the fools that hurt me
They won't call me a freak
They won't label me 'crazy!'
Goodbye Dream Town
Now nothing will faze me!

A P Richardson
Greater Manchester

Lost Chances

Sat here, the window reflecting my past,
Telling me of the things I've said and done.
Time has flown by, oh, so fast!
I want to run back, just get up and run.
Those rooms, those walls, like an animal I felt,
Caged in amongst the prisoners.
Yes, I laughed, I pranked, I had a joke,
Looking back I could choke.
The wardens, they had the key,
The window says it was all for me.
The warden, she'd murmur and chalk on the wall,
I'd look and I'd laugh, well, I've wasted it all!
If not twiddling my thumbs, I'd run about,
The warden, she'd scream and then she would shout.
She'd rattle that key, a warning to me,
Did she think me a lazy and tiresome lout?

Anita McErlean
Greater Manchester

In Him Who Is Fair And Just

J ustifying why we all are here
U nderstanding what life's all about
S ometimes these are the questions
T hat we just can't figure out.

H aving hope can help us
A nswers may begin to appear
V oicing our apprehensions by
E liminating fear.

F aith in our Creator
A sk and you shall receive
I nstead of doubt and insecurity
T ry trusting, learn how to believe
H e is there to offer assistance.

I n Him who is fair and just
N ow is the time to listen, in His

J udgement we all can trust
E very one of us will benefit
S o much does He do to please us
U nderstand His truth and wisdom, the
S on of God, our Saviour, Jesus.

Allan Ball
Greater Manchester

Unruly Kids

'Will you stop jumping on that sofa? Or you'll get a smacked behind.'
I don't care what this government says, smacking isn't unkind.
'Will you stop screaming the pair of you, and go and play on the stair?
I'm trying to watch a film with Ginger Rogers, and Fred Astaire!
For heaven's sake give her what she wants, and stop upsetting her now,
Just don't give me a headache, I can feel one coming on my brow.'
Why did I have to get married to have two whiny kids?
'Oh for God's sake, stop banging on those two pan lids!'
People think kids are lovely, they can have both of mine,
Then I might be able to watch the telly and everything would be fine.
'You two will go to bed in a minute, sit still, and behave yourselves now!
Hey you, don't talk like that to your sister, she's not a silly cow.
Come here and let me nurse you, just wait until your daddy gets back!'
It must be nice to be a fella, I'd love to give mine the sack,
It's alright for him to be out of the house, and not come home till late.
Men just have it easy, it's just a poor woman's fate,
If you're looking forward to marriage, I hope you don't have two kids like mine,
I don't know how you'll cope on your own, if both of them start to whine.

James Ayrey
Greater Manchester

Bury Market

A visit to the market
Is a trip around the world
Oranges from Saville
A cure for all our ills
Silk from China
Tea from Ceylon
Shoes from Italy
I always try them on
Salmon from Scotland
It has to be wild
Soda bread from Ireland
Sure to bring a smile
Cheeses from France
Spices from the east
Jewellery to enhance
Olives from Greece
Fruits from exotic places
Silks, satins and laces
Tulips from Holland
Over the sea
But after all this
What's for my tea
Because I'm in Bury
I just can't resist
Their famous black pudding
Served up on a dish

Elizabeth Thorpe
Greater Manchester

What If?

What if everything is random,
and nothing is planned out?
Probability and coincidence,
without a shadow of a doubt.
What if Old Testaments, New Testaments,
religion galore,
were just to control the people by score?
What if we're here and that's it,
and there's no answers at all?
No higher plane,
no God you can call.
Just human relationships and the sky at night.
A summer's breeze, and a bird in flight,
a heart full of love and a few special friends.
A life filled with memories,
and when it ends, it ends.

Vanessa Alvarez
Greater Manchester

Auntie Tracy's Monster

I go to Auntie Tracy's, I go there for some tea,
I've never ever been before, it's a special treat for me.
Auntie Tracy's really funny, I laugh until I ache,
So we stop for a little while to have some yummy cake.
But then I see something, the one thing that I fear!
It's coming right towards me, it's getting very near!
It knows that I'm scared but the thing it doesn't care,
It's going to come and get me so I had better be aware!
Its eyes are all narrowed and look like they glow,
It's crawling on its belly, at first it's very slow.
It's up on all fours, it's moving quicker now,
I've got to get out but I don't know how!
It's getting real close, it's going to jump!
It's big and it's furry, a great massive lump!
Its claws are all sharp and pointing right out,
I open my mouth wide and I scream and shout!
Auntie Tracy jumps up and spills all her tea,
'What is it?' she cries. *What! Can't she see!*
It's right by me now, it's stood by my leg,
'Take it away Auntie Tracy!' I desperately beg!
The thing looks up with eyes fixed on me,
I'm sure that it thinks I'm something for tea,
Auntie Tracy by now is trying not to laugh,
She picks up the fur ball and shoos it down the path.
'Francesca,' she said 'you're not frightened of that!
It's only little Ziggy, Auntie Tracy's pet cat!'

P Hoddinott
Gwent

Winter Pond

Standing catching weather
On the reeds of descant clay.
The silt gathered at base
And a folly of stone nearby,
Grasses italic in cutting winds
On a slate sky black and grey.

The ripples spreading from centre
And thoughts of you drift.
I feel the wind on my tongue;
Dry and cold with loneliness by my side

Winter's biting leaves left hung
On once smouldered cinders;
Sugar-coated for Mother Earth to taste.

Simon Jones
Gwent

The Outcast

Some people curse and swear at me
And others punch and kick
For they bully me every day
And drown me with their spit.

They threaten me with big sharp knives
So I'm their punchbag slave
They'll look and find to beat me up
I can't hide in a cave.

They punish me for everything
They say it's all my fault
There's no stopping these heartless ones
I beg them just to halt.

No matter what I try and do
They'll always strike me down
I cannot run from these foul fiends
Or hide in any town.

To them I'm always the outcast
The stranger and the freak
I'm no different from anyone
At least my heart is not weak.

Samuel Edwards
Gwent

The Sparrow

A sparrow comes to visit me
While I am drinking morning tea,
He sits upon my window sill
And doesn't make a sound until
I've drunk up all I have to drink,
Then - giving me a nod and wink
He calls, 'What do you have for me?
I'm not so very fond of tea,
If you've a drop of milk to spare
I'd quite appreciate a share.
You couldn't spare some bread could you?
I'd really like a crumb or two!'
I give him milk and crumbs of bread,
He picks and pecks and dips his head.
He picks and pecks and dips until
He's picked and pecked and dipped his fill
And then he says, 'My thanks, good day!'
And spreads his wings, and flies away.

Gordon Andrews
Gwent

Untitled

Wales, land of my father
A land full of song
Its beauty astounds me
It goes on and on

Wherever I am
In this country of ours
My heart comes back to *Wales*
With its magical powers

In life I can't ask for any more
My heart is content
Living in *Newport*
Living in *Gwent*

Come see for yourself
Please come to Wales
See all its beauty
And what it entails

You won't be disappointed
I'm not and can't be
Because Wales is my life
And forever will be.

John Horton
Gwent

The Dust Settles

The dust settles,
the wheels don't turn,
voices lay still like the echoes of years,
rust coats the artery of an industrial town,
like a heart ready to die,
like a heart ready to stop.

They closed the site and fenced it up,
they walked away,
they turned their backs,
open the stable gates and let the ponies run free,
as the harden'd paths turn to clay.

The yard will stand the last man out,
unkempt like the grave forgotten about,
with chains and locks that hold back the soul,
for every hand that shakes,
for every lung of coal,
as the dust settles,
and the wheels don't turn.

Matt Powell
Gwent

Nature's Fury

A polluted world,
Where the creatures choke,
Listen to the echo of the dolphin's cry,
A sound of forgotten hope.

The sun burns with fury,
The wind takes revenge,
The clouds burst with sorrow,
A message to send.

The tears turn to ice,
As flesh becomes bone,
The land crumbles,
And the creatures continue to choke.

The elephants show dignity,
As they lead to their nest of death,
Daylight fades into darkness,
The land becomes bare.

The sea brews a storm,
An almighty roar,
A warning to mankind,
Though the people still ignore.

Camille Metcalfe
Gwent

A Hundred Million Stars

A hundred million stars in the sky
And the one on the left caught my eye.
It's got some red and a bit of blue
And as soon as I saw it
I thought of you.

Fifty million pebbles on the beach
All the colours of the rainbow
From purple to peach
I picked one up, it was reddish-blue
And then guess what? I thought of you.

Ten million blades of grass on my lawn
All covered in dew in the early morn
Each drop of dew is a tear I cry
For the love I have for you
That will never die.

D T Baker
Gwent

The Bay Of Biscay

Endless war against sea-going men
Boiling cauldron of storms extreme
Waves as high as tall Welsh chapels
Howling winds and roaring seas that can
Persist for days and nights on end
Hanging onto a wild helm that swung
Twenty degrees and more either side
Rolling over onto her sides until she was level with
The loudly roaring waters, and often thinking
If she would ever become upright again
Watched in horror as the bows and the whole
Of the foredeck disappeared 'neath mountainous seas
And as a young lad I was truly afraid
Oh, Biscay, Biscay, why do you frighten us so?
This place of liquid mountains
This place of storms extreme
This place of lost souls
This roaring saline monster
This Bay of Biscay

Wyn Williams
Gwynedd

Welsh Rose 2

In the righteous hope that
Nature's true life symbolism
Will point this ravaged world
On the path to love and peace;

From Welsh kitchen window
Two pure rose heads sharing
Single, proud stalk, wing slowly into view,
Double the beauty, double the hue;

Two thriving roses, one proud stalk;
Arab and Jew continue your talk
Sunni and Shia continue your talk
People of Ireland continue your talk.

Combatants, world over, remember
Those roses subtly sharing same stalk;
Remember wily Welsh wizard
Who taught you to talk.

Chris Barnes
Gwynedd

Walking With A Friend

I walk beside the seashore
Each morning come what may,
My trusted friend beside me
Expecting me to play,
Throw a stick, a ball maybe
And also hide-and-seek,
Father Time has caught us now
We're both too old and weak,
When we walk along the shore
I thank the Lord above,
For all those years of friendship
And for my dog's true love.

Clifford Jones
Gwynedd

Love Went Away

My love is like the ocean,
Wild and strong,
My love goes on and on.
Across the sea to where you have gone,
My love is with you so strong.
My love goes on and on.
The sun is hot in your new land,
And cold in mine.
But in my heart the sun shines,
I will love you to the end of time,
You are always on my mind.

Beryl Elizabeth Moore
Gwynedd

Life's Pattern

Our lives are ruled by the way we are,
Our hopes, our dreams are special by far.
Friends and family, young and old,
Shy, adventurous, careful or bold.
We are what we are,
Because of what we do.
Hope for the future, fulfilling and true.
We hope we succeed, we hope we grow,
We'll follow life's pattern
Wherever we go.

Mary Plumb
Hampshire

Go Down Mill Lane

Go down Mill Lane in the twilight time
When birds sing their last song of day
And find their perch to sleep the night away.
Go down Mill Lane, where the meadow lies deep
In grasses and wild flowers and whispering reeds.

And as you watch, the red fox stirs from his earth
And by the hedge runs.
Swans hiss and cover their eggs on the watery nest,
The water rat jumps from the bank . . . and seeks the water's safety.
The red fox runs, tongue hanging out, pink and wet,
Eyes of orange brown and ears pricked.

Branches touch you on the shoulder as over the lane they hang,
Waiting for the spring
To burst them into green leaves and scented flowers,
The blue kingfisher flies to her nest over the stream
And the water rushes from the mill - if you stand very still in the lane.

The fox will cross and stare you out,
As for a magic moment you and nature meet.
And then . . . he's gone!
So, if I should grow old and die and you wonder where I am.
Go down Mill Lane and listen at twilight time
To restless spirits' laughter, as with me they meet
And take my hand and long to greet . . .
That's where I'll be . . . go down Mill Lane and watch the red fox.

Jennifer M Trodd
Hampshire

Just Trust Me

Just place yourself in my arms,
Everything will be OK,
I'll say what needs to be said,
I will never lie to you,
I love you too much for that.

Me and you will be friends forever,
There's no point in resisting,
Just close your eyes,
Fall back and I'll catch you,
Run and I'll find you.

Just trust me,
You won't regret it.

Rebecca Penfold
Hampshire

Through The Winter Windowpanes

Autumn has drunk the wine of summer
and left the moody earth.

Low to the horizon arc
that sweeps against an exposed, blue, fickle sky
a chameleon sun layers changing rainbow colours,
with thin, wispy cloud.

With each catching breath:
it is fresh! - It is cold!
with a crispy snap of icy frost
and the eerie whine of draughty breezes
across joyless, bleak ground.
Somewhere:
a hollow, paper bag rustles,
empty drink cans gutter roll,
topless bottles - moan.
It is the whispering sound of winter's glow -
a dirgeful lament
that hints of coming snow.

The garden is broody but, looks at peace,
through the winter windowpanes.
Flower blooms no longer nod
and spurt their pollen seeds wide.
Withered stamens are brittle dry,
and petals blown and fallen.
The humming humble bees have flown to rest
in hollow trees and warm, wax hives -
full-scented with sweet honeyed comb.

William G Thomas
Hampshire

Strangers In A Strange Land

At the entrance you cried.
Legoland at first . . . frightened you.
I took you in my arms, carried you.
'I'm a little bit scared,' you told me.
Everything was strange.
                        The crowd around you,
And those outsized colourful figures
Made with large plastic bricks.
I reassured you. I love you human girl . . .
From then on you had fun.
You ran around joyfully.
I never took my eyes off you.

'Not too far now Ellie . . .'

You discovered a miniature world.
No threat. No danger.
Small beings with no names.
All positioned in the right place.
Frozen in the right action.
Uttering not a word.
Everything tidy.
                All live in harmony,
With some smiling weather gods.
I saw you watching a model train going round
In a make-believe landscape.
Beside you, another toddler, a boy -
You were both trying to make conversation.
Shoulders almost touching.
Your hands resting on a low fence.
Smiles on your faces.
                        Fragile moment.
You - dressed in all shades of pink.
A pink hat covering your hair.
He - strictly dressed in the tradition
Of Orthodox Judaism.
You took no notice of the difference.

Claire-Lyse Sylvester
Hampshire

Release

Out of my barred window
I looked out for the last time
My name has been called for release
I gather the things that are mine
I'm leaving behind the smell
The awful prison clothes
The sad and gloomy faces
They're just staring as I go
The gate is unlocked for me
And as I'm walking through
I take one last look back
Then I'm led out by the screw
I am overwhelmed by a feeling
That I never knew I had
Filled with such high spirits
From being unfortunate and sad
Released from obligation
I am now no longer bound
Freed from the restraint
Unrestricted I have found
A condition of being contented
As I step outside the gates
Leaving behind the realism
My inevitable fate

Lucy Campbell
Hampshire

Noise

Once we listened to flocks of birds
The munching of bovine herds
The clip-clopping of horses' hooves
As they made their way forward in aligned moves
The cockerel's crescendo at the crack of dawn
The babbling brook on a summer-set morn
The hum of bees in their hives
The swish of the sickle and scythe
Now we listen to the noise of the street
Where everyone is trying to compete
Fireworks for our pleasure, with never a thought for our fellow creature
Music so loud, we can't hear the teacher
Planes taking off in quick succession
The noise they make leaves an everlasting impression.

L Warwick
Hampshire

Ode To Pesticides

We can kill and maim, destroy and slaughter,
We are the Death Squad, smartly dressed.
We can kill earth, air, rain and water.
All fall before us. We are the best!

We were created to improve on nature,
The whole new order would be nature, changed.
We're the guards, to wipe out all known hazards,
Against your enemies we are ranged.

We're not selective in our Blitzkrieg, advancing,
We just follow orders. Familiar words?
We're your four horsemen, stallions prancing.
All opposition falls to our bright swords.

Herbicides, pesticides, fungicides, biocides,
Smartly equipped and a mighty force,
All created to kill, destroy and slaughter,
We follow orders. Death takes its course.

You were so sure that we were no danger,
But the world you knew will not be again.
Remember the blame is in no way ours.
We are the children of your own brain.

M Reichlin
Hampshire

How Lucky You Are

The shimmering light from the sun
On the leaves of the trees
At dawn
Forecasting a new day
Raising hopes for some
Listen to the birds
Twittering in the trees
Listen to their song
Appreciate Earth's wonders
As time rolls along
Isn't it good to be alive
To be virulent and strong
To enjoy the things that you've been sent
And all from Heaven above
To have and to hold
Your loved one
All your long life through
Consider just how lucky you are
I wish I was one of you

Martin Selwood
Hampshire

Searching

For I am a bird
flying high and free
gliding and diving
for food in the sea.
My search is endless, far and wide
looking for untouched lands to hide.
I spread my wings, on Nature's course
my fate in her hands, I feel her force.
For I am the eyes
in your beautiful skies.
I see our planet decaying
but see no one on their knees praying.
I choke on your smog
from your cities' polluted fog.
What my eyes see
they can take no more
as my faith in humanity is tested once more
I let my tired wings take me
to distant lands to awake me.
As to when my journey will end
it's up to you to carry on my friend.
Please take a minute, and ask yourself this
hope I got your attention
whoever is reading this!

Lisa Read
Hampshire

The Wanderer

There's a lonely lane beyond the fields,
Which runs from Lumley Mill,
Across the water, rather wide
For 'Wu', who takes it in his stride
And then goes up the hill.

There's a great big bridge - for one small cat,
Across a busy road.
No chance if he should wander there,
No busy driver'd really care,
If one small cat was 'mowed'.

Keep to the fields, O small grey cat,
And do not wander so.
You're special now, to one and all,
So come back when you hear us call,
Be careful how you go.

Eileen Coates
Hampshire

The Swans

The waters of the creek were mirror-smooth
And the air was motionless.
The setting sun had cast streaks across
The evening sky of red, gold and orange.
The colours arrayed with finesse
Like an artist's brush strokes on his canvas.
A gentle hush had fallen on the scene
Only the geese could be heard, echoingly shrill.
Noisily wading along the water's edge
While the curlew piped his haunting song
As he skimmed and dived.
Then suddenly, from nowhere they came
Three gliding shapes along the creek.
A white swan leading her two cygnets
In silent movement towards the setting sun.
Their feathers tinged with pink
Their heads in graceful curve.
Dipping toward the still waters
And as they passed they did not even see
Their quiet watcher on the shore.
But I, in silent admiration, could only gaze
Until they were no more.

Barbara A Winter
Hampshire

The Merma Tale

A luffy-liffy mermagale
Was swishing in the frillick splish
When up there popped a pentapreyl,
The scourve of every mermafish.

The pentapreyl flied out its groils
And twyred the franting mermagale
Not spotting through its opticoils
The fast approaching mermamale.

A frac ensued of mammock vaibs
The ruckles floyed, the spingles spreed
But, after gours of gruelic staibs,
The franting mermagale was freed.

Oh blissops! Now no groils would twyre
The jocculd pair of mermafish
Who, wedlicked now, will never tire
Of swishling in the frillick splish.

Alan Millard
Hampshire

243

To Rowlands Castle

If in Rowlands Castle you should be
I bet you'd soon agree with me
It really is a delightful spot
With its village green and village shop
I'm sure you would like it here
As you stroll in the wood anytime of year

The village school's not far away
And in the park our children play
And this is something else you'd like
The big bonfire on Guy Fawkes Night

We have a station here, unmanned it's true
But we can catch the train to Portsmouth
Chichester and Petersfield too
And at Havant they have market day
And that isn't very far away

And if you have a need of a prayer
We have three churches here
Two in the village and one at Finchdean not far away
Where you'll be welcome any day

We have a post office and three pubs if you like a booze
All very good so you can pick and choose
So come and settle in Rowlands Castle and you'll see
You will enjoy life here, just like me

Pearl Williams
Hampshire

Devon Delights

Down in Devon something stirred
Was it just the singing of the birds?
All of the time I am thinking of you
Most of all when the sun comes into view
This countryside is lush and green
Like you, I think Devon is a dream
It's here that the famous clotted cream is sold
Lots of it makes you rotund I am told
Coast and beaches are a glorious sight
I view them all with sheer delight
In the evening when twilight creeps
Reluctantly I go to bed and sleep
Down in Devon something stirred
It's a wonderful place, no doubt you heard.

L A G Butler
Hampshire

To A Sweet Gem

The day my world stopped turning and darkness fell upon my life
was the grim day my wife passed on.
Although the sun shone on, in clear blue cloudless skies,
to me, a stygian gloom suffused my mind.
There was no light, no sun, no bright blue sky,
just utter misery, soul destroying loneliness
and dark, dark thoughts of death.

But there now has come, into my life,
a lovely girl who quelled my loneliness.
Her visits helped dispel the emptiness and
by spending a short time, now and then, with me
she had made me feel far less bereft.
It is surprising that one so young should have
such depth of thoughtfulness, kindness and feeling.

She has helped to make me feel that my life is worth living again,
with her happy smile and her inner light
which is now brightening my days.
My world once more has begun to turn . . .
The reason can't be sex, for I am far too old.
Nor love, for the beautiful child is much too young
to be affected by such feelings yet.

But she, by calling in and caring,
has brought back to my life a reason to exist,
I thank her from the depths of my being.

D G W Garde
Hampshire

Untitled

Awake
Stand up
This is it
Your day has begun
Stir your bones, sleep is done
By the ocean, watch a flying seagull
Circle down then swoop around a ship's hull
See wings above the low clouds and now below
Wait and feel the sun's orange, round, bright autumn glow
Watch crouched old men with walking sticks come and walk beside
Shingle beach waiting for their long, timely last walk - their winter tide

Sheila Cheesman
Hampshire

And We Sleep

Where the stark branches
cry out their solitude
and silvery drapes press
every hard, hushed field;
where quieted pools
glance up at a pink-streaked sky,
and bronzed-black leaves
are tossed to the fickle winds,
we should make friends with winter!
And thinking of that little Babe,
some other time,
some other country,
the star and the inn,
the midnight humming,
for comfort in golden silence -
a time for reflection.
Each furry stillness in the burrow,
each small feathery stirring
brings nature's promise,
perhaps we will prosper
to overcome our oddities;
and tangible love
and kind deeds dwelling,
as peace descends tonight
And we sleep.

Patricia Morris
Hampshire

Talented Lady

In the moonlight
Curves in shape
Pretty, slim bit
Ageless, timeless lady

In the morning
When she rises
Downtown into the city
Neat as a pin

In the evening
Timeless beauty
A woman of quality
Without a doubt: a talented lady!

S M Thompson
Hampshire

The Will

The will was writ on some post office form
And this is what it said
'My property I leave in trust
To my four children
And Mother may live there
For the remainder of her life.'

I wasn't given any option
I didn't want it on my plate
But she pleaded and Mother sobbed
And the afternoon was getting late
Like squealing pigs before the slaughter
Screaming words of hurt and pain
My mother and her daughter
I wish they'd never come.

Yet this woman, our mother
Had given everything as I could see
Her life was one of sacrifice
Make do and budget carefully.
It could all have been resolved with ease
Just four signatures upon the deed
But the eldest two would not concede
One can only think that it was greed.

The reality of the four-year-long feud
And it frightened me as much as her fear
Was the degree to which they pursued
Trawling Mother through the legal mire
What worth they placed on her appeal?
What incentive for their sordid desire?
Money, £8,000, was it a market deal?
For a mother's lifetime of love and care.

But I am also a mother just like her
And though I supported her to the end
It took its toll and left me in despair
Now I've no trust or loyalty to spend.

D C Mundell
Hampshire

Self-Sufficient In Suburbia

She found me lying on the floor.
Oh, what an awful waste.
She propped me up against the door.
Forget about good taste.

She stripped me off and left me there,
My clothes she burned to ashes.
She shaved off all my body hair
And pulled out my eyelashes.

She carved me into little bits,
Some stiff, some sadly flaccid.
She put me in the family bath
And covered me with acid.

She waited till my brew went thick.
It did not take too long.
She oft-times stirred me with a stick
And sprayed to dull the pong.

She went out to the local store
With all that I'd been saving.
She purchased things on every floor
And ordered yards of paving.

She chose a pleasant garden spot
With vegetation round.
She paced me out a measure plot
And dug it in the ground.

She waited, then, for night to fall.
Me, ladled in a bin.
She had to drag me through the hall
Before she poured me in.

She levelled all with fingered strokes
Then washed her soiled hands.
She phoned some local builder blokes
And told them what was planned.

She rarely spares a thought for things,
Now buried here below.
She sits admiring diamonds rings
Upon her patio.

Eric Hart
Hampshire

Innocence

Spread your wings little butterfly,
Flutter from flower to flower.
Before your wings are plucked
And your beauty is devoured.

Lift up your voice sweet nightingale,
Before you can no longer sing.
For life may dampen your spirit,
With the troubles it could bring.

Play joyously happy, fox cubs,
Before mixing with mankind.
For you will be disillusioned
At the cruelty you find.

Run swift graceful deer,
Feel the wind, wild and free.
For you may soon be trapped,
Where you don't want to be.

You fly, pretty butterfly,
Sing, heavenly bird.
Hide, happy fox cubs,
Deer, play with the herd.

Your innocence is endearing,
Although maybe amiss.
So shut your eyes and ears,
Ignorance is bliss.

Marlene Parmenter
Hampshire

Good Health

Never make a fortune, too late now
but I am happy anyhow
as my health is all I need
or my family to feed.
I cannot run a mile
but I do manage to smile
God gave me strength and courage
when the road grows long and rough.
I never ask Him for a blessing
as I am blessed enough.

Ann Thompson
Herefordshire

Haven: 1840

It was no day for man or maid
To be on the bleak moors
In howling wind and drenching rain,
Fain would they be indoors.
But they had neither cot nor byre.
The wind cut like a knife.
The man gazed long at the shiv'ring maid
He planned to make his wife;
At chattering teeth and bluing lips,
Whilst still she tried to smile.
He knew they must find shelter soon.
She would not make the mile
To warmth within the hay-filled barn,
Protected from the rain,
He wildly glanced about the moor,
It seemed he looked in vain.

Then saw a stone-built sheep pen
A hundred yards away.
He stooped to lift the cold, wet maid -
Carried her all the way.
Some sheep lay closely-huddled there
And all were loath to move.
But soon he made room for them both
By many a prod and shove.
They snuggled down amid the sheep
Secure in their warm place.
The young man watched; the young maid slept,
Fresh colour in her face.
They arose, stiff-limbed, at morning light,
Glad that the storm was gone;
Offered their thanks to grazing sheep,
Then travelled blithely on.

Jim Lawes
Herefordshire

Symmetry

Gentle journey bid the train
Leave its tracks in my refrain
And cast me on to you
For the joy of all that's true
And ease of heart bring ease of mind
That loves for you as you are kind
So long we've waited in-between
The times we lie together freed
By a skill of open heart
A mirror to another part
Of character that's less beknown
For in general talk, you are alone
But realising not of this
Until you love or love love's bliss
As wanderer, philosopher
Is want to leave the stars for her
As knows he from the start
No study tames his wilder heart
Since love she breathed her sigh
And mirrored him to what's inside
A pearl that bears no breath
Of fault upon her gentle breast
For all the law and tarnished wit
Cannot bear the truth that fits
But you quietly realise
The answer lies within her eyes
And all that's mocking be
A tribute to your symmetry.

Mike Thorne
Herefordshire

Let's Go

Come, go with me
Before it's too late.
Come, it's time for us to flee.
Here I am waiting at the gate.

Come, go with me
Before we are seen.
Come, let's go as if we
Have never before been.

Come, I'll take you to a faraway land,
Far across the sea we'll go,
Where we can wander hand-in-hand
And no one else will ever know.

Ruth Berry
Hertfordshire

Heart's Desire

Of all the shires that has my heart
is where I live called Hertfordshire,
the Great North Road and Watling Street
still bear the print of Romans here.
The ancient town of Verulam
is witness to the Christian creed -
of Alban, first of Celtic men
to die a martyr's death indeed.
The river Ver flows through the town,
a witness to our greatest 'He',
and should she ever cease to flow
the world will then the poorer be.
Then Hertford is its county town
with castle, school and buildings grand,
or Hatfield where Queen Bess was young
with manor gardens all around.
Then Chaucer lived at Berkhamsted
and Cowper born there later on,
or Whipsnade on the Chiltern Hills
where all the animals have gone.
The university is great,
and Watford sports a fine old team,
throughout the county shopping malls
meet all our needs as we might dream.
Luton/Stansted are close by so
if you fly in you're nearly there
to taste our priceless heritage
before the train takes you elsewhere.
The hills and dales of Hertfordshire
have my own soul and heart's desire.

Norman C Edwards
Hertfordshire

Rainbow Unicorn

The rain has stopped crying and the world is smiling a happy smile
Colourful shades climb down from the canvas sky
Golden shreds shine upon rainbow unicorn, a majestic sight
White as ice, graceful as the breeze
Hooves clatter on smooth blue rocks, kissed by a silent tide
Rainbow unicorn a wonder to everyone's eye
Flowing mane, white and pure dances within a glorious gallop
Fast as the wind and bright as the colours falling from the shimmering sky
A horn points the way on a journey through time
A perfect legend lost to history, but the rainbow unicorn picture will
Always remain a unique vision, as long as our eyes can see beyond what exists

Neil Mason
Hertfordshire

Crying In Waltham Cross

I met the most beautiful girl in the world at Waltham Cross
And I couldn't believe when she said she loved Natty Dreadlocks;
She had the most divine features and gorgeous big brown eyes
Looking into them then I could see nothing but eternal paradise.
Jezebel gave me love and I swore that we'd never part ways
And I gave her all I had and showered her with divine praise.

Now that was then, cos she kept me waiting for months in vain
Yet she knew it was over and played games with my brain.
One day out of the blue I saw her canoodling with another guy
And God knows at that moment I thought it was better to die.
I thought I was the luckiest man to have a woman so beautiful
But I feel like a fool, while I was chaste she broke all the rules,
And I'm crying cos I want to know how am I supposed to live?
Cos I'm beyond redemption and hate to even think of the word forgive.

I'm punching the walls thinking of every time I said - 'I love you'
And she laughed in my face cos I didn't even have a single clue
That she was an actress of distinction just playing the love feel
But now she's begging me to stay and telling me it's not real.
My mind is reeling and denying logic cos I'm close to the edge
And I feel like screaming cos I'm trying in vain not to lose my head.
I'm crying for God to help me cos I'm hurting and crying within
My world has come to an end and I feel my walls are caving in.

I'm home alone waiting in vain for true love to knock on my door
And an empress to confess that she loves me more and more;
My mind's denied reasoning and I don't give a toss, I don't care
I've got my knife and I'm about to commit murder in Hertfordshire
Cos I'm on the prowl and about to use my switch on that witch
And leave the bitch twitching in a ditch, not literally but lyrically.

Joseph T M Nthini
Hertfordshire

A Prayer

Just say a little prayer
with some care and maybe, flair
this world is for the living
and our God He did the giving
it surely is an amazing place
look, now I have a smile upon my face

Take a breath, the air is free
you could learn more from the humming bee
and while you grow
the more you'll know
just take the time to
say a little prayer.

Pat Murray
Hertfordshire

Earth's Harvest

August begins with hot days and nights
But this time of the year the cuckoo takes flight
For the summer is ending, the days will grow short
Harvest will be gathered, fish will be caught.

Farmers are harvesting fields of corn
Hurrying now before the violent storms
Prevent them from reaping their winter supply
Of oats, wheat, barley and rye.

Tractors are ploughing from dawn until dusk
Separating yellow corn from their husks
Field mice scurry from their precarious nests
Where they are taking their daily rest.

Now all has been gathered
The larder is full
Earth has given up its treasures
Once again for us all

Christine Hardemon
Hertfordshire

Motormorphopsychosis

The swift swoops and devours an insect, in flight,
The frog tongue flicks and another creature dies.

Nature takes its course.

The Peugeot 307 driver pulls out in front
Of the 20k exec' four-wheel vehicle driver of leviathan,
No room to manoeuvre for either,
Its driver oblivious to other road users obviously.

Jaws snap, bones crunch and a small mammal dies,
A wildcat family survive.

The boy racer in his Super Nova; Stellar with
Its spoilers, and omnipresent with its boom box, tailgates
The car in front; driver with mobile phone poised
Against the ear, under baseball cap, style
And weapon, too self-obsessed for the sudden brake lights.

Do people care so little about their cars?
Nature takes its course.

A J Barton
Hertfordshire

Behind The Fire

What is love,
a curse from above?
I doubt,
I speak,
I weep and show that her touch was so,
nothing placed unique elegance
I embrace for gleaming willows,
sound that dispersed through the change of the waking morning
and the sun's calling layer across her note was a breathing that softly spoke,
she grasped the light,
the movement was in flight,
under the changes the shadows became this
and cold winter tales spoke like purple stars singing like a flute
of gold man's fiddle toot and then the fairies simmered on the air's topping,
translucent molecules enveloped the sky
and up above a change of mine to show that her behind never spoke sublime.

James McBeath
Hertfordshire

My Tribute To Mo Molem
(Woman of true grit)

No more will she hear a seagull cry
Or see a north blue sky
She has gone to join a brave band
So we must say goodbye
She has gone to join a happy band
No more pain on Earth to roam
There will always be a place, for her in me
And forever in my home.

God keep you Mo.

Robert Henry
Hertfordshire

An Ashridge Invitation

A ll year round I am open
S unny, raining or snowing
H ere to enjoy, have lots of fun. Peaceful walks for everyone
R ead the notice, follow the trails, lift the logs and find some snails!
I n the woods there are lots of trees, connected by different leaves
D eer run through left and right and if you're lucky you'll see a wonderful sight
G ather up things to remember me by, a lovely collage you'll make with a lovely blue sky
E njoy your visit here with me, there's lots of nature for you to see!

Jasmeet Sagoo
Hertfordshire

It's Over

Painful words, like migrating birds
Come, and then they go
Your heart knows when it's over
Words, conclude it's . . . so.

A little spat, of this and that
A look, a breath, a sigh
Confirm what you've been thinking
Au revoir, adieu, goodbye.

Passion, doves, this one great love
Is over, why not say?
Honest words are rarely heard
In this painful game we play.

When you started out, such honesty
Was there, in all you said
As time went on, you longingly
Missed it, it was dead.

As both now part, with saddened hearts
Malicious, do not be
To have loved, been loved and parted
Is pain enough, you'll agree?

Maybe you missed those telltale signs?
You know what they were and how
But you were much too young then
You're wiser than that now!

Kevin Raymond
Hertfordshire

Faye Marie

With eyes the blue of summer skies
And hair of silken curl
I thank the Lord that I've been blessed
With this little angel girl

Her happy smile and gentle ways
Are like a breath of spring
She fills my days with happiness
And my heart just wants to sing

I hope she'll always live in love
And dark clouds never see
For she deserves the best in life
My darling Faye Marie

B J Benton
Hertfordshire

Under The Moonlight

They stood together silently
Under the moonlight,
Watching the sea
Crash against the rocks
From atop the cliff tops.

A beautiful sky
Full of bright stars;
Both gazing up,
Enjoying its splendour.

Never saying a word;
Both enjoying the surroundings
They walk away,
Leaving the crashing sea
And silent sky.

Sarah L Grigor
Inverness-shire

Contented Sigh

When smiles light every nation
And warm is welcome's hand
And everyone lives peacefully
As God the Father planned.
When streams of crystal waters flow
Where tears stain land so dry
Pray bless us with the music, Lord
Of Your contented sigh.

When thankfulness soars joyfully
Accompanied by the sound
Of laughter gay, as children play
'Mid caring all around.
When brimming cups of kindliness
Greet strangers passing by.
Pray bless us with the music, Lord,
Of Your contented sigh.

When written are new melodies
To all the love You bring
As fountains of sweet charity
And hope forever spring.
When rightfulness and friendliness,
And graciousness is nigh,
Pray bless us with the music, Lord,
Of Your contented sigh.

Violet M Corlett
Isle of Man

Take Your Compass Out

Commit yourself to an expedition,
Right here, right now, here's how:

Confused by being 'everything'?
You everything to everyone?

Step back a moment -
Breathe in deep; and take your compass out.

'My compass?' I hear you say;
Why, yes indeed, my friend -
And no, I ain't that round the bend!

For the compass of which I speak,
Is more than just unique,

None two are e'er the same,
Some of which go on to claim -
Renown and global fame.

The compass my friend, I think you'll find -
Is nought but your own mind.

One that makes its own decision;
Then routes its own position.

So every now and then,
Just take it out its little box -
And . . . *snap!*

Snap! your fingers go;
You've clicked, and clicked at last.

Once more you're in control again,
Found your way -
A destination,
Our constant source of fascination.

Carlos Phillips
Isle of Man

Blue Tit On Balcony, Camelia In Pot

180° this way, that way, a blue tit
Rotates its rigid tail feathers lightly
Hopping up the edge of the white slatted
Fence surrounding the balcony and transfers
Onto a bud-bearing camelia in a pot
As if sharpening its beak on the stem, it hops
Right up to the double flower's rust-tinged pink,
One among many in a chill wind this April,

Then does a flit.

B Lockyer
Isle of Man

Intrepid Women Of Paradise

Oh intrepid women of paradise
Come my affable lady, and dance underneath those glorious stars,
And kiss my eyes and heart,
Within the beautiful gardens of Utopia,

Be my princess, champion and guardian,
And live that wondrous dream,
Where heavenly miracles occur,
Your mysterious shadow is of natural beauty,

And read me furious poems of love,
Underneath a tempest hurricane sky,
Where heroines and heroes read muse,
Beside the temple of silent gods,

With potent force and courage thy intrepid women,
Command victorious glories,
Across the vast empire where Spartan women parade,
Welcoming home a thousand galleys and ships,

Conquest and triumphant with white-winged horses in flight,
Where water lilies, wild roses and fruits are picked,
Amongst marble waterfalls and perfumed gardens,
Ophelia of love, dances with Greek fair maidens,

Singing love songs of heavenly paradise,
Surrounded by luscious cypress trees,
Across a surreal, dreamy landscape,
They dance alongside beautiful water nymphs,

Within the great outside Roman theatre,
Where philosophers and poets exchange letters,
Oh Olympian men while Zeus watches,
Brave men who fight honourably,

Oh intrepid women of paradise and glory,
With the story of love and attainment.

James Stephen Cameron
Isle of Man

From A Distance

From a distance I saw the breathtaking view -
in the foreground cypress, larch and conifers fringed the scene.
Woodpeckers, robins, pigeons and doves arrived,
in leisurely succession, giving animation to
the still life beyond which rivets my attention.

From this distance I recalled childhood memories -
holidays in the sun, candyfloss, ice cream and all the fun of the fair.
Not a patch on what is before me now.
Memories of parents, grandparents, sisters
and brother all fade in a comparison to today.

In a distant future I will remember today,
the thoughts evoked like the memories reawakened
fringing the scenes of life,
to what lies ahead on a distant shore
is my true destination -
a heavenly home in a kingdom of eternal light.

Shireen Markham
Isle of Man

To Arundel . . .

Through a haze of spring-green
Where blossoms flatly clustered
Spill onto lush turf,
Past copses knee-deep in bluebells
Shrouded by ethereal mist
And, hiding their fragile beauty
In sheltered fissures,
Late primroses.

Here the river meanders lazily,
Winking a welcome to the early sun.
Against a backdrop of rape-covered fields,
Blinding in their intensity
The sum of its magnificent parts is defined,
The glory of Arundel.

Look upwards . . .
In medieval majesty, the castle,
King of this rural scene,
Serene in its rooted history,
Late sentinel, now benign surveyor
Of the wonders at its feet.

Vera Morrill
Isle of Wight

Trouble At Sea

Someone is in trouble,
In a boat off West Wight,
It could be in the daytime,
Or middle of the night.

A call on his bleeper,
Or on his phone,
So those unfortunates out there,
Soon will not be alone.

The Freshwater Lifeboat,
With the voluntary crew,
Will soon be launched,
By other volunteers too.

They will search the sea,
Until the caller is found,
Then brought back to shore,
We pray all safe and sound.

To maintain this service,
Has a very high price,
So a donation now and then,
Would be very nice.

Take a stroll to the boathouse,
There is plenty to see,
And would you believe it,
The entrance is *free*.

Will A Tilyard
Isle of Wight

Unseen

Foghorns are blowing
Through mist on the sea;
The notes they are playing
Sound eerie to me.

Vast, hidden vessels
Lurk out in the bay,
And familiar scenery's
Expunged for the day.

Perhaps the dank screen
Will lift in the night,
And blotted out landmarks
Return with dawn's light.
But today's phantom ships
Will have slid out of sight.

Julia Perren
Isle of Wight

Behind Closed Eyes

Behind closed eyes, I see -
Faces;

Faces which rise, morph and shape into being
From sepia smoke,
Or,
Push through skin-thin membranes,
Forcing themselves upon my inward eye,
Determined to be seen.

Elastic stretched, distorted features;
Lips move, forming unfathomable words,
Grimace, smile and laugh - or purse
In Monroe-kisses.

Eyes penetrate my own sightless pupils,
Or pierce straight through them
Into worlds of their own, beyond my head;
Or, ignoring me completely,
Seek other eyes in other faces.

The faces rise and fall,
Ebb and flow
One into the other;
Familiar to unfamiliar,
Known to unknown,
Flickering silent movie frames
On the screen of my close-lidded cinema.

Eyes open,
Vision is returned to the mundane,
To the very ordinary pictures of life.

The faces are gone,
But -
Close my eyes again . . .

Barry Jones
Isle of Wight

The Laughing Cavalier

Is it humour or disdain
that to his smile gives birth -
a compliment a lady paid -
or dalliance with a serving maid
of saucy mien and ample girth -
a victory in love's campaign?
Or can it be his rapier taught
a lesson in a duel fought
with one essaying to defame
His Majesty the King's good name -
a combat needing one parade
before the *coup de grace* was made?
A man quite conscious of his worth,
he poses there at ease, benign,
in lace-trimmed doublet super fine,
perhaps consumed with silent mirth.
With tilted hat and small goatee,
insouciant and debonair,
the essence of *savoir vivre*
which marked the age of chivalry.

T C Hudson
Isle of Wight

Tranquil Thoughts

Trees shape the landscape,
Sunlight flickers through the branches above,
Creating a dapple floor underfoot.
A shallow brook runs through the centre,
Adding a quiet melody to the otherwise silent place.
Hoofprints indented in the marshy land,
Created by a herd of cows brought through each day,
Thus making a pathway through the dense undergrowth.
Barbed wire cuts a crude line through the rugged beauty.
Dragonflies encircle the sweet-smelling pines
And fireflies glow in the night.
The dry brown earth cracks like dragons' scales
In the heat of the summer,
But when the rains come,
It transforms into an Amazonian rainforest,
With mudslides and the sound of drips
Splashing into puddles that form craters in the soft earth.
The tree trunks then part into a vast expanse of bright green grass.
When you look back you see the trees,
Waiting silently, patiently, for the apocalypse.

Charlotte Harris (13)
Isle of Wight

My Cat Amelia

My cat Amelia is so dignified,
She is a tortoiseshell
Who combines beauty with intelligence.
Her wants must be simple and sufficient.
Her food must be fresh and her bedding soft.

But what of her dreams?
One can only speculate.
Does she chase birds or little mice
Or surrender to the demands of some robust tom?
All this is none of our business,
We should leave her to enjoy her sweetest dreams.

Frank Bedford
Isle of Wight

A View In The Mirror

When I get home I will see,
a boy in the mirror looking back at me.
He looks the same every day,
with a rough day at school there's no more to say.

One year later he's back once more,
a little bit taller than before.
That day at school I had a dream,
thinking about him and where he has been.

He's got a driving licence and passed,
with a set of wheels, driving so fast.
With four A-Levels to his name,
a career in commentating on the beautiful game.

He goes out drinking with money to spare,
looking for that girl with long blonde hair.
Down the aisle with the one he loves,
she looks like she's been sent from above.

The father of three, two girls and a boy,
his life is fulfilled, and such a joy.
There's a shiny new motor outside the door,
who could ask for anything more?

A few less hairs upon his head,
no late nights for him, it's early to bed.
The wife's spending is out of control,
he feels like she's digging him into a hole.

It's 2050, I see an old man,
every day is a holiday, just look at his tan.
His face is wrinkly and very stressed,
with 10 grandchildren, just give it a rest.

William Bale (12)
Kent

Autumn Pace

The sun on my back
The breeze on my face
On this warm autumn day
I walk at a thoughtful pace

To collect my little girl
From her morning at school
And to hear of her adventures
Her stories always enthral

The cars pass me by at such speed
Their hurry is not my concern
As I drink in the beauty around
While the seasons take another turn

I kick the leaves strewn on the path
Their colours glorious in their demise
Few are left on the trees standing tall
More free-fall as the wind gently sighs

I think as I walk my even steps
The return won't be so sedate
We'll be running, skipping and squealing
Till we reach our garden gate

We'll be gathering spiky chestnuts
Filling our pockets to the brim
Making the most of this season
Until winter comes to replace him

So, for now I'll enjoy my slow stroll
For when winter reclaims its throne
I shall change my pace to an inattentive brisk
And quickly return to the warmth of our home

Michelle Borrett
Kent

Family

What is family?

Family is there for you when you are down.
Family picks you up when you fall
And is there for you when you need it.
Family has the key to open the door when all the rest are locked.
Family is there to hold your weight,
The weight that you can't lift by yourself.
Family is always with you
And always will be.

Luke Clarke (13)
Kent

Thoughts On The Arrival Of Autumn

Autumn slips in easily
Like a grub into an apple,
The harvest has been gathered in,
The leaves begin to dapple.
The church is decked with harvest store
An offering for our sins,
But things have changed with changing years
The harvest comes in tins.
The conker season has begun
To help the leaves descend,
The old trees take a battering
As fools their branches rend.
The garden tree is full of pears
With doubts I now peruse 'em,
And hope the wife can quickly find
Some recipes to use 'em.
The air is fresh with winter's edge,
Not yet quite there in force.
I can't walk far, rheumatic knees,
Perhaps I'll hire a horse.
But joy seems rare, and pleasures fade
As winter clothes are worn,
Yet, still, I'll count my blessings,
Won't have to mow the lawn.
The morning windows start to show
Initial signs of frosting,
Turn up the heating asap
No matter what it's costing!

Jack Scrafton
Kent

Girly Chat

Funny how a girly chat,
A glass of wine,
And a laugh at this and that
Can help to fill some time.

Funny how a girly chat,
A coffee and a piece of cake,
Can ease the strain
Caused by life's mistakes.

Funny that!
How a girly chat
Can help to put
The world to rights!

Rosie Heartland
Kent

There Is A Man Of Mystery

There is a man of mystery,
whose soul will be forever free.
He's tarnished not by thoughts of greed,
and values only word and deed.

He'll travel to most any place,
a cheeky grin upon his face.
A house he has but not a home,
as still his feet do long to roam.

He's loved by none except his kin,
a shame 'tis true but not a sin.
Of friends he'll only name a few,
this matters not for they're all true.

His greatest gifts no one can take,
until his deathbed they do make.
For respect, love and honesty,
are his to give and need no key.

Each day and night he dares to dream,
of willow trees beside a stream.
Where beneath a cloudless sky,
he'll rest and watch the world go by.

He's worth much more than gems or gold,
as friendships can't be bought or sold.
He'll always help when needed most,
a loyalty that few can boast.

Still I'm the one that reads him best,
a clearer vision than the rest.
I know this man of mystery
and know him well for he is me.

Dickon Springate
Kent

Old Silver Bin!

I am a smelly dustbin
I'm made of silver tin
Every time you lift my lid
You drop some rubbish in!
Full of stinky rubbish
I stand here in the rain
Waiting for the dustman
To empty me again!

Mary Anne Hammond
Kent

Mist Above The Clouds

At last, I am in the plane,
the routine is always the same.
Fasten your belt, sit upright!
Relax, no need to take a fright.

The wheels lifted from the ground.
With a shake and a loud sound,
we are flying high, up and away,
on a beautiful September day!

Bound for Florence, Tuscany, my birthplace.
Men drink wine, women knit dainty lace!
We are soaring up in the blue sky,
I am watching a few clouds going by!

There is a mist but it isn't very heavy,
no turbulence, we are going quite steady.
The mist's clearing up, the clouds are below,
looking like a carpet of white snow!

It is the same for the return flight.
We are reaching the normal height.
There is a mist, but it isn't heavy,
no turbulence, we are gong quite steady!

Descending, now I can see down below,
little houses, people moving like in a show!
The wheels are lowered down on the ground:
halting with a shake and a loud sound!

With my luggage in the waiting hall,
I can see my family, four in all!

Licia Johnston
Kent

I Am Me

I am not perfect,
I am me.
I have no long blonde hair,
No silicone, pert breasts,
I will not conform
To what a man thinks is best.
I have no pouting lips,
No gyrating hips.
No taut, tight arse,
Because it's all such a farce.
I will not conform to the caricature of a Barbie doll,
I have an imperfect body, and a unique mind and soul.

Susan Jenner
Kent

Rural England

Eynsford in Kent is not far away.
A beautiful place to spend the day.
The ford and bridge over the river there
Will entertain you from your chair.

The children paddle and fish in the river
The water's so cold, it makes me shiver.
There is a toot on a horn and the children flee
A farm tractor is making waves like the sea.

It is towing a trailer full of bales of hay
Shedding bits everywhere as it goes away.
The boys dare to ride their bikes through the water
They will get soaked if they should falter.

Next comes a lorry, followed by a car
The entertainment has been good so far.
The water settles, there is peace once more
As the clock on the church is striking four

Time for an ice cream before the sun goes down
And we pack up our chairs and return to the town.
We cross the bridge and drive up the lane
Promising the children we will come back again.

Lynne Walden
Kent

King Arthur

King Arthur did in olden days
A great magnificent table raise
Chivalry was the byword then
For the king pronounced equality for all women and men,
The knights weren't full of pride, greed, jealousy
But yearned to set good people free,
They had a tremendous gift of love
Faith to drive them onwards
Forgiveness, charity, care may have been their undoing
But they shone through the lakes, rivers, freedom bore no ruin
Vowed were they to return one day
When danger beset and tears wouldn't go away,
Despite the magic the men were Christian folk,
If they were to return
Surely the oppressed would be freed from their yoke,
Upon their horses they ride still,
In Christian myths and legends of beauty,
As most of Ireland, France, Wales, Cornwall
Indeed much of humankind learned in their youth.

Nigel Evans
Kent

Winner Takes All

I backed me a horse
at two hundred to one
and I hope and pray
that she can run.
I says to myself
go on, have a bash
so out comes me purse
and on goes me cash.
Now I'm stood here waiting
for the shouts of - They're off!
Will I end up stony broke
or a horse racing toff?
Everything depends now
on that knock-kneed nag.
Is she a champ
or an old windbag?
There they go running in a bunch
but about this nag
I have a hunch
she stretches her eyes
when the end is in sight
then kicks up her heels
and really takes flight.
It's that last burst of speed
that makes her jockey boast
there she goes 'God bless her'
she's first past the post.
Now I'm off to the bookies
to collect my pay
because that's my stake
for another day.

Pearl Ridley
Kent

White Cliffs

White cliffs, they stand, bold guardians of our land,
Defiant crags that overlook the sea,
Pillars of white shaped by a timeless hand,
A symbol of a realm that's proud and free.

The ancient Britons looked out from their height,
To view the Roman galleys cross the strait,
They lived in darkness, yet prepared to fight,
To save their soft green country from its fate.

The greatest poets were inspired and fed,
By these strong, silent cliffs we love to know,
And even Shakespeare climbed up to their head,
And gazed upon the raging sea below.

King Hal set sail to seek his cloth of gold,
And Charles returned, his rightful crown to claim,
The cliffs watched calmly every scene unfold,
And all the world would know them and their fame.

As deadly bombs and shells fell day or night,
The shrieking gulls gave warning as they flew,
As if to show contempt for enemy might,
And give support to all the gallant few.

Brave pilots flew above the cliffs so high,
Across the fields where once they ran and played,
Marked out the vapour trails across the sky,
A well made stage for friend and foe was laid.

The towering cliffs that through so many years,
Have warned all raiders from our precious shore,
Like sentinels they calm our greatest fears,
And stand more tall then all the knights of yore.

Geoffrey Elgar
Kent

Why Do We Ponder And Stare?

Why do we ponder and stare,
While each moan so broad, so bold,
Decaying amongst the whispered air?

The grey dome opens, with a god with glare,
Its great chasms shine ever so bold.
Decaying amongst the whispered air.

Each child tear glistens with none to spare,
Angered trees trapped within our hold.
Why do we ponder and stare?

Worthy men fight against prayer,
Each one smashed, by mere envy so cold,
Decaying amongst the whispered air.

Amongst the hills, the roars spare,
Tremble the winds of hope were we're told.
Why do we ponder and stare?

And it is the end, our faces turn grey,
It was our hope that we had sold.
Why do we ponder and stare?
Decaying amongst the whispered air.

Robert Winn-Rossiter
Kent

The Fire Hills In Summer

Bright silver lights glinting off the wide blue sea
On this edge of the land, by a low wind-bent tree
I hear gorse pods gently popping in the heat of the day
And the regular thrum from the coastguard's radar all grey
The view of Beachy Head shimmers and sways
And Winchelsea beach lies basking in the summer haze

Close-cropped grass like velvet with a scattering of seed
Where rabbits gather in the evening to frolic and feed
A fresh tangy sea breeze stirs the thistles and grasses
And rattles drying seed cases as it passes
Over these golden cliffs a myriad of butterflies flit
Like confetti they flutter, then on flowers they sit

Inland, Fairlight Church spire stands out tall and proud
Up the lane nestle homesteads all around in a crowd
Wide sweeping grassland where dogs romp and play
Colourful kites soar on thermals, this glorious summer day
Honeybees drone and chirruping crickets sing in the heather
Sussex beauty and quietude makes my heart light as a feather

Jean Selmes
Kent

Rochester Castle

Piled high, rugged stones against the sky
its ruined walls stand, still strong,
one time guardian of town and river
'gainst conflict and invasion strife.

Rivers meet within its gaze
sometime murky, or sparkling in sunlight,
then falling silent in haze and mist
while estuary fog rolls in.

Tidal press meets river flows
as moored craft, rocking astride
its contrary, moving, glistening splash,
lie at anchor awaiting sunrise freedom.

Past glories, now faded like those ruins,
remind of uncertainty and change
that face present times and things new
taking them into a challenging future.

Historic past stronghold and ongoing reminder,
symbolic walls stiffen the city's resolve to rise
above current needs, to become in deed
what it believes itself to be.

Jo Allen
Kent

Chance Meeting

We stroll hand in hand on a fine autumn day.
The leaves falling fast, as we go on our way.
On turning the corner, we almost collide,
with a couple we know,
no time to hide.
Who could guess our history,
as we four talk, casually.
I was content with being your wife,
until someone new, came into your life.
I hold the hand of your once best friend,
he cares for me, and on him, I depend.
Who could know, in the years gone by,
that we were an item, you and I.
What a coincidence that we all met.
It wasn't so bad, and yet -
a tinge of sadness, as I watch you go.
I remember the time,
when I loved you so.

Janey Wiggins
Kent

Living Our Dream

When you laid down close beside me
You made my body come alive
All those many dormant feelings
Had been pushed down deep inside
You brought them to the surface
As you gave your love to me
No man has made me feel so good
My reactions you could see
Your kisses lit the light bulbs
Shining dimly inside of me
Now they're glowing brightly
For all the world to see
Your touch sent my pulses racing
While your caresses did much more
We sent each other to new heights
That's never been done before
That day was oh, so blissful
We visited Heaven on the way
I can't wait to be there once again
And relive memories of that day
To feel your tender kisses
When your lips run down my spine
As you hold me to you tightly
And show me that you're mine

Margaret Ward
Kent

House Of My Father's Attendant

Up there are clocks.
Where toby jugs live on mantelpieces,
white as old marble.

You!
Winding up faces
to support an elusive hand shaking

looking like a pair of jacks;
top hatted and black
as vernacular night
on St Bartholomew's Day.

It never ends, Daddy Autumn.
Around the croak of rooks;
where everything is ancient,
timeless.

Graham Fairbrass
Kent

A Day In The Countryside

We drive through the beautiful Kentish countryside
On a summer's day it is a lovely ride.
It truly deserves its name 'The Garden of Kent'
To me this Eden is heaven-sent.

We pass by fields of sheep, cattle and horses too
Munching contentedly under a sky so blue.
We see the farmer and his tractor ploughing for a mid season crop
The gulls hovering, waiting to feed off the newly exposed earth on top.

We pass fields of rye, barley and wheat
So we can have our daily bread, or cakes for a treat.
We see oast houses which roasted hops in their prime
Now turned into residences because the hop brewers' industry is in decline.

We visit a quaint village with a river beside
Stop at a pub where good food and ale is tested and tried.
Take a stroll along the Medway's banks, so quiet and serene
Full of wildlife and swans presenting a delightful scene.

For our next stop we enter an ancient forest
Trees so old they are now coming to rest.
Having been part of Kent's history for hundreds of years
Witnessing the shire's good times and tears.

We climb to the top of our gentle rolling downs
Clothed in green, beset with yellow gorse, completing this beautiful gown.
We watch the sunset going to sleep to close this day
Dear Lord, may mankind and Mother Nature always keep Kent
                    in its green and pleasant way.

Terry Godwin
Kent

Quiet Light

The hushed light tiptoes
And shyly illuminates her,
With softness and serenity
It cuddles her aura.

With deep inhalation
It's drawn into herself
And dances with delicious delight,
Oxygenating with stealth.

One flick of a button
Can killingly cut, not keep,
But her eyes shut and so,
Like her,
The hushed light sleeps.

Joanne Gough
Kent

In A Flanders Field

We have walked amongst the graves in a Flanders field,
We have felt the sadness, where once, shells and mortars shrilled.
Young soldiers in their prime, though not their fault,
Life for them on Earth, had been cut short.
'I'll be alright Mum, don't you worry about me,
I'll take care of myself, just you wait and see,
Don't cry Mum, you won't see me through the tears,
It'll all be over soon, it won't take years.'
Fifty-eight thousand headstones, glinting in the sun,
Fifty-eight thousand heroes, every one.
Each grave tended with professional pride,
No place here for cowards in which to hide.
Only tranquillity, reigns throughout this field.
This is the place in which to shed the tears,
Though Man it seems, has learned nothing through the years.
This is the place where lumps are caused in throats,
This is the place where young men met their death,
No time for them to catch a second breath.
The cry went up 'this must not occur again',
But it did and it does, was it all in vain?
I can hear the last post, in the still air,
I can picture the uniformed bugler standing there.
Hill sixty-two, being a short distance down the road,
Today, deep in thought, as on that hill I strode,
Explosions, screams, death, blood and broken bones,
All a distant thought, but nonetheless,
Please God, take care of these men and let them rest.

John H Israel
Kent

Untitled

My baby I have is alive and well
But now I feel I have to tell.
The bump is small; I know it's wrong,
But the journey I've started is hard and long.

The limit is one, but I'll have two,
I don't want to be told what to do.
We need a boy to keep the family name,
I'm not trying to bring it any shame.

I know we'll manage with the money we've saved.
Now we have to keep being brave.
The workers will try and persuade me to have an abortion,
But I'm not getting rid of the baby,
You order the meal, you get the whole portion.

Danielle Wills (13)
Kent

The Golfing Mania

That morning was my birthday treat
To ride in a buggy on golfing land
Much too excited to eat
I sat in the driving seat, how grand!

What to wear, couldn't make up my mind
Style was important, I do have some flair
I set off in my buggy, the sun was kind
And all was set fair.

Monarch of all I surveyed, I felt good
Up dale and down dale, I was away
Past a little wood
Ended up miles away down the fairway.

Dark green, pale green the course, how blue the sky
My companions playing, a far away dot
The buggy took off again as though it could fly
I stepped on the pedal and away it shot!

What an amazing day, I wanted more
But my friends said, 'No, the sun has set
We will show you to your door.'
The best day I've ever had yet!

Joan Hands
Kent

A Day At The Fair

She'd been on this and
She'd been on that,
The swing flew high
She could have reached the sky,
The ice cream dribbled down her dress,
She was told, 'Don't make a mess.'
The man said, 'Surely you're not going on that?'
As she stepped into the carriage and lost her hat
She was whisked away and twisted around
So when she got off she collapsed to the ground
A voice from above came into view,
'Oh, there you are, I knew it was you.
Do get up, you've scuffed your knee.
Do you want to go for a . . .'
She straightened her dress and said, 'Shall we have tea?'
The money for tea she had to borrow,
Over a cup she said, 'What are we doing tomorrow?'
A chorus of voices and a look at each other,
An exclamation of, 'Oh Mother!'

Pam Eggleston
Kent

A Message From God To Humanity - Losing My Religion

Would you listen even when I told you?
What on earth was I to say?
Should I make you stop what you're doing
Or make myself go away?

I can't take the pressure anymore
All life is crumbling away
Your actions are causing annihilation
And you're doing it every day.

I thought you would be perfect
A happy mixture of difference
But My creation is ruined
I have now lost My omnibenevolence.

You all seem to defy Me
I have done nothing to you
I even gave you the power to live
I am the Creator and that is the truth.

It's not My duty to be there
For all of you to need Me
Although your lack of motivation
Suggests that I am the only one who believes.

So put down your guns
Put down your oil and end this silly feud
I can't continue to control
So I'm handing control over to you.

Your life is now in your hands
What else is there to say?
I can't stop what you are doing
So quite simply, I'm going away.

Chris Hayward
Kent

Refreshment

She creeps amongst the verdant bushes
Close against the brimming bath,
Prompted by the gleaming water warmed
By sunshine that entices urgent splashes;
Never heedless of the danger
Oft-times lurking in her way,
Lady Blackbird takes her pleasure
Then alights from swirling bath.

Carol E Margetts
Kent

Water

Water never takes no as an answer! Without a by your leave,
Clouds, themselves relieve, over land, hurricanes born at sea,
Hit punishingly with moisture lifted clear from oceans far and near
Up into stratosphere soaring, soon like a raging bull will
Misery sowing, rivers overflowing, Mother Earth goring.
In full flood over homes and fields dumping mid as if to drain with rain
Mankind's spirit, yet it survives and Man 'stays with it'.
Hurrying to the sea, millions of small grains, adding to beaches sandily.
Making at once a playground, and launching pad, for a boat or two
All of which, Man takes in his stride handily.

Out in the ocean, tranquil or in commotion, water,
Water everywhere, nor any a drop to drink
Salt-saturated, gift of land nigh obliterated water and its power can't be overstated,
So should not be underestimated, from river or creek, it is a gift-bearing Greek,
Delivering oft a bonus, but as a cherry bears a stone,
So too, there can be an onus, but sure as eggs are eggs, Man perforce
Takes the rough with the smooth, some to win, some to lose
Aware water means life, but looks on
King Neptune with regret, as drowned villages he can't forget.
Bells still ring in his imagination, from a doomed church and
Inside an organ is playing whilst phantom people are praying
Man's thirst, our village cursed, hear them saying.
And hymn singing, and bell clappers keep on swinging.
Hollow tocsin reverberating, sense of awe creating.
At one and the same time, water Man be loving and hating.
So goes the tale of liquid life, eternally renewing
Man bears this in mind past and present reviewing.
Children made aware for reservoirs they must care,
Remembering also, water never takes no for an answer.

Graham Watkins
Kent

A Bard With Only One Song

I wish it wasn't so hard to write a simple song
And tell a story that wasn't my own

I try

But the words just laugh
And take familiar paths
Leaving me still standing at the crossroads
Listening to the same story
Told a different way

Matt Doyle
Kent

The Surgery

I'm sitting in the surgery, with people all around,
There's a woman with her leg in splints, and a man, his head all bound,
There's pregnant ladies, spotty boys, and babies wailing out,
I'm sitting here in silence, with a bloke who's got the gout.
There's a boy who's playing cowboys, he's tied me to the chair,
And no one seems to notice, he's taken off my hair.
Well one by one, they all go in, and soon it will be me,
I've been sat here for just two hours, that bloke he's been here three.
A pregnant woman, she shouts out, she's got her labour pains,
That boy who's playing cowboys, he's now got my leg in chains.
The door it gently opens, and a woman steps inside,
Then tripped and fell flat on her face, I laughed, I nearly died.
They picked her up and sat her down, her face all drained of blood,
'I'm not surprised,' said one old dear, 'she went with such a thud!'
My shoulders are still heaving, poor woman looks so pale,
And the boy that's playing cowboys, he's now hung up on a nail,
His mother's had enough of him, and took him by the throat
She's hung him on a nail outside, then covered with her coat,
At last it's me and I go in, I sit down in her chair,
'Now what's the matter Mr Smith, you do look in despair?'
I look at her, she looks at me, her face it's all agog,
'I've just popped in to tell you, I've just mowed down your dog!'

Sandra Garrod
Kent

The Buffs

The sight I've loved to see
Are the soldiers marching as one
Having always lived in a garrison town
I've watched since I was young
The feet of the men as they passed by
Clad in boots so shiny and bright
Every step in unison
Such a wonderful sight
My brother was one of these men
And oh how proud he did look
When he marched through town on his own
To turn the page in the 'Buffs Book'
He wasn't really an army man
The country took him to war
But with buttons polished for Sunday
He was the best 'Buffs' soldier we saw.

Daphne Fryer
Kent

Sitting On The Fence

We often hear of politicians,
Other great decision makers,
Unable to decide which way to vote,
Which policy they should espouse.
Uncertainly they dither and delay
To make the necessary decisions.
We say 'they're sitting on the fence'.
To me that phrase has connotations
That are widely different,
Much more pleasing.

Such charming creatures sit upon *my* fence.
The blackbird in full-throated song,
The cheeky robin bobbing up and down,
His beady eyes watching me as I dig,
Hoping a juicy worm will be turned up.
Small blue tit pausing there awhile
Food in his beak for hungry nestlings
That await him in his box.
The plump wood pigeon softly croons
To be replaced by magpie harshly croaking.
These gone, the squirrels, bushy tails aloft,
Chase rapidly along the fence top.
Both sides of this have their appeal,
The field and trees beyond,
My garden's bounties this side,
But naturally I hope
That they'll come down on *my* side!

Roma Davies
Kent

Clouds

Sometimes loneliness gets in the way
Like dark grey clouds on a summer's day
And emptiness seems to come between
The need for a friend you haven't seen
Someone you can talk to, who will understand
Who will just reach out and hold your hand
But no one is there, only dark grey clouds
Breaking the silence that's sometimes loud
And you wonder to yourself, have they realised?
That loneliness is the colour of your eyes
For solitude is an isolated place
Where tears of sadness roll down your face
And all you need in-between
Is the caring friend you haven't seen.

Susan Hamlyn
Kent

The Garden Of England

Hills of pure green gold lining
Drowning out the song
Of birds up high,
As they soar the sky
And the lambs leap and bleat with glee.

The buttercups and daisies
Dance in time with the wind.
The uproarious scent
Of smoke's descent
From an old farmhouse chimney fire.

The farmers wander soft hills and vales,
Virgin earth underfoot,
The firm old soils
Full of troubles and toils
And rich with the cream of history.

The Garden of England so they say,
The enjoyment of all that nation.
Where a rolling hill hides
The crash of the tides
Yet they meet, in harmonious pleasure.

Karl Mercer
Kent

A Car Owner's Rant

To drive today is not much fun,
The lorries, white vans up your bum.

The speed cameras are everywhere,
Do you speed? Don't you dare!

The speed humps where you least expect,
Are ruining your suspension, what the heck!

Where do you park when you visit a friend?
Yellow lines are all about; they drive you round the bend!

Traffic lights on red, when they could be on green,
There's nothing around on the road to be seen.

Look out for the traffic wardens with their pen and board,
Are you parked correctly and within the time allowed?

Pedestrians and cyclists everywhere,
But look out for horses and take care.

It costs a fortune to own and run.
To drive today is not much fun.

Sharon Saunders
Kent

Flower Festival - 2005

Creativity, inspiration and happiness overflowed
as marking 800 years Smarden Parish Church celebrated.
A touch of magic, indeed a true presence
was bestowed upon us all
as we lovingly participated or viewed
three days of enchantment
blessed in an aura rare and beautiful.
Fun and camaraderie from dawn to evening,
floral splendour imaginatively presented,
embracing the building and centuries
in lively praise and thanksgiving.
The Saturday market and 3 day
home-made tea marathon
enhanced greatly the 'community umbrella'
as all generations walked through
the herb-clad porch in true medieval flavour,
into the sunbathed church,
heralded by keen bellringers,
ringing us 'in' and then 'out' on Monday.

Margaret Ann Wheatley
Kent

The Winter's Tale

Shakespeare in the garden of a Georgian house.
All seats are saved at the front.
The king is a tyrant estranged from his wife by jealousy.
Quality picnics available; bring your candelabra.
The king's wife is thrown in prison for treason.
The king's son dies of shame.
The king's mother-in-law saves her daughter.
The covered stand looks barely rainproof.
The king's daughter is banished to a mystery isle.
Wine, strawberries and cream are served in the striped tent.
Portaloos and parking by EU directive.
The king languishes in the error of his ways.
A tabby cat has a walk-off part.
The king's daughter loves the son of his rival.
A rogue steals from the gullible.
The king and party are shipwrecked on the mystery isle.
The dew falls; thank goodness we all have coats.
The son and daughter of their houses reunite the families.
Please don't start your cars at the same time.

Miriam Carney
Kent

Beautiful Kent

I've travelled to Yorkshire, visited Wilts
And been to the Welsh town of Gwent
But in all of my travels I've never once seen
A more beautiful region than Kent
See it in spring when the flowers start to bloom
And the orchards are oceans of snow
Take a walk in the woods on a carpet of blue
Where the bluebells are starting to grow
Visit in autumn at hop picking time
When the fruit is ripe on the vine
And see how the succulent grapes are grown
And made into fine English wine
Beautiful byways and country lanes
Churches with steeples high
Castles and mansions and palaces too
In which marvellous treasures lie
Visit a farmhouse in rustic style
And taste a traditional tea
Or take a trip down to the Kentish coast
And spend the whole day by the sea
Canterbury too is a marvellous gem
Its history is bound to enthral
And deep in the heart of the village of Leeds
Is the most beautiful castle of all
If I had to describe all the wonderful sights
I wouldn't know where to start
For the Garden of England's the jewel in the crown
To which I've given my heart.

Denise Castellani
Kent

Carols At Nightfall

Carols heard at nightfall, sounds praise for Christmas Eve,
the pastor brings this message, and prays for all to believe.
Love stirred in the heavens, long before the first star shone,
known throughout all creation, that God and love are one.

Carols heard at nightfall, and a message for all who will trust,
light entered into darkness, and Man was made of the dust.
Love wept for the fallen, as Man sought his own destruction,
while Word as flesh made known, that God and love are one.

Carols sung at nightfall, and a message to restore the contrite,
God's salvation is coming, His new covenant is at hand tonight.
Love comes to us as a baby, love comes to us as an only Son,
known to every Christmas believer, that God and love are one.

Keith Leese
Kent

Sherwood Forest

Beyond a village green where
a bowled sphere strikes the willow,
the great trees of the forest
stand . . .

The trees

To our feathered friends,
we are their destiny,
our ancestors were here long
before Man's laboured dawn;
we built the ships that strode
the deeps like queens;
and in praise of our creator
we built churches of tall steeple.

The birds

We are the masters of the skies,
our ancestral, winged dearth
settled these forest and glades
centuries before Robin Hood drew the long bow.
We and the forest are in harmony.

The waters

We are fed by the rains,
we are the rills, the veins that
feed the arteries of the land on
their journey to the sea;
our ancestors are the dawns of time.

The earth

I am the good earth untarnished by the plough,
nourished by the sun and rains;
I take the great oaks and all the forest to my bosom,
and give nourishment to all her needs;
I am as old as these hills that
have sailed the seas of time.

Peter Morriss
Kincardineshire

Summer

S wimming
U nder the water
M arvellous days
M um making the barbecue
E very day filled with sunshine
R estaurants are packed full of people.

Brett McLean
Kincardineshire

The Sea

I whisper upon the shores,
I push away the sand,
I don't have many chores,
I come from many lands.
Whenever I have left a place,
I leave salt,
Never have I shown my face,
I never drink, not even malt.

People put shells to their ears, like a telephone,
Thinking it's really me,
It's the blood rushing through their heads, I prefer to be alone.
I am a loner, can't you see?
When I get cross, I wail and roar,
I become 20ft tall,
Nothing is safe, not even the shore,
Everyone is screaming, drowning out the seagull's call.
At night I fall silent,
Quiet once more,
Whispering, not violent,
Quietly on the shore.

Melanie McLean
Kincardineshire

Messed Up Love

How could you do this to me, all your words, on how this love was meant to be?
Just like that you phone up out the blue saying how this love isn't true.
Leaving me in a pool of doubt shattered and shaking because you just ripped
my heart out.

You always talked about fate and how this love was so strong.
How can I believe that all your feelings have just gone?

I understand you are scared and confused about what path in life you have to choose.

I know you don't want to be tied to anything in life until you're really sure.
So that's fine, I will let you go, giving you the space you need to grow.

The days are so weird without you here, your face, your smile,
I miss it so much it brings me to tears.

I realise our love was not perfect from day to day but we had so much fun,
I can't believe you're going to leave me this way.

And if it was meant to be we will reunite, if not I have to be grateful,
I found an amazing love for one year of my life.

Claire Lithgow
Lanarkshire

John Thomas Montgomery
(In memory of a beautiful grandson)

We lost John Thomas
At the end of the year
He is one little soul
We all held so dear
We viewed him as an angel
And a beautiful boy
Cos in his short life
He brought us bundles of joy
He is a young life lost
While wonderful memories remain
But in all our hearts
We still feel the pain
With our aching hearts
We all sit here and cry
While he soars across
The bright, azure sky
The pain of his father
It's etched over his face
He prays that he's wrapped
In our God's good grace
We have weeping wounds
Which will never heal
So we all long for the day
That his spirit we feel
Goodnight, John Thomas
Sweet child of ours
Rest peacefully in your bed
Of sweet-scented flowers

Steven Wilson
Lanarkshire

My Friend

Little rabbit, you're my friend.
Since you left your hutch-like box
Round and round the yard you go,
Sniffing till you reach my socks,
Sniffing the soles of my shoes,
Sniffing all things, sniffing me.
Though your name I do not know,
I talk to you, you talk back
In a quietly sniffing way.
For we're alone and time's free.

Little rabbit, kept in hutch,
Since your roamings yesterday
Led you past a broken gate,
As you tried to run away
To the lane's verge, sweet and green.
Oh, the neighbour's gaze and shock
At the precious plants you ate.
Now, you're paying the penalty
For your sniffing, chewing ways;
Now, your hutch door's firmly locked!

Little rabbit, it's the end
Of my springtime holiday;
I've come to say cheerio,
Soon I'm going on my way.
I've brought you some leaves and shoots,
Dandelions, flowers and all
For you love them, this I know.
How I'll miss your funny face,
Sniffing snout and big dark eyes,
My dear friend and my cahoots.

Ken Millar
Lanarkshire

So Alone

I still can't take it in
You're gone, I am alone
How will I go on?
What do I tell our children?
So young they may not understand
I will have to be strong for them but I don't know how
Somehow you must help me, show me, and give me the strength
We had planned out our future together; we had so much still to do
Now you have been stolen from me
You were my husband, my lover, my friend and you made my life complete
Then came our children, our beautiful children
I'd watch you with them, you all playing and laughing
You were the perfect daddy and they adored you as much as I did
It breaks my heart to hear them cry for you
Such painful tears, they look so scared and confused
Asking me, 'Why? Why has Daddy gone?'
How can I explain when I do not understand myself?
When they are asleep, I cry so they don't see me
Our bed seems so huge now I sleep alone
I can still feel your strong arms around me keeping me warm and safe
Then I wake only to find I've been dreaming again
And another lonely day begins with my memories of our happy life together
You will live on forever in our children
I won't let them forget you
As for me . . . your love will hold my broken heart together
Until I am with you once more.

Jacqui Watson
Lanarkshire

Room Of Rain

Death is before me as I stand in the room of rain
As my soul begins to leave my body
Dead inside I feel, with my black heart in pain
All alone in the darkness and cold of night
I can feel water run down my cold face of shame
I cry out with all sadness but cannot fight
As I stand in the room of rain
The frogs of death are coming for me
Alone I stand with all my pain.

Stewart O'Connor
Lanarkshire

Hame-Sick For Glesca'

Och' a wish a wis in Glesca',
Strollin' by the Clyde,
Walkin' on the Broomielaw,
Wi' Jeanie by ma side.

Sure New York's grand - the jobs are here,
And the people are very kind.
They've made us very welcome,
But a miss folk left behind.

Here buildings are high, and scrape the sky.
Fifth Avenue's very posh.
But tae live or even shop here,
You need a lot o' dosh.

Broadway and Times Square, they say,
Are the places that excite,
But there's mair fun at the Barras,
Any Saturday night.

Och', a miss the Glesca' patter,
And the crack in the local pub.
There's nary a fish an' chip shop here.
A don't really like the grub.

So when a've made ma fortune,
Tae Glesca' a'll go home.
A'll settle doon wi' wife an' weans,
Never more tae roam.

Marjorie Quigley
Lanarkshire

Writing Myself Well

Yes I am. So let us
Float around that floor,
Keeping words simple . . .
One, two, three and four.

Step one; write what you see,
Move with words carefully . . .
So naturally,
Write effortlessly.

Write with joy some more . . .
Now your thoughts, outpour
Onto fresh paper,
Enveloped and stamped . . .

Open one new door!

Lesley J Worrall
Lancashire

Mosaics

You, me, we all have a few, forgotten for years
'N' brought out in tears,
Sometimes with a sigh, long remembered goodbye,
A time we felt cold, a love melted fast like snow,
The sluice gates opened but we wouldn't, couldn't, let go.

The music, the drink, the eyes that then winked,
Memories then stored, our own squirrel-like hoard,
A face lost in time, brought again to mind
When we've drunk too much wine,
Solid as coal, a mosaic of the whole, threads of life.

Who am I now? When bits of my past,
Unbidden for years, let me know who I was,
Sometimes, some bright rainbow mosaic,
Switches lights on in our eyes, a big beaming smile
To our own surprise, lets us know we've moved on.

Our bodies aren't stained glass, but we have survived,
Shared out our mosaics, in myriad other minds,
Not one burst a blood vessel, or scared us for life,
We can still hug and love, see the light of dawn,
We can still ride a rainbow, and still play our games.

And know we'll be remembered in others' mosaics.

Anne Jeanette Walker
Lancashire

The Jungle Beast

The pounding of the paws,
The creature's mighty roar.
It moves swiftly through the trees,
Like a child's terrible dream.
It moves near
And creates fear.
The jungle screams with fright,
But cannot be heard within the night.
I hear its growl,
I see its big eyes, like an owl.
My temperature rises to the highest point,
And every bone is removed from its joint.
The creature pounces from the bush
And the whispering trees are hushed.

Sarah Festa (10)
Lancashire

Black Pancake

The Isle of Ely, like a pancake is flat,
A beauty spot, people may grin with scorn.
Straight deep dykes are its various rivers,
But that is the place where I was born.

In winter, the east wind blew so cold,
Dark, clouded skies and black soil below
And if the wind changed, to the north,
Then the fens would get a blanket of snow.

From an old oak tree I would look afar,
See a farmhouse almost a mile away.
Sheltered by clumps of very tall trees,
A windbreak when gales came along to play.

When floodwaters to the 'Washes' arrived
And they remained frozen, both night and day,
Out would come, all those who could skate,
With moonlight, they would skate the night away.

Come spring, I'd watch the black soil ploughed,
Deep, dark soil, to the top being turned.
Those furrows would be straight as railway lines
And seagulls would come, to feast off worms.

To some people, the flat fens are like to Heaven,
To go cycling there, is something to enjoy.
Those lovely straight roads, without a bump,
I remember them, from when I was a boy.

Albert E Bird
Lancashire

The Powers Of Mother Nature

Ocean.
Vast, arms open wide.
Ready to swallow,
Anything that falls in its realms.
Man.
Possesses knowledge,
Knowledge of Mother Nature,
And her powers of constructing.
The tallest tree and the prettiest flower,
But not enough knowledge of her power to destroy.
Destruction beyond human control.
Wave.
Advances towards the land.
A wall of water tumbles and crashes its way,
Onto Man's paradise on Earth.
Paradise.
Turns into the complete opposite.
Man.
Knows not what to do.
Immense numbers suffer,
At the hands of Mother Nature.
And in the distance,
A small boy weeps,
Along with thousands more across the globe,
At the thought of loved ones,
Who will never be seen alive,
Again.

Mrinalini Dey
Lancashire

By A Babbling Brook

The sun wasn't shining,
But then it didn't need to.
The green leaves reflected
What light there was
And the woodland was bathed
In a serene glow.
All was still,
Except for the babbling brook
And the birdsong,
Which seemed to add a chorus
To nature's music.
I sat at peace and rested my soul.

A plume of water
Tumbles over a rock
And gushes through
To the pool below
Where, hardly pausing for breath
It joins a similar plume midstream.
Then hand in hand
They go, tumbling and laughing
Over the next set of rocks together.
I sat at peace
By the babbling brook, in the wooded glade
And rested my soul.

Eleanor Broaders
Lancashire

The Usual Rule

The even, fated uniform,
The archetypal standard norm.

The moral, ideal etiquette,
The second nature, routine set.

The rigid, certain, self-assured,
The egotistic power lord.

The father, top dog, alpha male,
The patriarchal social jail.

Tracy Green
Lancashire

Solstice

I stand on the bridge, between this world and the next,
Where I can watch the sun rise, like a ball of fire, way over in the east,
And to go and set in the oceans of the west,
You can watch the eternal cycle as the wheel of life goes round.

At solstice time and the quarter days,
Open your heart to the god you praise,
As the wheel of life turns round and round.

From your bridge you see the moon rise,
A great white glow up there in the sky,
It seems to smile, as you look at its face,
As the wheel of life turns round and round.

Clouds, fluffy and white, drift over your bridge,
But you will see storm clouds too,
And feel the rain on your face,
The wind warm and soft, or cold and harsh,
As you stand on your bridge,
Between this world and the next,
As the wheel of life, turns round and round.

This is your life and your wheel too,
So it turns around for you,
Your wheel of life, turning round and round.

Trevor Howarth
Lancashire

English Harvest

I've harvested the fruit of Eden's tree;
eagerly I've spread my empty net
beneath its umbral crown, unnerved to see
its ravening roots progress past vision's field
to subject soils ambivalent in its debt.
Impatiently I have willed the tree to yield
its eloquent harvest to my waiting tongue,
shaken the pregnant boughs until its fruit
has filled my net. Time's age-defying song
crushes its spicy seeds in every note;
the candied flesh cheers winter's cold salute.

But fresh-picked fruit secretes the song unsung
and in my quiet room, indulging greed,
I taste the juice of ancient fruit made young:
I suck its so-sweet essence, guaranteed
to water the desert of my thirsting tongue.

Rachel Davies
Lancashire

Broken Roots

Once a close-knit community
A way of life
You were so accustomed to it
You didn't notice the changes
Till you moved away

What you thought was there probably wasn't
What security was - only a mirage
To you whatever was there or thought
Was always there, isn't
What's lost or given up, can never be found or reclaimed

What you thought was yours, might never have been
For you - if it had - why did it never work in your favour?

Be satisfied with what you've achieved
By following the road laid out in front of you

If going back to your roots only proves one thing
That you have moved on - accept the hand
Of cards dealt to you - now, with head held high
Turn around, head back off the slip road and head home

The home you have made out of the patchwork
Left - given or chosen to take - be proud
You've come this far - there's nothing to go back for

David Charles
Lancashire

A Poem

To think and wonder what to write
When insomnia disturbs your sleep at night
Indecipherable scribble leaks from the pen
Words flow like water when you get the yen
Then when you're struck by writer's block
Your memory starts to run amok
Think what words will fill a line
And will the cadence metre rhyme
When you find the right words to fit
You have a poem you can submit
If accepted by the 'powers that be'
Another success we all agree
Made good use of those sleepless nights
Now everything has been put to rights.

Francis Arthur Rawlinson
Lancashire

Cellulite

To get rid of my cellulite
These things I'll do with all my might
I'm trying not to be too trite
I'll do my best to be polite
But Christ, I even weigh my shite
And every piece of food I bite
I've never really seen the light
I dream and crave all through the night
I wake and try to curb my spite
I try to do the thing that's right
But sadly I keep losing sight
Of all the things that cause the blight
So visually I cause much fright
People look and then turn white
I'm losing badly in my fight
I fail to fly my chosen kite
My willpower will not take flight
My future really isn't bright
I'm falling from a dizzy height
My hobby horse I now alight
Since I'm the master of my plight
I'll never really be all right.

Martin S Colclough
Lancashire

Self-Made Prisoner

It is better to hear laughter in the distance
Than to suffer silence in the dark
I lay down
Submitting to the gloom
Curl into a ball to protect myself

I can see it coming
Clouds gathering
The rain burning holes into people
Nothing is hidden
Fear is real

With all the pomp and circumstance, we talk about peace in our time
So we build the inevitable walls to keep the danger in
And refuse to let anyone out
Isolation breeds the idea to gnaw our own feet off
So we can use our immobility as an excuse
The fault lines no longer go past our front door
Someone else will have to pay the bill.

Rebecca Bennett
Lancashire

My Secret Hideaway

In my dream I'm there again
Slowly walking along the beach
Away has gone all my pain
And soon the sea I'll reach

I love this secluded coastline
And the quietness of it all
This secret bit of Heaven is mine
No intrusions and no one will call

The fine white sand is warm
As it slips between my toes
I play with the sand in my palm
A slight breeze and away it goes

As I gaze up at the pale blue sky
Realising that I am on my own
I laugh and give a huge sigh
As sometimes I need to be alone

There are plenty of hours ahead
Time to rest and relax at last
I'm no longer feeling that awful dread
And worrying about the past

Pieces of driftwood are on the ground
I can sit and dream and laze
Lapping water is the only sound
I'm looking forward to long, long days

A Burns
Lancashire

The Mystery Of Poetry's Soul

Some people say that poetry has a soul,
Like all the arts, it depends on who
First spins the academic ploy
For myriad students to follow through.

A touch cynical it may be,
But can any two experts agree
On a grade for the hours of thought
Put in by any poet, or even me?

The artist's magic knows no bounds,
As Picasso and Dylan often proved.
They break even the strongest chains;
Display talents and see spirits moved.

For years the written word was banned.
Its power gave others full control.
Don't shackle it now with rigid rules,
Let it run free, to be used by all.

Many tried to stifle the creative arts.
Just let Man show another point of view.
Still very important to make a case,
Than keep it hidden for the chosen few.

Poetry most certainly has a soul.
It's free as the air to rise and fall.
Maybe it will rhyme, but often may not.
Though no doubt, it touches the hearts of all.

John Troughton
Lancashire

October

September's sheaves are gathered in
Beech nuts lie thick on the woodland floor
Golden-yellow chanterelles and ceps
Raise their phallic heads and dance in the lower fields
Wild mushrooms, the first of the year
Damsons crowd in clusters along the bough
Ripe, purple and seductive
Scarlet-splashed leaves turn bronze and fall
Whipped into rills by skittish winds
And crunched underfoot
Holiday dreams from Skegness and Malaga
Fade and curl behind the kitchen clock
The spirit of Demdike and Nutter fly abroad once more
To plot and scheme their mischief
Amidst the covens on Ogden Moor
Scuff-toed breechy lads haul rotted timbers
Onto monumental pyres
That will burn Guy Fawkes in a thousand hellish fires
Lie easy King James
Lie easy in the warmth of Indian summer's balmy rays
All too soon Scorpio will open winter's gates
And let the nimbus hordes rush in.

Hayes Turner
Lancashire

The Trials Of A Teenager

As I lie in bed awake
Waiting for morning to break
What will tomorrow bring
Another teenage uprising?
The dos and don'ts of today's youth
Is that what makes them so uncouth?
Forever rebelling against law and order
Is this why there is so much disorder?
Trying to be free of old rules
Forever trying to make the government look like fools
To be young and out of work
My everyday duties I will not shirk
I forever live in hope that I won't
Succumb to dope
Who knows?
Maybe one day I will get employment
Be able to make ends meet
And pay rent to live my life
Without sorrow, who knows?
Maybe I won't be a lost cause tomorrow.

A Reilly
Lancashire

Hourglass

As the dawn starts to yawn
On a bright new morn
Songbirds sing a happy tune
As a new day gets underway
Strangers hurrying to and fro
No time to say hello
Life is such a pace
Is that why it's called
The Human Race?
No time to stand and stare
To see just what is there
The flowers and trees
Beauty in our towns and cities
It is all such a pity
We miss so much
Maybe we wouldn't
Be so tense
If we didn't try to climb
Too high a fence
And take
One day at a time.

Margaret Parnell
Lancashire

Sweet Tooth

The dentists say you shouldn't
You promised you wouldn't
Yet here you are with a chocolate éclair
Licking your fingers, spoiling your teeth and not a care!

Ah, I see, the work of Cupid
Any excuse! You must think I'm stupid
A box of chocolates from a boy
Sitting there looking all coy

So who is he? The milkman, postie, or boy next door
Who has re-stacked your sweet supply in the drawer
Yes, I know of all your hiding places
Filling all those tiny little spaces

What if all your pearl-white teeth were to drop
All because you're relentless to stop?
How precious are these sweets?
Enough to lose all of your teeth?

Samina Nazish
Lancashire

Nature's Blessing

There is a quietness on the fell
That lives where gentle breezes blow
Where brazen heathers kiss the air
And wild flowers reach the sky
Their leafy fingers spread the land
Exploring with caressing touch
Listening there to nature's voice
Fostering love for life

Where trees they glisten in the dew
Bowed through age and storm

Departing from this spectacle
My spirit moves in distant haste
As ear gives heed to brook's wild chatter
Where silver liquid cascades in splendour
O'er the staggered crags abundant
Ancient stepping stones of giants
Through the gap of earthern caverns
Therein grows that magic ribbon

Nature's blood in all its glory
Nature's picture, nature's story

Derek J Holt
Lancashire

Some Lancashire Logic

We all race round, like headless chickens
A common aim, hi-tech, rich pickings
But having a different point of view
With Lancashire logic - that's taboo!

Try giving an inch - most take a mile
'Thank you' more often, a po-faced smile
As for staying home, to care for kids
Such Lancashire logic's well on skids!

What if one day ASBOs were given
As tired grandparents being driven
To care, give back grandson or daughter
Would Lancashire logic be oil on water?

A common aim, before prepaid graves
Should be retirement plans, tailor-made
With *Number One* first, not inheritance
Use Lancashire logic - get it spent!

Betty Lightfoot
Lancashire

When Decorating A Smoker's House

Beyond terraced walls, I'd hear him
barking up decades of tar
that clung to his lungs and heart
like latex hot pants
or blackcurrant jam in jam jars.

Being a quitter wasn't one of his faults
but his heavy breath was paint stripper
for paint that wouldn't come off.

And his ribcage was a buttled stepladder
his chest was woodchip on rented walls
his cough was a toothpick for a scraper
and his muscles were lead pipe overalls.

His blood was emulsion spread in streaks
on window sills and doors
and his heart was a clogged up brush
stiff with neglect.

And his bones were made of asbestos
his past was of a velvet-red. His future
was of an ice-blue interior, his life
a plumb-line thread.

Paul Phelps
Lancashire

A String Of Pearls

Round her neck a string of pearls,
So wantonly she wears them,
Each one denotes a lover's tears,
Now haughtily disdains them.
I gave to her that string of pearls
And round her neck I placed them,
Then swore that through the coming years
Our love would surely bless them.
But what is life but hopes and fears
And love that could deceive them,
A cultured love no heart can keep,
The truth will aye displace them.
But true love runs forever deep
And endless does embrace them.

A J MacDonald
Lancashire

White Coppice

White coppice you're the place for me -
can't think where else I'd want to be!
Out amid all nature's scenes,
every walking rambler's dream.
Ivy clings upon stone walls,
tiny streams of waterfalls,
white cottages with cricket green,
lots of wildfowl seen!
Refreshment pauses on weekend days, for longer stays,
or passing through.
Walks from here are wonderful,
no path that's deemed too dull!
Spring and summer be the tops,
when beauty pulls out all its stops;
autumn's spring of heather sprigs;
how purple ye now be!
Every glance before my eyes,
nature's splendours no surprise -
Return I will via Healy Nab,
far-off views are just as fab,
Winter Hill seen from the rear;
illusive mast is far from near!
Through the forest pines I'll roam,
choose a path that takes me home . . .
views descending down front hill,
leave eyes that's never still.

David Pooley
Lancashire

To Greet You At Christmas

Mistletoe and holly mean Christmas
The loveliest time of the year.
Trees trimmed with lights and tinsel
And laughter, so lovely to hear.

Christmas cards full of good wishes
And presents hung on the tree.
Bangs from the crackers, and kisses
Everything for you and for me.

The carollers come around singing
Wrapped up in mufflers and gloves.
The good smell of turkey and mince pies
And Christmas cake everyone loves.

So let's give a cheer for Christmas
And all that we hold dear
Hoping that it will always be
The loveliest time of the year.

But let's not forget the new year
And all that we hope it will bring.
An end to all wars and suffering
The peace dove flying on the wing.

Good luck and good health to all people
Whatever their colour may be.
May peace reign again amongst us
The picture we all want to see.

Joan Smith
Lancashire

Summer

Far from a smoky town
So far from a winter's frown
Summer is such a treasure
The season that brings most pleasure
The countryside in full bloom
Trees everywhere bearing fruit
Fields of barley and golden corn
From sunset to a misty dawn
Time to unwind and have a rest
While summer is at its best
See the butterflies, hear the birds sing
All the inspiration that summer brings
For children playing in the park
Summer adds that extra spark
Cricket and tea and bowling greens
Soda pop and endless ice cream
Enjoy a summer holiday
Watch the surfers ride the waves
Sip ice-cold beer, take in the scenes
You know it's too good to be a dream
I could go on and write a story
Of summer in all its glory
The only season that lifts my soul
Summer is the seed - of love.

Frank Howarth-Hynes
Lancashire

Clouds Over Mull

(Inspired by the picture 'Clouds over Mull' by C John Taylor)

Wispy, high white cloud
Gently strokes the Ross of Mull
A bright, crisp morning.

In the Firth of Lorne
Steel-grey water, now turned blue
Reflects the high sun.

In the island's green
Small cottages dressed in white
Shimmer in the sun.

Alan McKean
Lancashire

Four Hundred Years,
The Gunpowder Plot 1605 - 2005

Four hundred years have come and gone
Since the date that Guy Fawkes tried
To kill King James with gunpowder
And the parliament beside.
Now on this date we celebrate
It's 'Penny for the Guy'
When fireworks blaze with coloured lights
And rockets rise up high.
Bonfires are lit and we remember
That certain date, fifth of November.
If Guy had done the dreadful deed
He had been sent to do
It would have changed our history
And so, for me and you
We'd have no need to have our fun
Or light our bonfires too.
Each year before the Queen goes to open Parliament
The Yeomen of the Guard go there
And all of them are sent to search the cellars down below
For those who have intent to plant their bombs in secret
Before this great event.
Why should we celebrate this date in the year 2005?
When other great events have been
We keep this one alive?
Because it's easy to remember
Guy Fawkes - the fifth day of November.

Margaret B Baguley
Lancashire

Close To Me

No prayer of rote on Sabbath knee,
no doing good so all might see,
no judging others as worse than thee
will bring thee ever as close to Me
as the ordinary folk who humbly pray,
and quietly try to serve Me each day
with kindness, compassion, laughter and love,
of such is the kingdom of Heaven above.

Susan Carr
Lancashire

Mr Thomas P

Mr Thomas P is single and free
This latter day saint used to paint
At decoration he was a master
At decision taking, Tom could be faster.

I've known him now for many years
With ups and downs and many tears
We have a friendship, the sort that lasts
We had many a laugh and good repasts.

Nowadays Tom has to be slower
In the past he's been a grower
Perhaps his garden will play its part
To help him rehabilitate his heart.

That fitter man rode a bike
Championship status, you never saw the like
Over hills and dales and countryside
Now it's the bus and cadging a free ride.

In lots of ways he will never change
It is a shame Tom lives out of range
To Chorley, Lancs, I've had to go
Tom called on me at old Langho.

I too am on the buses and train
It means, like Tom, I'll have to refrain
From flying about and always rushing
Slowing down to stop the 'flushing'
Red in face is when Tom glows
When slowing the pace he tries to show
That he can do it and do it well
That's another tale to tell.

Ellen Spiring
Lancashire

Air Display

The sky is bare, overcast.
A panoramic screen of greyness.
Suddenly! They streak into view.
Scarlet brush strokes boldly
emblazoning an empty canvas.
Jet streams: red, white, blue,
trailing rapidly in their wake.

Initially the formation is rigid.
Seamless patterns interwoven,
transposing each chameleon colour,
zigzagging, through the clouds,
deceiving like a mirage.
Complex movements subtly made,
performed with consummate ease.

Abruptly the skies empty!
Spectators stare in confusion,
unaware of what comes next.
Then at last the planes return,
divided into twos and threes,
revelling in unbridled freedom.
Happy to shed their composite yoke.

Gasps greet each manoeuvre,
applause ripples through the air.
The squadron resumes formation.
Giant-sized jigsaw pieces,
slotting smoothly into place,
circling the sky one last time.
The audience cheers, ecstatic.
Affection dislodging respect.

Paul Kelly
Lancashire

Haven't I Been Busy?

When I was born, I became,
A daughter,
A granddaughter,
A sister,
A niece,
And a cousin.
I have not yet spoken a word,
But a lot of people know me.

When I went to school, I became,
A pupil,
My teachers taught me so much,
For this I thank them.
A friend,
We shared sweets and things,
We still, after all these years, meet up for lunch.

When I married I became,
A wife,
A daughter-in-law,
A sister-in-law,
Then best of all, a mum.
I am now a mother-in-law,
Hopefully one day I will become a grandmother.
But most of all I am myself.

Pauline Smale
Lancashire

The Despondent

Despondency is not what I wanted from this wretched life,
With no prospects, no expectations nor wife.

Where did I go wrong? Was it really my fault?
Or was it government policies or recession that
Brought prosperity to a halt?

There is no one to turn to and I'm considered too old,
Yet I'm as fit as a fiddle and healthy too, so I'm told.

There is nothing around here from what I can see,
Jobs are far fewer and there is nothing for me.

Things will get worse, I know it, I fear, and the worst
Is to come . . . I will be in my mid-fifties this year!

Mike Graham
Lancashire

When I Saw You

When you were standing in the sun
And I saw you
You were Icarus
Riding through a storm
Of golden sand
Your need to populate the world
Was shining spirit and song
You were dauntless
As a winter sea
Moving everything before you
You could have stood
With sword in hand
A shining banner carried before you
To the battlefields of Rome
You were Mars
Moving through the heavens
With fire and heat
Hand to shoulder you strode
With Bacchus at your heel
Mercurial and sharp
The flashing dagger entered my mind
Even now your magic
Is mine to keep.

Glenda Stryker
Lancashire

Doctor's Misdiagnosis

As I look at my mother
snuggled up in bed, dying,
my mind wanders to when as a child
she was always there
to cajole or inspire
the hope or desire
that all will turn out fine
which it invariably did.
Now she lays dying
after years of being misdiagnosed
by people we are expected
to have faith and trust in.

James Ashworth
Lancashire

Selfish Actions

Can you listen - one moment
Then have a good look around
Our world - set for dying
No friends has it found.

It gave us so much - offered
Enough food for us all
We so wastefully plundered
Ignored that wake-up call.

Now, we are all starving
No fresh water, or shelter
Our own sad existence
Upon Death's helter-skelter.

Too late to make changes
There is no goodness left
In our wake - pure disaster
The world, left so bereft.

So, no more left to say
No more words, could explain
Our own selfish actions
Led to suffocating pain.

Death, has consumed all
Wastelands and rotting flesh.

Maureen Westwood O'Hara
Lancashire

Kaleidoscope

Give me the sunset in a cup,
So I can fill my heart with warmth.
Give me the blue sky on a spoon,
So I can enjoy its special taste.
Fill a bowl with jewels of rain,
So I can quench my raging thirst.
Give me the moon in a velvet sky,
So it can always light my way.
Give me the rainbow with a pot of gold,
So I may stay young and never grow old.

Janet Lorraine Peel
Lancashire

The Weeping Of Madrid

Sultry, rising, crimson sun;
Cloaked by majestic blue sky,
Yield spellbound shores,
Sharp-toothed sierras high.

The heart of the Mediterranean,
Warm, haughty land of Spain,
Islands of music and dance,
Olives, lemons, landscape stain.

Wild, eroded, high altitude,
Sculptured capital, Madrid,
Warm, carefree culture,
'Buenos dias,' each other bid.

The landscape fell silent,
After the explosions roared,
Terrorist target, busy trains,
The fate of 11th March 2004.

Twisted, tangled wreckage,
Lives lost, injured and cold,
Brave Españols toil, rescue,
Loved ones, sad memories hold.

Thousands gather together,
In faith candles light,
To show the whole world,
Gallantly, in solidarity unite.

Again, let cantadours sing,
Children laugh and play,
Fun-loving people dance,
The sun come out to stay.

Patricia Carter
Lancashire

Town Of Change

My town of today, how it's changed, since a boy,
When with school chums we did many tactics deploy,
To get into places we should not have been,
Skulking and creeping so we wouldn't be seen.
Exploring old buildings that were derelict and empty,
Signs saying *Danger, Keep Out*, were aplenty.

Old houses that were, with new ones replaced,
And countryside also, sees building in haste,
Trees so mature, cut down for new village,
Fields where corn grew, no more will see tillage.
Farmland is shrinking, so much all around,
Concrete replacing the grass on the ground.

Old town with its character being nibbled away,
Demolition continues within it each day.
Not just great mills have to history gone,
But the houses of workers, now hardly a one.
Old Market Place where cattle once sold,
Hosts parking meters, your money to hold.

Pedestrian zones where traffic once 'flowed',
Host patterned brickwork, where once was the road.
Shops are rebuilt, old frontages gone,
Two or three might be made into one.
Old family businesses, nearly all disappeared,
All this it is 'progress' . . . just as we feared!

Roads they are narrowed, speed humps to fit,
More dangerous now, most motorists admit.
Supermarkets now part of the rural scene,
Of late this was meadow, all peaceful and green.
Is this then the norm we have to accept,
When so many believe, it's all most inept?

Jay Smith
Lancashire

Born In The Night

Like upside-down mushroom caps in the sky
much milky and beige-coloured cloud drifts by
as they have since morning mist disappeared -
and born-in-the-night strangers appeared.
Where trolls or hidden hobgoblins once stood
or wherever they have found rotting wood,
where they fancied making a fairy ring -
now who can tell what may be lingering?
Nearby trees are fast losing their leaves.
A quick glance shows you a vole that retrieves
a button mushroom it dropped by its stream
that winds in its own melancholy dream
of fungi spores flung out everywhere
spiralling about
unseen
in
the
air.

Lumpy and bumpy, some white on the ground,
others yellowish, uncanny when found.
Yet most mushrooms that cluster at your feet
you'll discover are delicious to eat.

But remember Emperor Claudius
famously poisoned . . . could be one of us.
Also, unless you want to run berserk
red and white spotted toadstool you must shirk
whose 'magic' may make you hallucinate -
a flying sensation you may well hate -
(though fine for Santa's reindeer on Christmas night?)
or any shaman's other-worldly flight.
For the human forager, just the wish
to pick safe mushrooms for a tasty dish.

Chris Creedon
Lancashire

Saturday In Southwold
(A very hot Saturday, 18th June 2005 on Southwood Pier, Suffolk)

They stood, these two people, their bodies an inch or so apart,
Yet fused together like a fossil to a stone.
She was dressed in white, a simple garb, white roses in her hand.
He was beside her, so crisp and smart and handsome, a steadfast presence.

The room was hushed, but charged with power, drawn naturally, from two souls
and strengthened from the hearts of those around.
This was a union of love, the aura of which was felt so strongly it was almost visible.

Before the time it took to gently bat an eyelid and detect a falling tear, they were joined.
Two small boys went, one to each, and nestled into the scene.
A family of four - a marriage of four - bound by love.

All around a framework of sea and sky, white woodwork and decking, white gulls
calling in celebration.
Then laughter with clapping and hugging, more tears, champagne.

My daughter, so beautiful, was wedded to her man.

Janet Scrivens
Leicestershire

Dreamscape

The night
is never still.

Twilight speaks
of winding down,
the sun draping
her weary limbs
across the window sill.

The world
seems to reverse,

slow motion,
crowds thin and wane;
shop windows droop
their lids, enchanted
by night's curse.

Beneath shades,
folds of vestment,
day looms;
a sphere of restless
slumber breathes,
rippling through false moonlight.

Kirsty Smith
Leicestershire

Spring Grace

Nature is born with colours of hawthorn green and blackthorn white
Bursts into springtime after winter's long fight
Away to the fields from concrete grey faces that stare without care
Carried along the miles on wheeled rubber and black tar.

Away to the green solitude among the buds and beauty of creation
As nature dawns, spawning new life without hesitation
Billing and cooing are the bunches of feathers in trees, yet bare
Globes of dew twinkle like stars on cobwebs and spider's lair.

Beauty is being born once more, year on year it goes on
As we, with nature, travel side by side, living in unison
This power, this love from the cosmic source, giving sustenance
Knowing we are a part of all this creation gives this life substance.

The sickness that is abroad is only the face of ignorance
Of those who do not see the flowers, always in a monetary trance
Lost are they too, to the perfume of love and giving
Never to see the eye of the blackbird or hear the robin sing.

For me it is everything to touch a scented rose
To feel the strength of a tall oak tree, only love knows
Knows all and everything, of our life, our time and space
All is written in the skies of love and is acted on in good grace.

G Hall
Leicestershire

The Tree, The Dream

I dreamed that I was standing beside a large tree
with branches that spread like a very wide umbrella,
and under this tree sat a couple on a bench
cuddling together, hand in hand;
while the world around them carried on, with cars whizzing past,
and the occasional child riding past on their bike.
But the couple took no notice of the things around them;
because they had found each other
and, to them, time had stood still.
I turned and looked again, but now they had gone;
the silence was broken by a car passing by,
and the bird nearby started to sing.
I suddenly sat up in my bed
was this really a dream or was I really there?
The answer was yes, I was there
for although you cannot see,
the couple that were sitting on that bench,
were really you and me.

T Gibson
Leicestershire

Thoughts From A Motorway Bridge

Looking down upon the scene below,
What is their hurry? Where do they all go?
The sounds of the motorway cloud over the mind,
Is this really what God planned for mankind?

The rush of the traffic, the noise and the dirt -
Surely all this can do nothing but hurt.
Internal combustion has reached into our souls,
Modern day living is taking its tolls.

Consider our world in ages gone by,
The sweet sound of silence where green fields lie.
No terrible scars tore up our land,
Just Man and his animals walked hand in hand.

God gave us land to love and to cherish,
No wish did he have that under asphalt we perish.
But Man does not seek a simple solution,
He has taken the path of dust and pollution.

And now - oh the change - that has shattered our peace,
The roaring inferno seems never to cease.
I look down on the traffic and consider the past,
How long must we suffer? How long will it last?

But there might come a day when the call comes - 'No more!
We've heard all the reasons and judgements before.
We don't want our lives to be ruined by cars,
The land that we love is just as much ours.'
And the future . . .

One day geologists made up their mind -
'Sorry, we've looked but there's no more to find.
The fuel for your engines has dried up forever,
We can't find any more despite our endeavour.'

And now once again we hear the sounds that we love,
The skylark is singing his sound from above.
The cows in the meadow low as before,
The sweet sound of silence is with us as before.

Ronald Moore
Leicestershire

Water

Will kill
but will save lives of some,
the murderer,
the spreader of disease,
a crude criminal,
a superior saviour saving lives,
never-ending, flowing furiously
but suddenly without a sound
coldness creeps across the surface
with one blow, frozen,
shiny, slippery, wet.
Married to life,
delightful drink,
super for swimming,
freedom for fish.
In league with light,
floating in the sky
like huge lumps of candyfloss.
Creator of rainbows,
gushing down waterfalls,
crashing on rocks,
trickling through cracks,
water is the world,
we're just tiny specks floating on its surface.

Charlotte Bradshaw (12)
Leicestershire

Love In The 21st Century

Where does love start?
It is endless and boundless.
I am born and am loved,
Guided to grow with loving hands.
I love my parents, siblings, friends.
I fall in love, a different love,
We marry to share this perfect feeling.
I give birth to a child,
Oh wonderful feeling of love.
I guide my child with loving hands,
She grows in love for siblings and friends
And falls in love, marries and gives birth.
She guides her child with loving hands,
To grow in love for siblings and friends.
Soon she will fall in love too
And the circle will go on,
Endless, boundless eternal love.

Joan Gray
Leicestershire

Moonrise

Silence and stillness
And all the shining grasses
Loosening their lights.

High on the hillside
The moon becoming more pale
Without any sound.

Silent nothingness
And absolute emptiness
In the quiet sky.

Streams catching pale light
To bear it in their bosoms
To a lower plane.

Nothing in the sky
But the round moon of autumn
And unfeeling light
So frostily reflecting
The light of the other orb.

Dan Pugh
Leicestershire

Who Am I, What Am I?

Who am I, what am I?
Sometimes I don't know!

I try to be good, 'cause I know that I should.
Then sometimes I feel being good doesn't work,
so then I go the other way.
And when I'm bad, *I'm bad,* and then I'm sad!

I want to be happy and live a good life,
so give me the love that I give to you.
'Cause love and happiness go together -
without one you don't get the other.

But most of all we need peace of mind,
so forget your troubles, leave them behind.
Sometimes you have to turn a blind eye,
then you see things from the other side.

Life is what you make it, be happy with what you've got.
Sometimes it's a little and sometimes it's a lot (God bless).

Yvonne Cooper
Leicestershire

Grandad's Egg Spoon

It always sat by Grandad's plate,
Not to be touched by anyone but him
Or Mam, who laid it out and put it back
To bed, and never said a word.

He'd say it was a rabbit's shoulder blade;
A rabbit cursed by an old barren known
To all the village as a witch: and left
For some unspoken reason, on his step.

And then he'd give a sudden wink and rub
His callused thumb across the hollow of
The yellowed bowl, decapitate
The top of his brown egg and winkle out

The sunlight from its shell. He never said
Just what he might have done to call
Such curses down upon his head: and Mam
Would only say, 'In time you'll get to know

More than enough - now go and play,' and turn
A silent back. He stayed a man of mystery
And wonder, till the day he died: the day we read
'Made in China' stamped on the plastic bowl.

Dylan Pugh
Leicestershire

My Mum

My mum can make me laugh and cry,
I just as often, make her sigh.
My mum works as hard as hard can be,
As is evident for all to see.
My mum loves to shop all day,
More than my mere words can say.
My mum is loving and giving,
With a penchant for food that is nice and filling.
Count the stars and multiply by ten,
That's how much I love her always,
Not just now and then.

Aisha Opoku (18)
Leicestershire

Curious

What is forever and what is now?
Does the dreamer ever see his dream come true,
Or is it something in the sky?
What goes round comes round, in the old-fashioned way.
Nature sorts everything out or
Is it hearsay?
Things seem to mellow as the years gather speed,
Then sometimes I wonder, is that all I need?

Mary E Wain
Leicestershire

Old Codger

I know a crabby old codger
I cannot divulge the name
Who had a cash dilemma
Himself the source of blame

Excited by the chance to greet
A handsome published poet
Arrived too early for the meet
No cash he had, you'd know it

So in a panic off he went
No thought of time of meeting
To stash some cash, to be spent
After the initial greeting

The handsome poet was on time
No codger there to greet
And so he penned a simple rhyme
Whilst waiting for the meet

Old codger came a-rushing in
To greet the handsome poet
And explained his silly whim
To get some cash, then spend it

The handsome poet was amused
Old codger was astounded
'I'd have lent the cash you used'
The kindly poet expounded

The moral of this little tale
Is simple in its making
Believe a poet not drinking ale
And forget the Mickey taking

Nigel Lloyd Maltby
Lincolnshire

And Yet Knowing

Lying here,
I feel the breeze caress my skin.
Softly,
A lover's touch.
Tentative - yet knowing.

Lying here,
I hear the whispering of leaves.
Soothing,
A lover's voice,
Seductive - and knowing.

Lying here,
I taste the saltiness of tears.
Lingering,
A lover's kiss,
Gentle - but knowing.

Lying here,
I have memories that burn.
Cruelly,
A lover's goodbye,
Hurting - but still knowing,

You're gone.

Deanna Dixon
Lincolnshire

Clouds

Big fluffy balls of cotton wool
Rushing across the sky
Changing their shape as they go
Oh, how they seem to fly.

Suddenly their appearance changes
No longer fluffy, soft and light
Heavy with rain they race towards us
Now it's our turn to take flight.

The wind increases with the rain
Dark clouds race towards the sea
The rain has stopped. Where did it go?
The clouds have fled, now we are free.

Big fluffy balls of cotton wool
Rushing across the sky
Changing their shape as they go
Oh, how they seem to fly.

Ann Elizabeth Bruce
Lincolnshire

The Future

I went to the future and saw what is to be
The cars are so tiny there's only room for three
All my school friends are successful, but
There's not just you and me
Mother has given birth to a number three
There are no schools, just streets of kids
Playing football and making skids
They all have bikes that squeak pretty loud
And there is quite a lot of yelling, happy sounds
There are people drunk all over the place
The town has become a mega disgrace
People walk across the street
Scared to show their face
Little kids still use the tricycle
But the world still will not recycle
We need to be a careful bunch
We need to make amends
Apologise to people and treat them like friends
The fields and trees have been pushed aside
To make way for developments instead of the countryside

We can stop this happening in the future
By stopping development and teaching kids manners
We find an easy way out all the same
But sometimes it's easier to just take the blame!

Charlotte Whitehouse (10)
Lincolnshire

Tattershall Castle, Lincolnshire

As Lincolnshire's treasures unfold,
Tattershall Castle is one to behold.
Across the field, behind the tree,
Its beauty is there for all to see.
Cross the moat to the castle door
And go inside and look some more.
Wander round each detailed room,
Feel the excitement and, alas, the gloom.
Battles fought in every war,
Lives lost, then many more.
Climb the stairs, see every nook,
Read about the lives it took.
Stand up high towards the cloud,
Look down at the peacocks standing proud.
Such beauty within these walls so bold,
Such treasures here for all to behold.

Stephanie Lynn Teasdale
Lincolnshire

As Fresh As Mint

A leaf of mint crushed in my hand
can take me back in time,
to a time when I would take
the sprigs of mint,
strip from them the leaves,
releasing their powerful scent,
their fresh perfume,
their deliciousness of nature.
I'd place them
on the chopping board,
the old one that was
slashed and scoured with time,
then sprinkle the leaves with sugar,
take the heavy knife,
lay it sharply across those leaves,
rock and chop,
releasing their sweet aroma,
gather them up into a jug,
add the sharp malt vinegar,
mix together for mint sauce.
The meal was not a meal
without that sauce.
Let me smell mint even now,
I can recall the meal,
the day when everything
was as fresh as mint.

Gilly Jones
Lincolnshire

My Special Someone

When I first met you
I knew from the start,
You would be the one
Inside my heart.

Just getting to know you
I thought you were great,
I just knew from then
It had to be fate.

I always miss you
When I'm not with you every day,
I get a strange sensation
That won't go away.

Louise Chafer
Lincolnshire

Sirens' Song

Creaking speak of weathered beams, curving wooden planks
burnished bows, riding the spray of sea-swelled ranks
salted spume coating face and lips, angry waters crash
rising rollers enveloping decks, fists of fury downward dash
grizzled mariners flounder awash, work-worn fingers vainly grope
seeking life-saving purchase, desperately clinging rigging rope
unwary sailors, gently lulled by the pull of drifting song
tantalising glimpse of diving mermaids, imaginations ocean throng
full-breasted sirens, teasing the surf with thrashing tails
stealing broken hearts in a plunging flash of iridescent scales
fluctuating female forms, robed in trailing free-flowing locks
offering sylphlike succour, luring innocents onto jagged rocks
falling into life-leeching waves, softly stolen minds elope
seafaring stragglers stumble empty decks with abandoned hope
enjoying the ocean's caress, accepting fish-tailed warm embrace
invading ballads gentle allure offers sweet mental bliss
enduring the final solution, silent suffocation of drowning kiss

Paul Birkitt
Lincolnshire

A Knock On The Door

Blackmail: extortion with menaces,
The vilest crime when, as is
The custom, to succumb to pressures
Is inevitably the precursor to further measures.
Yet, to take a stance and demands ignore
What are you letting yourselves in for?

When the knock came on the door
I was expecting it, for sure
Though that did nothing to assuage my apprehension.
My pounding heart did raise my hypertension.

The two stood there in aggressive mode
While I felt vulnerable as a land-locked toad.
The younger of the two was the spokesman
And words came smoothly, as was the plan,
To leave the victim in no doubt
As to what their mission was all about.
It was a 'demand' rather than an 'ask'
Enhanced by the grimace on the Hallowe'en mask.
The dreaded words, far from discreet,
Were, 'Hello mister! Trick or treat?'

John W Skepper
Lincolnshire

Deep Waters

At vision's edge, grey horizon
Where sky embraces silver sea,
A soul reflects in silent motion
To find serenity.

Elusive sun's hazy face,
Misty shroud low suspended,
Briny breeze's warm embrace,
Broken heart slowly mended.

Sea air healing; sand's appealing
Damp caress between the toes,
Nature's mending; her peace amending
Life's unyielding woes.
Gloom depleting; heart's a-beating
Running on the shore.
Joy awakening; soul uplifting
At nature's store.

Vast, eternal shimmering wet,
Fires the soul and land defines,
Slapping water's boundaries set,
Right now, somehow, is mine.

Moody water's lunar dance,
Sometimes monstrous, sometimes still,
Invisibly restrained; ordered to advance;
Decides limits - then takes at will.

Whispering waves yield to sky and weep
Of enigmas kept beneath the deep.
Birds from out the Stone Age fly,
Waving shadowy ghosts goodbye.

Joanna Malone
Lincolnshire

The Newborn King

Once again the bells ring out
To welcome the newborn King.
Let us kneel and worship Him
And Christmas carols sing.
The birthday of our loving Lord
We celebrate with joy,
Born in a stable, so long ago
For man and woman, girl and boy.
He came to us as a helpless babe
And was laid in a manger bare,
Angels, shepherds, kings led by a star
Came to see him there.
The angels sang, 'Hosanna!'
The shepherds brought a lamb,
Kings gave gifts of precious things
To honour the Son of Man.
Once again it's Christmas time
What present will you bring?
Just give your heart and give your love
To Christ, the King of kings.

Vera Hankins
Lincolnshire

Winter To My Mouth

Morning brings winter to my mouth
Shadows race across my eyes,
But holding you close and tender
Will bring me no great surprise.

For your love never has limits
Everlasting as time itself,
Countless times you've trusted me
Overflowed my heart with wealth.

I need you to bring me sunshine
I need you to bring me joy,
Your love always does that and more
Just like my favourite childhood toy.

When you rise and beckon me to you
I know I am born again.
For my life begins as always
Down your enchanting lane.

Sharon Grimer
Lincolnshire

Barry The Barber From Bardney

In Queen Street, Bardney there's Barry's barber shop
Barry gets there early and you won't see him stop
He is very well known for many a mile
He says, 'How would you like it?' with a grin or a smile

'What is it today, is it number three on the top or is it two?
I think we'll make it a number two
Because next week I have a holiday due'
If you're in a hurry and little time you've got

Then you want to be early when he opens the shop
I have called for a haircut sometimes before
And he is ever so busy, I have queued out of the door
After a month, Albert and I are looking rough round the ears

So we jump in the car, it's not very far
We have done it for a good many years
You often see friends there; you always see someone you know
They come from Horncastle, Langworth and Louth

And a car load from Sturton by Stow
Before you leave home you must look at his chart
Because it's a long way for Albert and Len
We once got to Bardney and couldn't open the door

Begger me, he was holidaying again
I have only used one other barber besides him
He must be a great barber, the queue tells us that
I shall keep going to him whilst I have hair under my hat

Len Woodhead
Lincolnshire

Don't Make Me Laugh

Don't make me laugh.
How often do we say that word
On a serious occasion
When a titter should not be heard?
Don't make me laugh
Because I am in pain,
If you make me laugh,
I think I will go insane.

Please make me laugh
And you will laugh I can tell.
People who cry get sick and ill
And people who laugh keep well.

Jenny Bosworth
Lincolnshire

Autumn's Promise

Now come the misty mornings and the mellow muffled days
The silent shadowed woodlands wrapped in silver cobwebbed haze
The narrow aromatic lanes where secret paths unwind
Through avenues of trees all ivy-draped and bramble-twined

When evening steals the sun's glow and the twilight comes too soon
When days are short and night is softened by a haloed moon
Rainbowed in a watercolour haze as clouds pass by
And stars are frosted diamond shards that pierce the velvet sky

On such a night, in solitude, to highest hill I'd go
Up to the point within the cloud that shrouds the ground below
And peering through the misty haze would glimpse the softened edge
Of sleeping trees and mysteries that bound this grassy ledge

With blind awareness, night-bound eyes, release that mystic sense
That brings to me the essence of the forest, dark and dense
Breathe wisps of mist that swirl and light the shadows from within
With ancient awe to bow before the autumn closing in

Jane Johnson
Lincolnshire

Life In The Past On The Farm

Way back in the nineteen fifties
When women worked on the farm,
We had our backs bent many hours of the day
When the weather was cold or warm.

When we filled our baskets we had to get up
And walk to the riddle nearby,
Where we shook them and shook till the dirt fell off
And they were almost dry.

Then back we would go and pick up some more
And do it all over again,
Back and forth, and up and down,
Unless it started to rain.

We didn't need exercise to keep us fit,
After a day at work in the field,
The proof was there that we had worked quite hard,
With the bags of potatoes now filled.

Iris E Covell
Lincolnshire

Our Lives Around The Clock

The clock it counts our lives away,
It counts the hours, night and day,
The minutes and the seconds too,
It counts them all our whole life though.
As a child I sat and watched the hands
Upon the old school clock,
Time seemed to pass so slow
All those many years ago.
When you were a child, time seemed to stay
Longer than it does today.
Then off to work I had to go,
Working on the factory floor,
Looking at the factory clock -
Waiting for the line to stop.
Homeward bound on the train,
Looking at the clock again.
Teenage years pass so fast,
No time for feet to touch the grass.
All spent trying to beat the clock,
No time to wonder if it will stop.
Marriage came and children too,
The years flew past as they do,
All spent looking at the clock,
Wondering when it's going to stop.
Rushing here and rushing there
With no time to spare.
Old age has soon appeared
And time flown by - year by year.
People and places now fade like dreams,
Our lives are not what they seem,
It's just a race against the clock,
The clock of time that never stops.
And what do we do with the time we've saved
Before we all go to our graves?
We keep on looking at the clock,
Waiting for our lives to stop.

W J Oliver
Lincolnshire

The Only One

(Ronnie Barker, never to be forgotten)

When Ronnie died the other day,
A really good friend passed away,
A friend I never could forget,
Though he and I had never met.
Not ever . . .

When one is getting on in years,
Laughter is better, far, than tears,
And Ronnie never let me down;
He never even caused a frown.
No, never . . .

Poor Granville's mum he'd criticise,
To customers he told white lies,
And as Nurse Gladys he pursued,
He was just funny - never rude.
Well, hardly ever . . .

Slade Prison was his home from home,
From which we thought he'd never roam.
Mr Barraclough would miss him sadly,
Although he treated him quite badly.
He was so clever . . .

So, may I say to Ronnie Two,
I miss him as I'm sure you do,
Our screens will never shine so bright,
As when you two hove into sight.
Truly, never . . .

Harry Cooper
Lincolnshire

Spring Canvas

Tenderly, carefully, threading through the blue-
Bells carpeting the woodland floor, green
Grass bordering; stunning, picture-
Perfect, shimmering; above, bird
Song sprinkles the air, joy-
Ful inspiring, heart-warming
Air filters through the canopy, tree-
Tops stretching to the sky, vivid hue
Tones, painted perfection of a nature
Walk, tempting me to touch,
Tenderly.

Donna Parry
Merseyside

The Changing World

Listen to the news and you will begin to piece together
Just what is happening with our changing weather.
Hurricanes more frequent than ever before
Plus they seem to be knocking on everyone's door
Earthquakes happening more frequently than I can ever remember
The weather is much more unpredictable in months like September.
Do you remember when summers were hot and winters were cold?
There is something going on and we are not being told.
England has had floods in the south and tornadoes in the north
There is enough evidence for all to see coming forth.
We have to sit up and take notice of just what is going on
Or before we know it, this world of ours will be gone.
Look at how society has changed as well
For lots of families on estates it's a living hell.
Children out of control, without parental guidance
That's why society has such a severe subsidence.
Gun crime is rife and drugs are the norm
This generation just seem to slip in and conform.
People are scared to go out of a night
Is this what remains for mankind, is this our plight?
We need to act now to change this spiralling direction
This world of ours needs our protection.

Tom Roach
Merseyside

Caring Hands

Actors left the stage that day
To play Santa Claus in aid of a good cause
Stallholders behind heaped tables of Christmas fayre
Caring hands, taking delight in creating fantasy
A winter wonderland of make-believe.
At Formby Little Theatre
Proceeds of the bazaar going to relieve
The lives of the local hospice
Provide a bit of Christmas cheer.
Candlelights reflected the smiling looks
Villagers bought books and charity cards
Knitted toys and antique bric-a-brac
As they went back, like Dickensian day
To acting out the message of goodwill
To all.
The baby in the stable, painted on
Victorian cards, a flicker of warmth
Like a candle-glow held steady in caring hands.

Freda Grieve
Merseyside

Just To See

To see the glorious sun rise in the sky
To see the migrating birds pass by
To see the shapely clouds above
To see the sweet flowers that I love.

To see the colours a rainbow makes
To see the winter fall of snowflakes
To see the people I hold so dear
To see the things I can only hear.

To see the leaves fall from the trees
To see the grass shimmer in the breeze
To see the changes that autumn brings
To see the songbird as it sings.

I can only imagine what it's like to see
But the gift of sight was not meant for me
God in His wisdom gave me ornamental eyes
All I can do is visualise.

So unfair is how it sometimes seems
Visions for me are only dreams
He must have reasons for leaving me this way
But I wish I could see, just for one day.

Mark Ainslie
Merseyside

Cestrian Childhood

Yes . . . there's the little row of shops
The post office - the school
The shop where we all bought our sweets
On the way to the paddling pool
The traffic mostly horse and carts
A car was a rare sight
The sleepy village atmosphere
Our bedtime prayers at night
Strange - the absence of our parents
Gave us a unity
Looking out for one another
As any family
On Sunday we'd all troop to church
Nurse at front - nurse at rear
Like collies shepherding their sheep
By cuffs around the ear
These warm memories of childhood
This village where I grew
Or has distance lent enchantment
To this idyllic view?

John Smurthwaite
Merseyside

334

The Climber

At last I am ready and raring to go,
To conquer a mountain, now covered in snow.
My rucksack is packed. That's all I am taking,
And creep from the house, before anyone's waking.

I pick up my guide at the end of the lane,
And off we both go, into unknown terrain.
I've said my goodbyes to the one that I love,
And prayed for a safe journey to the fellow above.

We now are on rocks and a slippery path,
My feet ache like mad and could do with a bath.
Upwards and onwards we both still scramble,
To get to the top is still a big gamble.

My guide says, 'This mountain is haunted.'
I will admit, at times I've felt taunted,
And now, above the clouds we stand,
Deep in snow and cold in the hand.

A biting wind leaves us chilled to the bone.
'Oh God! I wish I'd never left home.'
One more night in a tent, pinned to rocks,
Our clothes are frozen and holes in our socks.

And now I know I'll never reach that wretched peak,
My breath is going and I feel so tired and weak.
In no-man's-land now I lie,
Between the Earth below and the Heaven on high.

And on this barren mount, I now await,
For you, dear Lord, my battered soul to take.

Florence Bullen
Merseyside

Come To Me In Dreams

Come to me in dreams my love, when you're no longer here
Lay upon my pillow and whisper in my ear
Kiss me on my cheek and then wipe away the tear.

In the shadows I will see you stalk
In the echoes I will hear you talk
In my footsteps I will know you walk.

So come to me in dreams my love
I'll sleep and wait for you
For now I say a fond farewell, goodbye but not adieu.

Frankie Shepherd
Merseyside

Rainbow Dawn

Turning as a planet, a star far out in space,
As you are motionless just standing in this place.
Relentless as the incoming tide or a smile that's gone too soon
And a heart that is beating to the song 'The Whole of the Moon'.
As the sand that runs in an hourglass that time has no face,
Your heart is filled with emotion as it drifts out in space.
The present is the confusion set in the rainbows of your mind,
As you come out of the dark shadows not knowing just what you will find.
There's a pathway that you follow where you have never been,
Passing through the depth of wonder in a dream that you've once seen.
There is a thought that keeps repeating in a half-forgotten dream,
Like the fish that keeps on swimming against the current of the stream.
As lovers we held the rainbow and hoped others would understand,
Or was the sound of your heart beating just the tapping fingers of your hand.
Your picture is hanging in my hallway within the dream of our song,
Then we saw the names and faces, but did not know to whom they did belong.
You were looking back at yesterday waiting for tomorrow to show,
As the sun started rising you were still trapped in the night,
In the night you drifted into dreams where you still saw the light.
My dreams are sometimes the answer to the questions never asked,
Finding the truth people tell me is just a lie well masked.
We are now standing in the emptiness as the memories flash on by
And we knew the truth was in a future tear we both would cry.
There is no answer to our question until we see tomorrow,
For even alone and apart we will know each other's sorrow.

Jim Anderton
Merseyside

Sadness

My heart is filling up tonight, I really don't know why
All I seem to want to do is cry and cry and cry
I find life so bewildering, I wish that I could die
I know there's much to live for and I must really try
But somehow loneliness sets in, for since my Peter died
I've lost the joy that was within, it's left me open wide
My family are quite wonderful, they do their best I know
But will they ever understand your death was such a blow
There's no one here to talk to, to share my cares and fears
I lie here on my own in bed and wash my face with tears
It's now the middle of the night, the world is fast asleep
But I am here quite wide awake, it's no use counting sheep
The moon and stars are shining bright, they bring me close to you
For somewhere in that far beyond I wish that I was too.

Barbara Hampson
Merseyside

The Little Girl

The little girl waits at the gate
For her friends to come out and play
She arrives when they're home from school
And she is there every day

The little girl waits at the gate
Even when the weather is cold
And the children are kept indoors
And have to do as they are told

The little girl waits at the gate
And watches until it gets dark
Then she walks away so sadly
And disappears into the park

The little girl waits at the gate
But doesn't say a single word
She keeps up her silent vigil
Because she knows she won't be heard

The little girl waits at the gate
She likes all the children the most
Because the grown-ups can't see her
Since she became a tiny ghost.

Ann Blair
Merseyside

Megan's New Friend

Megan to the moon:
  'Moon, shine through my bedroom window
  And make my nursery bright
  Be my close companion
  And stay with me all night?'

The moon to Megan:
  'Yes Megan I will be your friend
  And brighten up your day
  For even though the sun is out
  I'm never far away.'

  'Thank you moon,' said Megan,
  'I'm sleepy now, goodbye.'
  'Thank you dear Megan,' said the moon,
  'I'm lonely in the sky.'

Pauline Scragg
Merseyside

A Christmas Dream

Dreams of long forgotten throwing snowballs in the snow.
Sledge rides and long ice slides a long, long time ago.
There was a Christmas tree in the corner with flashing lights of red, white and blue
And the presents underneath it were saying with love from me to you.
At nightfall when fast asleep in bed, Santa would finally come, leaving presents
in our pillowcases,

Oh didn't we have so much fun!
Then on Christmas Day we all would play with our new toys on the ground,
Until the turkey was ready cooked then we all would gather around.
The table was set just right with crackers to be pulled
And then the dinner was all served up with drinks that were oh so cold.
When the evening time had come all was said and done,
This was a special time for us all to sit down or lay upon the floor
And watch whatever they were showing on the television box.
As I sit here now thinking of them all
Wondering if they still do the same, now that they all have their own families,
I wonder if times have changed.

K Thompson
Merseyside

No Evening Stars

Clouds seek revenge on the sunlit day
Darkening the land where the evening lay
Bringing an omen that is ominous and nigh
As they encroach upon the blue laden sky

Brutally and suddenly the day becomes cold
Whose journey into darkness, a prophecy told
The air becomes damp, obnoxious and cruel
Inviting the rain now the sun cannot rule

Upon the invaded land, came tears of rain
Driving the parents and the children insane
Pouring the spite of its anger and rage
Upon the valiant few who dare the cascade

A miserable evening is programmed and tuned
Hiding all signs of the romantic moon
The rain gods have used their heavenly right
Ordering the clouds to reign through the night

Voices summon the weather they hope will obey
For sunshine next morning, they whisper and pray
But the words of repentance are going nowhere
With no evening stars guiding their prayer

David Bridgewater
Merseyside

Bing's Day

Where's she gone? She must be up there
My little legs struggle to get up these stairs
That bed she's in looks comfy and wide
I jump up and snuggle in at her side

Morning comes and up gets Mummy
She cuddles me and tickles my tummy
The light blinds me as she turns on the switch
I stretch for a while and scratch that itch

I hear the clinking of the chain
Walkie time is here again
I see all these feet pass me by
Why is everyone else so high?

Here's a friend of mine coming my way
We stop and chat - I long to play
I'm so excited, I can't be slowed
We're off to Nana's, I know this road

Grandad gets out all my toys
Jingles or squeaks - they all make a noise
I get told off when I jump on the couch
I land on Grandad's head - he says ouch!

Nana's in the kitchen - I run to see
What she's getting me for my tea
Walkie time again - I jump in a puddle
I'm dried off and then get a cuddle

I'm scared - I start to run and moan
They're coming at me with that comb
But I sit still and they're all pleased
I'm rewarded with a piece of cheese

They all stare as I droop my big brown eyes
I yawn and stretch and give a big sigh
It's been a busy day, so after one last treat
I curl up on my bed and go to sleep

Martine Corrigan
Merseyside

Shades Of Grey

The sky is blue, the sun is out
So why do I feel like I want to shout?
Vibrant flowers in the park
But in my heart all is dark

I only see in shades of grey
I don't know why I feel this way

Children's laughter fills the air
But do I hear it, do I care?
A radio plays my favourite song
The notes are flat and sound so wrong

I only hear in tones of grey
I don't know why I feel this way

Exquisite food upon my plate
I cannot eat; I hesitate
Sweet is sour, spice is dull
Butterflies flutter, so I feel full

I only taste in flavours grey
I don't know why I feel this way

A crisp white room that's newly painted
Has aroma musky, old and tainted
Home-made bread and fresh brewed tea
Seem bland and odourless to me

I only smell in scents of grey
I don't know why I feel this way

Kisses and hugs from you still come
I don't react, I feel so numb
Will Prozac make me feel more sane
Make me feel myself again?

I only touch in textures grey
I wish I didn't feel this way.

Vanessa Dineen
Merseyside

Come With Me

Come with me
this Christmas morn
to stand beside the tree,
then side by side together
walk the lanes of memory
and as the years roll back
each brightly coloured light
caught by the tinsel
splinters out across the room,
each glint, each gleam,
reflection of a happy day
the sparkle of our love
the glittering strand
that binds each year on year
So come with me
before the world awakes
and for a moment
there beside the tree
hold me close
hold me tight
then slowly turn and hand in hand
steadfast face the year ahead.

G R Bell
Merseyside

We Must Treat It Right

The Earth is our home
We must treat it right
All through the day
All through the night
Poisons in the sky
Poisons in the sea
Put there by you
Put there by me
We know it is wrong
We know it is not right
The Earth is our home
We must treat it right.

Greeny
Merseyside

Never

Never to see your lovely face
Lighting up my lonely place
Your shining eyes and happy smile
Or hear your laughter, rich and warm
Your voice like velvet in the room
That I long to whisper words of love
Close to me.

Never to feel your lips kiss mine
Or run my fingers down your spine
Sit with you and watch TV
Laugh about the BBC
Share with you a late night drink
As I wake you from your 40 winks
Next to me.

Never to hold your hands in mine
Or see the lovelight in your eyes
To talk and put the world to rights
Both relaxed and full at ease
To hold you close in warm embrace
Secure in the knowledge
Of your love.

To know that you are in this world
Out of my life, my mind in a swirl
The miles between us, 10,000 long
Never to speak, feels so wrong
My heart is empty, my love unrequited
And scalding tears run down my face
Because of you.

Judy Dix
Merseyside

Ode To Music

Music, sweet food to feed the soul,
That makes my mind and spirit whole,
On Elysian fields, all thoughts aspire
To greater heights, my heart to inspire.
From deep melancholy to perfect bliss,
There my inner being finds happiness;
Nectar for my spirit, mind and soul,
Music, sublime art, your praises I extol.

Joan Thompson
Merseyside

Contrasts

The new life of spring,
The earth's awakening
And buds burst into bloom.
The lovely colours of azure,
For the sky,
Purple, white and yellow
For the early flowers.

Our friend has departed
A sad and sudden experience.
No more the early snowdrops
Will he see.
No more to smell spring flowers.
His loved ones dressed in mourning
A life still young has been taken away.

The green shoots in the garden
To start a brand new cycle.
The absence of that friendship
It had been one for life.
No more advice be given
No friendly chat at noon
The croci are not daunted
Birds sing out in full tune.

It is a time of contrasts
Arrivals and farewells
A prayer for rest eternal
For light to shine as well.
There's also light around us
The sun's decided to shine.
Our memories immortal
All part of a plan divine.

Joan Peacock
Merseyside

Sand Dancer

When I turn round to look there is no one there.
I turn round again, this time she's standing there.
With a pretty smile she holds out her hand.
I look with amazement and gaze as I stand.
What does she look for, is it romance?
No! I realise she just wants to dance.
I don't know why, but I extend my hand
Towards this pretty lady, this vision in sand.
She places her tiny hand within mine,
With her head on my shoulder we appear to entwine.
We are dancing away for an hour or so,
Sometimes quickly, sometimes quite slow.
The tide comes in rapidly, our feet are now wet
But we still dance and turn and run the gauntlet.
As she lifts up her head, I can feel her tears,
Her sad eyes look up and she just disappears.
I retrace our footsteps, looking into the wet sand,
Yes! There are four with this girl in my hand.
I saw her once more, this time smiling at me,
She then turns her head and slowly fades into the sea.

K D Benson
Mid Glamorgan

Alba

There cannot be another as beautiful as you,
Oh Alba.
Your ruggedness is not compared anywhere.
The beauty you possess is copied nowhere else,
Oh Alba.
There are mountains all across the globe,
But none compared to yours.
And sure there are lakes and hillsides everywhere,
Oh Alba.
You were so blessed by the Earth's creator,
So blessed and lucky too.
There really is nowhere else like you,
Oh Alba.
Don't you ever change!
Stay exactly as you are.
Years and years you have been you
Deflecting anyone who dare try to change you,
Deriding anyone who wanted to become you,
Oh Alba.
My Alba.
I miss you every day.

Brian Lamont
Mid Glamorgan

The Song Of Kantakeewis

(A homage to Longfellow)

From the glare of sun-baked mesas,
From the canyons where the heat is
Comes a song, a hymn to nature,
Sung by chieftain Kantakeewis.

'See the flash of flowing water.
See the wonder of the river,
Making deserts green and fruitful -
Source of life and pleasure-giver.

Hear the rhythm of the river.
Mark the measure of its lapping.
Listen to its constant gurgle
And the lilt of ripples slapping.

Taste the juices of the berries.
Gather them in deerskin pouches.
Have your fill of all their sweetness
Then lie down on grassy couches.

Smell the fragrance of the pine trees
And the potpourri of flowers.
Savour all their subtle perfumes,
Heightened by the sudden showers.

Touch the gold where maize is ripening.
Feel the cobs as they mature.
We must pray to the Kachinas
Then good harvests we'll ensure.'

So sang kindly Kantakeewis
To his grandson soundly sleeping,
Unaware of spear and basket,
Unaware of salmon leaping.

Celia G Thomas
Mid Glamorgan

My Wales

Green valleys and dark mountains,
A land of laughter and song.
Of coal, steel and sailing ships,
Black dust, blue scars, hard men.

A land of a thousand voices,
A land of belonging and smiles,
A land of hymns and funerals,
A land of fighting back to survive.

Snow, sparkling, high on the mountains,
Hazy smoke, peace in the valleys below.
Sheep, ponies, cows standing close together,
Gently touching, a peace we could never know.

A place where you could walk anywhere,
A place where you could walk day or night,
A place you could be happy, not worry.
A place without anger or fear or fright.

That was Wales when I was young.
That was the Wales I grew to know,
That was the land of milk and honey,
That is the land where my soul should go.

Grahame Garfield Evans
Mid Glamorgan

Open Your Eyes

Open your eyes at the great world about you,
at the wondrous beauty that lies within.
See all God's creatures in their countryfied setting,
all of the birds, as they soar on the wing.

Open your eyes to God's own creation
then you'll see with your soul the beauty of God.
See what the Lord has given His children,
it's truly a symbol of love.

Open your heart to our own Redeemer,
let Him teach us the way we should live.
His love will sustain us through every trouble,
open your eyes to all that God gives.

Remember His Cross on which He did suffer,
with forgiveness, that all might be free.
Open your eyes, the Lord is always with us
Heaven's grace to both you and me.

Jean Parry
Mid Glamorgan

Now And Then Pen-Y-Bont Ar Ogwr

Then,
Better by far the warp of time and fuss
In Co-op store, London House, Market Place
Of hats, gloves, shopping bags and big red bus
Run to time and left from its allotted space.
Town Hall's grim colonnade no place for us
By day, but friendly dance hall come the night
And missing last bus home the only fright.
Bobbies strolled the beat, no stick in sight,
Sidewards glance, antisocial kids took flight,
Cinemas three but still we had to queue
For back row double seats to an early few.
That huge bus station, valleys to the sea,
Svelte Red and White, mysterious N and C,
Took folk distant places quite unknown to me.

Now,
Croeso I Pen-y-bont, what is there to see?
More jeans and trainers, bare midriffs, don't stare.
Doorway vomit, beer cans and grown-up pee,
Big Issue, time-share begging boys, don't glare.
Cast-off shops the new antiques, fast food curse,
Instant-money banks, robotic cash machine,
Over-shoulder, underhand your secrets seen,
Urban clone, no class, no style, getting worse.
More boxcar buses than travellers to take,
Cars banished from brick walkway for whose sake?
Trapped trader, shopper folk or skateboard clown
While no safe-haven car parks fill and cost,
Lucky you on your return your car's not lost
Like Charm and Chic. Who next to quit this town?

Once proud market town where does your future lie?
Success is at the margins, diversify or die.

Mike Hayes
Mid Glamorgan

Wales

Is it true?
That music seeps through the blood
and poetry through the soul,
of people who live in this fair land?
This wet, windy, sunny, glorious place.
A haven for nostalgia,
and *hiraeth* for the past;
a byway for the future
a culture that is old
a landscape even older.
Northern Eryri mountains,
the heartland next,
followed by a scarred coal landscape
and flat southern plains.
Was Eli's prayer
a hymn to ancient gods
who weep the rain
that mists these valleys?
Valleys carved by water and ice,
mountains from eruptions and quiescence.
It is true?

A T Williams
Mid Glamorgan

Living With Memories
(Dedicated to Evelyn)

Why don't people understand me?
Why can't people see?
My life is but a memory past.
I'm caught up in a time warp
Of how I used to be.

Why can't people understand me?
Why can't people see?
My mind happily wanders through my past.
From this day on and evermore
This is how I'll be.

Why don't people understand me?
Why can't people see?
My mind's locked into the past.
How long will feelings of utter confusion last?
It will continue endlessly.

Robert D Hall (12)
Mid Glamorgan

The Friendly Garden

(Chris Needs' 'Friendly Garden' is a programme on BBC Radio Wales. A late night music and phone-in programme, it has been called community radio with a worldwide community for, as well as local calls, presenter, Chris Needs, regularly receives calls from Europe, Canada and the United States. In the 2005 New Years Honours list Chris Needs was awarded the MBE for services to broadcasting and for his charitable work)

There's something strange occurring in the land of Wales,
People are quietly stirring in the hills and vales,
Bonding close together in the small hours of the night,
Brought together by a man with a voice that's clear and bright.

Wherever you may wander you will hear this loyal call.
'We're in the Garden' with Chris Needs, the one who leads us all.
Bringing us together in the small hours of the night,
He was brought up to know respect and taught wrong from right.

So all his listeners follow the example that he sets,
We will teach our youngsters that they have to give to get.
Spreading love and kindness all throughout the land,
There for one another, with a helping hand.

As the flowers grow and spread the message that he sends,
Those who thought they were alone will find that they have friends,
'If the world was like the Garden?' One day it just might be.
We can make it happen. Just you wait and see.

Pamela Evans
Mid Glamorgan

Follicly Challenged

Trying to conceal his balding patch
With so little hair, he was hoping to thatch
His shiny crown that kept getting bigger
Despite hair restorer that he rubbed in with vigour.

Rapidly receding he gave up the fight,
Being follicly challenged, it was part of his plight,
His best kept secret was exposed in a gale,
That shining dome of the alpha male.

A victim of vanity, he vowed no more
To tinker with nature or try to restore
His balding head, that was genetic,
It's only hair, simply cosmetic.

Willard Griffiths
Mid Glamorgan

Raisons d'Être

Because life is nasty, brutish and short,
cruel, intractable, unforgiving,
it gives me satisfaction to report,
three good reasons to continue living:
Eros, Amour, Agape.

Eros: the god of sexual desire,
stirs impulses of passion, life and lust,
the body's consummation, sacred fire,
the flames of love without which all is dust:
Eros, Amour, Agape.

Amour involves an opening of the heart,
a yielding up of selfhood, the giving
in to the one who is your better part,
union with whom is the true end of living:
Eros, Amour, Agape.

Agape is the love of God for Man,
love that is selfless, Christian charity
for all mankind, purer and higher than
all other forms - perfect philanthropy:
Eros, Amour, Agape.

As agony or as exultation,
love, and the chemistry of its weathers,
gives life meaning. Its manifestation
prompts Hosannahs, celebration - whether
Eros, Amour, Agape.

Norman Bissett
Midlothian

Time Trap

A need to escape, a need to relate,
Remorse thick in the air, soon changes to despair,
A need to be me, a need to be free,
When ambition is dim, faces are grim,
Conversation is sparse, becoming harassed, morality stretched thin,
Time is hard to catch,
Live for the present, forget the past,
Time in a cage, it's time it was smashed,
Endless winters on a never-ending plain,
Banging your fist against a wall, trying to stay sane,
Worry, uncertainty, drifting personality,
Friends long-lost, suicide has its cost,
Live for the present, forget the past,
We live in a vacuum that should be reversed.

William Lightheart
Midlothian

Saint Jane (Haining)

Auschwitz, the kiss you didn't have to take, lips eagerly pursed,
Inviting the Nazi tongue to lick
You with gas.
Amongst the mass of strangers you died,
Sacrificed.
Name almost forgotten because of your gender.
Left   Right
Left Dumfries to end up on your knees for a race forgotten
'I have found my life's work' your tune, but the world didn't dance.
No rest in Budapest as you sewed stars of yellow
Onto your chosen children.
Light of Scotland, rejected the Church offering of safe return
Held tightly the hands of those who yearned
Your protection,
Affection enough to lay down your life.
'Even here on the road to Heaven there is a mountain range to climb'
You whispered,
As you were gassed
With a mass of Hungarian women
Such a German chore.
Left   Right
Left the world on August 16th, 1944.
The only Scot to be slain . . . martyred Jane,
Remembered only by a sliver of Glasgow glass and plaque.
Yad Vashem, men declared you 'Righteous' 55 years
After you'd died.
No libraries, films, memorials, tutorials
Lest we forget St. Jane
And the day you were crucified.

E Pomeransky
Midlothian

The Wishing Well
(I wrote this for school homework when I was 12 years old and got C+ for it!)

Down by the grotto in the dell
Throw your coins in the wishing well.
Over your shoulder, what can it be?
Don't break the spell by telling me.
Could it be that in one go
You'd know all there is to know?
Perchance you'd be all full of grace
And show much kindness in your face.
Over your shoulder, what can it be?
Don't break the spell by telling me.

Caroline Carson
Midlothian

A Scottish Soldier

I've walked these streets for two long years,
Experienced all the soldiers' fears,
A soldier dies, the locals cheer,
I wonder what we're doing here,
They put her shilling in your hand,
You're going to fight in some strange land,
The New Lodge Road, the Divas Falls,
You're on the streets when duty calls,
The Scots and Irish, nearly kin,
To send us here's a bloody sin,
They say to us it's Britain's fight,
It looks to me like England's might,
The politics are not for me,
I just believe what I can see,
The Irish folk I've met are fine,
Their Celtic roots the same as mine,
The day they take us out of here,
Now that's the time for us to cheer.

John Fraser
Morayshire

Scar Tissue

Sometimes it feels like I'm all alone.
Sometimes it feels like all I love is gone,
drifting away from me like the tide.
Trying to hold on, it slips through my fingers.
Hope washes over me as I travel my memories,
reminding me of who I was,
showing me all I could ever want to be.
I try not to fall apart and only time will tell.

I don't want to feel that I've been left out here to roam,
take me back to where I feel safe, there's no place like home.

It's hard to imagine there's someone out there for me,
it's hard to imagine I'll ever be whole.
At least I'm dreaming, seeking love on another horizon.
I may be lonely today, tomorrow it could change.

A heart full of scar tissue, picks up its broken pieces.
A heart full of scar tissue, skips a beat once more.
A heart full of scar tissue, forgets about what it's lost.
A heart full of scar tissue, gives itself over to oblivion.

I don't want to feel that I've been left out here to roam,
take me back to where I feel safe, there's no place like home.

Kate Ransom
Norfolk

To The Other Side

You're tugging at my heart,
So persistent, every cell
In my body screaming to respond -

Yet there was no need to fear
You would depart; slipping
So unexpectedly away -
When suddenly that dark November day
Became still and strangely silent.

In that same second, straight upon the clock
There was no pulsing beat, no second hand,
No ticking, no tick-tock.

The telephone shrilled, screeching loud and clear,
His soft words whispered gently in my ear -
Your life crushed in the palm of Fate's cruel hand.

Had I listened when first I felt your call,
And understood that loud, though silent scream;
Had I left when first you willed me to -
I would have been there, just in time
To speak of love and say goodbye to you.

Then I could have held you close to me -
And let you quietly drift with peace away;
Across that swift, fast flowing stream.
That dark, cold, sad, long past November day.

Anita Richards
Norfolk

The Daily Grind

Who wants to be a housewife and stay at home all day
drinking cups of coffee, free in every way?
Watching daytime telly whilst eating Custard Creams
it sounds a perfect way of life, but only in your dreams.
Try and do the washing piled up on the floor
the washing machine has gone all weird and is not working anymore.
The baby has a tantrum as he tries to squeeze the cat,
the dog is eating grass again and has thrown up on the mat.
The soufflé is deflating, the veg has boiled dry,
the washer is still silent, the laundry piled high.
Call centres ring me often with deals too good to miss,
I haven't stopped for coffee, how did it come to this?
I want to be a working girl and mingle with the best,
if I became employed again then I could have a rest.

Jean Reynolds
Norfolk

Elegy To Motherhood

(Inspired by Tichborne's Elegy, 1586, 'And now I live and now my life is done'.)

You were so small, a mite, when you were born
too soon to leave my womb, too fine for home.
Your careful nurturing could not conform
to routine parenting till you had grown.
I could not ask, not then, what you'd become
'And now *you* live, and now my life is done.'

You were a small-framed child, with words writ large,
a code to tease and stress each break and dash;
your patterns read each stage with sounds less harsh.
Watched close, you shone conformity's fine badge.
I could not hide the pride now you'd begun
and now you live and now my life is done.

You fill my dream-mind with your peopled state
and laugh and play and make each game a start.
Too early, not too soon to be, nor late,
developing fine style, a work of art.
I could not ask, not now you have become
and now you live and now my life is done.

Wendy Webb
Norfolk

After The Ball Was Over . . .

Sylvia Sedgwick delighted them all
When she offered to help with the Townswomen's Ball
She was young and beautiful with a figure to tease
And Mrs Fitzperkins viewed her with unease.
The others thought she was quite a find
But Sylvia had other things on her mind.
Plans went ahead like a military campaign
With rotas and details from seating to champagne.
Invitations were sent out to the Mayor and Mayoress
To businesses, local radio and to the press.

Mrs Fitzperkins organised with precision
And woe betide anyone who questioned a decision
(Little Mrs Hapless did at one point try
But was swatted away like an irritating fly).
On the night of the ball all the ladies were there
Looking very festive, some had flowers in their hair.
The only one missing was Miss Sylvia Sedgwick
So runners were despatched just in case she was sick;
They found a note saying: 'Apologies to his wife
But I've gone with Mr Fitzperkins to start a new life'.

Betty Nevell
Norfolk

Knowing Jesus

I love to talk about the Lord
And what He means to me
His joy, His peace, His mercy
Means so much more you see.
I could not live in my own strength
To help the weak and needy
But Jesus knows all people's needs
And is always there beside me.
His love and peace surround me
As day by day I grow
A silent prayer He answers
So I know the way to go.
Knowing Jesus makes my life
All it could ever be
Jesus is my special friend
Who meets my deepest need.
He suffered cruelly on that cross
Bled and died for you and me
Do you know my special friend?
He longs to set you free.
Free from worry, free from pain
And any constant fear
He really wants to love you
And show how much He cares.

Hazel Gladding
Norfolk

Grow Old Gracefully

'Grow old gracefully' the saying goes
A lifetime has quickly passed me by
Birthdays out of the window did fly,
Never allowing me the time of day
Exasperating all I say,
Judging the life I wish to pursue
Never enriching anything I do.

'Grow old gracefully' the saying goes
I'd rather be capable of touching my toes
Not having to hunt for magnifying lens
Whenever I read or look for pens,
Finding when dressed, clothes are inside out
Dropping the teapot, breaking the spout
I would much rather be in my prime
Working and making a dime.
'Grow old gracefully'.

B Lockwood
Norfolk

I Have A Dream

I have a dream,
That one day all my pains will vanish,
No more hurting,
No more tears.

I have a dream,
That one day I can walk again,
Without my special shoe,
I'll be wearing shoes like you.

I have a dream,
That a little girl will call me Mummy,
I will love her and care for her
And every night after her bedtime story,
She'll kiss me and say, 'I love you Mummy.'

I have a dream,
That one day people will see me,
For the person I am,
Shy, but loving and caring.

I have a dream,
That one day we all can live together in peace,
No more fighting, justice will be done.

I have a dream that one day we can all live happily,
Never wanting bigger or better,
Neighbours living in harmony.

If I was ever granted a wish,
My wish would be this,
Sickness and illness gone,
With our loved ones around us,
Living in a happy and peaceful world.

That is my dream.

Katrina West
Norfolk

Doing The Right Thing Isn't Easy

Knowing right from wrong,
knowing where I belong,
coming back to the Lord,
keep trying to be strong,
saying sorry over and over again,
then giving it all to God,
so it's not so much of a strain,
why so much bad happens,
I haven't a clue,
being a mum isn't easy,
I don't always know what to do,
finding the church that works for me,
now the girls are growing up,
we're working together for all to see,
missing my mum with so much pain,
why cancer happens, why'd she have to go,
daily still such a deep drain,
but I'm getting there, you see,
God please give my mum a cuddle for me.

Nina Bates
Norfolk

The Oval Dish

The night the lights went out
caught me standing in the kitchen,
jumped by a dark
so thick
it squeezed my throat and seemed to hurt.

You had just left.
I scratched around for matches
with new, invisible hands;
fumbled through drawers full of ordinary sharpness,
careful of fork prongs, peelers, knives.

I lit one candle from the stove,
then tipped each new wick to the next,
joining dots with hands that shook;
pleased to trace
what little shape.

I watched the wax sink into light
and placed them in the oval dish.
Then - careful, careful, not to touch -
I lowered my palms
to find the heat.

Isabel Pierce
Norfolk

Razor Blades

Your silent laughter
Deafens me
Unlocks doors to feelings
Trespassing in my head

It's the skeleton key
You use to unleash
My poisonous self-doubt
To make me suffer

You think I can't escape
From this isolated prison
Can't break free
From your suffocation

But, I've found a way to defy you

Pain is your punishment
It washes over you

A cleansing river

I watch the crimson spread
Feel the metal biting
At your worthless flesh

You deserve it

Satisfaction surfaces
And I smile at you
As I stare in the mirror.

Sian Jenkins (16)
Norfolk

That Certain Delivery!

Life is but, a major and minor key
That possesses an unknown identity
                amid an unrequited melody
Of a profound harmony.

The harmony that comes from the
                depths of its tranquil delivery
Amid the simplicity of its
                                basic reality
Behind the basis of its needed
                                spirituality!

Dave White
Norfolk

358

Will Tomorrow Be The Same As Yesterday?

If I told you I had feelings, would you hurt me?
If I said I had a smile, would you wipe it away?
If I told you I could laugh, would you silence me?
Will tomorrow be the same as yesterday?

If I told you that I loved you, would you scorn me?
If I said that I'd be there, would you run away?
If I said I had a heart, would you break it?
Will tomorrow be the same as yesterday?

If I told you I was brave, would you scare me?
If I held my arms out wide, would you push me away?
If I told you I remembered, would you forget me?
Will tomorrow be the same as yesterday?

If I told you I was strong, would you crush me?
If I told you I was free, would you lock me away?
If I told you I was safe, would you desert me?
Will tomorrow be the same as yesterday?

So I sit here all alone with my belongings,
My heart, my soul, and all my feelings packed away,
And although for you I feel an ache of longing,
I know tomorrow's just the same as yesterday.

Sarah Evans-Wrench
Norfolk

Inspiration

For inspiration
I cast around
Meadow, field
Nothing of interest
Do they yield.
But something low
Scuttles over the road
Perhaps a stoat or a weasel?

Within the mind, I draw a blank
Sky is high, mind bare
As the branches of that tree.
Nothing for my poem do I see,
But wait, I look too far,
Here by the window of my car,
Small inspiration for a poem,
'Norfolk County Council
Take your litter home'!

Barbara Robinson
Norfolk

Insanity Of Humanity

Hamburger bap
fast food crap
late night shopping
TV channel-hopping
daytime chat shows
with celebrities no one knows
Botox face injections
instant Viagra erections
anti-wrinkle lotions
skin peeling potions
false summer tans
fag smoking bans
Big Mac Whoppers
gun slinging coppers
nagging cocaine crave
secret midnight rave
got stomach irritation?
get colonic irrigation
no more plain bread
ciabatta and foccacia instead
implanted silicone breasts
gay rights protests
vandalised park seats
filthy littered streets
peaceful tree-huggers
violent street muggers.
I stand alone and stare
at the madness everywhere.

Carrie-Ann Hammond
Norfolk

Time

Is time in the category of sense;
A beginning and an end?
Is it a recognition of before and after
Or does it hide between measured beats,
That tempo will defend?

Is it not the duration of utterance,
Bringing forth thought and action? Or is it a moment that flies,
When rhythm is lost
At the moment of birth
Or the moment one dies?

All movements require the presence of time.
It is lifeblood to the ballroom dance;
A regular beat to the movement of feet.
It is a regular measure
For a movement of chance.

Time can be gentle and sometimes kind:
It can soothe the troubles
Of a troublesome mind;
It can help the sick and sanctify the spirit;
It can straighten out a problem
And all the worries within it.

It's not the judge of evil voices,
It's full of wisdom;
With aid for others and their choices.
It's never seen; we know it's there;
And we know time is so important.
That is why we have to take
The greatest care.

E S Peaford
Norfolk

My True Self

True self,
where have you been?
Lost in time past,
I didn't think I could remember you,
but I've found you now at last.
The grief had washed you away,
through the loss of people that I loved.
True self, you had just hidden from me,
as my life was in dismay.
As I heal myself from past wounds,
you start to emerge.
I am finally awake to the wonders around me,
simply looking out into my garden,
I see the abundance of life,
I see colours; greens, yellows, oranges, reds, to name a few,
before, black and white was all I seemed to view,
I see trees, flowers and a sky full of clouds, all shapes and sizes,
great appreciation of nature in all its forms.
My senses have awakened,
filling me with possibilities to expand my imagination.
When I stop to take a quiet minute,
and let my consciousness bring awareness to my life,
birds I hear singing, the miaow of a cat, rustling of trees,
all this I missed when you, my true self, was asleep.
I have the ability to feel,
and love finally radiates from my heart,
helping me to create a new world around me,
what was once dark is now light,
now that you, my true self, is awake.

Emma Jane Lambert
Norfolk

My City

Norwich is a fine old place
Its gardens there are full of grace
The castle on the hill so tall
Looks out above us one and all

The cathedral spire stands so serene
The cock shines out in sunlight gleam
The large oak door is open wide
For everyone to come inside

The city hall with clock on high
The clock it strikes across the sky
The shadows of the tower on high
Over the market it doth slide

The cobble street you hear from afar
The little streets with cafés and bars
With quaint old shops for you to find
For some have been there a very long time

They're old and new, they're all mixed in
The roads run thro' since time began
The river flows its weary way
Thro' the city day by day

So Norwich you are home to me
To other places I have been
I still return to this place of mine
No other place you will ever find.

R Claxton
Norfolk

The Skeleton Tree

Standing tall in the dark, dense forest,
Branching out into open spaces,
I am lost within the depths of despair,
There are hundreds of faces everywhere,
Voices are heard from the road afar,
I hear the horn from the passing car.
The skeleton tree stands ahead on the hill,
Glorious and so wonderful to see,
It's hard to imagine, but it's so real.
Winter is here and every year,
A tree so brave, does not fear,
If you could talk a little to me,
You have a friend for eternity.
You are beautiful oh skeleton tree,
I will protect you forever you see.

Maggie Hickinbotham
Norfolk

Time

Katie
How is one so in love meant to pick up
The thread after my heart has broken in two?
How can I go on when in my heart I
Realise and understand there is no happiness
Or love ahead of me?

There are many things that time can heal and
A few will not, and my heart is one of but a few that
Time will never heal.
Some hurt goes too deep that sadness takes
Hold inside and I realise the only ones
To heal my heart and bring happiness to my life
Are you and the girls that I miss so much.

I also know inside that in my life you three are
Meant to be, as we can be a happy family,
My body will not let me carry on
As things must be put right that went so wrong
This is what time can help mend
I want more than to be just a friend.

Marry me, let our souls be one.
I will never give up.

Gary Miller
Norfolk

Trees

Trees are unimaginatively beautiful
To ponder over, to sit beneath and wonder at
Listen to the leaves' crispness
Watch them fall to the ground.

They are tall and majestic
Small and loaded with berries
Covered with leaves and uncovered
Home to jays and the like and pleasantly cool.

The shades of green are endless
A perfect cover on a hot day
Friendly and welcoming the branches
Stretching and growing ever wider
To encompass oneself without thinking.

Long may these wonderful trees
Shelter us in their shadows
Look gorgeous in their autumn
Dressing and winter starkness
At their own expense.

Hazel Cooper
Norfolk

Blanket On The Ground

Out under the stars
We lay on the ground
That blanket under us
Keeping us warm and sound.

On nights crisp
When the air was chill
Giving us our comfort
Its warmth a thrill.

Those summer nights
The breeze just a flow
We'd lay upon it
And watch the sky aglow.

Of natural wool
Its weave so tight
Keeping out the rain
And wind at night.

Summer and winter
It would keep us warm
From a light summer shower
To a winter snowstorm.

Old, but still in use
Rolled up tight
It lays by the door
Stopping the draught at night . . .

Alan J Morgan
Norfolk

Tempting Providence

TV ads, leaflets, offers of money
Banks also plying their trade
Will you spend your money?
I'll have to watch, even a piggy bank they'll raid.
We know your name from registers
That you work, even that you own a car
Perhaps we'll tempt you to buy a house
Or a holiday home in Russia, next door to the tsar.
I hear your income is good
And that status means you can afford something new.
We can accrue, prosper through investment
Meeting your target or two.
You'll gain a home for family
With security and comfort along the way
It's never easy, you'll work hard
Pay your tax, plan for events to save the day.
Sacrifice can bring reward, happiness and sometimes sorrow
But time years of planning will be a requisite for tomorrow
Whatever option I should take will depend on income, old or young
I shall make sure throughout those years
There'll be time to have some fun.
Pills and potions, healthy diets, care of myself
And others could save the day
May we live long, remaining young at heart.
Spending time wisely with care
Our loyalty and love to impart.

Margaret Jowsey
Norfolk

Gone But Not Forgotten

We started off as friends
Our love just grew and grew,
After just a few months
Came a ring, all sparkly and new.

Then our love got stronger
And a house we went to find,
We found a two-bed semi
The first time buyer kind.

In May it was our wedding
A very emotional day,
'The best one we've ever been to!'
Everyone would say.

The next year we had a daughter
A perfect family we'd be,
It was a house of love
Not one, not two, but three.

After a few years we made a move
To village life you see,
But then a tragic accident
Left two and not us three.

We've gone through lots of feelings
Anger, hurt and tears,
But I know he's on the other side
And with us through our years.

When my daughter gets awards
And I go to clap and cheer,
Although I sit there on my own
I know her daddy's there.

Andrea McDermott
Norfolk

August 4th, 1914

Was it really ninety years ago that
Ignorance ended abruptly and the world imploded?
That we stood, young and eager to
Watch the storm of Satan's wrath well up?

That we clambered in awe to
Witness the devastation of his lightning and thunder,
Pressing up against the glass of life
Lest we missed it all pass by?

And go it did . . .

Taking thousands of young men to
Fall as drops in that thirsty metal rain:
Thousands, thousands of old men saw
The harvest rendered, cut down, never returned

Left untended when the storm was broken,
Little remains of where the hailstones once pitted
But here, in the minds of the crop, nine
Decades have gone since they smote the land

Ninety years since the crosses started,
Names scoured into hearts as well as wood;
Branded, tattooed with the pen of 'Survivor's Guilt'
Others, still crushed by ghosts desperate for home . . .

S J Robinson
Norfolk

Dwellings

I see that Diss is fast expanding
On virgin soil new houses standing
Take Ashbrook Meadow by the station
For an instant confirmation.

Here and there some plots remaining
Salesmen have received a training
Pointing out the salient features
First time buyers - eager creatures.

Our town perhaps will not recover
As more arrivals now discover
Picturesque - The Mere - so fetching
Services quite overstretching.

And yet her charm is still retaining
Pleasant vistas - sun or raining
A green belt should be placed in order
By the Norfolk/Suffolk border.

Steve Glason
Norfolk

Memories

Memories, are all I'm left with,
Where once I thought I had it all.
Now these years I've spent without you,
What would I give to hear you call.

It was not your fault you had to leave me,
Although we knew you had to go.
You tried so hard to help prepare me,
It broke my heart, I loved you so.

My life, today, has no real meaning
And family do not feel things as I do.
Their lives to mine, though not demeaning,
Are leading lives they must pursue.

One day my love, we'll be together,
Until that day, we've had to part.
My memories of you are mine to treasure,
In my mind, my soul and in my heart.

A G Revill
Norfolk

The Forgotten Soul's Prayer

I sit here in my wheelchair,
Paralysed from head to toe,
Wondering if You've forgotten me Lord;
I'm still alive you know.

Most people pass me by Lord,
Some even stop and stare,
Few utter words of sympathy
But they don't really care.

I want to speak just once Lord,
If You're listening up above,
I'll use the chance to thank my mum
For her sacrifice and love.

I won't ask for any more Sir,
You're a busy man I know,
Please grant me what I ask Lord,
Before I have to go.

It's nearly time to go now
And I've had my little pray
But I'll speak with you tomorrow Lord,
When I've thought of more to say.

Paul Harris
Norfolk

Awake Or Asleep Thought Remains Deep

When I'm awake I breathe with the sky
I sit there pondering asking myself why
when I'm asleep thought lost so deep
I lay on my bed just a snoring heap

When I'm awake your distance is there
not far from the truth but as close as you care
when I'm asleep you are right by my side
holding my hand together two tied

When I'm awake I know you are around
you are very elusive just happy unfound
when I'm asleep you are the girl of my dreams
when I awake nothing's all as it seems

When I'm awake I wait for the night
then you are mine until dark night turns bright
when I'm asleep I dream I will stay
that time again your smile wishes me away

When I'm awake I'm waiting for you
you never once came my dream never came true
when I'm asleep your kiss so sweet
in this world of dreams our only place to meet

Shaun Cook
Norfolk

Golden Wedding Anniversary

Your love has become stronger than ever
    As you celebrate fifty years together

As you make your vows anew
    May all good things come to you

May your day bring lots of pleasure
    With lots of memories to treasure

As you've now spent fifty years together
    Your love will last forever and ever

Suzanne Reeves
Norfolk

Across The Breydon Water

I note, marshes that stretch for miles
A lush green land, with waving smiles
Cropped with dots of cattle and sheep
In trim, their task, the marsh to keep.
Wind hovers haunt the endless skies
Huge herons hunt the dykes close by
Starlings swamp the telephone wires
Lapwing wheel like titanic tyres.
Farm tracks curve on their wavy way
To B&Bs where hikers happily stay.
I see a scattering in this sea of green
Of desertion, decay, somewhat obscene
Of blackened withering wind pumps
Feigning lace topped tree stumps
Spurious sails no longer propelling round
Unlike the turbines towering above the town.
Excited, I feel like shouting ahoy
As I spy the river's sandy buoys.
And with a splash, I swoon in a blue lagoon
Then I know my journey's over, oh so soon.
A few slough land aspects have I noted
Too multifarious for all to 'ave been quoted.
The train, like a sloth, slowly trundles in
As the masticated marshland wavers thin
And like the sails, all grinds to a halt
And I smell the sea spray and pinch the salt.

Chris Preston
Norfolk

Walking Under The Influence

Pedestrian left his local
Driver almost ran him over
Pedestrian drunk
Driver sober
Driver yelled obscenities
Pedestrian yelled, 'It's OK
I'm an organ donor!'

Paulie Pentelow
Norfolk

Wellingborough

O Wellingborough, since the beginning of the railways, you have been growing.
How you have grown!
O Wellingborough, from the twenties to the thirties, the first of the council estates
went up in Wellingborough.
How you have grown!
O Wellingborough, in the fifties and sixties you had more and more people
from other places to fill your houses and roads.
How you have grown!
O Wellingborough, in the seventies and the eighties, a new era, you grew
like you had another limb with more and more roads, and more and more houses
and people that came to you from other places.
How you have grown!
O Wellingborough, in the nineties and to now, you have grown to the east
and you have grown to the west. What lies in the future for you, as you keep on growing!
O Wellingborough, when will you ever stop?

Rodney Pope
Northamptonshire

Farewell

Leaning across him,
I permit myself the luxury of one last kiss,
Forbidden, but exciting.
His so-familiar lips a bas-relief,
Bearing the marks of all our joys and sorrows.
Our battles,
Our times of lasting peace.
Whose deep reserves often have yielded me
Sweet waters of a mutual and dependent love.

His journey is not mine, not yet,
And I would gladly wrench him back to me,
To hold against my heart,
Whose edges, like a new-stripped burn,
Only now start to bleed.

But conscience chides me. So soon parted,
Why can I not see life without his presence?
Silent in homage, I await the trumpets.
Then, from closed eyes, tears fall,
For he too hears, and looking with amazement,
Knows that they sound for him.

Diana R Cockrill
Northamptonshire

Blooming Northampton

'Blooming' Northampton
A very nice place
With hundreds of people of all different race.

All working their business with quiet aplomb
To earn a good living, it shouldn't take long.

There are cafes and shops in all different streets
The choices are many, you couldn't compete.

The buses and trains seem to run quite on time
With bus passes for the elderly not much more than a dime.
The taxis are many and don't charge much more
And they offer to take you from door to door.

The cathedrals and churches built to suit all religions
But you have to be wary of low flying pigeons.
As you walk unafraid to the entrance nearby
You hurry along, sitting down with a *sigh*.

The cinemas and theatres put on a good show
And the holiday coach's booked ready to go.
To the seaside and country, all with lovely views
Also the factories that used to make shoes.

Then homeward bound at the end of the day
To a home warm and cosy, there's nothing to pay.

Nancy M Harris
Northamptonshire

The Butterfly

It has been by scientifics, reliably stated
That a flutter of a butterfly's wing
Could cause havoc unabated
Through progression from breeze to hurricane wind

But if the butterfly broke wind
Through indulgence to excess
If one can imagine such a social sin
How would the result be expressed?

It would be of cataclysmic proportion
To the extreme of scientific scale
And present laws of physic distortion
All past weather into insignificance pale.

Brian Norman
Northamptonshire

Dad

If you could come back for a day
I'd have so many things to say
I'd want to tell you loud and clear
I miss the fact that you're not here
I miss the face of love and care
The empty space, the empty chair
I miss the moments lost in time
Those precious days of yours and mine
The memories will always be
A part of you, a part of me
They're etched forever in my heart
So somehow we are not apart
Each day you're here inside my head
In prayers I pray when in my bed
For you will always be the man
Whose son is still his biggest fan
So, Dad, I wish, just for a day
That God would let you pass my way
So I could say 'I love you Dad'
And bless you for the life we had

David Whitney
Northamptonshire

Arty-Farty

I'm not going to get all arty-farty,
And use words nobody understands,
I'm not going to try and make you believe,
That I had this poem thoroughly planned.
In my verse, it's all straightforward,
To read it, you don't need a degree,
It makes it far more enjoyable,
If what I mean is clear, you see.
I'm tired of reading poetry,
That has words only a professor would know,
Not everyone has a brain like Einstein,
How about some poems for the average Joe?

Michelle Rae
Northamptonshire

Quirk Of Nature

By quirk of nature
And rebel gene
A life was quelled
That should have been

Genetic flaw
Tossed dreams aside
Blueprint error
Cast shadows wide

Mother weeps
Over imagined sin
That taints the infant
Deep within

And parents' tears
They try to hide
Though crushing blow
Is felt inside

But sunshine floods
That dark recess
Where troubled souls
Know such distress

By quirk of nature
And rebel gene
A life adapts
To what could have been

Ann Peat
Northamptonshire

Fire, Fire

Fire, fire burning bright,
It kills someone each day and night.
When they're in their sweet little dream,
They wake up to death and steam.
Don't just sit there and lie,
Before you know it you might just die.
Climb out a window just in front,
Don't let someone say *don't, don't, don't.*
Before you know it you're safe on the ground,
Just listen all, you hear a banging sound.
Make sure your loved ones are safe and near,
If they're not you will drop a tear.

Louis Dickens (11)
Northamptonshire

Cancer

My nan, she was the first where the cancer began.
She found a lump within her breast
but didn't want to have the test.
She tried her best to carry on,
pretending she was fine, nothing was wrong.
The pain she must have suffered and beared,
so our worries and tears would be spared.
So brave, so strong,
but all too soon my nan was gone.

Then once again I heard that dreaded word.
No, not my dad, that's the craziest thing I've heard!
He's never ill or off his food,
although I've sensed a change in his mood.
It's here again, within his lung,
an operation must be done.
But once again 'twas not to be,
it took my dad away from me.

Now wait, there is one more,
my darling big sis who I adore.
She too was told it was within her breast,
waiting for the results of that dreaded test.
They did what they had to do,
part of the breast, a few lymph glands too.
She was so brave, so strong,
and fought this disease on and on.
She too was suffering and so afraid,
I just hoped and prayed and prayed
that she too wouldn't leave and go away
but I'm glad to say she's here today!
And that's the way it's gonna stay.

Lisa Card
Northamptonshire

Stranger

A dream can be a step which drifts from your hand,
dropping like a moment, which has a secret.
Time walks away like a stranger
who keeps my undiscovered word from my heart.
How can I clear the smoke from the water
that blinds the moment?

Mark Allibon
Northamptonshire

The Swimmer

I swam in a beautiful sea,
Azure, blue and white,
And tiny silver fishes
Flashed in shoals of light.

I swam in a dazzling sea,
Under a blazing sun,
And gentle golden wavelets
Caressed me one by one.

I swam in a murmuring sea,
Washing the white-hot sand,
And green and glassy seaweed
Made a necklace on the strand.

I swam in a darkening sea,
With coldness all around,
A plaintive seabird's cry
The only mournful sound.

I swam in an angry sea,
Under grey and leaden clouds,
Great waves dashed against me
And the breakers roared and howled.

I swam in a raging sea,
Cruel currents dragged me down,
I fought to stay afloat
But in the end I drowned.

Pauline Halliwell
Northamptonshire

Passage Of Time

I feel as if time is running away - I panic
I'm trying to stop it, my mind can't keep up
Running away as quickly as the sand in an hourglass

That is just what is happening, that's why I can't stop it
No one can stop time, I should relax
Enjoy the passage of time, savour each minute

In my mind's eye, the sands of time, I relax
Enjoying this new found feeling I'd lost
All because I tried to stop the passage of time.

Carole A Cleverdon
Northamptonshire

No Place Like Home

The North East is crazy
Battered and old,
The weather is horrid
Raining and cold.
The countryside's pleasant
Quiet and green,
The ocean is freezing
Salty, unclean.
The streets are littered
With rubbish and slobs,
The people look scary
But they're not just yobs.
Beneath all the dirt
Graffiti and grime,
This place has heart
That's there for all time.
Each street tells a story
That's treasured and old,
Each house has a memory
Never to be told.
So you can have
Sydney, Paris and Rome,
But at the end of the day
There's no place like home!

Kim Akwei-Howe (14)
Northumberland

The Old Oak Tree

In the lane there is a lovely oak tree
Many a tale it could tell you and me
Rural development took the other trees away
Now this tree stands alone to sway
Lovers who kissed and walked in the dark
Carved their names into its bark
Maybe a meeting place for a first date
This could be the beginning of the couple's fate
Somewhere for children to climb and play
Also for birds to rest and welcome a new day
New life from this tree will spring
From a tiny fledgling on the wing
An acorn dropped onto good earth
This will bring trees of new birth

J Parker
Northumberland

A Mother's Fear

The mother held her daughter's hand,
As she walked her round the park,
Till she looked up at the deep blue sky,
And found it was getting dark.

The mother went to collect her things,
Left her little girl gazing at the lake,
But the second that she returned,
She knew she had made a mistake.

Her baby girl had gone,
She was nowhere in sight,
And the thought that she had lost her,
Made her shout out in fright.

Then she remembered her little girl,
Was admiring a big oak tree,
For she thought that among the twisted roots,
The little fairies would be.

She ran to find that tree,
She could not have run any faster,
She would never forgive herself,
If she had forever lost her.

Her heart was in her mouth,
She whispered a silent prayer,
As she peered around the tree,
And found her sweet child there.

The child was fast asleep,
Dreaming her fairy dreams,
And as her mother carried her home,
Her tears of relief came in streams.

Jessica Shakespeare
Northumberland

Butterflies

Butterflies are beautiful, delicate things
flying elegantly on gossamer wings,
Flimsy and fragile, gently fluttering by
glints and glimmers of colours in the sky,
Flitting to and fro, from flower to flower
in sunshine or shower, hour after hour.

From creepy, hairy caterpillar to chrysalis
hidden away, a cocoon waiting for summer's kiss,
Inside, a magical metamorphosis is taking place
and out will emerge an exquisite thing of grace,
A nectar gatherer, one of garden's helping hands
spreading seeds and wild flowers all over the land.

Mother Nature is the most wonderful thing
bringing us this joy, on two wondrous wings,
Red admirals, cabbage white or misty blues
a rainbow of colours, a myriad of different hues,
Navigating their way through with majesty
these creatures capture you with their glory.

Greta Forsyth
Northumberland

Muddy Boots

Mam goes mad about my muddy boots.
  It's not my fault!
If I played ball saying, 'Don't pass to me, it's muddy,'
The lads would laugh at me,
Call me a fuddy-duddy.

I cannot say, 'Mum says I am to keep them clean.'
They would think I was crackers, you know what I mean.

Last week she put my trainers in the washing machine!
  Boy, did they look clean.
My best friend, Dean, said, 'Where have they been?'

It took me weeks to get them just right,
Then, overnight, they got white and bright,
  What a sight!
I know what to do, when new ones are due
Put the white ones back
At the back of the stack
And choose *black!*

Sally Hall
North Yorkshire

Tsunami, Boxing Day 2004

How powerful was the hand of God
That shook the ocean floor
And caused the fearsome mighty wave
That wrecked the Asian shore?

People fled in disarray
But didn't stand a chance
Thousands were simply swept away
In the mighty wave's advance.

This thing they call 'tsunami'
A giant wave to you and me
Destroyed things like an army
Like flotsam on the sea.

How could a God, if kind, let this occur?
Maybe our consciences to stir!
For men whose hearts so fickle, now are stirred
Immediately responded when the call for help was heard.

Then to all the nations
That to waste were laid
Made good relations
And rebuild with massive aid.

Then, having helped with this great and worthy cause
Now help all other nations with disease and poverty
Not for one moment should we pause
Forget indifference, greed and apathy.

Dennis Bowes
North Yorkshire

Only Dreaming

If I could win the Lotto, oh the things that I would do,
I'd share with friends and family but, most of it I'd share with you.
I'd take you travelling everywhere, around the world and back,
We'd live in a grand big house, not our poor little shack.
The kids would want for nothing; houses, cars and things,
But I've never been one for fancy cars and diamond rings,
I would still go shopping in our local town,
I'd wear my jeans and jumper, not a tiara or a long silk gown,
But yes, I'm only dreaming and dreams just don't come true,
But I will be happy to share what there is now, with you!

Patricia Munzer
North Yorkshire

Nell Gwyn

Nell Gwyn sold oranges in pairs,
The king looked down from up the stairs,
He said, 'Now there's a charming thing,
Perhaps to me you would them bring;
They look quite fresh and full of juice,
And if they are, I'll have a deuce.'

Nell said, 'You are a saucy lad,
Of course my oranges aren't bad;
They are quite large and firm and sweet
And you can have them for a treat.'

King Charles replied, 'I cannot wait,
But tell me, do you have a date?
Perhaps someone for you has spoke,
Is that him there in hat and coat?'

The orange seller gave a wink,
She said, 'Perhaps you'd like a drink?
I could squeeze you some orange juice,
But don't start thinking I am loose;
I might right now be on the shelf,
But just keep your hands to yourself.'

The king replied, 'That is a shame,
I thought we might just play a game,
Especially since you're not wed
And upstairs here I've got a bed.'

Nell Gwyn then flushed and went bright red,
She said, 'You just heard what I said.
This job I've got might be the pits,
But just keep your hands off my fruit.
About you I have heard a tale,
But fruit is all I have for sale.'

Bernard Johnson
North Yorkshire

Untitled

Waving sea of lands lost true
regret unfound and force unto
how weave we not to seek the day
that finds the one within the fray
I hear the sound of long-lost love
I see the sight of truth above
to temper these, the force of leaves
how whisper they throughout the breeze?

Steve Brooks
North Yorkshire

A Young Girl's Wish

Her world is new - and, as young girls do,
she'll wonder what will see her through,
towards a perfect womanhood.
That is good, but, let it be understood,
a youngster needs to use her brain, to gain:
to improve her looks; her beauty too.
I'll tell you how: just watch my lips,
I'll offer lots of little tips.
That present nose - a grafting job -
will cost her quite a tidy bob, or two!
Well, that is what she'll have to do.
Her legs must be as smooth as silk:
not rough; not hairy - not in that ilk.
With lovely ankles; twinkling toes:
all even spaced in neat, sweet rows.
Her muscles taut - not soft and flabby.
Her voice controlled - the speech not gabby.
That's my vision - it's the same as *perfection,*
for that's the game.
However, will all that be enough
if her genetic bits are duff?
Because her forbears couldn't wait,
when they went to seek their perfect mate?
Then, her problems grow - they're really huge.
What can she do? Use subterfuge!
A cover up - under duress - to hide away the sorry mess:
a little more? A little less?
Well, she'll have to guess -
unless she learns how best to dress!

Eric Chapman
North Yorkshire

North Yorkshire Moor

Stand you atop a hill on North Yorkshire Moor
in morn's magical twilight moment,
the moment a ground mist kisses heather's waking face
before it slips away, ghost-like over yonder tor.
Witness the majesty of burnished sun's ascent to the sky
as breaking dawn slowly lifts the darker hour,
a moment heralded by songs of birds taking to air
and the scurry of God's creatures in search of their fill.
Yes, stand you atop a hill on North Yorkshire Moor,
watching, with grateful eyes, this very special moment,
seeing there the splendour of the Day of Creation,
that special moment which fills you with *awe.*

T D Green
North Yorkshire

The Wonder Of You

When I first came to know of you, I must admit you scared me,
You turned my life upside down and still I knew you barely.

And still, before we'd met, I spent days wondering how you looked
And when that special meeting came, would both of us be hooked?

That sickly feeling that I had, surely couldn't last forever,
Would it all be worth it, when we finally got together?

But the butterflies you gave me, they felt oh so right,
All the time the wonder of you, kept me awake most of the night.

I still needed so much time to prepare, for the special day we'd meet,
But you were making me so tired and draining me, my sweet.

I wondered was there such a thing that they call 'love at first sight'?
How can love be brought through the pain that you are giving me tonight?

And now the meeting day has come, the answers are so clear,
The pain you gave me has disappeared now you are finally here.

Not just love at first sight, I'm thinking as I look into your eyes,
I love you more than life itself, it's a love that never dies.

And now I wonder what you're thinking, as I softly stroke your hair,
You're sleeping very soundly, like you haven't got a care.

I'm hoping you will grow to love me, as much as I love you,
And I'm going to try and do my best and make you proud to have me too.

And so, to you, my newborn child, here are my feelings bared,
But to meet and bond as mother and son, means I'm no longer scared.

Amanda Waggott
North Yorkshire

The Ultimate Sacrifice

More than sixty years ago,
Many nations went to war,
To fight against a common foe,
And reclaim peace for rich and poor.

Family life was torn apart;
Children left each danger zone,
Young men were parted from their wives,
To face grave perils far from home.

Despite social class or creed,
They responded to the call,
To regain freedom and much more,
They all gave some, but some gave all.

Brian M Wood
North Yorkshire

The Caring Cosher

They'd lurked in the alleyway, week after week, to watch Mr Percival Frank,
Arriving at seventeen minutes to eight, deposit his cash in the bank;
'A creature of habit, our Percy,' said Sid. 'He's someone we know we can trust -
It must be so hard when they're haphazard, like.' 'You're right,' agreed Bertie, 'it must!'

The two would-be robbers: the young Herbert Snert and veteran thief, Sidney Snosh,
Had armed themselves suitably; Bert had a knife and Sid had a good, solid cosh:
They'd laid their plans carefully - here they were now, so stealthily lying in wait
To take by surprise the old faithful cashier at seventeen minutes to eight.

They knew when the clock had chimed half-past the hour, the man they were waiting to rob,
Had balanced the books with meticulous care (old Percival valued his job).
He'd open the safe where the money was kept and empty it into a sack,
Then, carefully locking the premises up, would leave by the door at the back.

They pictured him briskly beginning the walk that took seven minutes in all -
He'd shortly appear with the small heavy sack to post in the safe in the wall:
The robbers were tense with expectancy now - 'It's nearly the time,' Sidney said,
'Remember to grab all the money as soon as I batter him on the head!'

Young Bertie said eagerly, 'I'll grab the cash and run down the road for my life . . .'
. . . 'No wait,' replied Sid, 'he may struggle, you know, and then you must plunge in the knife.'
'But Sid,' exclaimed Bertie, quite anxiously now, 'I've never stabbed anyone yet!'
'If you want your share, then you'll do as I say - I'm running this show, don't forget!'

The darkness had thickened; the clock struck the hour. 'He's late!' complained old
                                                            Sidney Snosh;
He moved around restlessly - shuffled about and tested the weight of his cosh.
'You don't suppose anything's happened to him? I'm worried,' declared Herbert Snert,
He tested his knife for its sharpness and said, 'I do hope he hasn't been hurt!'

Rosemary Y Vandeldt
North Yorkshire

The Joiner

I am a joiner
do you know
I get in my van
and to work I go.
I saw up wood
and bang in nails
I waffle my head off
if all else fails.
If I can't make it
as a poet
then I'll plant a lawn
so I can mow it.

Steven Rodwell
North Yorkshire

Ending It

(The Astronomer Royal, Sir Martin Rees, is said to have concluded that the human race has only a 50% chance of surviving the 21st century. ('Our Final Century'))

If it's curtains for twenty-fifty,
We might as well start being nifty,
And love as never before.

We should give the world a big hug,
And say sorry for being a mug,
Homo sapiens, the world's biggest bore:

A bore whose imbecility,
Poisoned the air and the earth and the sea,
And let the forests fall.

So now, whilst the globe waits for grief,
Let's cherish each flower, each leaf,
Say goodbye to them all.

Forget all the national ditties,
Sing songs of the Earth and its pities,
And our need to be as one.

Look again at our nations and churches and wars,
And education gone wrong, and our crazy laws.
Their course has been run.

Poor kids! Cut the tests, cherish arts and leisure,
And feelings that help them to grow, even pleasure,
And end the great stress of our schools.

Let the animals at last have their time.
What we've done to the Earth and to them has been crime.
We reap the harvest of fools.

End the making of weapons, but rather make balm,
To soothe and comfort the coming great harm.
Use lost imagination again.

If there's light at the end, a god may say,
'You've got it right at the end of the day,
But you've been a bloody long time!'

Roy Stevens
North Yorkshire

Just Dreaming

As I sit and ponder and think on things gone by
And let my mind just wonder to where, and when, and why
It makes me think of a pebble on a beach
Tossed by wind and tide
Until at last, beneath the sand, I'm buried and glad to hide.

Hetty Launchbury
North Yorkshire

Christmas Glad Tidings

Peace on Earth, goodwill to men
When will it happen, what time and when?
With the love of God and our Saviour who was born
In a stable on Christmas morn
Anything is possible; our prayers can be heard
God in His wisdom listens to our every word
His messengers listen and pass on our thoughts
The whole world knows of the words our Saviour taught
Some thousand years have passed but His teachings we still hear
God's glad tidings came when Christ came here
Each Christmas life changes and all for the good
Peace will come when love is understood
Christmas glad tidings, are all about peace
United in God's love will make wars cease
Most nations love Christmas, it's a time of great faith
It overrules differences in the human race
So let's all hold hands and give praise to God above
For by giving us His Son, we have His undying love.

Sue Brooks
North Yorkshire

The Rose

Roses of red, yellow, pink and peach
A lovely perfume comes from each
Roses on standards, bushes and trellis
The loveliest flower, we should always cherish

Roses mean England, and the winning of wars
Roses in my garden, and also in yours
Roses in hedgerows, with thorns aplenty
Roses never leave any space empty

Their petals are all of a lustre
Their flowers all in a cluster
Leaves of greens, golds and browns
This lovely flower never lets you down

You feel the tranquillity and the peace
They leave the heart, all at ease
You would not leave your garden bare
By not planting roses here and there

From a lovely country cottage garden
Choose a rose, when you need to say pardon
With this gift, you'll be forgiven
As the rose is sent from Heaven

John L Pierrepont
Nottinghamshire

Impulse

Has impulse changed the world
Its true power belittles its *name*
Without its power nature's delicate
Beauty or histories, couldn't be the *same*
In the book of time recorded some pages
Tell of sudden impulses *acted*
The consequence to life's stable
Charade *distracted*
If defining, the impelling force
Or motion it *produced*
Our mind's convinced it's logical
Thought not whim *seduced*
Mankind's ability
To alter *fate*
Raises his intelligence level
To *investigate*
So no blaming,
No *recall*
An act's been sanctioned
That's *all*
Common sense demands more evidence
Needed, to convince, quell *doubts*
Yet impulse, often happens because
No time given for thinking alternatives *out*

B Wharmby
Nottinghamshire

One Wish

If I had but one wish dear
You would still be here with me.
No more the future would I fear
For safe with you I'd be.

The day you left you broke my heart
Shattered all my dreams.
I thought that we would never part
But life is not as it seems.

I wish you would return to me
And take away my pain.
Back in my arms you would be
To share my life again.

Memories are all that now remain
Of precious days together.
Without you life will never be same
But you will stay in my heart forever.

Josie Rawson
Nottinghamshire

Love Can Be . . .

Love can be
a beautiful butterfly-winged cloud
which surrounds me with showers and sugar
and makes me forget
that I am not only this.

Love can be
a sweet marshmallow forgetfulness
where my body becomes like a cushion
giving to melt into yours
and I forget that I am also hard and brittle
like sugar.

Love can be
a straight narrow path
with a house full of happiness
and dogs at the end
which makes me forget
that I have been wandering the fields
and the mountains.

Love can hurt my all-togetherness
so I give the heart of my meaning over to you
and forget that I have been building a ladder
strong as stone made of my bones
and my wetness.

Caroline Stancer
Nottinghamshire

Gypsy Woman

Her short black hair was neatly cut
Her skin was dark and wrinkled
Her bony fingers were dressed in gold
With her teacup she made a circle
She read the tea leaves
It had made her quite famous
Twenty pounds she had charged
And history was in the making
She foretold the future to many a man
Some cried, some laughed, some hated
Her crystal ball was her powerful tool
There was no mistaking her for a fool
This gypsy woman with her big heart of gold
She held a piece of jewellery
Visions had come to her fast
For now she saw her own destiny
And the lottery was up for grabs!

Sharon Lambley Dzus
Nottinghamshire

To Be A Waitress

Oh to be a waitress now that summer's here,
Serving chips and ice cream, coffee, tea and beer.
Dashing down the tables, clear the pots away,
It's hard work being a waitress on a busy summer's day.
We open bright and early to catch the morning rush,
A busy motorway restaurant, clean, but not so plush.
We cater for the driver, to stop and rest awhile,
Where he can take refreshment and service with a smile.
We serve a hearty breakfast, a light and tasty lunch,
Or if it's in-between, we'll cook you up some brunch.
Oh to be a waitress, we never seem to stop,
Serving eggs and burgers, milk and fizzy pop.
Writing down the orders in our little books,
Tear out the carbon copies and give them to the cooks.
They have a row of orders, each one done in its turn,
So if you've never cooked before, now's your chance to learn.
We fill the sugar basins, salt and pepper too,
Remove the crumpled place mats, replace them all with new.
Sterilise the cutlery, polish it so bright,
Scrub and bleach the wooden shelves 'til they are almost white.
Arrange the fancy cream cakes upon a silver tray,
Wash out and fill the milk machine, this must be done each day.
Then stock up the bar shelves with spirits, beer and wines,
Polish the big mirror until it really shines.
And then there are the customers, each one we have to greet,
Extend a friendly welcome and show them to a seat.
We hand to them a menu to choose a favourite dish,
Whether it be omelettes, salads, meat or fish.
We each have our own tables to wait on and to clean,
Filled with different people, from old to early teens.
From toddlers through to pensioners, such a lot we see,
And old familiar faces call once again for tea.
Oh to be a waitress when lunchtime comes around,
The crash of pots, and clink of cups becomes the only sound.
The cooks shout out the orders, 'Five plaice for table eight,'
And table three says, 'That's for me, I'm running rather late.
I haven't time to wait for long, the service is so slow,'
And all the time you're thinking, *just hurry up and go!*
Two egg and chips for table ten the cook shouts out to me,
But when I reach the table they say they ordered three.
And dashing down the restaurant, table six shouts, 'Here,
I'll have another plate of chips and half a pint of beer.'
'Could we have some ketchup?' asks table number two.
'And cheese for me,' shouts table three, 'I'll have some Danish Blue.'
'I'll have a pint of lager, a sherry for my wife,
And could I have a spoon please, and for the cheese a knife?'
Sliding down the polished floor with six plates on each arm,
It's hard to smile all the while and dish out constant charm.

Oh to be a waitress when rush hour is all through,
And we can put our feet up and have a decent brew.
We love our teatime cuppa, our daily little chat,
We even sneak a sandwich, we know we won't get fat.
The miles we walk in just a day will keep us slim and fit,
Sometimes we'll share some supper, a tea cake or some chips,
Catch up on all the gossip and count our daily tips.
It's nice to have a minute, how busy we have been,
A hundred different faces, and people we have seen.
Everything is tidy, neatly put away,
Ready for the morning to start another day.
We've washed down all the tables and set them all just right,
We never thought we'd get it straight for eight o'clock tonight.
The floor is swept and polished, we've worked without a fuss,
But driving round the corner is another bloody bus!
We stare in desperation and everyone just sighed,
As fifty hungry people come hurrying inside.
Oh to be a waitress in this busy little diner,
But I wouldn't change this job of mine for all the tea in China!

Jane Swann
Nottinghamshire

A Jewel In Our Crown

State of the art in submarine style
21st century, two thousand and three
Compartments waiting in single file
Ferrying passengers - you and me.

Not the first to be seen of their kind
The eighteenth century giving its call
By horse power pulled through the streets they would wind
Ferrying passengers - one and all.

Technology offered an electric outlook
Nineteen hundred and one giving power to grow
Animals spared as their duty it took
Ferrying passengers - to come and go.

On through the ages to reach present day
Cumbersome, slow then, sleek now, with speed
Travelling as centuries faded away
Ferrying passengers - fulfilling a need.

Shining like diamonds, enhancing our town
With lions to guard them, not standing alone
The tram is the new jewel in our city's crown
Ferrying passengers - Nottingham's own.

Linsi Sanders
Nottinghamshire

Christmas Time

When I was a child at Christmas time,
There was no such thing as yours and mine,
You get one thing, I get another,
It's time to share with a sister or brother.

Colouring books and crayons, an apple or pear,
Whatever we got we had to share,
Barbie dolls, Action Men or a toy car,
Whichever it was they were the best by far.

When I was a child at Christmas time,
Whatever we got it would be fine,
Dominoes, a football, a game of some kind,
Whatever it was we didn't mind.

Whatever we got we didn't care,
We never moaned once, oh that's not fair,
But most of all we had each other,
Sisters and brothers our father and mother.

It's who you're with that really matters,
Even if you're dressed in tatters,
So at Christmas time stay close to home,
And be thankful at Christmas you're not alone.

Jacqueline Appleby
Nottinghamshire

Inspiration

There are memories of my past life
In the verses that I write
To look at them, to read them
Brings pictures back to light
So many things forgotten
That suddenly appear
This and that and other
Lots of memories so dear
Putting pen to paper
Is not much at the time
It's just you have the feeling
Which ends up in a rhyme
Today is just one moment
A letter sent from you
The acceptance of some verses
From 1942

R Harvey
Nottinghamshire

Bulwell

My home town got its name many years ago
When a bull drove its horn into a rock and water started to flow
It flooded the ground which became known as the Bull's Well
That's how it derived its name, or so the legends tell

There has been a community here for over a thousand years
Built around the marshland which surrounded the River Leen
This area is still known to many as the Bulwell Bogs
The marshes have gone, but a bustling town can still be seen

Bulwell grew gradually into an industrial town
With hosiery mills, quarries and a coal mine
Many local people established businesses of repute
The community had many qualities easy to define

Its transport system was amongst the finest in the land
Three railway stations providing trains to everywhere
Two golf courses and many open spaces
And churches of every denomination represented there

Now the Main Street has been pedestrianised
In an effort to improve the environment
Most of the local businesses have disappeared
Replaced by amusement arcades and betting shops where hard-earned money
can be spent

The passage of time has seen many other changes
But any improvements are hard to perceive
I believe the Bulwell of yesterday was much better
A truth in which I earnestly believe

Ron Martin
Nottinghamshire

Culex

The setting of the Roman sun,
My day at end, hers just begun.
Sweat-soaked sheets upon the bed,
On blood the Devil's daughter fed.
Dreams deranged, exquisite pain,
White plastered walls your sister's stain.
From tortured sleep I lie awake,
A second helping her mistake.
With outstretched hand and deftly sly,
I look the beast straight in the eye.
One swift whack, her life finito,
That curse and scourge of man:
Mosquito.

Mark L Moulds
Nottinghamshire

Where Do You Go From Here?

In dreams you walk the strangest track, in life it is the same,
You dare not dither nor look back for then you'd feel the pain.

From the darkest corners of your mind, deep within your soul,
You keep on searching, trying to find a way out of this deep dark hole,
    Where do you go from here?

Your sanity controls your might, you're frightened and alone,
In this unventured sight, feeling the unknown,

Within this zone you can't see through, familiar landmarks forsake you,
In this whirlpool you are blind, no doors nor pathways can you find,
    Where do you go from here?

This load you carry is so great, no comforting arms await your gait,
You're pulled within an endless spin, and there you stay locked deep within.

Your silent screams of resounding fears, flow through streams of desperate tears,
    Where do you go from here?

All that's left for you to do is know your faith will see you through,
This pain and wrath that blocks your path, that's where you go from here.

Ann Crampton (Roony)
Nottinghamshire

Old Age?

Why did I go downstairs and have to go up again?
Did I forget my hanky, do I need a pen?
Did I switch the gas off, did I lock my door?
I really can't remember what I've done for sure

I must be getting old; I'm forgetting such a lot
Putting tea leaves in the cup and milk in the teapot
I'm getting absent minded, losing things as well
What I'll forget next you never can tell

I must try to concentrate on the job in hand
Otherwise I fear in trouble I will land
Oh to be young again and remember everything
But I suppose being young would other troubles bring

So I'll just be contented to do the things I can
Try not to worry if things don't go to plan
I have many blessings even if I am old
Good friends, food, clothing and shelter from the cold

Mary Shepherd
Nottinghamshire

The Life Story Of A Teddy Bear

A long time ago, I am a brand new bear, a gift-wrapped present
For a pretty little girl called Millicent.
A pampered, spiteful, wayward child,
A monster in her tantrums wild.
She stamped on me, ripped off my head,
Kind Nanny fixed me up again with her magic thread.

A damaged toy confined for years in a dusty attic,
Then along came Rosie, she thought I was fantastic.
I am her treasured special bear,
She kissed and caressed me, nibbled my ear,
A poor dumb teddy, see this frayed patch on my paw
That is a scar from the nursery floor.

A lady now, she gave me to a little boy,
He cherished me, I am his only toy.
Happy days, childhood with sweet sticky things,
Ice cream cones, lemonade, playing on the swings.
It is over now, I am bagged and ready for the bin,
I peep out, *ahhh*, he refused to drop me in.

I am off to the boot sale to be sold as tat,
Fiver for the bear, my bow tie's worth that.
Some patina, sticky, damaged, very old
Tat, or worth my weight in gold?
With a price reserve, a low expectation,
I am packed up, sent to the auction.

The auctioneer values me with a little smile,
'This bear is a veteran, he should make a pile.
Lot two, beloved toy, start at one hundred, any more?'
Someone on the telephone, just bid four.
I am distinguished, well preserved, quite unique,
Charming old ted, is now a genuine antique.

Violet Sinclair
Nottinghamshire

My Day In Sherwood Forest

Today in Sherwood Forest,
I wandered through the glen,
And wondered if those tales were true,
Of Robin and his merry men.

I came upon the Major Oak,
Hideout for Robin Hood,
Still majestic, but poles and ropes,
Now support the old man of the wood.

I sat beneath a nearby tree,
And gently closed my eyes,
'Tell me stranger, from whence came thou?'
I woke and gasped in great surprise.

There before me stood a man,
Lincoln green was his attire,
Behind him an oak, quite young and strong,
'Neath its branches stood a friar.

I told him since he'd roamed these woods,
Centuries had come and gone,
But his name was known around the world,
And his legend it still lives on.

Then that day I spent with Robin,
Romped with his band of men,
We fought the sheriff, robbed the rich,
Met Maid Marian in the glen.

While singing round the campfire,
The scene soon faded fast away,
Was it real, or but just a dream?
With Robin Hood had I spent the day?

Pauline Wilkins
Nottinghamshire

Ode To A Butterfly

OK! Where are you?
I'm a very patient lass,
Honest!
I catch a glimpse
Of your flashing colours
Then you fly away.
Nestle awhile
This shoulder won't stray.
You fly amongst the flowers
I marvel at your beauty
God created surely
On a beautiful summer's day.
So, alight my delicate creature
Maybe we can walk awhile.
Your wings brush my face
I will not look . . .
Perhaps one day
You'll just be there
Hitching a ride on these broad shoulders
Lending your colour to my soul.

Liz Osmond
Nottinghamshire

Someone's Wife

I thought there should
Be more to life
Than being someone's
Mum and wife

I'm not sure what else
I would be
If I was someone else
Not me

Perhaps ambition
Passed me by
I'm quite content
I'm not sure why

To just be here
And live my life
As someone's mum
And someone's wife

Sheila Jane Hobson
Nottinghamshire

Seasons

Spring has sprung again and so
Gardeners put ground to the hoe
They dig and plant for all their worth
Vegetables and flowers in the earth
Soon they grow and come to bloom
Flower and fruit will come quite soon
Summer steeps us with its rays
Of hot sunshine unbearing days
Evenings fall and cooler nights
Sometimes they stay quite warm and bright
The summer days and longer nights
Begin to change and birds to flight
For warmer climes they need to go
As leaves turn brown and golden glow
The swirling wind plays with the leaves
In autumn days fall from the trees
They cannot stay up, up aloft
But flutter downwards to the ground
They fall so softly on the ground
That hardly a whisper made of sound
Wintry weather is here again
Snow may fall and wind and rain
Damp wraps around you every day
Whilst watching children out to play
Garden's drab and dreary now
As farmers' fields to winter plough.

Bryan Maloney
Nottinghamshire

Love

Love knows no bounds, it has no caring
It is selfish to the very least
Like a sickness it overpowers you
A small taste, just like a feast
A constant dream in fevers of the heart
Quietened easily with tender touch
Of great elation of excitement
Quelled by words, I love you much.

John H Stafford
Nottinghamshire

Food For Thought

'How to have a good healthy life',
now often this statement I see,
and every time I read these words,
I wonder if on the planet I should be?

I've read fry-ups, crisps and greasy chips,
should not pass over my lips,
don't eat chocolates, leave cream cakes off my plate,
such things are a recipe for increasing weight.

I'm told don't drink pop unless it's sugar free,
use decaffeinated coffee, make herbal tea,
drinking water from the tap, I should never be,
as for enjoying a beer every night, how silly of me!

I can't sit outside on a hot summer's day,
that old sun will damage my skin in some way.
Should one smoke when the telly is off?
No way! Those fags will make you cough.

Oh dear me: once more on my TV,
there is someone telling me,
don't drink this, never eat that,
I'm getting confused, that is a fact.

Now I'm thinking, is it no more fry-ups for me?
Stop drinking Irish coffee, and ordinary tea,
keep crisps and beer away from my lips,
never again put salt on greasy fish and chips.

If everything I've seen and heard is true,
to have a good healthy life, what can I do?
It seems next time we have a hot summer's day,
I'd better stay indoors without a fag,
and slowly - fade away.

John Booth
Nottinghamshire

Can I Help You?

Those girls on hospital reception
have perfected the art of deception,
they manage quite well, their hysterics to quell
whilst offering the patients direction.

Hairpieces and wigs are amusing
when positions on heads they are losing,
the girls hide their mirth for all they are worth,
pretending their work they're perusing!

When wheelchairs are in short supply,
some patients are left high and dry,
but there goes our Shirl with a dance and a twirl,
to commandeer one on the sly.

A visitor commonly noted,
is Barty (brain surgeon, demoted),
he gathers fag ends to give to his friends
and eats leftover scraps till he's bloated!

Take heed of the advice suggested,
ensure that your hair's tried and tested,
don't stammer and stutter, nose dive in the gutter
and make sure that your food's well digested.

For when you are asking for X-ray,
or seeking the quickest and best way,
a burp may transpire, or worse, something dire -
and the 'team' will two dozen fat eggs lay!

Janice Mitchell
Nottinghamshire

God's Love

My love goes deeper than the ocean
it surpasses the length and breadth
of the largest rainforest
it scans every globular section
of our universe -
it ripples like a never-ending stream -
its sparkle exceeds the most expensive
vintage of wine -
it is full of love itself
like a big balloon
bursting to expand its inflation -
I am never deflated
if I acknowledge your love!

Mary Skelton
Nottinghamshire

Cyril The Squirrel!

Cyril the squirrel was lonesome,
In love with 'Babe Beryl' next door!
She made his heart go boom, boom, boom -
He was nuts on her for sure!
Each time he saw her leap the fence
His heart would leap for joy -
He hoped that they would soon be friends,
Yet Beryl played it coy!
The little minx! She played it cool,
As if she didn't care . . .
His love for her made him a fool -
He wondered, should he dare?
The babe had teeth, the babe had claws,
So cautious he must be . . .
He played it casual, took a pause,
He simply let her see
That guys must pick their moment, too.
Today may be too soon.
It isn't always, 'I love you!'
And then the honeymoon!
It isn't always, 'Now, now, now!'
The wait is worth the while.
Beryl caught on to this somehow
And thought, 'This guy's got style!'
In time, as nature took its course,
Cyril and Beryl grew close . . .
They simply learnt that love has laws -
As each good neighbour knows . . .

Denis Martindale
Nottinghamshire

If I Was

Superman
That comic strip hero
That magician, juggling balls
A fire-eater, running around walls
I'd change the world - I would
Not for me
But for the greater good of all!

Josh Brittain
Nottinghamshire

A Drunkard's Dream

Miss Peabody has passed away; they think she may have drowned
Her deathbed was a soggy mess when she was finally found
Her petard was well hoisted, and I think you will agree
That dandelions have caused her fate of drowning in her wee

Let's not forget the benefits she gave in her demise
Where would we be without Miss P and her true sacrifice
If she'd not stumbled headlong that night so long ago
The dandelions' secret - no one would ever know

The world would be so different, a sadder, drier place
We must not underestimate this improved human race
We can drink and have a skinful without that nagging dread
Of waking up six times each night and leaving our warm bed

The dandelions they work their charm as everybody knows
They bring on enuresis you just lay there and it flows
Damp beds each day are nothing when you've had a full night's snooze
It's thanks to Lady Peabody that we can sup more booze.

Shirley McIntyre
Nottinghamshire

That Place

Take me by the hand
And lead me to the place,
Where life is cotton-candy
And happiness is lace,

Where everything is well
And no one knows no sorrow,
Where all that matters is
The coming of tomorrow.

Take me to the place,
Where no one tries to win,
Where laughter is the cure
And sadness is the sin,

Where nature is unspoilt
And everything's 'let-be'.
Take me to that place,
Where everyone is free.

Elena Uteva
Nottinghamshire

The Winning Ticket

Sitting in front of the television with my lottery ticket and pen.
Waiting for my numbers to be called, the first one out is ten.
I quickly give a little tick, I only need five more.
The next ball rolls down the shoot and it is number four.
One more number to go and ten pounds will be fine.
I could not believe my eyes when out rolled number nine.
This is so exciting, it is too good to be true.
My heart started jumping when out came number two.
There are four ticks altogether, my hands are starting to shake.
Are my eyes deceiving me, is this all a big mistake?
Two numbers to go, I cannot take much more.
Now I am jumping and screaming, because out comes thirty-four.
My whole body is trembling, I'm in a terrible state.
I have won the lottery, because the bonus ball is eight.

Family will share our fortune, and never want for more.
Maybe we will buy a farm, and have animals galore.
Or a cosy mansion built on a few acres of land.
All this is possible, now we've won a few grand.
The telephone line is hot, we are telling all.
That 'the winning ticket' is on the wall.
Celebrations have started, champagne is on ice.
It's all unbelievable, but it's all very nice.
Drinks are being poured, more whisky and gin.
Glasses are raised to our lottery win.
Have I had too much to drink, everything's fading away?
I am struggling hard to gather my thoughts, of such a perfect day.
Suddenly the alarm goes off, I want to scream and scream.
I haven't won the lottery, it was all a bloody dream.

Barbara Russell
Nottinghamshire

Colours Of Scent

Violets, lavenders, crimson rose reds,
Adorned with emerald green leaves,
Waving their dainty petal heads,
Fragrance drifting on the summer breeze.

Delia McGregor
Oxfordshire

The City

The chill of the winter drills holes in his toes,
Frost crystals crackle beneath his feet,
He lives in a city where anything goes,
No one knows who he is on these streets.

Ice carpets the lawns by the first breath of dawn,
In shop doorways tramps battle the cold,
Within themselves so withdrawn, tired eyes so forlorn,
Their stories are never heard and untold.

The filth of the pavements lit orange by street lights,
Just above, the sky looms starless and Bible black,
Knife fights on weeknights are a memory past midnight,
These quiet hours belong to the insomniac.

A heartsick romantic transfixed by the city,
Yet blind to its borders of green,
Treads a well-trodden path with a laugh of self-pity,
While she sleeps he is alive in-between.

'Neath the dreaming spires of this monarch of shires,
Wired eyes drift skyward in awe,
A life lived in a city he reviles and admires,
A city he both hates and adores.

Cheradanine Ridgway
Oxfordshire

Dratted Midges

My garden isn't very big,
It isn't very swampy.
What brings this plague of midges
That makes my legs all lumpy?

Can it be the tiny pool,
Or a hedgerow hawthorn tree?
They've opened up a snack bar here,
Their favourite food is me!

One little thing I'd like to know,
How long do midges live?
I hope one 'sting' is all they get.
Have you advice to give?

Patricia Lindsay
Oxfordshire

The Final Word

So no more words - books, poetry or song
Take back your Homer, Shelley, Virgil and Donne
The page lies flat, unturned by day or night
And no comfort gained by its recite.
Have your couplets, lofty rhyme and thoughts
Its healing kind cannot be seen, hugged or felt.
Take this useless verse to be the final say
That we do not need such literary play.
Swallow them all, these mighty tomes,
And just bring me the tongue on which it is done.
The veins that stream with red hot blood
Far surpass these stringy lines
And so outclass
By ways and matter so much more profound.
You, your love, your touch, your life
They cannot bring or come even close,
So no body of work should even be called
Using a term so undeserved.
For you are gone and in your place
Are empty icons that just chase
With now seen feeble gestures
Floating, fighting, preening
Never to fill
Your empty space.

Selina Lim
Oxfordshire

My Teddy Bear

My father bought a teddy bear
When I was very small
It was a treasured gift to me
I loved it best of all
The years soon hurried by us
A wife I then became
But teddy still came with me
Although I changed my name
I've now become a granny
And my father passed away
But when I see that teddy bear
That love will always stay.

Sheila Elkins
Oxfordshire

The Unknown Writer

Many stories I have to tell
Creative is my mind
But what I write I'll never sell
So nobody will find

A chapter, at most I usually write
Loose to easy interest
A struggle to continue fight
But I need to rest

Mistakes annoy me, I must confess
I make too many to ignore
But it stops me writing less and less
My interest always soars

A muse I seek, to keep me writing
But inspired I am not
Descriptions turn to words like 'thing'
And responding back with 'what!'

Is it me, or have we got that bed
Television has clouded our minds
Creation is lost in people, it's sad
Empty brains is what I find

'I'm a writer,' I say aloud
'Nobody listens,' I sigh
But there, I stand proud
The unknown writer, am I.

James R Shewell
Oxfordshire

Star Lore

Sages deep in star lore
Say there's life out there,
Primitive, definitive -
Does anybody care?

Fossils tombed in space rock
Soulless science loves -
Have they half the interest
Of what breathes and moves?

Sterile, arid moonscapes -
How could they surpass
Snow slopes of December,
Fields of summer grass?

Dreams of zooming sunwards,
Some cosmonauts delight;
Oh, give me dusk and noonday,
Not dawnless, stellar night.

Cease hubristic probings.
Moon dust's hueless stuff,
Leave the stars their secrets,
For me, green Earth's enough.

Cold facts for me are often
Far better left untold.
Oh, leave me stars of silver,
Oh, leave me suns of gold!

Emma Kay
Peeblesshire

A Triolet For Bradley

He is the boy to be our pride and joy,
Don't look far, Bradley is our boy,
Happy go lucky is his fame, but hoy!
He is the boy to be our pride and joy,
He is a precious bundle, not a toy,
Alert he is, but somewhat coy,
He is the boy to be our pride and joy,
Don't look far, Bradley is our boy.

Mary Lawson
Perthshire

The Rose Of Glenlyon

Petals pink to white
Soft touch
Velvet
Still a starlight

Mist prances
Round
Trying to steal
The sweetheart's advances.

On the stem
Thorns
Maiden pure
Dewdrops light them

Thirsty the rose
Drinks
The water of breath
That chose

Sweetheart broken
Lovers' bough
Kiss
Always unspoken

Blood shed
In memories
Head
Flower is never dead.

Jan Ross
Perthshire

Guidance

Sailing like a ship caught in the wind
My sail takes me where the waves win
A crew aboard, working against the tide
Rolling as the body is caressed
Crashing, controlling water powers her every move
Trying to steer against, to fight and be strong
Heading in the opposite direction, this must be wrong

Can't seem to win, she's tired from the fight
The ocean lay her soul to the floor
But tides are beginning to ease off
And the sail once again takes control
The wind ushers her along guarding their safety
Every crewman tired from the journey
They've reached the sandy beach
Small grains beneath their feet, feel so safe

Lying down on solid ground, a place of haven
Can breathe out a sigh
They're in one piece
Alive she is and so are they
Sunshine from the shore, the life they can see
Tides below that surrender from peace
Thief stole their fire, their rage I have felt
Before you they pleaded to your mercy they knelt

All aboard they set sail with she
Access to creation leaves them with he.

Zoë Thompson
Perthshire

Venice In Peril

City like no other in this world,
exuding grandeur, art and style.
Her colours permeate the soul -
pale gold sunsets over Grand Canal . . .

Oro pallido . . .

City born from shimmering lagoon,
her stunning skyline so serene.
Bridges, churches and domes abound -
vaporettos and gondolas, the only traffic sound.

City where footsteps soft echo,
whispering through lanes and alleys.
She entices us through her maze
and we're blissfully lost once again.

City of romance? None can compare -
forget Paris and Rome, let me take you there . . .
Until you've seen the Grand Canal at dusk
from Rialto Bridge - you've never lived . . .

City so vibrant as sun goes down -
St Mark's Square by night is divine.
Musicians tune up as we sip
chilled Bellinis and Prosecco wine.

Oro pallido . . .

City sinking in crumbling decay,
yet retains her charm and beauty.
Venice-lovers all round the world -
please save her from the acque alte.

Irene S Johnston
Perthshire

Untitled

The tiredness creeps over my brain
Like a slug leaving a trail behind -
Still tired from yesterday - not enough sleep last night.
Head is buzzing . . . body feels alright.

Eyes will soon be popping,
Bags below will show,
Face will show a pallor
Where there used to be a glow.

Sleep - sleep . . . come to me
And caress me with your touch
My body and my brain
Both need to rest so much.

I feel so tired, I want to cry,
If only I could rest.
To lie down and sleep the whole night through
Would be the very best.

Lorna Grant
Perthshire

No Entry

The road back is thick with thorns,
Brambles hug the way, strewn glass
Waits with cutting edges of pain,
Dark thickets, where every danger lurks,
It's too far back along that road.

For tired-already folk
No good will venture forth
From the heavy branches, drooping
With tears, dark, silent
Dripping wells spring up
Beneath the soft soil;
Grass cannot grow in that place
For no sunlight lingers there now.

A once beautiful place, it broods
And frets, on its spindle of decay,
Chained and guarded by time's embrace,
You will not be able to find a way
Through, never,
Back to the past.

Janet Hughes
Powys

A Native Pony

Short, square
An engine far too big
For its frame
Character. Intelligence
A stance of importance.
Weaned, branded, gelded
His welcome to mankind
Forced restraint, girth
Galling his skin
Metal hitting his teeth
Bruising his bars.
Predators, all bidding for his meat
Or if he's lucky his mind.
He's worked out so many evasions
In human form there's no doubt
Borstal for naughty boys.
Show him a bridle
He'll show you a 'giraffe'
Show him a saddle
He'll show you an unfriendly bottom.
Head collar? Well OK.
As long as you move as though on the moon
Weightless, quiet and painstakingly slow
Move too quickly and you've lost him -
For today.
You cannot ask for trust
If you cannot be trusted yourself
He will never forget
But he will, inexplicably
Forgive in *time.*

Floella Nash
Powys

Christmas Stars

Snow fell down one starless night
From out the plume of lonely clouds,
To decorate the land with white,
Adorn the hills with pallid shrouds.

The eyes that gleamed behind the glass
Watched the weather rage outside,
Saw the darkness come to pass,
Filled with wonder, saucer-wide.

Then from the ether, from the swirl,
Through a split in clouded night,
A silver shaft impaled the world
And lit the earth with vibrant light.

Upon the eve before the day
Iconic magic rose and shone,
At once the darkness cast away,
A Christmas star to wish upon.

In modern times of strife and war,
When hatred reigns a harsh regime,
It ill behoves us to deny
Our children of a better dream.

So on the eve before the day,
Make the demon year be gone,
And teach them of a better way,
Of Christmas stars to wish upon.

Tony Bush
Powys

I Am Not Gone

I am not gone, I am still here always by your side,
Forever watching over you, smiling with golden pride.
I am not gone, when you need me I am here,
I could never desert you, one I hold so dear.
I am not gone, my presence you may sometimes feel,
My love will always nurture, my spirit forever real.
I am not gone, I live on eternally as an everlasting light,
Caring, bringing comfort in the saddest dark night.
I am not gone, the veil between us is not what you think,
Just a thought away and our souls do link.
I am not gone, we exist still in the universe of being,
Remember that I am happy, paradise I am seeing.

Marlene Mullen
Renfrewshire

Empty Spaces

This world is full of hatred, violence and drugs,
Whatever happened to that simple thing called love.

So many empty spaces in this world today
So many people having to fight to even get a say
Innocent lives taken from us every minute of our daily lives.

Brothers, sisters, husband and wives,
Screaming to save their families
So they can get on with their lives.

War, violence, bloodshed
So many tears shed for innocent ones dying instead.
What has happened to this world of thine.

So many pray for peace today
But what can one do or even say?

Empty spaces, broken hearts
So many families' lives torn apart.

Please no more violence, no more war,
No more racism, no more drugs
Then no more innocent lives taken and given to God above.

Anastasia Williams Cowper
Renfrewshire

The Victims

Why is the world still filled with hate?
Through centuries it's fed the fire,
the innocents left to their fate,
by tyrants bent on vengeful desire.

How is it that men never learn
to live their lives, forget the past?
They plot and scheme, their minds still burn
to maim, to kill with violent blast.

When will it end, what will it take
to change their minds, settle for peace?
Start life anew, their choice to make,
lay down their arms, let warring cease.

Where will we be this time next year,
facing new hope fearlessly?
No longer have to shed a tear
for those who suffered needlessly.

Ann Odger
Renfrewshire

The Remedy

It is so hard, this getting old,
My neck is sore, my feet are cold,
And when I hear my kneebones creak,
I'm feeling like a human freak.

My eyes grow dim and slow my walk,
I start to stammer when I talk.
I used to hear the green grass grow,
Alas! this is no longer so.

My memory used to be fantastic
But is no longer so elastic.
Events that did not worry me
Seem like a nightmare now you see.

At night, in bed, to flee the pain
I toss and look for sleep in vain,
And when I wake, start getting busy
I stumble, for my head gets dizzy.

As life was really not much fun
I thought, *I'll ask my doctor son*
For doctors know and always will
Prescribe a potion or a pill.

'My son,' I asked him, hopefully,
'Perhaps you know a remedy?'
When smiling kindly, I was told:
'There is one thing, *not getting old.'*

Gertrude Black
Renfrewshire

Music

The food of life to me is music
It revives me, enlivens me
Bringing peace, relaxation
Hope for the future

The type of music, must be live
It can be light, classical, modern
But it must have depth of feeling
Life is only worthwhile with music

May it always be there for me
Whether in house, on disc, in theatre
In the plush opera house, the quiet living room
Music is the food of life to me.

Carol Habrovitsky
Renfrewshire

The Dreamless Dream We All Dream

I went to sleep and dreamt;
That an angel stood at my bed.
The angel looked at me and said, 'It's time.'
'I haven't done anything yet,' I said.
'Please don't take me.'
'What do you wish to do?' asked the angel.
'I wish to dream, to desire.'
'And what do you dream and desire?'
'Love and happiness,' I said.
'Do you believe in love and happiness?'
'It is what keeps me going.'
'And do you hope to one day find it?'
'Yes, but I won't if you take me.'
'Very well,' said the angel, 'I shall come back
When you have loved and are happy.'
And with that, the angel was gone.
And I awoke to find my angel
Asleep next to me, and I was happy
And I wished for sleep no more,
For I would dream the angel would come
And take me from my angel.
Oh! How I wished for sleep no more.

Naveed Arshad Saleem
Renfrewshire

Evening Thoughts

When darkness falls
It is a sign,
Another day is at an end.
And with the evening
Comes the thought,
Was this a day well spent?

Did I do all
I should have done,
Did I think of my fellow men,
Offer to comfort
And to help
Just how and when I can?

If this should be
My last day here,
I want to leave no task undone.
Would it be so, then
Don't be sad.
Think of me when I'm gone.

Helga Dharmpaul
Ross-shire

The Stone (Lia Fail)

Far it travelled, Scots child of dreams,
Much it felt, much it has seen,
So you ask, where this pillow lies,
It is kept in heart, till the time arrives,

To those who have met upon the stone,
Secret of life it has shown,
Where came the thoughts of Tele wise,
That transcends the mind,
To a future's kind,

For the one who is ready,
For the one who has come,
The stone shall sing,
It is I . . . destiny.

David Harnetty
Ross-shire

All That Jazz

Take a moody moan,
From a moonlit mellow saxophone,
Make a loving groan,
From a tinny, tempestuous trombone,
Imagine a moonlit lake,
With you and me alone,
A tender kiss,
From my young miss,
Give it all a man can take
Think about a big brass drum,
Or a harmonica and hear it hum,
When each note,
Sends you afloat,
Let the rhythm surround you,
Let rhapsody confound you,
What is this bunk,
What is this junk,
A recipe for love,
Sent from above,
A boom, a bang,
A ching, a clang,
Add a dash of phizaaz
What is this?
It's all that jazz.

Alan Pow
Roxburghshire

The Village

At the end of the lane does the village begin,
mellow thatched cottages set in gardens serene
together with splendid old coaching inn
surrounding the sycamore shaded green.

On a warm summer's day hardly anything stirs,
just the clip-clop of horseshoe on metal road.
A black and white cat in dusty porch purrs
and the distant sound of a lawn being mowed.

An old man his garden does lovingly tend
surrounded by colourful scented flowers
and a vegetable patch over which he does bend
hoeing and weeding for sun-ripened hours.

The school is all quiet, the children within
absorbed in their lessons as the world passes by,
but soon a bell rings and playtime will begin
as they all tumble out under azure blue sky.

The grand village church with lofty stone spire,
adjacent to manor house, walled garden and lake,
accessed by a lane edged with campion and briar,
its weekly communion the vicar will take.

In a shady side street, two ladies do talk,
the door of the village shop opens and closes,
a man with his dog goes out for a walk
and the summer air's filled with scent of the roses.

A war memorial stands close to the well
remembering two wars of bombing and pillage
by recording the names of the soldiers who fell
and will never return up the lane to the village.

Alistair L Lawrence
Rutland

Rain In The Garden

In random clusters descend the whispers of cloud
With radar precision strike - and victory cried
Sun sacrificed palms dance to the tune
Where succulent bombs bounce and vibrate to feather wound
Tulip kings bow their heads for their reign is right
To weep cold tears from petal platforms and raw stem pipes
Wrapped in vapour, like cotton sheets in dew
Sweet scent penetrates each second the crusade is through
Blades and blooms breathe to give today's blessing
How rich is the carpet of goodness that follows the torment of shelling

Tracey Powell
Rutland

Frothy

Funny little things excite me . . .
like a visit to the beach
the morning after a stormy night
when it looks just like a bucket
of frothy coffee has been spilt
all over it . . .
or could it be
the resident mermaid
has left soapy bubbles to fade
after washing her beautiful ebony hair
before secretly performing at the local fair
on the eve of a summer full moon
and sometimes on a Tuesday afternoon . . . ?
Or is it nearby fairies
playing out late and forgetting to tidy up
after painting and spraying each other's wispy wings
and leaving behind telltale rings . . . ?
. . . I like to sit and smile awhile
and think such childish thoughts may still
happen occasionally . . . blocking out neatly
all traces of reality . . .
I recall your words just hours ago . . .
tomorrow looks like we may get snow . . .
makes me laugh to her your precise forecast
every morning over toast crumbs at breakfast . . .
how would coffee froth show up on your weather charts . . .
which direction, which colour the arrows and darts . . . ?
Funny little things excite me . . .
most of all the sight of spilt frothy coffee . . .

Netta Irvine
Shetland Islands

Winter

Winter is here cold and clear
Kids out to play, so fun to hear
Scattered snow upon the ground
Sounds of laughter all around

Steven Evans
Shropshire

Images

Oh weep for the false images
Of self and others,
The starved, emaciated images
Retreating,
Fleeing into the depths
Of time,
The fugitive images.

Weep for the false images
Broken like garish idols,
Swept from the sanctuary,
Whipped by the winds
And scattered -
Who will collect
The broken, painted pieces?

Weep for the false images
Nursed in safe places,
Secretly;
When they are threatened,
Save them!
Flee with them into the wilderness,
Alone.

Dorothy Buyers
Shropshire

WINNER!

Looking Forwards

No longer sunshine - from that day
Only darkest skies of grey
I wait and wait for skies of blue
Sunny skies when I met you
Because of you my life began
That golden day, you took my hand
And showed to me life's golden way
No longer raindrops on that day
Then time just went on winged feet
But no my empty heart does beat
Till you repeat, repeat, repeat
Your love for me is mine alone
Now no one to call my own
Till stormy grey clouds turn to blue
Like summer days I spent with you.

Joan Winwood
Shropshire

The Clock Struck Midnight

A whispering voice could be heard
In the silence
In the silence of night
In the deep dark caves of my mind
And behind that soft voice of reason
I thought I heard the faintest sound
Of an angel's harp
Playing upon my heart strings
And a hand
Reached out from the mists of time
And pointed to my future.
The clock struck midnight above the hearth
And the full moon's ethereal light
Forced back the dark blanket of night
To reveal familiar colourless shapes
Embers glowed red amongst the ashes
Of the dying fire
And the muffled sound of an owl
Drifted upon the mists of silent night
Through the open window
And so I rose
At the first minute of a new day
In quiet solitude
And waited for the dawn.

David M Walford
Shropshire

The Tree

With lessons for all
Standing majestic and tall.
A tree shows us what we should be
Succour for all who to your canopy flee.
Giving shade from the heat of the day.
Shelter is offered to creatures in need
As they gather to feed at your feet.
Then when shadows lengthen and sunshine fades
The brightness of colours you show.
These lift the spirits, give hope, till the dawn,
When winter's past and spring is born.
Yes a tree standing majestic and tall.
Really does have a lesson for all.

Alice Turner
Shropshire

A Rhyme To Make Earth Sleep

Silver moon over countless mile,
Spinning Earth under dark sun dial.
Rivers burn with liquid heat,
Animal and human with nothing to eat.
Forests move and birds are still,
No air or empty space to fill,
or need to sleep or need to kill.

Technology and nature, lost and found,
No notice to us of things around,
Hills see valleys, ground sees sky,
Left sees right and low sees high,
Clouds are gone when stars are here,
People rejoice when far is near,
or dark is light and they do not fear.

Cradles rock, songs are sung,
Time is done when bells are rung.
In cold and dark, creatures alive,
But humans destroyed where they would thrive.
The Earth rotates and dusk is dawn,
People wake, their life goes on
And cannot imagine when it's gone.

Random things we cannot tell,
Like how or why our cities fell,
Why Earth was mad,
For her nature gone bad,
Perhaps it's just the things we reap,
And though the pain, it makes me weep,
I pray for the Earth, a peaceful sleep.

Pency-Rhaine Byrne
Somerset

To Be Or Not To Be

It won't be long before I retire,
When I could be lazing by the fire.
It would be nice to be wrapped up warm
Instead of getting up at dawn.
But then I think of the girls' night out
And all the friendly faces,
Making residents cups of tea and
Tying up their laces.
The pension isn't very much,
I know that I'll feel poor, but
If my aches and pains don't cripple me,
I'll stay for one year more.

J Faulkner
Somerset

Admiral Nelson

(I have written this poem for the celebrations of the 200th anniversary of the Battle of Trafalgar)

Horatio Nelson, an admiral so fine,
Commanded the Victory, flagship of the line.
Although he had only one arm and one eye,
He inspired his men to keep fighting or die.
Shouting, 'England expects,' as they faced that great fleet
Of the French and the Spanish. 'We will defeat.'

The battle raged on, full of gunsmoke and noise.
'Twas gallantly fought, though some were mere boys.
Injured or dead, they watched comrades fall,
Then Nelson himself was hit by a ball
From a sniper's musket, and carried below.
The surgeon knew that it was a death blow.

To encourage his men, he grimly held on,
Refusing to die 'til the battle was won.
And so Admiral Nelson, both gallant and brave,
From Napoleon's hand, our England did save.
To honour this battle we've Trafalgar Square
And Nelson's Column, rising high in the air.

Gwen Hoskins
Somerset

The Dragonfly

I'd love to be a dragonfly,
With elegance and grace,
Moving swiftly and dynamically,
An arrow steak in space.
Jinking and darting,
Dazzling to the eye,
Shaft of brilliant colour
In a summer sky.
Still as a statue,
Resting after flight,
Sphinx-like, enigmatic,
A mesmerising sight.
It is my favourite insect
'Bove ladybug 'n' butterfly,
Whenever I glimpse one
I just sigh and sigh.
In that slender form I see
All those things I'll never be!

Sue Cann
Somerset

The Walking Boy

He says that autumn always brings him change
As everything leaves green, he feels the empty stage
Kicking through the trees' dry tears, he says it's strange
That this time of year should always raise a little fear

He says he's walked these fields for liberty
Cap within his hand, evenings spent in certain doubt
With November air, the fair of carnival
Like another world, one night that turns your head around

Working in a rhythm that will disregard time
Thinking in a circle, with no reason or rhyme
I'm talking to the walking boy
I'm talking to the walking boy

And he knows the time he has spent wandering
In-between the windy lane and the garden with his graves
And he feels that all those days remembering
Were just like another autumn, when two became a crowd

And he's sad to feel the new morning chill
Thin silhouettes of trees, fingers at the breeze
And the earth's new gown of yellow, red and brown
So he walks again and still he feels down

I'm talking to the walking boy
I'm talking to the walking boy

James Bull
Somerset

Love And Peace

When all the world is yours
Bright and clean and shiny
The sun extends its warmth on us
The seasons thread all over us
The trees go green then brown
We go round and round
We age - get old
Wonder what we are doing here
Where are we going?
Who are we?
Find the answers, don't despair
Love lots and have no cares
God grant you health and happiness
Wealth would be nice
But love is the greatest gift of all, we know not why

Rita Jane Williams
Somerset

The Irish Fisherman

I'm sorry I didn't ask your name,
This fisherman of mine,
Who helped me put my bait on and re-arrange my line.
You told me you lived on a small island,
Just off the Southern Irish Shore.
In your lilting soft voice told me, you were fishing as a boy of four.

At first I didn't see your tent, way up upon the shore,
A funny sort of blue thing, with lines from top to floor.
I did not know at that time, that this was your small abode,
A small pod of solace, below the quiet, and windswept road.

It's a hard life I believe you've had, with your weather-beaten face,
The distant stare when fishing, far out across the bay.
There seems to be a sadness there, which, like a cloud of rain,
As quickly as it comes, a twinkle of the eye shows
And the sunny smile, is back again.

A helicopter passed overhead, at this you really stared,
'I've been in a few of those,' you said, pulling on your line tightly.
With mind made up I queried this, 'How come,' I said, so brightly,
He didn't answer straight away, then,
Twenty-seven years I served, in the Paratroopers. He smiled and said,
'It's hard to settle down you know, after many years of fighting,
So I walk and fish my way around the coast,
I'm always just a passing.'

It's a strange life of ours, on this green and sun blessed planet,
We come across a stranger, from where we do not know.
It's just a chance of crossing paths,
You never had to plan it.
Fate takes a hand, and off you go, along life's chosen way.
To dream and think of many things,
Like my fisherman, on, firth of Solway.

Elizabeth Turner
Somerset

Wedding Photo

How did it come to this?
We were talking
Then
We were shouting.

We were laughing
Then we were crying.
How did it come to this?

My ears bled to hear you
- a high squawking monster -
As plates sliced by me
Cutting chunks out of the wall,
Desecrating photos
    flimsily held by failing strings
And a failing us.

How did it come to this?

I fear it was just a matter of time
And that was all we had left holding us together,
A sweat clasp, silk on a river,
Marble skimming, skimming
Then drowning.

The years had been good
Just not to us.
Sun and sea and sun and sea and sun and
So much sea,
Barbecues, family, friends, children,
Everything for a 'picture-perfect family'
But pictures tell of a moment,
A second or less.

Peter Cole
Somerset

Nostalgia

The weather's nice today my dear,
come lift your eyes, come wipe your tears.
No time to mourn the sighs of past,
bequeath the lark to sing at last.
Let your spirit touch the sky
raise up your wings and flutter high.
Colours of the world shall shine,
flowers at your feet are thine.

The grass so green upon the hill
with daffodils and falling bells.
Blue are they in summer sun
I cannot count them one by one.
For if I do my eyes would see
so many cowslips mingling free.

The weather's nice today my dear
come hold the hand who follows near.
Today come live upon a throne
reach out your heart to Heaven's home.
Pleasant pastures come with age
old windmills turn of love's assuage.
'Tis often I would see you smile
if now for only just a while.
Angry were the years I know
where leopards hid beneath the snow.
How lambs they bleat in pastures new
they bleat of love so young and true.

Nostalgic of the thinking years
remembering such with childhood tears.
Running through the knee-high wild
Campion's flower, and poppy's child.
Countless primrose and cuckoo flower
Buttercups and timeless hours.
Where violets basked in proud esteem
beside the chattering old mill stream.

Comfort then my stolen child
be comforted, be reconciled.
Come feel the soft and fresh wind blow
Lift up your heart, your gentle soul.
I am of old and ever new
I come, I wait in thoughts of you.

Michael A Massey
Somerset

Shangri-La

Green fields stretch languidly
Towards mountains rising
On the far side of the valley.
The water sparkles in canals
Irrigating a generous landscape.

Terraces climb the valley sides
To dwellings hewn from mountain rock,
Clinging to ledges.
Homes, workshops, temple and palace,
Rising up the steep mountainside
On it and of it - part and parcel.

Shambhala in deepest Tibet
Hidden from strangers,
Hidden from politics and celebrity.
This last has been gained over centuries.
Legend of loveliness, peace, dreams.

All was lost long ago.
Strangers found you and were welcomed
But their dream became envy.
There followed war, kings were killed
And peace deserted you
All that was left was the valley
And the ruins
And the legend of the dream.

           *   *   *

Now the dream exists.
The green fields full of cattle
Cut by rhynes of shining water.
Blue lias from the hills
Builds homes, farms and church,
Rising up the hill,
On it and of it - part and parcel.

A place welcoming strangers.
Not hidden from politics or war -
Not making those important.
Not hidden from celebrity
But not needing it.

A place of peace, dreams and loveliness.
Not hidden from view
But not easily seen.

Penny Allwright
Somerset

Before You Live In Somerset

Before you live in Somerset
There's something you should know,
Red deer come roaming on your land
In rain, in sun, in snow.

They prune your hedges, eat the buds
Of crocus, tulips, thyme
And the fragrant scarlet roses,
All gone before their time.

This morning I saw a young fawn
Relaxing by my stream.
His mother came to move him on,
I watched as in a dream.

It's worth the disappointing sight
Of losing a few stalks -
When you can see the wild red deer
Reclining in their haunts.

West Somerset is where I live
And hope I always will.
Each season brings new surprises
Yet beauty stays here still.

Evelyn Golding
Somerset

The Sandy Beaches

The sandy beaches lay empty
The children no longer play
For winter is upon us
Cold winds sweep across the bay

The waves are rough and boisterous
Bringing the seaweed to the shore
Which will wait for the next ebb tide
To take it out to sea once more

Gone are the sailing boats
Gracefully floating on the sea
The sandy beaches have seen it all
And now blows about quite free

The sky is dark and overcast
We are in for rain or snow
People are all warmly dressed
When on their way they go

Violetta Ferguson
Somerset

Somerset

I love the fields of Somerset,
To walk across the grass -
Buttercups and daisies
I am a country lass.

Primroses and violets
Along the woodland way -
To walk among the bluebells
A heavenly carpet lay.

Springtime and summer
Colours ever changing -
Scarlet poppies in the corn
Wheat and barley growing.

The olde worlde village,
The church where we were wed.
Happy are the memories
Here I was born and bred.

The farm on the hillside
Where I love to roam,
This is my Somerset
This is my home.

Ellen M Lock
Somerset

Spring

Light
Bright
Across
The
Countryside
Trees
Beside
Lanes
And
Ditches.
Farms,
Fields
Like
Nests
From
Last
Year.

Nicola Barnes
Somerset

Summer . . .

I pushed my chair into undergrowth
crushing honeysuckle that walled
the sun from me.
Deep into straggling wild roses
(once my father's tended pride) . . .
breathed in nectar
as my eyes slid shut,
warmth and breeze enveloping my bare skin.
The nearby humming bumblebee
sucked the honeysuckle
flower to flower,
never dreamed of bothering me
as I found respite from August heat.

Plunged in the midst of August heat
appear signs of autumn's advance.
Bleached grass lies beneath
clusters of green berries and fat red rose hips . . .
the laden summer apple bough
has dropped its fruit to rot,
whilst the heavy autumn crop
is reddening at an alarming rate.
Loathe to leave hot scented days behind
autumn marches towards us . . .
(moments of doubt and a longing to kick off shoes and lay back
in the heat of the sun)
but he draws the drapes of darkness
each night earlier than the one before.
Golden blessed, but trailing
dead leaf debris behind him
to banish that shining summer.

Jane Isaac
Somerset

Somerset

Somerset - county of sea and sun
Rolling hills and levels and moors
Coombes and farms with frolicking lambs
Cider apples and cheeses too
Strawberries so delicious with cream
Somerset is more than a dream

Joyce Beard
Somerset

Temples Of The Gods

Sssh, softly, solicitously step;
rooted well, a tiny tremble talks,
but yes, they have been dancing,
see their twisted trunks?
Silent statues,
forest guardians
hold their breath
so we can't tell
that they are living
spirits of the green-wood,
architecture of the gods.
Cloaked with umbrage,
sacred space,
nests in tired flight,
furniture, fuel for fire,
food for foraging,
friends for hugs,
forgotten for their gaseous use;
Trees of life, knowledge and enlightenment,
wiser than the aged sages,
stories in their rings re-tell;
climb aboard
but do not hang,
from the gallows pole, remember,
resurrection sprang.

Alexandra Rice
Somerset

Somerset County

S easide towns and countryside too
O ver Cheddar sometimes skies are blue
M arkets selling clothes and bric-a-brac
E ver friendly townsfolk chat
R ivers and seaside pure and clean
S omerset sets a beautiful scene
E very cake, well most have cream
T ake a trip down yonder and you'll see

Peter G H Payne
Somerset

Immortal

Like a snowstorm in the desert.
Like a sunbeam in the night.
The past becomes the present,
the soldier flees from fight.

A memory long forgotten.
A pinprick in the past.
Repeating raw emotions.
Fear that's made to last.

Like an echo in a crowded room.
Like a ripple in a storm.
The past comes back to haunt you,
forgotten pain reborn.

A single word,
a smile.
Attention from a foe.
Enough to make you reconsider,
what you forgot so long ago.

Like history repeating.
Like enemies on your side.
The black, merging with the white.
No longer free to cry and hide.

A struggle and a test.
Reborn within your mind.
A second chance . . . tempting!
But can the Devil become kind?

Amy Caiels
Somerset

A Little Learning

The books are stacked on shelves and piled on chairs
as knowledge overflows capacity
of any library to store its wares.
The Internet will quickly set us free
from space constraints: we can embrace with glee
the bits and bytes and Ebay. Critics scoff
in vain; until the day the power goes off.

Rose Docherty
Somerset

In Tribute

There is something I will ne'er forget,
The time when Joyce and I first met.
And we both knew right from the start
That we had touched each other's heart.
Love at first sight is very rare,
But we just knew that then and there
Our own true love we both had found,
And with love's shackles we were bound.
So many happy years passed by
Such wedded bliss for Joyce and I.
With our family, such happiness
And fifty-seven years together we were blessed.
Now those years, fond memories must be
A comfort and a solace for all the family.
My love for Joyce forever lives within my heart,
For all the time that we may be apart.
And God alone knows when the time will be
When once again my own dear Joyce I see.
She was ever gentle, loving, kind,
The sweetest lady you could ever find.
The same if you were husband, family or friend
And on that note this tribute I must end.

Dennis Brockelbank
Somerset

Seasons

Now the winter fast approaches,
Withered is my field of dreams,
Sadness in my heart encroaches,
Shattering souls, the vision screams.

Summer's halcyon days have ended,
Autumn steals with latent shade,
Gold and brown to amber blended,
Winter's chill soon to invade.

Life to barren landscape harnessed,
Never more will spring resurge,
Time has gathered in my harvest,
Dreams too late to re-emerge.

Days drift down to final number,
Shiver under laden sky,
Wreathed in snow-clad icy slumber,
In my field of dreams I lie.

Dorothy Neil
South Glamorgan

Changing Seasons

Summer's gone, winter's here, nights are drawing in,
The memories of those sunny days are slowly becoming dim,
Days of sitting on the beach surrounded by the sea,
Children running everywhere, happy to be free.

Smiles upon their faces, laughter in the air,
For this time we do forget all our daily cares,
The sound of children laughing is more precious than gold,
They fill our lives with happiness and give us wealth untold.

The sun is sheltered by the clouds, no longer shining bright,
The days are getting shorter, soon the day becomes the night,
But in these changing seasons, there's only one thing that we lose,
An hour of daily sunshine, so why are we so blue?

Let's look upon our children, for they seem to know what's best,
They found the gift we're looking for that brings us happiness,
It's nothing to do with seasons, nothing to do with rain,
The only thing we need to do, is become like a child again.

They don't care if it's raining, so what if the sky's not blue,
Who cares if their new coat doesn't match their new shoes?
Only one thing that matters, that stands out from the rest,
Is that someone loves them, forget all about the rest!

Sheila Johanson
South Glamorgan

Glamorgan

From Cardiff to Rhossili,
With its rugged coastline and powerful sea,
The towns that you pass through
And all the history,
Cardiff's museum and art gallery
And its wonderful impressionists
Given by the Davies sisters
One of their most treasured bequests
The gentle vale,
With the occasional thatched cottage
On the road to Porthcawl,
Passing through Newton and Nottage,
The docks and the pits,
Which are now memories,
And the museums which are built
To remind us of these
Now, with the Millennium Stadium and Millennium Centre,
So many people enter
Cardiff and wish to stay.
It's the service industries that are now the order of the day.

Rachel E Joyce
South Glamorgan

A Poem From A Story By An Alien Insect Queen
(A poem for posterity)

In nineteen forty-five they watched
Them through an envelope gate
Watch the Jews with fear
Watched the Germans hate
To them the Jews
A waste of space
To be destroyed
By the master race
Yet England and America
Won the war
And said no to what
The Reich had in store
And said at Nuremberg
The war is won
And said to the Jews
Your freedom's begun
Yet in the year
Nineteen fifty-two
Picked up by an army
Radio crew
Bounced off the moon
A signal transmitted
Earth co-ordinates
Were what they envisaged
Over Nevada
The co-ordinates crossed
Once understood
The signal was lost
So over Nevada desert air space
With the American Army
A meeting took place.

Jack John Georgion
South Glamorgan

The Explorer

Let the pavement be the carpet under *my* feet,
Let my battered *Adidas Superstars* walk miles,
Let the brassy builders boner, as I bolt past.
Let me get caught in gridlock, not trapped in wedlock,
Let my poignant perfume pierce prejudice's nose,
Let me tie suave stiletto strings, not apron strings.

Let me smell stale Sambuca scent upon my shirt,
Let my cuisine be palatable *Pot Noodle*,
Let me compulsively scour the catalogues.
Let me dice with debt, not chicken,
Let my belly bulge with Brie, with no kids to feed!
Let me stir among bitchy friends, not his porridge.

Let me watch re-runs of *'Spaced'* till my heart's content!
Let me smoke cigarettes solemnly and reflect,
Let me dye my old *Levis* green for eco cause.
Let me smell the green of weed and not *Fairy*,
Let me cater for communism, not a man,
Let me be a sloppy Cinderella out late.

As one day the tarot cards tell,
As one day the tea leaves read,
As one day the crystal ball predicts,
I shall only care for housework
With callus-covered mitts.

Sarah Parry
South Glamorgan

Friendship

Not made with pots of gold,
It's made with caring deeds,
Then forged with kindliness and love,
When riches and good health prevail and worries only small,
The need for friends seems not so great,
Until misfortune strikes us all.
True friends are those you never ask for favours large or small.
They are the crutch that breaks your fall.
Then when the last goodbyes are said and tears begin to fall,
Feel not ashamed of misty eyes, we will all meet again;
Maybe in that far 'beyond'.

Jack Jenkins
South Glamorgan

Lament For The Snows Of Kilimanjaro

I saw a sad photograph the other day
showing Kilimanjaro with snowless summit.
The photograph was taken from the air
and a carpet of foamy white clouds
mocked the grey and barren crest
and in a mere blink of time the scattered snow
will dissolve like the skin from a rotting corpse
and no more feet will crunch on magical white.

So next time you drive feel a little shame
for it's not just others who are to blame.

How sad Johann Rebmann would be today,
for snow lay deep when he stood here,
the first European to discover a place
bedecked with snow two hundred miles from the Equator.
Mawenzi and Kibo peaks peer pitifully out of the clouds
invisibly shorn of their claim to fame
now just an ordinary rocky mountain
as it was eleven thousand years ago

and the people who stare from far down below
see it with no glistening crown of snow.

Guy Fletcher
South Glamorgan

The Long, Long Goodbye

And as the morning sky opens, stream of light
Shadow of the ground predator, in the green wild
Nest strangled friend not alone;
Fly, fly against the empty sky.

Though cries lost, knowing the mind shines
Into another universe, not the first of losers
As candles blue, blow out in this life.

And in this world so strange, blinded by a shield
And learned too late, in breaths dark and desolate
Eclipse, do not fly into the empty sky.

Men in white long gowns frail by life, felled
In a cloak of darkness, so sad as the night sky burns
And live their lives as ghosts; close to the wind men alone.
Fly, fly against the burning sky.

Journeys end in the long, long goodbye, too late
Lost to the grave, in the universal light, one day.
Hold hands, as we dance in an empty cloud.
Fly, fly against the burning sky.

Garrett John
South Glamorgan

On Reflection

How long have I known you but not known you?
I'm sorry I left you standing there
in the playground,
no one would play so I left you in shame,
your heart must have sunk as you stood there bewildered,
when I walked away.
You went into hiding,
locked yourself away in the closet,
waiting to be set free.

Now I want to make up for
all the time spent apart.

Now I'm getting to know you,
learning to love you with all my heart.

Taking off those heavy garments
of criticism and dogma
that they dressed you in,
re-recording over those ancient beliefs they taught you,
and I've stopped scolding you,
no longer at war, I accept you as you are.
When you're scared and hurting I'll be there for you,
together anything is possible.
You and me.
We can dream and live those dreams,
we can love and be loved,
we can feel safe in this world,
I'll make sure of that,
I say to the mirror.

Coral Raven
South Glamorgan

Questions, Questions

Why fill in this form when you and I are here to talk?
I can answer you any question, just speak to me.
This question misses the point.
Will there be a section where I may write freely to explain?
I can't answer yes to these, yet plain no wouldn't be the whole truth.
None of these bald facts will be of help to you.
Some of these are unnecessarily personal.
If I could tell you the right things now it would save so much time.
This I don't understand, could you explain?
Could you?
Didn't I give all this to you the last time?
Don't you have records to draw from?
How can it take a month to process, I need help now!

Steve Gorvin
South Glamorgan

The Green Giants

Man is outlived by trees, green
giants of the woods withstood
the years and tears of his brief time.
As he, an eager huntsman, passed,
cut down like grass.
Knew his mount foaled, his rider
grown old and saw the fledglings
leave their nest each year.
Where lovers tryst, a maiden
kissed, her prayer, her fear.
Breeze shakes to sudden gale,
plans fail, no choice, sad voice
of moaning wind.
Here man return to sigh, wood-stillness,
given passer-by.
Roots delve the past, small feet
of children come and go
whose thoughts a-thistle-down the
wind until bright hair has thinned.
Striving each one the same in love
experience strife for all the things
that might.
Green summer boughs, high hope bespoke
plans swept away.
Like fallen leaf, in grief, a man,
a friend to seek.
Dwarf giant trees he tramps the ground,
in every place he haste there's no
solution found.

A E Doney
South Glamorgan

Our Wales

I travelled by car over hills and dales
Drinking in the beauty of this land called Wales
The sheep grazing in the fields so green
Ramblers stopping to view the scene

Water running down the mountainside
Gushing and dancing into the rivers they glide
Horses munching on green, green grass
Scenes that could have come out of the past

Yet we have all this in this present day
Simple things to view in our own special way
Mother Nature still strives to give us perfection
Whatever havoc we cause to her creation

The coal tips are mostly covered now
With grass and trees covering the brow
Of mountains of slag left to rot
Dumped by the pits time has forgot

The scars that are left on the valleys and hills
May be covered now but in the memory still
We remember the price we paid for coal
Of the lives that were lost in the black holes

Children dying in school when the tips slithered down
To cover the school and houses in town
Remember, remember what has been
Yet rejoice in our Wales so lovely and green

Be as proud as those who have gone on before
Take pride in this country which is yours
The mountains and valleys in all their glory
Have been depicted in many a story
But God has given us the real thing
That's why we are able to sing
We tell of our lives in poem and song
Of the green valleys and hills where we belong

Glenys Hannon
South Glamorgan

Growing Old

The bell has rung. Since I was young,
My world has changed, been rearranged,
Once family, now only me,
I was once bold, now getting old,
Once loved to dance, now of bent stance,
I loved to bake, now I buy cake,
With greying hair, in mirror stare,
I see not me, but an old lady,
Make-up I wore, now sagging jaw,
Vision spot on, but now part gone,
Was full of zing, now got no spring,
I battle on till day is gone,
Then off to bed, to lay my head,
When will I sleep, and just how deep?
Then when I wake, my muscles shake,
Sit up and rest, my legs to test,
My legs will hold, and will not fold,
With smile on my face, body to brace,
I smile to greet, friendly feet,
My friends are gold, though getting old,
I have good days, and those I praise,
Some days are not, I lose the plot,
If not a hit, I have to sit,
To write or read, do what I need,
To pass the time, make up a rhyme,
Paint, draw, maybe, let mind go free,
Till better day, then work or play,
Do garden, clean, washing machine,
Cannot do all, that's my downfall,
Though full of strife, I'll live my life.

Nicolette A Thomas
South Glamorgan

My City

Now here's a little ditty
About our hundred-year-old city
And fifty years, the capital of Wales
And all the people on this date
Will be sure to celebrate
With a sense of pride that never fails
For Cardiff City has it all
With its rugby and football
And a history colourful and long
Though our ships with coal are past
We have a castle built to last
And a stadium that echoes with our song
But it's the people on the street
And the kindness that you meet
That makes this city friendly and with heart
For no matter what they say
About the buildings and the bay
It's the people who make up the major part
And it makes me proud to hear
From visitors staying here
How they enjoy just everything they see
For I know so very well
That this city casts a spell
And that's why Cardiff City's dear to me.

June Davies
South Glamorgan

Perfect Love

A child is born, the message springs eternal;
The word of peace, re-echoes through the land;
God's blessed Son, lies peaceful in a manger
Christians awake, God's time is near at hand;

Let every man that's born to every nation;
Live to revere the Son of God most high;
Until the clouds of Earth are rent asunder
And we in Christ, shall live no more to die;

The perfect love, has triumphed through the ages;
May it inspire our hearts to be like Him;
And may we share the joy of full salvation
When lights of Earth, grow dark and strangely dim;

And one day soon, to hear the trumpet of angels;
When we will share, the rapture of the blest;
No more to doubt, for we shall dwell forever,
In perfect love, and peace and joy and rest.

Ernest H Cottle
South Glamorgan

Howden Valley

I have got to go to Howden Valley, I need to feel good about myself
I am going to leave my cares behind me, put my worries on the shelf
And climb the purpled hillsides and see the crystal streams
I have got to go where my heart is, the place of my dreams
Howden Valley

I'm going to leave this dirty city with its stresses and its strains
Where the people crush around me in the buses and the trains
I have got to roll around in the heather and walk the pine-fringed lakes
I have to go to where my heart is, for my sanity's sake
Howden Valley

How long can I take the strains of modern life in the city?
I don't know, but I will tell you this
I could live forever, where the windswept, rain soaked, green-reflected lakes
Are washed by crystal streams
In Howden Valley

I'm going to go there with my darling and walk the waterfalls and streams
We will climb the hills together and be happy way beyond our dreams
We will roll around in heather beneath the mountain ash and pine
And bathe our feet in water cold as wine
In Howden Valley

And when I'm tired of living and it's time for me to go
Please take whatever is left of me through the rain and snow
Across that lonely packhorse bridge, beside our favourite waterfall
And bury all that's left of me right there
In Howden Valley.

Keith Skelton
South Yorkshire

Contentment

A simple life is my desire, I do not seek renown!
Good health and friendship will suffice, far better than a crown.

The humble things, a hearth, a fire, a meal of good plain fare,
My sweetheart's gentle smiling face and ever loving care.

I take no joy from others' woes, nor envy them their gains,
I share my neighbours' highs and lows and suffer with their pains.

With strangers I will gladly share the tidings of the day, then wish
Them well in all they do, to cheer them on their way!

I'll seek enjoyment out of life with every fleeting breath,
For time, ephemeral in life, eternal is in death!

And, thus contented with our lot, together we will go
Through life's uncharted waters, to meet whatever foe!

Leonard Muscroft
South Yorkshire

My Precious Child

The moment I saw you
Was the moment I knew
My life's greatest wish
Had finally come true

As I held in my arms
My new baby girl
My heart full of love
My mind in a whirl

You arrived in the world
Without making a sound
Your eyes were wide open
Having a good look around

Your nain she was with me
And also your aunt
Telling me to push
And then when to pant

We all had a cuddle
With our new precious child
We were all overjoyed
That's putting it mild

Taid came to see you
He was ever so proud
He rang everybody
Well, I guess that's allowed

And as I start my new life
With my beautiful girl
My hopes for her future
Begin to unfurl.

Andrea Ashmore
South Yorkshire

Secret Love

S pecial glimmers of hope, outshining the dark,
E yes to guide us when we're blind!
C onscious, some way, somehow you've made your mark,
R ecognising there's treasures we've yet to find!
E very day, I discover what I couldn't see,
T hinking you may be discovering me too?

L iterally hoping we're really meant to be,
O ften find myself dreaming, that is true!
V oyaging onwards and upwards, being bound together,
E verlasting, still believing, through the stormiest weather!

Simone Dempsey
South Yorkshire

Fosgail An Dorus

Sitting by the fireside, one dark December night,
Looking through my window and the moon was shining bright,
A feeling it came over me, like something was not right,
So I grabbed my coat and got on up and made my way outside . . .

. . . Off to the pub! Off to the pub! Fosgail an dorus!
Ah, here's to all my drinking pals, away off to the pub!

To all here present I'll raise a glass, to friends both near and far,
No strangers, but friends who haven't met, whoe'er, where'er you are,
To friends north of the border and o'er the water too,
To Scots and Irish, Yorkshire, kin, I'll raise a glass to you.

To all who've gone before us, to the place from where we came,
To the closing of an dorus and it's opening again,
To absent friends and times gone by, the laughter and the craic,
If e'er you stray, may you find your way, to a smile and welcome back.

Paul Andrews
South Yorkshire

Patchwork Blanket

In the beginning, Heaven and Earth
were created from love and purity
a patchwork blanket was woven
to cover this new world
colours from the rainbow
were hand-picked to create
the contours of land and sea
all stitched together with golden thread.
As time went by, Man
created wars, devastation and pollution
leeching off the world with a greedy
hand, the stitching began
to fray, holes appeared as
disaster struck, the blanket was
once a protection, but we forgot
how to darn and live together
in peace and harmony.
Now the stitches have widened
delicate threads breaking as another
disaster raises its head
leaving behind a trail of destruction
when we remember how to darn
the blanket will once again
protect our precious planet.

Karen Canning
South Yorkshire

Without You

Without you I could not be me
For there is no other person with whom I'd rather be
Without you I would not be free
But with you I'm all I can be.

Our paths crossed and it was meant to be
Soulmates I believe that's you and me
It's a power so strong that goes on and on
Without you I could not be me
Without me you could not be you.

When you look at me across the room
I see the fears behind your eyes
I know you try hard to disguise
Your thoughts are mine and mine are yours.

Life is full of uncertainties
So I hold each memory close to my heart
Knowing one day we will be apart
Sometimes I look up and question why?
I shed a tear and have a cry.

You will always be by my side
We have two sons of which to be proud
I treasure the joy you have given to me
Because without you I could not be me
Without me you could not be you.

Positive Poetry 2005
I am glad to say that I'm still alive
The future's never certain you see
So live each day preciously.

L White
South Yorkshire

Twinkle, Twinkle

I sing a lullaby to the moon and stars hoping one will hear my thoughts
I've waited so long for this the feeling of contentment and love
A satisfaction unavailable to some I pray that I am able to receive
What I've longed so much for time will tell me if it comes true
If I'm one of the lucky ones chance and fate watch me closely
As I try so hard to attain it a single thing can mean so much
Seems so out of reach right before it arrives
At the point where you think it's no longer available
A lightning bolt surprise hits home there it is in front of your eyes
Your one hope
Your one prayer
Your one wish.

Barbara Fox
South Yorkshire

New Season

Heartbeat of the earth, once dimmed by touch of winter's hand
begins at last to reawaken from its long appointed sleep.
Soft and low the word of life through root and tendril passes
echoing the call of spring in voice unheard by Man.
Slowly and from a dream awakening, the golden sun
bestows the gift of warmth upon a grateful land.
Freed at last from its icy prison, the gentle stream begins to stir
and with each passing precious moment prepares itself once more to sing.
In search of food, a lonely robin perches high in greening tree,
no shelter yet its branch affording but rich with promise for days to come.
And as by unseen hand conducted, the early shrub does now reveal
the tender bud tight-wrapped;
whilst 'neath the verdant spreading carpet that cushions foot falls as they pass
lies silent beauty, whose life safe shielded in the bulb, now reaches upward to light of day.
Such sweet perfection, what joy to see your life revealed;
to catch upon the warming breeze, the first faint perfumed scent.
O season of spring, short-lived yet filled with wonder, what human voice
could call you forth to work your magic still?
Show me now the hand of man that can from nought bring glory to this land
and lest he swell with pride of heart let him recall how few his years in number be.
Heartbeat of the earth, though dimmed each year by winter's hand, beat on.

Lisa Alexandra Smith
South Yorkshire

One Wish (For Peace)

My one wish - could it be granted?
Is for peace in 2006.
I am sure so many would agree
We need peace throughout the world.

During 2005 we have witnessed the most horrific scenes
Scenes which have brought death and destruction.
We had the tsunami, earthquakes, floods and gales
Terrorism beyond belief.
Warfare; all killing thousands of people
People's hearts were broken beyond repair.
It was as though the world was at war with itself.
My wish for 2006 - is for peace
Calm weather and calm tempers
So that we can all live together
In brotherly love, unity and concord.

Janet Cavill
South Yorkshire

This Colourful Life

Green, green, everything is green
Hair spray, politics, even the Queen
Note the latest colour on the media scene
It's rather boring, this monochrome green

Global warming, greenhouse effect
How many more phrases will they select?
To describe in detail, the damage we've done
To almost everything under the sun

Green, green, what is the theme?
Clearly controversial, but always clean
Not just a colour, more of a scheme,
A plan for the future that mankind has seen

Our planet is sinking, the scientists say
But nations together must find a way
To get things moving and clean up our act
Or there'll be no future and that's a fact!

Pauline Harvey
South Yorkshire

Contract Unknown

It wasn't part of the contract
When you took him as your own
It wasn't in the marriage vows
Or at least they didn't make it known
That you would have to be the one
To forgo a life of leisure
The joy of washing underpants
Was thought to give you pleasure
Oh to be the faithful little woman
An unpaid skivvy in the home
They gave you the greatest compliment
Mankind could ever bestow
Made you part of the bricks and mortar
Calling you a housewife
Was it all part of a cunning plan
To catch you by surprise?

Phil Clayton
South Yorkshire

What We've Got To Live Through

Have you ever wondered,
How life would be,
If there was no loving,
And no fish in the sea?

Would we all stick together,
Like a big family,
If the end of the world,
Was close enough to see?

Do you really think,
That you would cope,
Living so worried,
And all you've got is hope?

Could we ever change,
How life is today,
But in the future,
Will it still be this way?

Because this is the world,
That we've changed it to,
This is the life
What we've got to live through.

Scott Smith
South Yorkshire

My Trusted Friends

I have good friends around me,
I know how much they care,
It's such a help just knowing
If I need them they'll be there.
We've swapped so many secrets
There's nothing I can't tell
After all the years we've shared
We know each other so very well.
So I thank you for your friendship
It's just a shame we can't stay together
All of us
You're always in my thoughts
And a piece of you, lives in my heart.
Sheila, Sylvia and Graham.
Ernest xxxx thank you.

Ernest Stokes
South Yorkshire

Want

The places where the plough has been,
She heaves the land into furrows of expectancy.
Now she sits awhile on the headland, at rest,
Her silver breast shines in the moonlight,
Waiting for daybreak and the coming of man.
That was yesterday!
Today she rusts away, like me,
Old and useless,
Replaced by five silver breasts and noise.
I don't hear the ploughman singing or the lapwing cry,
But rejoice, like men before me,
When the corn stands high
And famine slinks away.
When the harvest is home.

Les Dernie
South Yorkshire

Tears

Tears from a clown
A smile that's now just a frown
Sadness that fills the air
Where there is no hope, just despair
A fool with a fool's hope
No, just a fool
No words need to be spoken
Just a heart that's torn and broken
Behind a mask, does a clown shed a tear
When all are gone and no one can hear?
Ask yourselves, who can this fool be?
Well, look no further, for that fool is me
Still, what more can I say
A fool waiting for that day
When you will come back to me.

Karl Smedley
South Yorkshire

Summer's Demise

In darkness I rise, a sure sign of summer's demise.
Razor winds herald autumn's golden treasure.
Darkened days hide a guilty pleasure.

Sheila Prime
South Yorkshire

Washed Out

When land and sea, in battle meet
The loser is the land
And ill it bodes for what it goads
It grinds its finds to sand.
So it is with England's coast
Where most of it gave up the ghost,
And left, bereft, an irate host
Midst shattered dreams he'd planned,
Not only eastern seas confound
The boundaries of the land
For those out west as well contest
What tempests all demand.
When east and west, in concert meet,
And each shall wash the other's feet,
Then England's shores will face defeat
Beneath King Neptune's hand.

Ben Stone
South Yorkshire

From Status Quo To Sinatra Via The Smiths

Funny how I've always been drawn
To the S's in the record rack.

It began as a pre-pubescent preoccupation
With middle-aged men
With long hair
You could shake your head to.

It moved to the box bedroom rebelliousness
Of an adolescent obsession
With introspective,
Shoe-gazing miserablism.

And finds me now
Crooning at karaoke
To the velvet voice
Of a toupeed trooper.

My three musical ages.
Which should leave four more,
But please God, no room,
For Andrew Lloyd-Webber.

Whose quality counts
As an 'S'.

Jayson Burns
Staffordshire

A Childish Kind Of Magic

I walk in a kaleidoscopic landscape,
With waterfalls of flowing sands.
Large ceramic-faced clocks,
Are dotted around this strange realm,
Imparting no real information,
As all the time pieces register,
Every conceivable hour,
Which is not really surprising,
As several suns vie in the violet sky,
Along with another lunacy, numerous,
Waxing and waning, party balloon moons.
I stop at one of the bizarre chronometers.
It is the dial which turns quite rapidly,
Rather than the ornate fingers.
The second finger is held within,
A separate revolving disc,
With flying pigs engaged in acrobatics.
This place is truly fairytale fantastic.
It is a domain somehow as childish,
As a kid's first attempt at painting.
It holds a toytown kind of magic,
Though here peopled by strange adults,
Rather than growing minds of little folk.
I do not have the type of free thinking,
To take in all this wisdom or wizardry.
For I am sleepwalking in surreal kingdom,
In the garish ideas of the very young,
Where everything dreamed is conceivable.
This place exists near the Tower of Babel,
Trafficking the ideas of inventors unhinged.

Julia Pegg
Staffordshire

Time

It's nice to have nothing to do
Let things lie, let things stew.
To appreciate nature, memories sort
Time is the essence, time is thought.
Locked away memories to search and see
Untold feelings; only one key!
Brought back to present with ticking clock
Past laughter and tears put back under lock.

Vera Collins
Staffordshire

The Pink Blossom

The pink blossom
Calls to me
Pierces the depths
Of naïve innocence

The eye beholds
Delicate swirls of colour
Envelops the soul
And drags it away

To another place
The perfect one
Pure, like a teardrop
That splashes as

It falls tenderly upon
A solemn white cheek
Much happiness
The pink blossom exudes

A world of innocence
Betrays the doom
The flower blows softly
In a wind that gently

Echoes and stirs the heart
With a sensitivity too great
The two worlds merge and
The eye consumes the flower

Kay Deakes
Staffordshire

The Sun And The Moon

The hills are silent, as the sun slowly dies.
Soft as a whisper, the night owl flies.
A breeze barely stirs through the trees,
Gently, so gently, just rustling the leaves.

A full moon glows from the night sky,
A guiding light for all to rely.
In shadowy woods and leafy retreats
Nocturnal creatures move on silent feet.

But soon they must leave, the sun is awake
The moon and her creatures their leave they must take.
Sleep through the sunshine and rise with the moon
Be patient, so patient your time will come soon.

Catherine Lambert
Staffordshire

The Neighbours

She must have been nearly eighty,
And the children called her a witch,
She lived in a scruffy cottage,
It was rumoured she was rich.

Her hair was grey and greasy,
Her clothes dirty and ripped,
Her smell preceded before her,
Until one day she tripped.

I went over to help her,
An ambulance was called,
She was taken to hospital,
And they were duly appalled.

A dear frail old lady,
Now clean in a hospital bed,
A broken hip the outcome,
But now warm and fed.

And now we all visit,
And help all we can,
She had been too proud to ask us,
And I a selfish man.

But now this dear old lady,
Has given us a wake-up call,
We will all make amends,
A shame it's because of her fall.

S P Cockayne
Staffordshire

Footsteps In The Snow

You cannot live upon the Earth and leave no trace,
We will not age with no lines on our face.
Old Mother Earth is a violent place,
She glides effortlessly through space.
These seas of anger and storms of rage,
They have left their marks on every page.
We are only Man we live and learn,
The perfect balance is what we yearn.
To live as one with nature's gifts,
Into the harness in which it fits.
The conquered skies are now within reach,
Seas and mountains lie on the beach.
Man will soon the seasons and elements teach.
For he was born with all these things within his reach,
Look on, observe but don't ever knock.

Alan Hulme
Staffordshire

Just Who?

Just who do you think you're fooling
When you say you're feeling fine?
Just who do you think you're fooling
When you say love's not for you?
When love is recommended
By God and angels too.

Just who do you think you're fooling
When you give out that sad line?
Just who do you think you're fooling
When you say love's not for you?
When it's clear, love light's melting
That big heart of moody blue.

Just who do you think you're fooling
As you pull your gaze from mine?
Just who do you think you're fooling
When you say love's not for you?
You know, you know you need me -
And you know I need you too.

Just who do you think you're fooling?
You're only fooling you!

Sylvia Anne Lees
Staffordshire

An Ode To Ambition

The need to know
The urge to go
Ever onwards and upwards
Always this has been Man's story
Ever looking beyond yesterday's accomplished goals
Restless Man takes scant joy
From transient personal glory
Restless in his need to further
Man's unending story
Untiring in his God-given inspiration
To free his soul
And at journey's end when the
Candle of life flickers and wanes
The balm of fulfilment
Appeases life's final pains.

William McGinnis
Staffordshire

Farm Labourer

Rubber boots standing outside the farmhouse door
stepping stones of newspapers across the kitchen floor.
Farm labourer waiting patiently to receive his wage
earnings do not go very far in this day and age.

All the overtime could not cover his outgoing bills
so he entered a trade that was as old as the hills.
Hunting for rabbits was the order of the day
to feed a growing family with another one on the way.

'Do you want me to stop over boss?' was a regular request
'Not today Son, get yourself a well earned rest.'
Checking his wage packet on leaving the big house
he felt as poor, as a little church mouse.

Halfway down the path his heart began to race
he could not believe what was staring him in the face.
Have I been overpaid or was this my lucky day
do I keep it, I do not know what to say.

The end of the path he could not reach
he knew in his heart, he must practise what he preached.
The farmer and his wife were waiting inside the kitchen door.
They said, 'Son we know what you have come back for.
We have not overpaid you or given you too much
your hard work and dedication we appreciate so very much.'

JHB
Staffordshire

The Old Windmill

Four huge sails have I
That are harnessed by the wind's power
Standing tall towards the sky
I grind corn into flour

I look into a distant field
Full of maize and wheat
Seeing a farmer gather in his yield
The combine harvester slashing with every beat

The miller with skilful hand
Tips the maize and wheat into my jaw
And there I grind it like fine sand
Till the coarseness is no more

My old oak timbers creak with age
As I was made to last
Catering for the village
A relic of the past

Walter Mottram
Staffordshire

Ernie

I don't think that Ernie can remember me,
My rich pals can go on a spending spree.
They might even go for a cruise, on the sea
But, I've got to stay at home with a cup of tea.

Ernie's Premium Bonds? Don't come my way,
So try to have a bet, on Lotto, on Saturday.
My dreams of having a fortune, well, it's nil,
I wonder if? It's because my name is Bill.

It would be great, to have a substantial win,
Then I could celebrate, with a glass of gin.
My days are numbered, those bonds won't come,
No wonder I'm miserable and feeling glum.

My roof wants repairing, my car is getting old,
The carpets need replacing, the floors are cold
But, I'll look on the bright side, I won't be forlorn,
Maybe one day, I'll own a Jag, with a windtone horn.

I always pay my way, when the bills are due,
I try to enjoy myself, then I don't feel blue.
I say a prayer for Ernie, at the end of each day,
That my prayers might be answered, soon, one day.

Will of Endon
Staffordshire

Baby Boy

With chubby hands and tiny feet,
He lies there sleeping sound.
I can't wait for him to start to toddle
And put his feet on the ground.

He has big blue eyes and curly hair
And fingers soft and smooth.
I hold him when he starts to cry
And his hurt I try to soothe.

I love to hear him giggle and laugh
And squeal with such delight.
I lay him softly in his crib,
For him to sleep at night.

He's warm, soft and cuddly,
A little bundle of joy.
He's the sweetest thing in the world,
This little baby boy.

Sandie Smith
Staffordshire

Blessings

I can see the golden sunshine
I can feel the falling rain
I hear the children's laughter
And the birds' happy refrain

I can feel the cool wind blowing
I see the trees' gentle sway
They are some of God's blessings
We enjoy them every day

I see the flowers blooming
They have a delicate perfume
With their lovely colours
They take away our gloom

We are part of a family
We have many a good friend
We have so many blessings
They never come to an end

The greatest blessing of them all
Is God's unconditional love
He sent Jesus our Saviour
Down to Earth
Who now reigns in Heaven above

We have many blessings
Some great, some small
God's unconditional love
Is the greatest of them all.

Doreen Swann
Staffordshire

A Thought

People without imagination, never feel despair,
They do not see, or seem to care,
For the troubled world, we share.
Like rolling stones; gathering speed,
They enjoy the ride, wherever it goes.
Caring little for the havoc that ensures,
Living only for the moment! No time to lose.
If only they would take the time to reflect,
Look at nature's treasures.
Realise without help, this Earth as we know it,
Cannot exist forever.
So, when the day comes to a close
And all is still, think about tomorrow,
Do something worthwhile, something new! Imagine!

I D Welch
Staffordshire

Our Holiday

My daughters and I decided one day
That we would go on a holiday
We thought about Scotland and places we have not been
Then we said we would go to Dublin in the green
We went to the ferry at Holyhead
The weather was very calm
I had not been on a ferry before and
I kept falling in people's arms
When we arrived the weather was good
The hotel was quite new
I think they had just finished building it
Because we did not think much of the view

Part 2, The Driver

Frank, we think that you are great
Your sense of humour is out of this world
You would make a good mate
Because you make my hair curl
You have a good word for everyone
And you were very helpful and kind
What more can I say you are full of zest
In other words you were simply the best.

May Ward
Staffordshire

Lads' Night Out

When out with the lads
We never are cads
We always are pleasant and charming
So we never know why
All the girls passing by
Can find us so strange and alarming
We'll buy them a drink
And then we would think
They'd become much more willing and pliable
We see them all smile
And think in a while
That they are looking at us as reliable
They listen and smile
As we put on the style
And we think they're forgetting their rules
But they just up and go
And what do you know
They shout, 'Bog off you silly old fools!'

MAW
Staffordshire

First Home - May 1958

In the early 50s, homes were hard to find
No matter how we tried, six months with Mother-in-law
Two years bedsit, with Mum and Dad
Then one May day 1958, a friend of ours
Came and said, 'I've found you a house,
Vacant, early 1900, you must go and see.'
We were thrilled, and very glad, so off we went, the house to view.
But, oh dear, not a pretty sight. Outside, nice lawn,
Sash windows, nice little walled garden, up an avenue.
Inside, musty, no electric! Gas lights.
Property had stood empty two years, one cold tap,
Long shallow, grey stone sink,
Black lead range and a brick boiler.
My heart sank, 'I can't live here,' I cried and sighed.
'Don't think how it looks now,' my husband said,
Imagine, what it could look like, in time.
We collected the key off the landlord,
No furniture, only two armchairs and a bed settee,
Small table, a cot and a little bed.
My husband worked, day and night, painting, plastering,
Filling cracks and installed electric light.
The old wooden loo, with a hole removed,
The stairs, ceiling, came down, along with the bedroom one.
Months passed, paper on walls, an doors,
Lino on the floors, new cooker, still old tin bath!
By autumn, it was clean, bright and warm.
In November, a new baby daughter was born, upstairs!
A new home, a new start, first Christmas,
All with love, from the heart.

Irene G Corbett
Staffordshire

Beyond The Tears

We rake the grass
The rigged leaves
Anthems
Static winter's picture
Beyond the tears
Past emotions
The broken chain
A learned tuition
In silence.

Roger Thornton
Staffordshire

Without Christmas

Where would we be without Christmas?
Where would we be without hope?
When we were down and full of despair
How would we ever cope?
Without something there to sustain us
Without faith and hope it's futile
So pray that our faith will be constant
And make Christmas last, for a while.

Grace Divine
Staffordshire

Guardian Angel

The hand you are dealt
And the way you play the game,
Through the hardships of life
One thing stays the same.
When you've hit the very bottom
And you feel like giving up,
All things will change
And you rediscover luck.
This might be coincidence,
But you must believe it's true,
It's your guardian angel
Watching over you.

Melissa Hadnum
Staffordshire

Human Nature

If a duck can live among swans
And a swan can swim with the coots
If a cat can reside with a dog
And a frog share a pond with the newts
'What happened to people?'

Marji Tomlinson
Staffordshire

Man O' Steel From Stoke-On-Trent
(Dedicated to the memory of Mr Frank Jones)

'Up all night and in bed all day,'
words to me, my stepfather would say.
Working most of his life on Shelton Bar
six till two, two till ten, nights and more.

Twelve hours on or a double 'un to do,
without thought, off to work he'd go.
On his old boneshaker bike pushing pedals
toiling through the war years, no medals.

For thirty-seven years he sweated in all
punch, tool and die shop in his overall.
Mending, fixing, greasing trains and machines,
to be replaced by yuppies in designer jeans.

Upon retirement he got a watch and 37 quid,
one single pound for each year that he did.
Grafting hard for days, nights and noons
I wish instead that he'd had a snooze.

If only he had, then I could have said,
'Don't criticise me for laying in bed,
I'm building up to a life of work
and just like you I'll be a jerk.

Making money for all of the bosses
as they cleverly hide away the losses.
So until then I'll do things my way
better off, up all night and in bed all day.'

Carl Nixon
Staffordshire

When Time Stands Still

When time stands still the pain is frozen
Etched in your heart

When time stands still life passes you by
You make an attempt to live
But it isn't worth the try

When time stands still you think and think and think
Too much time to reflect on your life and why it stinks

When time stands still the pain isn't really bad
Your heart accepts that you have a choice
To stand still or to live

Will you stand still or live?

Sue Rogers
Staffordshire

For Better Or Worse

My childhood was a happy one,
Lots of freedom, lots of fun.
In parks and fields we did play,
Tired but happy at the end of the day.

Then came the war, everything changed,
A job that tested guns on the range.
Travelling back home each weekend,
Rationing and blackouts were the trend.

When the war was over, what had we got?
Back to work, a job in the Pots.
That soon changed as they were sold,
Making room for motorways and roads.

I love our city of Stoke-on-Trent,
The changes I see are not well spent.
It hasn't made us happier today,
Never able to park where you really want to stay.

Evelyn M Harding
Staffordshire

Different World, Different Life

Watching these people on our TV screens,
Individuals dying, from water unclean
So little to eat, people starving to death
Struggling to take each and every breath

Watching in colour on our TV screens,
Conflicts all over, no one intervenes
Soldiers dying from the constant war
Watching, but still, we seem to ignore

Watching in colour on our TV screens,
Natural disasters, changing the world so green
Houses and lives destroyed by hurricanes
Bringing much sorrow, causing much pain

Watching these people on our TV screens,
Then retreating back, to our daily routines
Switching off from this life outside
This consumerist world too pre-occupied.

Sarah Bibb
Staffordshire

A Yorkshire Stream

Winding and twisting, flowing so free,
Dancing with pebbles a sight for to see.
Shaded by trees so tall and so proud,
With gaps here and there to see a white cloud.

Swirling around to gather up speed,
Pretty yet wild, caressing a weed.
Stopping in places enjoying a rest,
Then onward again now full of fine zest.

Where has it come from, where will it go?
Nature's decided the path it will flow.
Sparkling like diamonds scattered about,
From a blanket of daylight of that there's no doubt.

Speeding so gracefully without a care,
Such beauty beholds for us all to share.
Colours will change as the seasons go past,
In winter the water will flow not so fast.

A fountain for wildlife, so fresh and so cool,
Insects and beetles will bask in the pool.
This treasure to find, what is its worth?
More priceless a gift from our Mother Earth.

Betty Hattersley
Staffordshire

War

Tell me why I went there, what was it all for,
I went to be a soldier, in 1944,
One hundred thousand soldiers, one hundred thousand men,
One hundred thousand soldiers, one hundred thousand dead.

Not a bird is singing, there's not an earthly sound,
There's thunder in the distance, there's crying on the ground,
No shooting stars are falling, just banging in my head,
One hundred thousand soldiers, one hundred thousand dead.

Tears fill my eyes now, for me this war is done,
I've cast aside my anger, I've cast aside my gun,
I see the railway station, my mother's calling, 'Son,'
I try to shout and call to her, but I know my time has come.

No shooting stars are falling, no banging in my head,
I'm just another fallen soldier, who makes
One hundred thousand dead . . .

Graham O Gallear (aka Fuzz)
Staffordshire

Ochil Hills

He breathes in harmony with the hills,
eternal Ochils 'neath changing skies.
Music falls swiftly from craggy face,
entwines and dances with stream below.

A startled curlew sounds his reed note,
still he echoes as he takes to flight.
Trumpet-necked geese herald the springtime,
with a gaggled wave high overhead.

He climbs to the top by gnarled path,
made more narrow by mountain briar.
Gentle wind teases and whispers low,
kisses his cheek like a lover's song.

Yet he had known, when drums had thundered,
with silver flashes in perfect time.
Stormy wind piped his pibroch loudly,
calling Wallace's men to rise again.

Old man looks out at the distant hills,
remembering when he roamed there free.
He feels their music touching his soul,
in a sweet encore of symphony.

Hannah Bateman
Stirlingshire

Empty Inside

Empty, barren womb,
an infertile land where nothing will ever grow.
Sadness and longing has gripped
my soul and tugs my heart strings
into playing out a strange, woeful song.
Maternal sickness will never plague me,
nor will the pains of labour wrack my body
when it's time as a host is done.
My arms ache to hold my own bundle
of innocence and joy.
My child.
My body's guest.
My gift of greatness to the world.
My baby . . . a girl or boy.

Pam McCormack
Stirlingshire

The Old Bridge

I stand fascinated, hypnotised, on the bridge
looking down as the river races, swirls
and churns around its several arches
before rushing on, by many loops and curls,
in its tireless, perpetual journey to the sea.
Was this indeed, once a busy waterway?
Aye, but sadly now long since disused,
traffic preferring the faster moving motorway
to the slower pace of bygone age.
The bridge itself is old, indeed, too old
to take the pressures of this modern life -
better by far, if truth be told,
left as it is, its five centuries old stones
a testament of its ageless, natural beauty -
so that we, today, can walk its cobbled way,
seeing it as it used to be.
To touch the worn parapet, as countless
hands have touched it down the years -
they are still here, those fleeting shades,
once people like us, with the same basic joys and fears.

Joyce Hockley
Stirlingshire

An Ode To James Gordon
On His Birthday

A sweet little fellow
With limbs full strong
He howls in the night
When things go wrong
An empty tummy, a need to burp
And cry my little darling
It's a sign of many a quirk.

Sleep and dream too young to know
The perils awaiting you as you grow
Enjoy the pamper and tender breath
My soul enjoys the sight of your rest
Grow brave little darling, my love is all yours
Our togetherness will conquer the love humane
And joy be with you, a glad refrain.

Jean Bald
Stirlingshire

Sunny Hunny

With a gentle breeze we sat on Hunstanton town green,
looking out to sea for miles at a beautiful scene.
Walkers passing by, with their shadows ahead,
seagulls hovering for scraps of fresh chips and bread.

Some of the amusements are closed until Easter,
always a favourite and special in our calendar.
Suddenly, a glider flew over the calm sea,
having lunch was my son, wife and me.

Behind us, was the clock at the Tourist Information Centre,
and passing traffic wishing to travel a bit further.
A man stripped flaky paint off the beach huts quickly,
as the sun went in, it became very chilly.

We then walked into the town to the shops,
looking at jackets, trousers and tops.
We also went into Fudgetastic to the smell of sweets,
made on the premises for all who deserve treats.

The old bakery stood on the corner,
displaying fresh cakes in the window delicious and super.
We walked back along the promenade whilst the sun was out,
with a lot of aircraft doing their military exercises out and about.

Now, tucked up in our warm caravan for the night,
Taylor is ready for his travel cot with delight.
We are due to go home tomorrow,
having to pack will be hard and slow.

Adrian Bullard
Suffolk

Another Nail

Another nail in the box, the body is the grave,
The part that rots, the part we try to save.
So as ashes drift onto obscurity,
We ponder over eternity and purity.

Another painful induction, each joke a nail,
So what does it mean to truly fail?
The comedy of our degradation
Heals the truth that hurts the nation.

Another dose of life, the body is the box,
The part that begs to stop the clocks.
So we must think beyond existing
To affirmation of souls persisting.

Matt Annis
Suffolk

Dad

I saw you today as you crossed the road,
I knew it was you
By the tilt of your hat
And the arch of your back.
Two years ago you were there
On my holiday.
That same grin,
The way your hair wouldn't lay straight.
That earnest expression in serious conversation.
That furrowed brow.
The way your rubbed your head in exasperation.
I caught sight of you in the street,
With friends, happy, joking
Hands in your pockets
Crinkly eyes twinkling.
You were there at my uncle's
Wide-eyed, forging a tale,
Your whole body laughing
Showing the gap in your teeth.
I pass you by in the car
With your beloved dogs walking.
Last week I glimpsed you in the garden
Busy digging.
It was you.

Margaret Newson
Suffolk

Grief

We cannot live our lives without grief's pain
bereavement is a hurdle we all cross
but life goes on and we will laugh again
yet never will forget a loved one lost.
Thoughts overflow in torrents of despair
as memories and regrets agonise.
Heartache and guilt are a tormented pair
displaying sorrow's shadow in the eyes.

Time is the healer - anguish will subside
as happy memories replace distress.
The comfort and the cheer good friends provide
confirm their loyalty and thoughtfulness
so precious are true friends who lend their ears
and give their time to wipe away sad tears.

Joy Saunders
Suffolk

October In Lowestoft

They came in their scores
By train, or by bus.
The herring to put on a truss.
Their knives slashed as they sang a song
In their Gaelic tongue - a sea's lament,
Their backs bent.

Fish barrels rolling, hammers banging
Like a gun and weighing a ton.
Eyes could never take in the speed
Of those deft fingers - the Russians to feed.

Salted herring, packed tight in wood.
We joked and teased
And ran, if we could,
On barrels rolling over and over.

Yet when their working day was done
Those fingers were never still.
Huge balls of wool were tucked under the arm
Knitting needles to fill.

Large, buxom women
With weather-gruff voices
Laughing and talking away.
The strong smell of fish hard to escape
I will never forget to this day.

Pauline Burton
Suffolk

Field Machines

Voices stilled, work done,
They stand
Bulking in the field,
Summer fret
Misting their outlines.

Cut swathes baled,
Red-gold grasses
Gone from the land.

Soon,
The inexorable year begins again;
Sheep dotting the field,
Ram busy begetting his future.

Baler,
Autumnal and still,
Re-grouping, ready.

Richard Maslen
Suffolk

Hubby For Hire

My hubby is a lovely man
A regular top geezer
He buys me flowers and chocolates
And lets me use his Visa

He lets me use the remote control
And provides the cups of tea
I watch all the sport with him
He watches Sex In The City with me

He's the king of DIY
Does every task with a smile
He says he'll do just any job
If I make it worth his while!

He gets lost in the garden centre
Nowhere to be seen
He's hugging all the power tools
Yep he's in a dream

He cleans the car and cuts the grass
What would I do without him?
He likes me just the way I am
Doesn't care that I'm not thin

My hubby is a lovely man
He is my little flower
But if you want to hire him out
I charge ten pound an hour!

Mary Daines
Suffolk

Freedom

A blessing on the natural world.
Balm of the sea on Aldeburgh beach.
Wind blown jazz in trees by the Ore.
High seas at Slaughden Point, freeing poignant emotions.
Homage to the water god who tends my garden
encouraging brilliance and pure pure white.
Subtle splendour filling my day.

And when winter blankets all with snow
a thank you to my hearth and home
where I am free to voice
a curse
on arrogants and misers all.

Su Laws Baccino
Suffolk

Look East Weather Girl . . .

Where did you find that accent, Jules,
That challenges all normal rules
Of stress and intonation?
The emphasis you sometimes base
On syllables so commonplace
Defies imagination!
For prepositions often drawled
And some conjunctions badly mauled
We wait with trepidation.

But Julie, please don't change your ways,
You bring the sunshine to our days
With your prognostication.

Grahame Godsmark
Suffolk

Mallow

Long, low, laden spurs
of bright pink trumpets
lean and languish,
shading the grass beneath,
that place, the greener
for its covering.
Above, a bee's incessant hum.
Perfect pink promises
waving high
against still, blue, cloudless sky.

Greta Robinson
Suffolk

Didn't You Know?

Come back.
Footsteps black,
In the snow.
Didn't you know
You can redeem
The lost dream?

U Johnson
Suffolk

Maturity

An aged, wizened man,
Sat solemnly beside the fire,
His trouble face, marked with time,
Of recollections, hard to bear.
This mellow man, so kind and fair,
Deserved a life, devoid of tears;
What justice then, is this that prays,
On goodly folk, of gentle ways.
A tempest raging, all around,
Propelled the window, of his library open;
Extinguishing the candles,
That barely lit, the thought-filled room.
Relighting the candles, without a sound,
Then returning to his seat,
To meditate upon, the glowing embers;
Staring hard and seeing well:
What he senses, at this time,
Could cure the world, of all its grime.

Paul Cutting
Suffolk

The Gift Of A Child

From their soft curly hair
To the top of their toes
Nothing is more precious than a child
For every father and mother knows.

Every cherished smile
Each innocent grin
The soft warmth of their skin
Nothing more can happiness bring.

The sleepless nights and endless nappies
Is more than worthwhile,
As the excitement mounts in their eyes
At everything each new day brings.

Is it our right and privilege
Or a precious gift from Heaven,
It's certainly a gift I would love
Whether it's one, two, or seven.

Jackie Williamson
Suffolk

Our Little Bit Of Heaven

We sit on the seat
In the corner of our garden,
We take in the view
Of the fields in the distance,
And the two church towers as we look towards the east.
We wonder at the large open skies so blue
With the puffy white clouds floating by.
The swallows are swooping overhead
And the occasional plane writes in the sky.
The boughs of the apple trees
Are weighed down with their fruit
Not quite ready to be picked.
The Michaelmas daisies are blooming
Bright pink and mauve,
Whilst the fuchsias are still producing
Red, mauve and pink blooms like
Ballerinas dancing in the gentle breeze.
The passion flowers so beautiful for a day
With fruits that hang like lanterns, orange in colour,
A few roses still blooming,
A deep red one planted for our Ruby wedding.
Most of all we admire the sunflowers so tall
Yet such a tiny seed was planted,
Sown in faith, fed with love and prayer, harvested with joy.
We feel gratitude in owning our dream bungalow
With its colourful and tranquil garden
Where we sit and meditate,
We thank God for the beauty of His creation
And our little bit of Heaven, where we feel close to Him as
We sit on the seat.

Peggy Courteen
Suffolk

The Swallows' Reconnaissance

They came safely last April, then looked around
Our garage eaves, where their nests were hidden from gales
And storms. Mud for rebuilding can always be found.

As proof of the summer. Their air show seldom fails -
With such flight skill, they have no need of songsters; tunes.
Let nightingales and warblers please us with wassails.

Sounds of twittering reach our astonished ear . . .
The nest, once again, is in busy possession.
Once more, our South African friends have arrived here
To add more members to the species' progression.

Gillian Fisher
Suffolk

September

Golden days, sunlit trees
Smell of earth and harvesting
Boys out working late at night
And girlfriends sitting by their sides

In tractors, trucks and harvesters
Sun setting, mist coming on
Sunlight shafts pass through the trees
And casting rays, caught on the breeze

Earthy hues as fields are ploughed
Sounds of deer barking loud
Calls and chants of evening owls
Rabbits rustle, foxes howl

I love September in its golden light
For me it's just like paradise

Rachel Wood
Suffolk

Summer Wood

Step the forked path
Into lazy green hue
Beneath resonant blue
Lost to broken time

Drenched light funnels beech avenue
Oak cradle dappled sky
Silver birch shimmer on broken wavelets
Beneath pine heady pyres laden velvety fume

Milky fern holds secret ways
Crackling broom scatters stardust gaze
Ragged robin face enlightens shadow
Blackberry pour forth summer lease

Rabbit delves the collected voice
Squirrels capture the tide of canopy
Deer hang to silence
Bird whisper tunes temple glow

Forged path draw an ugly hue
Back to Man's caged time
Still the wood walks temple mind
And sounds wash in the heart tides.

Nicholas Heleine
Surrey

Cards

Cards are fun
Cards are great
Yes we'll find one
Never late.

Bunny rabbits
Birthday cake
Please give Mum
A special break.

Father Christmas
On his sled
Hope you all
Are tucked in bed.

Sad occasions
Have their place
Wipe the tears
You'll spoil your face.

Twenty-one
Well fancy that
On my knee
Once you sat.

Cards for babies
Cards for Nan
Let me help you
All I can.

Trouble is
There's so much choice.

Rosemary Povey
Surrey

One Wish

If I had only one wish
I wonder what would I choose
With just one wish I'd be careful
Because one wish is so easy to lose.
Would I wish for more money
Perhaps a house in the sun?
I'd have to choose so carefully
For wishes, I only have one.
Perhaps I'd wish for more wishes
That seems the logical thing to do
And if I had some more wishes
I could give some wishes to you.

Trudy Simpson
Surrey

The Last Goodbye

Goodbye Tom, dear uncle of mine,
My mother's brother, the last of that line.
An unobtrusive man, always there,
With his gentleness and wisdom, you know he cared.

His character was part of his charm,
But some would say, it was his strong right arm.
He liked nothing more, than a drink in the club,
As a young man, it would be down the pub.

With his brother and friends, he would prop up the bar,
Putting the world straight, with another jar.
We're sure his life was a happy one,
A wife, two daughters and a son.

He had to leave his family to go to war,
His character was built on that foreign shore.
Strong and reliable, broad shouldered to bear,
All the things that he saw and the pain that he shared.

To his grandchildren, he was a special man,
He was proud of them, that they did the best they can.
The little ones could always sit on his lap,
With his strong arms around them for a chat.

He will be missed for his stories and so much more,
His place in our lives, his knock on the door.
The one of his kind, no one can replace,
We will always remember, the smile on his face.

Linda Walker
Surrey

Christmas Eve

The door has closed, out goes the light.
Will Father Christmas come tonight?
Our chimney stack is tall and thin,
How will he squeeze his body in?
And bring his sack all full of toys -
Some for girls and some for boys.
Perhaps I'll hear him when he comes,
Will there be trains and sets of drums?
I've tied my stockings to my bed,
In just the way that Mummy said.
My eyes are shut, I'll try to sleep
But when he comes I'll have to peep
To see if really it can be
Santa Claus who's visiting me.

Norah Dale
Surrey

Every Child

Every child born, is born without choice,
Innocent and beautiful, they have not yet found their voice,
From the moment you hold them close, resting on your arm,
That is where they must stay, safe and out of harm.

As precious to you as treasure, as important as life itself,
It takes your unconditional love, it does not come from wealth,
Safety and security should go without saying,
Joy should fill your heart when you first watch them playing.

A happy place should be, what you create of your home,
Somewhere they can be children and never feel alone,
They need calmness, not a life of ups and downs,
You should be the magic to take away their frowns.

Never leave them lonely, never become their fear,
Treat them like the person they are and never forget to hear,
Listen to them as they will be listening to you,
Learning the world through the things that you do.

Emma Yvonne Johnston
Surrey

The Heart And Mind

A woman knows her own mind as well as her heart.
Sometimes she is impulsive, other times guarded.
She requires the space to fulfil her dreams,
A chance to prove her independence,
The opportunity to make a difference;
At times she strays searching for something better.
Then again remains the same person she always was.
Someone you can depend on.
A person you call a friend and a soulmate.

Ise Obomhense
Surrey

Mars Walk

After many years of trying
And years of deep space flying
After journeying across the stars
We finally land a man on Mars

He begins his walk at sunrise
And then he finds to his surprise
After exploring near and far
An Irish pub and a burger bar.

Paul Curtis
Surrey

Smile

The someone with the beaming face,
All shapely round and wrapped in silk,
Whose open welcome calls to me,
As raises smile as twinkles by.

Can't stop myself, it's in my genes,
To think the things I'm shamed I thought,
I thought these thoughts would drift away,
Yet years they pass and still they come.

All ages bring their own reward,
I see the things I missed back then
And know them as they truly are,
Yes, youth is wasted on the young.

James Melrose
Surrey

Dearest Mother

Dearest Mother;
Through the two score and four years,
I have mentioned, I have remarked, I have reminded,
I have asked, I have urged, I have implored,
I have explained, I have preached, I have rambled,
I have told, I have foretold, I have warned, I have forewarned,
I have yelled and screamed and danced and hopped
And cursed and multiples all thereof;

And, nonetheless - here come you again - smiling abroad
and carrying the salads,
Which you've again doubtless doused with
malt b*****d vinegar.

Tom Hathaway
Surrey

Discs

There can be little else - save perhaps clothes
- Treated in so irreverent a fashion,
Despite their worth being far more than their lightweight nature would say,
Empty or open,
Contents right or wrong
They spread like a multicoloured, many faceted cow pat
Across the floor,
Slipping, sliding, edging further
From the source,
Threatening to engulf all.

Catherine Saunders
Surrey

Falling

Feeling like all of the eyes of the world are on you,
Pacing through them all,
Falling to rock bottom.
You're screaming, but no one's listening,
No one ever was.

Never has anyone cared about you,
What's so different now,
Still, the ignorance holding you tightly,
Its arms grabbing you.

The darkness covering you,
Exasperating, you try to catch your breath.
The light has gone out,
Along with the pain.

What has happened, why are you lying down?
Still falling, slowly trying to grip reality
But it just slips out of your grip
And out of sight.

You feel stone-cold and lifeless,
Like someone has covered you in a sky of storms,
Pushed down into a world where everyone has to hide.
Then in your hand a black rose appears and you realise
You have . . . died.

Lucy Elliott
Surrey

Grief

She slipped away with the morning
and hid herself like the setting sun.

In light sleep he was aware of the dawn
and sensed a billowing light.

Now she would never again be there.

The hollowness seemed without depth
and the longing without end.

Trees they had passed hand in hand
shed blossom in remembrance.

The sky changed pattern and
rain dripped from the leaves.

How many springs before
the sun rises again?

Godfrey Dodds
Surrey

School Dinners

When sweet Jamie Oliver lay dreaming in bed
A strange sudden fancy came into his head
He thought, *the children of Britain are not that well fed*
So what can I do? as he fell out of bed
I know what I'll do
I'll go to the school
To see what they can tell me about their
Golden Rule
When he got there he had such a shock
To see what they were feeding the dear little flock
Things will be better I'm sure very soon
Now he's been on the telly with his golden spoon
And seen the recipes that our mothers knew
Thank you, dear Jamie, you've done a good job
The children will rise up to bless you a lot.

Linda Johnson
Surrey

Smiling Ventnor

Everyone smiles in Ventnor
We now know the reason why
It's the healthy fragrant wind
Blowing in under the clear blue sky.

Ventnor's huge botanic gardens
Lying to the west
Have an international reputation
For fragrant flora, the best!

Bracing winds from the Atlantic
Streaming from the west
Carry all these healing fragrances
Directly onto our chest.

So come and stay and sample our air
Breathe in as much as you can;
Then you'll return again and again
(And you will also collect a nice tan).

We shall welcome you every time
Though you may travel many a mile
But it's worth it, to feel so young again
With your permanent Ventnor smile!

Wilfred John Parker
Surrey

The Winter's Grip

Now at the late time of year - deep into winter's gripping wrap
there seems no choice - one must stay indoors - yet not all
is lost - one can recall the days of spring - that time of year -
when all was new - all was fresh - one was eager to explore
to find nature's delights - some hidden in quiet woods - others in
meadows wild and free.

On to the long summer days - recalling the pleasure of a gentle breeze
enjoying the shadows cast by the full-grown trees
to escape for a while the beat of a hot summer's day.

Return one must to winter's days and nights
once again to learn to enjoy the real comforts of the home
protected from winter's gripping ways - finding a pleasure recalling nature's
world from those early days of a new spring
can be a real treasure in one's thoughts
helping to escape the long winter days and nights.

R P Scannell
Surrey

Life Is Now

Life stands still a little while
A cloud blocks bright sunbeams
Can't absorb this medical file
An unreal moment it seems
What is this mistake . . .
Not me, but another poor soul
Got wrong file, give me a break
Not me, haven't reached my goal
I will forget in a short while, so I can move on . . .
To all those well planned things
I will wake to find this madness a con
and enjoy pleasures that life brings
Big mistake, it's so wrong
I have targets, places to see
A voice yells
'Be strong!'
. . . And with a roaring flame of fear

I realise it's me.

Rita Pilbrow-Carlsson
Surrey

Via Carshalton To The Thames

Why not visit Carshalton in Surrey
Where there are lots of things to see
Especially at the village beyond
Where there lays a wandering pond

Two graceful swans swim side by side
While squirrels, seem to want to hide
Playing around the willow trees
Amongst the sunlight and gentle breeze

Those squirrels are so very tame
Maybe life can just be a game
Feeding them with nuts from our hand
Perhaps, thinking life, is so very grand

Visit the pond, it's a nice little treat
Especially where the rivers meet
Flowing towards the Thames, it really does
Where tourists view London, from an open-top bus

Going to the mighty sea, so wide and vast
So as we go back to Carshalton, at steadfast
Especially through spring and summertime
When each different bird sings in rhyme

Where there are so many different parks
Listen to the proud shrill warbling of the larks
Flying high, then soaring towards the ground
So much beauty in abundance lies all around

Lovely to see the beauty of God's creation
It really does give one a surge of inspiration
Where the best things in life are so very free
And costs nothing to learn of Carshalton's history

If visiting Surrey, you will be welcomed there
Where the sun shines down upon this land so fair.

Jean P McGovern
Surrey

Remembrance Day

For the blood that was shed all those years ago
is now a place for poppies to grow

In the fields or on the moor
and the other places that witnessed the war

In the cemetery where the gravestones stand
friends and family with flowers in hand.

Tara Harris
Surrey

This Night Of Dreams
(A pantoum)

This night of dreams, this magic night
The woods are quiet, all is still
A languid moon casts silver light
Pale ghosts are seeking good, not ill.

The woods are quiet, all is still
Sprites are calling, a fairy's bell
Pale ghosts are seeking good, not ill
Open your heart, all will be well.

Sprites are calling, a fairy's bell
Angels are dancing, come and see
Open your heart, all will be well
Believe in love, you can be free.

Angels are dancing, come and see
A languid moon casts silver light
Believe in love, you can be free
This night of dreams, this magic night.

Patricia Smith
Surrey

Nauplius, Nauplius
(The baby who doesn't make a fuss)

The oceans of the world abound
With tiny babes, pear-shaped or round.
They are formed in the eggs of lobster and crab,
Of prawn and krill (none of them drab),
Of copepod and barnacles, all of them crustaceans,
And the babes are known as nauplii to men of many nations.
At this early stage they have only one eye
And six little legs with plumose setae,
The Decapoda young in the eggs they stay
Others prefer to go out and play.
As they grow quickly, skins they shed
(These no doubt drop to the ocean bed).
Neptune's toddlers they now become
And take on appearances more like Mum.
So just as a baby is born to us
Many crustaceans produce a nauplius.

A E Joyce
Sutherland

Ladies In Waiting

You daintily feign your most elegant waddle
And speak with conviction about senseless twaddle.
But it matters not that your brain is like jelly,
All that's important is there in your belly.

What will they look like? His/her mum or dad?
Either way you will both be so glad.
Another angel on the Earth . . .
Once you make it through the birth!

You're anticipating an 'inappropriate gush'.
From Tesco or Boots you may have to rush.
Good job the suitcase is all packed and ready;
Old T-shirt, some sleep suits . . . at least one teddy.

You're falling apart and those hips are aching.
Hubby wonders about all the fuss you are making.
Pictures need dusting: there are shelves to re-sort,
When the rest of the year they don't merit a thought.

Not long to go now and everyone's calling.
'Haven't you popped yet?' 'Der, no . . . I am stalling!'
And all the while . . . your legs are inflating.
Oh, what it is to be ladies in waiting!

Vivienne C Wiggins
Tyne & Wear

I'm Not One To Moan

I'm not one to moan
But today I am unwell
My thyroid is causing problems
And my knee is beginning to swell.

There are large warts on my fingers
And there's no feeling in my arm
My depression is deepening
With a mind that's far from calm.

My boil is extremely painful
There's spots on the left lung
Migraines are now permanent
While there's fur beneath my tongue.

I feel I am weakening
I'm only skin and bone
But don't feel sorry for me
I'm not one to moan.

Alex Branthwaite
Tyne & Wear

My Linda Louise

Linda Louise, Linda Louise
My sweet loving angel Linda Louise
As I walk all alone
Through the pouring rain
My lonely heart is breaking
And I can feel the aching pain
Flowing slowly through my body
For no longer, my sweet angel
Of the night
Have I you to hold
Tenderly but tightly
In my arms
And close to my heart.

For your love was so warm and tender
Your love was so soft but strong
Your love was that of an angel
I long to hold and love
My whole life long.

But now I'm all alone
With a heart like a stone
And a life filled full of sorrow
But when will my broken heart
Stop loving you
And when will my broken heart
Stop caring
For an angel no longer here?

Donald John Tye
Tyne & Wear

Miracles

'I believe in miracles,' I heard the blind man say
'I've heard song of a nightingale at the end of a perfect day
I've tasted honey nectar-sweet, I've breathed the autumn mist.
When you speak of miracles, don't leave these from your list.'

'I too believe in miracles,' the deaf man said, in sign.
'I've seen the sunset crimson like a fire in the sky.
I've touched the velvet softness of a silky summer rose.
I've watched a mother smile as she held her baby close.'

The dumb man then said nothing as he took me by the hand.
He showed me children laughing as they played upon the sand.
He pointed to the pounding surf with white foam crested spray.
He smiled, a knowing smile, then he turned and walked away.

Evelyn Kane
Tyne & Wear

Reg's World

'Hello. My name is Reg and it's a pleasure to meet you.'
An ironic smile.
'Hello. I'm Reg and I'm delighted to be here.'
A knowing smile.
'Hello. My name is Reg, the scared one in the corner.'
A truthful smile.

The gilt-edged mirror held its silence.
Non-judgmental but non-comforting.
Reg considered his reflection,
Harshly and self-deprecatingly.
He didn't like the mirror.
The mirror laid bare his soul.

In the cold, white snow he was a ski instructor,
Strong, confident and bold.
In the yellow, hot sun he was a lifeguard,
Tanned, muscled and courageous.
In the fierce, blustering wind he was a sea captain,
Adventurous, fearless and brave.

Fearful of living in the real world.
Scared to fully embrace the fantasy.
Terrified that as he tried to exist in both,
He would belong to neither.
Lost and alone, forever searching for peace.
Trapped in the confident man's web.

A memory sparked in his mirror-eyes.
The awkward stance; the fidgeting fingers.
Dark hair; darting eyes. Recognition.
Her name? He didn't know yet.
But just a few practised words could remedy that.
'Hello. My name is Reg.'

Anne Marie Latham
Tyne & Wear

Lord Let The Needy Have My Heart

The people of the world Lord, they need prayer,
And all I can do is show, or reflect that I care.
Many truly need hope, courage, and Your love,
Maybe myriads of angels, from Heaven above.
Countries well off, often forget those in pain,
And slip into their luxury, time and time again.
Lord if as a man I see this, and know it's true,
Then much more in Heaven, You also see it too.
I know words of the Bible say all will be well,
With depth of my heart, Lord let my word tell
That I ask You in Heaven to take all my hope,
Spread it about so others worse off, may cope.
Lord, depth of my heart wants to outwardly give,
Take from me dear Lord, bless others to live.
What thoughts and magic Your spirit flows out,
Give to those needing, through famine or drought.
Rich and greedy cannot take this from my heart,
Seed You sowed tended by angels at life's start.
Lord, use me to speak to all of entire creation,
Speak through me words to say, use in deliberation.
Take the love in my heart, spread it among needy,
Not for myself Lord, nor for glory or being greedy.
The Heavenly Spirit within, can surely grow more,
Take from my being, and carry too tired and sore.
Send my love globally to my sisters and brothers,
Children, parents, all folk, fathers and mothers.
The love of a stranger, a brother to give hope,
And help them, dear Lord, to have faith to cope.

C R Slater
Tyne & Wear

The Great North Run 2005

Spectrum of colours and kinds mass together
in vast staggered swarms, as they start the big race,
blessed by their beauty of spirit. The weather
is generous: for most, it determines the pace.
The spectrum extends to the motives: the reasons
that so many people are deeply involved
in forcing their bodies so far out of season
and over a distance, so firmly resolved
to push to the limit their edge of endurance -
a matter of pride to prevail through the course;
prestige is the prize for the prime; reassurance
for others, sufficient to know they endorse
what boast they have made on their way to the start.
There's mirth and there's laughter and friendship all round;
for everyone here, in his way, plays his part,
his moment in history; joy-whoops resound.
While many are here for the glory, yet others
indulge aspirations to prove themselves fit;
still others a fun run among friends and brothers
is all that it means. But for some, this is it:
the height of their year, regardless of status,
their hopes to enhance how co-humans may fare
by dint of this effort to fill the hiatus
that some institutions have failed to repair,
relying on charity, sponsorship, mission,
yet join in enjoyment, rejoice in their play,
the sense of occasion confused with their vision
of those whose misfortune this run can allay.
This spectrum of people and purpose, when done,
is positive proof we need the Great North Run.

Adrian Brett
Tyne & Wear

Mouth Of The Tyne

Barking dogs, gulls' angry, screeching chatter
Grating on children's melodic laughter
Dancing whitecaps embrace rocky shoreline
Lapping the groin in homage at a shrine
Dunes sashay and sway, their rhythm sublime
Unheeding of North Sea's tears for the Tyne
Percolating breeze with soft, briny spray
That captures and spirits days' care away.

Echoes and aromas subtle combine
Ambience created by hand divine
Angelic graffiti artists sketching
Luminescent clouds with gold-tipped etching
As sun succumbs in her dying throes
Bathing the Roman fort in blood-red glow.

In folklore souls long lost carry on the cry
Of foghorn blasting their warnings on high
Spectral Bernadine's roam in reverie
Poised for flight from a ruined priory
Once shipwrecked sailors' only sanctuary
Caught on Black Middens near river entry
Vessels sunk in watery cemeteries
A patchwork of ancient memories.

A cruise ferry bobs on far horizon
Ploughing lazy waves, headed for Bergen
Air alive with melodic evensong
As twilight creeps up casting shadows long
Visions of myth, history, mortality
Potpourri stirred with harsh reality.

A captured snapshot of nature and Man
Jigsaw of pieces in a master plan.

Kathleen Potter
Tyne & Wear

Wensleydale

Wensley, oh Wensley, thou art the dale of my heart
I would grieve for thee dearly, if we were to part
You fill my life, my soul and my dreams
Your beauty surrounds me with meadows and streams.

I gaze at your trees, hedgerows, old stone walls
I hear the birds warbling their different calls
As your beauty unfolds before my eager eye
Breathtaking as ever 'neath yon lowering sky.

The mist hangs o'er the hills, clouds threaten with rain
Bringing balm to my soul while easing my pain
You are my true love, my future and my past
As into the river Ure I throw out my cast.

Hoping I could lure a fish from the river
Quiet and contented with my senses all aquiver
As I wandered thro' the dale, I strolled at my ease
No cares! No worries! Myself only to please.

I gaze at your beauty in all wonderment
As I think of the days and hours I've spent
Embraced in the warmth of a fine summer's day
The springtime, the autumn or a cold winter's day.

Wensley, oh Wensley no more will we part
You are my life, my soul and my heart
Embrace me oh Wensley, deep in thy soul
When I have departed this mortal coil.

Albert H Gormley
Tyne & Wear

Look At Me!

Nurse!
What do you see,
When you look at me,
All hunched up in my chair.
My nightie needs changing,
The blankets rearranging,
Do you really care?

You dash about,
I hear a shout,
'Your breakfast is getting cold'.
How can I feed myself,
When the food is left on a shelf,
I'm not stupid, just very old.

Throughout the day,
I hear you say,
'Can't wait for this shift to end'.
You're lucky, my dear,
That you can leave here,
While I'm going quietly round the bend.

As I lie in my bed tonight,
I pray with all my might,
That God will come and rescue me,
From this prison they call a home,
Where my free spirit cannot roam,
Back to how I used to be!

Marion Brown
Tyne & Wear

Shivers

I watch three candles burning bright,
Into the darkness of the night!
Creating shadows, full of woe,
Dancing wildly to and fro.
Alighting fears in my mind,
They dwindle common sense, 'til blind.
They chill me through, freeze the bones,
To such point, I hark for groans.
Of some bedraggled destitute,
Who roams the darkness, in pursuit!
Seeking me to suck my blood,
Or chop me up, like firewood.
And so I yield, turn on the light,
Then douse three candles, once so bright.

Sid 'de' Knees
Warwickshire

Hallowe'en

There comes a time in every year,
  Which older folk have cause to fear!
When darkness falls and doors are closed,
  These older folk feel quite exposed!

They come to dread that fearful knock,
  An opened door could bring a shock!
A ghastly visage peering in,
  Albeit with an eerie grin!

The frightful question, 'Trick or Treat?'
  While peering from beneath a sheet,
The elderly, wish it would stop,
  A shock could well induce a drop!

Or even, if they closed their door,
  Afraid to face what they might score!
A stolen garden gnome or worse!
  A painted slogan - or a curse!

For Hallowe'en they'd rather shun,
  But know that children have their fun,
With scary pranks beyond belief,
  And other kinds of pure mischief!

If only there could be a way
  To make those children stay away!
Although they do it for a joke,
  It really scares those older folk!

R Bissett
Warwickshire

Don't Believe In Love!

Today I woke up loving you,
Tonight I'm going to sleep hating you,
I can honestly live without you and your lies,
I'm worth more that that,
I've broken all the ties.
Now you're single, you're free to find,
The girl of your dreams who's got to be blind,
The only words that remain to say,
Are that, I'll regret every moment of time spent together with you every day!

Nisha Tanna
Warwickshire

A Special Anniversary

From Venetian skies
  Of deepest blue,
To waters reflecting the skies
  Through and through.
From waves gently lapping
  The sides of the boat
To the sound of the seabirds,
  Though somewhat remote.

From tables all laid to
  Perfection and style
To immaculate waiters
  With always a smile.
From food often dreamed of,
  Remaining untried,
To the friendship of others,
  With nothing denied.

From basking in sunshine
  And lounging at ease
To swimming and dancing,
  Just as you please.
From enjoying the theatre,
  Away from sea view
To relaxing and dreaming -
  Could all this be true?

From the porthole which signals
  That land is in sight
To the end of this dream cruise -
  A week of delight.

Joan Mathers
Warwickshire

Beauty

Oh! radiant beauty
Starlit wonder.
How the moon pales
Next to you.

Be it my curse
That I cannot
Hold you
Next to me.

Be it my downfall
That I have
Been struck
By your charms.

Venus hangs
Her head in shame
When she
Sees your beauty.

If you would
But choose me
I would
Consider myself blessed.

But your light
Does not shine
Upon me
In my life.

I cannot hold
Cannot touch
I must join
The faithful.

Many may come
Worship at your feet
I am but one
Will you choose me?

Anthony Lees
Warwickshire

The Still Halt

Sometimes there is a silent space in Time
When thought hovers suspended:
A moment that offers lucidity
And a lifting of the year's invisible load:
    The leaden weight
Of constant consideration.

The trick is to recognise the gift
Of the Still Halt between Now and To Come.
If we snapped the strings attached
We could rise and surrender things
Past and Future - as a swimmer,
Using the steady flow of a tidal river
On a calm day, leaves behind the green bank
Of known events to meet, without fear,
    The unseen mysteries ahead.

We could soar the power of thought
That tethers us here - Earthbound.

We sense when Time stands still;
Withheld, for a split second, the shrinking fabric
Of life, when all Nature holds its breath in awe:
Then, in the potent seed of Silence,
Intuitive awareness reveals the promise of peace
Beyond our understanding, holy and sublime,
Within the haven of this brief, Still Halt
In the intangible tissue of Time.

Dorothy Thompson
Warwickshire

Untitled

I love to go out dancing
bowling I like too.
I do a bit of keep fit
and quizzes one or two.
I'm not looking for a toy boy
to take me on a date -
no I'm a new-age pensioner
no rocking chair for me.
For every day's a bonus
when you're seventy-three.

Zena Brown
Warwickshire

Something Unpleasant

One warm summer afternoon
a peaceful place of rural rest,
St Martin's Church at Barcheston.

Taking a brass rubbing here
of an effigy on an ancient tomb,
a man, a teacher by profession,
not given to fanciful invention,
suddenly had a cold feeling of fear
which made him so uncomfortable,
his brow to sweat, his skin to crawl.

Tried to concentrate on his task,
ignore the awful atmosphere,
but the sensation intensified
until he became quite terrified.

Unable any longer to endure,
he rushed out of the church door,
leaving the rubbing incomplete.
Once outside, he felt the gloom
and dread sensation disappear.

Two carvings, neither unnerving,
a ram's head in the nave roof,
a green man on the entrance arch,
continued quietly grinning.

David Daymond
Warwickshire

The Old Home

Why do I have such affection for our former home?
Why do images of it often appear in my dreams?
I see it clearly still, though forty years have fled
A pleasant garden in front with a lovely rockery
Flower beds line the path, filled with pansies and primroses
A longer garden at the rear, a brown trellis fence
With wandering clematis and scented yellow roses
Glorious vegetables and luscious blackberries
I remember the details of how every room looked then
But why do I still retain such fondness for the old home
After all it is but bricks and building materials
Much later I realised it is not really the house
That I hold dear but the memories of the time spent
There when my wife and I were young and the children were young
Memories of our marriage and growing family
Yes, it was a lovely time, gone now but not forgotten.

Terry Daley
Warwickshire

Monty

Monty the cat had a black eye
It was caused by a ginger tom
But he had pride and plenty of style
So he walked off with aplomb
He had had many a fight
Usually over some female or another
Some of them liked to play the field
One even cheated on him with his brother
Oh, the tales that he could tell
And the battles he had won
But he'd finally met his match
When in his street came the ginger tom
Then one day when he was out
He came across a terrible sight
Some toms were beating a lone cat
So he waded in with all his might
He dispatched each one in turn
Then went to look at the injured cat
But to his amazement he found
It was the ginger tom on the mat
He helped him up and helped him home
But not a word was said
He licked the wounds and cleaned the fur
And then put him to bed
A week went by, then one day
The ginger tom paid him a call
Thanked him for all he had done
And said they shouldn't fight at all
Monty agreed and they shook paws
And Ginger told him his name
Reaching this peace with the ginger tom
Was to Monty his *El Alamein.*

Diana Daley
Warwickshire

Finding The Way

The day I had depression - I thought the end was near
My gosh how I did panic, every day I shed a tear
Every hour was darkness, no light could I see
'Why or why,' I would say, 'is this happening to me?'

If we only knew the answer, if there was a magic cure
No one would be suffering, there would be no cross to bear
But life just isn't like that - we all do get our share
Sometimes it's just not easy, and it really seems unfair.

As I sit here writing this, I know there is a way
Yes you will come through it, you will have your day
Give yourself some freedom - accept the way you are
And you will find in doing so, you really will go far

You have the power within you - it's there you cannot see
Just remember that true saying, *what will be will be!*
Make yourself feel happy, be yourself, *be you*
The clouds that all surround you, one day will all be blue.

Veronica Buckby
Warwickshire

November Skies

Tears of November
Falling onto the golden hands
Of trees in autumn
Branches embracing the sky.

A lonely raven cries
To the clouds of stirring coldness,
Waiting for answers
That will never be heard.

The icy breath of dusk
Draws the last of the evening light,
Guiding the darkness
To the face of the sky.

The tide under the moon
Listens to its silent commands,
The moon's looking glass
Of the sky in the sea.

Natalie Holborow (15)
West Glamorgan

Terry's Loss

Terry's eighty-seven
At the twilight of his life
He's lived through war
He lives next door
And lately, lost his wife.

They'd only had each other
For sixty-seven years
The war took both their mothers
And their children . . .
And their fears . . .

It came not to him sudden though
He'd nursed her for an age
He'd come to terms with letting go
And cursed her not in rage
He cursed her not for leaving him
He cursed her not at all
Her mind had left so long ago
Had night, but yet, to fall.

The Social Service lady came
And then she went away
She came again, forgot his name
But took not, from his day.

At night I hear him sobbing
Talking only to his cat
Asking if she's missing
Curling up, on Mattie's lap!

His time to mourn, his curtains drawn
Within so, on his own
A simple man, forever worn
And living . . . all . . . alone . . .

No one else has visited
No one gives a toss
'Tis only he, and you and me
Have suffered, Terry's loss.

Mark Anthony Noble
West Glamorgan

Call Of The Mountain

Over the mountains a summer breeze sighs
A whisper of breath under the clear blue skies
Deep down in the valley, far-reaching below
Sprinkled droplets of gold in the sun's morning glow.

The mountain is still, with the heavens at rest
A time of the day that I so love the best
As I drink in the balm that nature instils
I gaze up in awe at the beautiful hills.

They thrust through the valley and stretch to the sky
On silent wing a lone hawk hovers by
My mind is at peace in the quiet of day
As serenity washes my troubles away.

Wrapped in pockets and folds, little farmhouses stand
Lost to the world on this green fertile land
Sheep steadily munch, playful lambs have been born
Each drenched in the joy of this mystical morn.

But a sour-faced mountain can often be tough
Gripped in jaws of a thunderstorm cruel and rough
Aggressively wild when blustery winds blow
When the lamp of the storm lights the valley below.

Changes occur as the seasons unfold
From the rich blaze of autumn, to a snap raw and cold
When winter holds court as a powerful king
Then agrees to submit to a soft gentle spring.

There is charm in their magic, nature's contrast we find
A look fresh and vital, a beast savage and wild
They stand as forever, majestic and tall
For strong is the voice of the mountain's call.

Barbara Davies
West Glamorgan

Why?

If only someone cared
Instead they stand and stare
Some others pass you by
As you sit and cry
A figment of their imagination
Some crazy hallucination
They pretend you don't exist
So they can live their life in bliss
You need a friendly hand
To pull you up and help you stand
But no one cares at all
And if I try to get up I'll fall
Living in the world alone
All faith and hope is gone
Happy memories do remain
Never to be lived again
Hardened by the cold
Strengthened by the wind
Your mind is old
But your youth shows in your skin.
The storm is on the horizon
The sun will never shine
And all I ever wanted
Was a home to call mine.

Natasha Brand
West Lothian

Thank You Mr Blair

Thank you Mr Blair,
For winning another election,
For bringing us terrorism,
And not much protection,

We asked you,
Not to go to war,
But you went right in,
With a patriotic roar,

We asked you,
Not to listen to him,
But you can't help it,
You jump right in,

'But Bush said so,'
We hear you cry,
But please don't think,
Of those who die,

Thank you Mr Blair,
For causing us pain,
I hope you enjoy,
Your political gain.

Alan Gordon
West Lothian

Seasons

When spring appears snowdrops are the first to arrive.
There are buds on the trees, and the squirrels are alive.
The hedgehog appears with leaves attached to spikes.
Here come some children out on new bikes.

We know summer is here
When the trees are all dressed in their fine array.
The flowers of every kind out by night and by day.
The weather is warm, and wild animals know.
It is time to be lazy there will be no snow.

The autumn is here, there is colour everywhere.
The foxes are looking everywhere for their fare.
The badgers and rabbits are out hunting too,
So are stoats, weasels and hedgehogs, to give them their due.

Autumn has gone and now winter is here.
The branches are bare except for the snow which is everywhere.
It carpets the ground all thick and white.
Even in the dark it is still very bright.

Zoe French
West Midlands

One Wish

One wish,
What would it be,
To see my parents again,
What a sight it would be.
Peace on Earth
And happiness all around,
To see my parents again,
Raised up from the ground.
If the Lord would grant me just one wish
To see my mom and dad once again
It would give me such a lift,
It would lift my sadness
And take my loneliness away.
Please give me my one wish
And bring them both back again to stay.
I'm forever wishing
To see both my parents once again,
I'm forever crying, alongside the rain,
Alongside my parents.
They could bring the love and peace,
This Earth needs so badly,
But I will always keep my love
Waiting, for you both
The day I reach Heaven
And we meet again
And share our love.

Mary Woolvin
West Midlands

Fear

We live in a world full of fear
Shut up, be quiet, don't let them hear
Frightened to express our own point of view
For fear of assault, or maybe even killed.

It seems we are scared to take any action
Afraid of reprisals, negative reactions
Terrified, we may have too much to lose
Open to all kinds, of possible abuse.

Remember that fear, is all in the mind
Move through your fears back the tide
It doesn't matter, if this all shatters
Because nothing in the end really matters.

Andrew Nokes
West Midlands

Missing You

Missing your kiss, missing your touch,
Missing your smile so very much.
Missing the gentleness of our embrace,
Missing the love that lights your face.
Missing the soft touch of your hand,
Missing the way you understand.
Missing the love that pours from your heart,
Missing every second that we're apart.

Missing the times you dried my tears,
Missing the way you calm my fears.
Missing the laughter we both shared,
Missing your comfort when I've been scared.
Missing the strength your wisdom brings,
Missing the safety of your loving wings.

Missing the chance to tell you true,
How much brighter my life's been since I met you.
Missing the chance just to hold your hand,
And show you I love you and I understand.
Missing the times we just used to hold,
Missing your warmth for now I'm left cold.
Missing the days you showered me with love,
An angel before me, sent from above.

Missing the times we just used to walk,
The pride I felt when hearing you talk.
Missing the chance to comfort your pain,
Wishing every second I'll see you again.
All these things I miss, all these things and more,
For now my love I miss you like never before.

Helen Dunford
West Midlands

Faith

Faith is a virtue that cannot be forced.
Faith is devotion, trust and religion.
Faith shall always be recognised,
Whether to God or just a friend.
Faith is the bright light in darkness.
Faith can't be destroyed, nor can it end.
Faith keeps you strong in the most difficult times.

Samyukta Aryasomayajula
West Midlands

Please Tell Me Is There No Way Out?

Walking through a crowded street
Where no one knows your name
Another person walking by
All faces seem the same
Where broken hearts lie hidden
Underneath designer labels
Pain and hurt just logos
Found upon bargain tables
Life is what we make it
Yet make it we never do
Too much competition
Stands before me and you
How can we ever win?
When all we do is lose
No trophies for us to hold
Just the morning blues
Days and nights roll into one
So do months and years
Our youth of yesterday
Drowned in sex and beer
Burned away like a cigarette
As we awake in ashes of doubt
The same four walls keep drawing in
Please tell me is there no way out?

Lisa Jane Mills
West Midlands

The Little Mind-Dwelling Creature Of Wonderment

'Thought's a word,' I thought it said;
That cursèd voice within my head,
'That deserveth not the time o' day.
These words I speak, not simply say.'

'Why not, my friend?' I ask in jest,
Playing up to my personal pest.
'Is't not a word without thought?'
Say I swiftly in sweet retort.

'To think, you see,' he helps me find,
'Is to slaughter dreams of the innocent kind.
It's to gaily grow into sweet dismay,
So this, you see, is why I say.'

David Maidment
West Midlands

I Couldn't Win . . .

I knew 'Death' was on a visit,
Felt his presence near.
Found out who he had come for,
Cos in Mitzi's eyes was fear.
Death waited quietly on one side
My Mitzi close to me.
With my hand I held Death at bay
Hoping he would leave my Mitzi be.
I saw Death creep around my guard,
To rest on Mitzi like a cloud.
I was helpless with the happening
And mentally prepared her shroud.
A single thread bound her to me
A thread I was holding tight.
Alas, felt it slipping through my fingers
And I knew I had lost my fight.
My senses say it isn't up to me.
But my heart didn't wish to know.
Ah well! My heart will hurt but will not break
As I bow my head and let her go.

Rosie Hues
West Midlands

Looking For A Rainbow

(Dedicated to my lovely husband - 1938-2005)

My heart is sad and weary *Lord*
I don't know what to do
Everywhere is dark *Lord*
No light is shining through.
I've lost someone so precious,
My heart is broken in two.

I start each morning with a prayer,
And ask that you be near,
When footsteps falter on the path,
Please take away my fear.
My faith and trust I put in you
Please guide me on my way.
That I may once more see the light
And a bright new lovely day.

We cannot stop life's changes,
Or re-open a closed door,
But if we don't look back too often,
We may find peace once more.

Jacqueline Claire Davies
West Midlands

The Lost Hope Bar

Somewhere in the street of life, there's a flashing neon sign
Where lost souls visit from time to time.
The Lost Hope Bar, all are welcome there
Broken-hearted and all who carry despair.
Inside this bustling place
There's music for all those with sad taste.
Come drink a glass of humiliation
Cocktails served of emancipation.
Pints of sorrow, and agony snacks served in bowls
Drinks and snacks to serve and suit all souls.
As the bar tenders lend ears to sad tales
Of the down-trodden over misery ales.
On the dance floor is the dance of pain
The dance that others do over and over again.
The regulars come back for more
The way of things, they know the score.
There is the odd new face
Who visits this mournful place.
To get intoxicated and drown their sorrows
Looking for hope to fill those hollows.
Maybe to meet a new friend and be a pair
To tell each other sad tales and compare.
So if you're passing pop in and say hello
And who you meet you'll never know.
Open twenty-four hours a day, seven days a week
A place of mournful stories, you are free to speak.
Come in mix and speak at the lost souls' bar
All are welcome from near and far.

Terry Powell
West Midlands

Free Range

I went down to the farm to buy some eggs,
They should have walked home but they had no legs.
So I rolled them gently down the hill,
Some went on rolling, some stood still.
Some of them ambled,
Some of them rambled.
They all got broken
And so they were scrambled.

Olive Allgood
West Midlands

Dance Of Life

Energy,
Flows throughout the universe,
In a constant stream,
Connecting each and everything,
In the dance of life,

Creating patterns,
Spirals and circles,
Bringing to all,
The divine sparks of life,
From the eternal flame,

The supreme power,
From which all outpours,
And once more returns,
In a never-ending cycle,
Participating in the dance,

A pulsing beat,
Of vibrations and rhythms,
The heartbeat that never ceases,
Which was before the Alpha,
And radiates forever infinite,

In each and everything,
The essence exists,
If it were not so,
Its presence would not be seen,
All unfolds from the source,

Our Earth and all upon it,
Remote planets in the cosmos,
All that God unveiled,
Each and every cell,
Dances, to the Creator's melody.

Ann G Wallace
West Midlands

Autumn

The leaves change colour
Like my mother.
The plants die
And start to lie down.
The plants scrunch up
And you can feel them munch in your hand.
The animals start to hibernate
While we get ready for Christmas.

Matthew Skelton (8)
West Midlands

Pause To Remember

Pause to remember . . .
As Poppy Day nears -
Pause at the Cenotaph.

Pause to remember . . .
Yesterday's years.
In the garden of remembrance.
In a cold November
Shrouded in haze,
Place poppy crosses,
Feeling tears through your gaze.
You remember their youth -
Now you have got old.

Pause to remember . . .
A corner of England -
A grave and the cold.
They went off to war
Feeling tense and numb,
A premature death -
Was yet to come.

Pause to remember . . .
And show that we care.
Our loved ones departed
Know how we feel,
In planting those crosses
The pain - in time it will heal.

Charlie Hughes
West Midlands

Changes

I may look fine but I'm all at sea
I wonder if it is really me
Be it work or family
The changes and uncertainty are plain to see
The time has come to make a choice
But my head is screaming with everyone's voice
Which one is right I'm not sure
Confusion reigns and logic is out the door
I want to do what is best
And make my choice then I can rest
Changes create major uncertainty
I almost want to flee
It's not the answer that I know
Confused and upset which way do I go?

Dave Slade
West Midlands

Know Your Friends . . .

For every day that you're not here,
I close up tight and shed a tear,
I know one day you will return,
My eternal flame will forever burn.

The times we shared both good and bad,
Gave us fine memories, for that I'm glad,
Problems that come were solved together,
Friendship was formed that will last forever.

The lives we lead are so compact,
It's amazing our friendship stays in tact,
There's never an hour, a minute or date,
So our one reason must be fate.

Relationships start and finish so fast,
Soon yesterday's news is now the past,
But friendships last a lifetime and more,
Because friends are people you love and adore.

We all have mates and people we know,
The ones in the street that say hello,
But the word friend means that special bond,
The one that's compact, and still so *strong!*

Kevin Mytton
West Midlands

The Tree

The tree stands still
On a lonely hill
Under rolling dark clouds
As thunder and lightning strike
A burst of fire
Branches snap
Crashing to the ground
The tree looks dead
Yet it's alive
Standing one hundred years
Roots are strong
So life is prolonged
People remember the tree
And write songs
The tree lives on
When time is gone.

P Bennett
West Midlands

I Miss You

When you left me you broke me.
I didn't feel like talking, didn't feel like walking.
We grew close together and you just went away.
No explanation just upped and left.
Confused my mind, it died a mental death.
I missed you.

I thought we were doing life.
Knew all about me, like an open book
Been exactly 10 years since it had been shut.
Now it's torn again and it's all my fault.
Should have stopped you, should have made you halt.

Didn't know what was going through your heart.
Dropped you home, you gave me a smile.
How was I to know you were going to leave me?
Why didn't you talk? Why didn't you explain,
Why didn't you make me see?

It's been too long and I feel lost without you.
Wondering if you're alone and whose been with you.
Are you still mine? Will we meet again some time?
Now I know why you went away,
You loved me too much to stay.
I'm all alone, and I wanna cry sometime.

Why did you have to leave.
I miss you.

Az Chaudhry
West Midlands

A Perfect Afternoon

The lamps are lit
The fire aglow
The curtains drawn
It starts to snow
The table laid with tea and cakes
A cosy feel the room it makes.

The tape is set to sit and watch
A film of romance an era lost
But over it is all too soon
To end a perfect afternoon.

Susan Bamford
West Midlands

Our Wedding Day

It seems a hundred years since we first met,
Did not know then and yet.
As time went by it was plain to see,
We got on well you and me.
And now we stand together side by side,
Our love combined, love now defined.
Holding your hand in mine.
As we say I do,
Now sharing a life for the both of you.
As we stand here saying our wedding vows,
All around can see,
Our pledge to marriage for eternity.
We hear the distant music playing,
It's our wedding song.
A unique togetherness two as one.
It is so long since we first met and love has slowly grew,
Now family and friends gathered as we say I do.
This is a journey all will share on this our wedding day,
Our bands now complete at the altar we pray.
We'll take a little time together on our honeymoon,
Romantic love then coming back to our home soon.
Yes we will always remember the first night we met,
Our beginning yet we were so blind.
And now our hearts united,
Saying I am yours and you are mine.

Carol Boneham
West Midlands

Dymock Dreams

I came along your many winding ways
and found you dressed in yellow daffodil,
that flowered in the orchard's dappled shade
and filled each field and cottage window sill.

To where your story lies in sacred stone
held fast in Norman Arch and Saxon chapel.
Where marched the Roman road, long overgrown,
now tread the weary feet of English cattle.

To see where once your poets stood in awe
to praise the singing stream and quiet wood,
till summoned by wild trumpetings of war
to spill their verse in foreign fields of blood.

I left you sleeping in the warm spring sun,
where dreams and daffodils still linger on.

John Eccles
West Midlands

The Silent Severn

The silent Severn softly flows
  Across the pleasant Shropshire plain,
Meandering in shapely bows
  To scan the distant hills again,
Remembering the laughter still
  Of splashing down Plinlimon Hill.

One bow, with tender whim,
  Has wound a comforting moat around
Old Salop town, hemmed it in,
  All but a neck for the castle mound,
Protection Welshmen voted loathsome,
  Howsoever, Salop throve some.

On from here the river plies,
  Listless by the high blue Wrekin,
Until through Coalbrookdale she glides,
  To come upon a simply sweet thing,
Hi, Bridgnorth! You can date me surely,
  Then on she swans to dazzle Bewdley.

Down at Worcester, Tewkesbury too,
  Where Teme and Avon meet the flow,
Where Malvern's blade surveys the view,
  And Severn winds a silver bow,
She hears an unexpected roar
  And curtsies to the tidal bore.

And all these ancient towns they grew,
  Along with Gloucester, and lush lands,
For flats got up by sail, a few,
  And hordes more by drays or gangs,
But silent Severn fast and free
  Finds at last the beloved sea.

Terence Belford
West Midlands

What's Religion?

Solace in a time of pain
It's there through all bad times
A comfort there to cling to
As life's mountain we do climb

A cause of war and hatred
A cause of blood and death
Calling out your saviour's name
With your last dying breath.

Stein Dunne
West Midlands

Oo Needs Bleedin' Snobby Class?

Alright a' kid, ow am yow?
Cor stop nar I gotta goo!
Ow's the werter, is it gud?
Ar's just off to meet me bud.
I cor tell yow ow I lernt,
To talk like this, it's abserd!
Ar've lived in Walsall all me life,
Me accent's never caused me strife.
Apart from when ar went to Wales,
They tek the mick, but me accent hails!
Rule Britannia, never mind that,
Rule Beechdale, ow's that!
Ar'm Black Country, born and bred,
Jus' like Noddy Holder sez!
'E's Black Country through an' through,
So cum on da'n, and join the crew!
Ar'm proud to be a Beechdale lass,
Oo needs snobby bleedin' class?

Clara Ann Louise Preston
West Midlands

Thoughts On Leaves

Green, gold and mustard,
Secret all year round
In this chestnut tree.

Here's green. Calm gentle green
Of annual meadow grass,
Sweet continuity,
Beneath the paddling pool
It never dies.

Gold dominates. Reminds
Of gifts from those
We believe to have wisdom
And gleams in the sun
Of worn wedding rings.

Perhaps. Ah! Mustard leaves!
See them come down,
Vivaldi's quavers, darting.
Feel sharpness of mustard
In heart and mouth,
Catch at the throat of an older mother
At another year's parting.

Jennifer McDonald
West Midlands

Lost Paradise

This morning I woke forty some years ago
in the forever meadow fringed by the eternal wood
that chameleon fantasy of jungle or Sherwood in a whim
where the soft foes of fancy suffered
their losses obligingly as the birds perched
and wooded or wheeling sky bound sang their hours away.
Each early holiday sun morning
we, a coterie of actors
uneducated as the stones sliding away beneath
our sandled feet on the baked farmyard track
blowing pink sweet bubbles smashing onto our faces
past heifers and cowpats, horseflies and stiles
reached our Heaven's destination
where in a Wild West moment
three boys lay dead for a while
two blew their smoking fingers
one brown as a berry girl giggled
and innocence shivered.
All day long in the revisionist wood
we made our statements which meant nothing at all
skipping home in the humming eve
to hotpot and love.
Then, quick as a flash a second
the time it took to snatch our protector king
from our grasp
I return bedded in lead
and draw the shroud on this holiday sun morning
over my death masked head.

Nick Godfrey
West Midlands

Grandad A Terrorist?

If you want a laugh, then I'm your man,
I can tell a joke with a face deadpan.
The grandkids, they have come to stay,
We are really having a great fun day.
Grandma who is so sweet and gentle
Says, 'Oi, Husband, have you gone mental?'
A change of mood, the police knock door,
I open, ask, 'Who are you looking for?'
'Sir, we are arresting you, do not resist.
You're on our *fun-day-mental-list.*'

Albert Watson
West Midlands

Sweet Meadows

One morn, I stepped out of my cottage,
looking at the freshly fallen raindrops,
glistening in the morning sunshine, like
thousands of jewels sent down from Heaven,
on this sweet meadow.
Listen! I hear the song of a skylark
across the coppice. Wait, what stirred
inside it? Mother rabbit pops out with
her offspring, behind her a fox,
looking for a quick meal.
In the trees a song thrush sends forth
its beautiful melody. All this is laid
out before you, if only you will be quiet
and wait for God's creatures to appear.
On returning from the meadow,
I spy cheeky Charly, my blackbird,
sparrows and later, from my cottage window,
partaking of a drink from the bird bath,
a squirrel,
what joy this brings me.
These are all God's creatures and
I thank Him for creating them.

Maureen Margaret Huber
West Midlands

Last Lesson Of The Afternoon

When will the bell ring and end this weariness,
Of the boredom that congests the room so rapidly,
And the thoughts of my mind vanishing blankly?
Now the clock is ticking slower than a snail,
Making the time seem immovable,
I cannot stand this anymore,
Even the trees outside are more interesting.
I can feel his staring and burning at my neck,
'Kamini Manivasagam, the answer please?'
I feel the sweat dripping off my tiresome face.
'That will be a detention and a D-merit!'
The teacher smirks in his sinister way until,
The bell, my saviour rings loud and clear to end my day.

Kamini Manivasagam (13)
West Midlands

I Am The One

I am the one
You chose to ignore
I am the one
Who waits
By your door.

I am the one
Who sits up
At night
I am the one
Who leaves on the light.

I am the one
Who knows
How to cry
I am the one
Who has to get by.

I am the one
Who feels your pain
I am the one
The pawn
In your game.

I am the one
Who's left
Feeling lonely
I am the one
Who pines for you only.

I am the one
Who begs
Your forgiveness
I am the one
To be your witness.

I am the one
Who loves you best
I am the one
You put
To the test.

John H Foley
West Midlands

Happy Memories

From Yorkshire by coach on a summer's day
Came my sister to Birmingham for her holiday,
I planned days of interest for us both to share,
Discovered a castle, canals and rivers everywhere.

We climbed into a long boat, received cups of tea
Sat by a window, enjoyed Birmingham's canal history,
Chug-chug-chug went the engine, as slowly we did glide,
Passing trees and greenery, an interesting, relaxing ride.

Joined a bus ride from the city, to Tamworth we came,
High above the river, stood the castle, historically fame.
We walked through flower gardens, folk picnicked by the river,
Explored castle rooms, a ghost gave us - quite a shiver!

Thursday, a special morning film show to see,
The city's 'Odeon' senior's ticket, included biscuits and tea,
Happy chatty seniors, soon filled each and every seat,
A weekly enjoyment, where groups of friends meet.

The new Bullring Market, with long stalls we did see,
Aroma of onions and hot dogs, wafted over to me,
A hive of activity, many voices filled the air,
Silently looking down, St Martin's Church gave a welcome there.

B'ham Cathedral and art gallery offered interest to all,
Botanical Gardens grew tropical plants and trees so tall,
White glass houses, colourful flowers, rolling lawns so green,
Peacock family, singing birds, peaceful gardens, so serene.

One hot sunny day, travelled to Stratford from the city
Discovered the River Avon hedged by trees, tranquil and pretty,
Saw river boats, canal boats through locks slowly passed,
Ducks, swans and geese swam, found ice creams at last!

The ride back to Birmingham was our last trip too,
My sister had to pack, her return coach date was due,
So if you have a relative, come for a holiday,
Give them happy memories to keep, and take away.

Stella Bush-Payne
West Midlands

Autumn Leaves - Haiku

Crumpled, they fly on
Multicoloured gusts of wind
Winter's blank eyes stare.

Brenda Dove
West Midlands

Squirrels - The Neighbours From Hell

At the start they seemed such friendly neighbours,
They all welcomed us with open arms.
They called round a lot, but we thought so what,
We were captivated by their charms.

We invited them round for some supper,
Not thinking they'd be messy eaters.
They chucked food around and dug up the ground,
We tried not to let these things defeat us.

They no longer seem quite so endearing,
Since they came and dug up our sweet peas.
Their habits are crude, they eat the bird food,
By the way, did you know they've got fleas?

Now they really have outstayed their welcome,
Their behaviour has just gone to pot,
And oh flippin' heck, they've chewed through the deck,
So they'll have to be poisoned or shot.

I have heard they make rather good eating,
Stuffed with herbs, brushed with good olive oil,
I'm sure they'd taste fine with a glass of wine,
Slowly cooked in a nice casserole.

Susan Guy
West Midlands

Control Freak

Put that there listen to me
Can't be out of place you *must* see.
Need to be organised, has to be in order
Please don't be late that's pushing the border.
Where are we going? Give me the time and place
Need the information to put in my database.
Have to think ahead, need to be aware
It is important, I need to be alert and prepare.
Colour-coded, matched I want my dress sense to be
They say wake up and look to reality.
No time for that have to get it done now
Not enough time in that day for who, what, where, when or how.
If there's something to be done but out of my reach
Impatient I become so easy to teach.
Out of my hands but the situation is there
Please let me sort it out I'm reaching despair!

Elisha Mesquitta
West Midlands

Wish You Understood

What's that inside your mouth
Another bird I fear
How I wish you understood
When I say get it out of here
I found one yesterday
Underneath the bed
Almost gave me a heart attack
Well I thought that it was dead.

You're doing it again
Jumping on the sink
I wish you understood
From your dish to have to drink
That's broke another glass
The last one in the house
Is that what I think it is
Another blooming mouse.

Leave them all outside
Don't bring them in the door
Wish you understood
I don't like that anymore
You are such a loving cat
Especially when you're good
Just don't bring dead things inside
How I wish you understood.

P M Stone
West Midlands

No Going Back

Once something is done, it can't be changed
You made the choice, it can't be rearranged

Things are done for a reason, and that must stand
Even if things aren't super, or even grand

That choice was made, and that must stay true
No one can change it now, not even you

There's no going back, never will be
It will be OK in the end, you will see

But what you have to do now is live your life to the max
Never look back, always forward, don't hide your tracks

For life goes forward, not backwards to the past
Live life to the full, for it goes too fast

Gemma Steele
West Midlands

Katrina

A natural disaster at its worst
Or is it nature's curse?
We will never know
No mercy did it show.

Nothing will stop nature - no way!
As humans we have no say!
Race, colour or creed
Wealth or poor, nothing agreed.

Was always down to fate
If in New Orleans on that date?
A lot of people left dead
Not a tear did Katrina shed.

Katrina did not care
Nothing for her to share
Kind, good or bad
She gave everything she had.

As humans we do not understand
Large, small or grand
A disaster to the end
This we do not pretend.

Katrina left floods and destruction behind
For New Orleans this was so unkind
This is nature's way
Or is it? So they say.

Garry Bedford
West Midlands

A Man's Oil

She was not very pretty
Her smile was somewhat witty
And unhappy sitting still
In the noon wet winter chill

When night came, she wished to stay
Nay said I, be still I pray
But away she strolled hostile
She'd enough of her false smile

Her soul on canvas captured
I took those thoughts discoloured
On the journey of my life
As a decayed, deceased wife

Seeyam Brijmohun
West Midlands

No Glory

This story ain't pretty and at times ain't clean.
But a story of life and a story of death
Is seldom what it seems.
The day in the life of a Coventry kid,
To play in a tree and always keep falling,
Was never the same when Hitler came calling.

His mum and dad, the cornerstone of life,
Now stand broken and divided by strife.
His dad sees Romel.
His mum sees men.
The kid's life, never the same again.

Times can change and they always do,
A luxury prefab, a concrete block.
Built from hope, but more in despair.
The landscape bleak, no one there.
Can they go on? Do they care?

The kids take over, their turn to live.
Their fight never physical always subliminal.
Coventry the phoenix, from ashes of the past
Tries to fly but it doesn't last.
Foe and enemy are not so clear,
The city still fights on
IRA, father dear!

John Hiron
West Midlands

Freedom

Do you think the world's gone bonkers
When our kids can't play with conkers
Can't throw a snowball in a fight
Just in case they might
Go and hurt one another
Or distress a little brother
Can't play on the swings
Or those roundabout things
No matter what MP's say
Our children should be allowed to play.

M Watts
West Midlands

A Mother's Love

A mother's love is like steel;
Strong and firm and unshattering,
A mother's love is like a mirror;
Honest and true yet flattering,
A mother's love is like a dewdrop
Refreshing the early flowers,
A mother's love is like the sun
Illuminating darker hours,
A mother's love is like the sky;
Infinite and indestructible,
A mother's love is like a drizzle;
Gentle yet unpredictable,
A mother's love is as unique
As the kind soul who gives it so freely.
So we thank you Mother
For the constant shower of love you supply us with,
We mean it deeply.

Vinothini Manivasagam (14)
West Midlands

Mr Wonderful

My bloke thinks he's got it all;
he's toned, he's tanned and he's tall.
With his dark brown eyes and hair to match,
he thinks he is quite a catch!

He won't wash the dishes
and leaves wet towels on the floor.
We have a lovely coat rack
but he insists on using the door.

He snores so loudly
it makes the house shake!
Our neighbours must think
that there's an earthquake!

When he watches his football
it drives me insane!
As he 'conveniently' goes deaf
when he's watching a game!

But it doesn't seem
to bother him at all;
because according to him,
I've bagged Mr Wonderful!

Elysee Rafot
West Sussex

Time Is Like Gold Dust

'Time is like gold dust,' she said
As she watched the grains of gold
Cascade through her fingers
Unable to prevent the precious metal
From flooding to the floor
Desperately clutching it tightly
As it escapes, lost forever.

'Time is like gold dust,' she said
As she watched the clock hands
Tick-tock, tick-tock
Stolen, another hour
Stolen, another sixty grains
Tick-tock, tick-tock.

'Time is like gold dust,' she said
With her last breath
As the last few grains slipped
Through her tightly-clutched palm
As the grains of gold sealed her fate.

Ida Petretta
West Sussex

From Time To Time

Find a quiet corner in your mind
And come sit with me
It can be as dark as an empty soul
Or it can be what you want it to be

Feel the isolation, discover what it's not
It's troubled in here, I know
I need to get a firmer grip
I can't let this feeling show

Touch on a pain that hurts and does not heal
See an emotion then look away
It's too painful to unreel
Hold on to it all

Keep it together, not long now
Please hold onto my hand
I will close the door on all of this
As I still can't understand

I might always be afraid of every emotion in me
So many different sides
Some I like and some I don't you see

Karen Langridge
West Sussex

Astrus

From the void detected
A UFO entered our sphere
Were we to cheer
Or were we to fear?

Called Astrus, it descended
Against background of brilliant blue sky
Uniform in motion
Were there beings on board?
From where, what, who and why?

Final resting place awaiting
On so solid ground
People rushing to the point
From miles and miles around

Emerging from this object
Came parachutes now too slow
Spectacle of heavy impact
That chance now a little low

Astrus it was so called
For it came from amongst the stars
It fell from Earth intact
They discovered, though, it was a secret Russian unmanned probe
That had just come back from Mars!

Ivan Sepp
West Sussex

Obstacles

You speak soft words that barricade my ears,
I wish that they made sense.
Instead they tangle like briar-sharp thorns,
weaving intricate, deserting me.
I offer them a safety net,
a space to feed and breathe,
then I somehow reject them and helplessly let them bleed.
I tried and failed to let them in,
maybe not enough.

Perhaps I'll hear them if they sing me a song,
maybe I'll keep them playing sweet for long.

I'm trying to understand your words,
I know they are for me,
and once I get to hear their sounds,
eventually they'll set me free.

Anna Green
West Sussex

Auntie Dotty

I love my auntie Dotty
I see her every day
She gives me lots of cuddles
When we have a little play.

I love my auntie Dotty
She always shares her food
I get all sorts of tasty things
That's why I'm always good.

I love my auntie Dotty
When I stay with her at night
She lets me sleep upon her bed
We snuggle up so tight.

I love my auntie Dotty
When someone knocks her door
I bark so very loudly
As I race around the floor.

·I love my auntie Dotty
And when she needs to rest
We curl up on a comfy chair
I like that bit the best!

Mike Wenham
West Sussex

Dew On An Early Rose

I walked along the garden;
The air was quiet and still.
My eyes went off to a distant scene
Of sheep upon a hill.

The birds were not yet risen;
The foxes were at home.
Looking at my garden,
I felt no need to roam.

Dawn shone on the roses
With their dewy stems,
While violets and lobelia
Adorned the borders' hems.

Cob spiders' webs were shining
In the rising sun.
I stood and watched as it rose,
And saw the day begun.

Roger Tremethick
West Sussex

A Sussex Journey

Rolling downs, rolling up
Combed by tempered wind
Creased by verdant combe
Footed by mattes of green
Dotted by Man's squared touch
Threaded by ribboning tarmac.

On these, as I watch
Vehicles hiss and roar, snarling speed
Loud in their passing insignificance
From the wheel, some, I fear
Witness the surrounding magnificence
And foolishly think it is all for them
And foolishly pass it as timeless.

How wrong, for if I look
I can see how in aeons' time
Long after their journey is over
The bigger journey will still be going on
Rolling downs will be down
Grass mattes will be drowned
Trees layered charcoal
Vegetation layered peat
Strewn with fossilised fauna.

And one will stand where I do now
Alive with the only things that can ever survive
The invisible threads we fail to see
Love, consideration and dignity.

Dan Sewell
West Sussex

The End Of Frustration

In view of the friendship we've shared in the past
I've come round to tell you I've got one at last;
She really is lovely, her body's sublime,
I'm sure that I'm in for a wonderful time.
I saw Dr Brown on account of my nerves -
Oh boy, when I think of those beautiful curves -
He said he was sure, there was no doubt about it,
He could see at a glance I'd been too long without it.
I know it has taken some time to achieve
And you may find this very hard to believe,
But I never imagined that I'd go that far . . .
Not a woman, you fool! I've purchased a car!

June Marshall
West Sussex

Corvus Frugilegus

Nesting time is over;
High in shredded treetops
Colonies of rooks collect,
Moving their clock to match the twilight hour.
Their rasping calls cutting the roof,
Clashing discordant music, alerting all below.

Countless arrive, jostling for space.
Silence falls.
Two pathfinders float out,
Giving an ordered signal
Wave upon wave, flood like autumn leaves
Driven in a storm,
Screaming their release
Across pearl and orange sundown sky -
Aeroplanes stacking, then revving with energy
To drive a course to distant woods
Where night must still their tongue.

In the field below
A woman lifts her arms
Wishing to protect the flight;
Swept up by Homeric force,
Pin-like in their presence.

Deep in a valley
An old man is content
To close his eyes and sleep,
Secure the rooks will arrive,
Moving their clock
To match the twilight hour.
Their rasping calls cutting the roof,
Clashing discordant music, alerting all below.

Veronica Charlwood Ross
West Sussex

Spring

To wake - to fling abroad
and drink the sunshine's vital potency.
This fire of life leaping at roots of trees,
touching curled leaves within the bud,
the blackthorn - startled into white.
What a moment of glad recognition,
bringing delight in body and mind.
A time to give thanks,
dynamic earth is waking
as spring breathes a blessing over the land.

Idris Woodfield
West Sussex

White World (Without Sound)

Morning grows
street lamps fade
below these blue, forgotten hills
winter winds
Siberian
froze the stars and stole the sun
for now the Earth becomes spellbound
here in a white world without sound

No one knows
who can say
when silence wins the day?
Not the church bell's hollow tone
nor the dumbstruck marble moon
for now the Earth becomes snowbound
still in a white world without sound

Peter Lacey
West Sussex

A War Poem Without Rhyme

In 1944, President Roosevelt sent his top envoy, Ed Murrow, to BBC
To suggest a quick end to World War II
By cleverly bribing Hitler to atom-bomb Moscow
But this fell on deaf ears at Broadcasting House and Ally Pally
When we discovered that other cities were secretly listed as well
Not ending World War II but starting a new atomic world war race
Unfortunately with Churchill leading in first place
Most backroom boys at Ally Pally were stunned by these proposals
Many of us, including myself, succumbed to 'war-psychosis'
In my case requiring hospital operations to remove head cancer
A shocking price to pay for Ministry of Defence planning
Who are still withholding my wartime salary
Refusing to give the answer *why*
But I will live for another *try*
Sadly *no* tomorrow for Ed Murrow.

Paff-Pafford
West Sussex

Those We Have Loved And Lost

Those we have loved and lost,
Like a bright and shining star,
Shine from above and let us know,
We are not alone as we think we are.

Gordon E Miles
West Sussex

Conflict

Can this be true? Are the storm clouds gathering?
Is this the beginning of the end?
Can it be possible that you and I are now facing each other as enemies?
It seems but a short time ago that we stood facing the challenges of the world - together.
Overcoming the adversities - together.
Side by side and hand in hand we were proud to declare our love - together.
Now those two hearts that beat so strongly lie broken, the dreams shattered!
Harmony has been replaced by conflict, agreement by opposition.
The eyes that shone and sparkled with love now stare blankly - with indifference.
Not hate, I could never hate you.
But what went wrong? Why do we hurt each other so?
And where do we go from here?
Can this be the final chapter?

Joseph Brough
West Sussex

Curse Of The NCT

Miss Blakenwell was very calm,
She never saw cause for alarm,
But she really hated mice,
Their scurrying tales were not very nice.
Oh no, oh dear, alack, alas,
This was not known by her Year 9 class,
So when one of her pupils found a dead mouse,
They quickly ran right out of the house,
And put it in the teacher's desk at school,
If only they'd known, little fool!
The word had spread round the school the next day,
All wanted to see, no one stayed away,
The teacher walked in and opened the drawer,
Held out the mouse and the class gave a roar,
Miss Blakenwell sighed and rolled her eyes,
'All right then, who did this? Tell me no lies!'
No one raised their hand, so she uttered a verse,
The children were horrified, it was a curse!
'Study hard and do your best,
Prepare for the National Curriculum Test!'
Then there was a boom: when the smoke had cleared,
Miss Blakenwell had disappeared!
And in July that very year,
Many a teenager shed a tear,
For no one escapes it, not you, nor me,
Beware and prepare for the NCT!

Sophie Bridger
West Sussex

An Ode To The Credit Card

Oh yes, I'm a f**king millionaire.
My freshly signed plastic is with me and I'm out before the ink is dry.
Where to?
Anywhere!
I could go to the moon if I wanted, with my new friend,
No questions asked and first class you know.

Old friends, new friends, everyone is my friend.
D&G, CK, Armani, Boss, Adidas, Timberland, YSL and Burberry.
The real deal too, paid for with gold; no s**t.
B****cks to public transport; b****cks to the mayor's dream.
I travel in style; do you want to come?
This roller coaster only goes up, live it up; live with me.
Come on!

Week after week, oh yes; I'm a f**king millionaire.
Spring, summer, autumn, winter and a card for all seasons.
Suddenly I can speak every language on the planet.
Everyone listens to me you know.
Yes Sir, can I help you Sir?
Of course you can.
The Ritz, The Savoy, The Hilton, The Carlton, the obsession and then depression.

I forgot to open the post today.
Your transaction has been denied.
Spring, summer, autumn and winter, the long, dark, cold winter.
I stand here alone on my pedestal.
Where are my friends now?
I'm a millionaire you know.
I put my head into the noose and suddenly my pedestal is gone.

My life flashes past me as they say it does.
Champagne £40, taxi £25, dinner £80, jeans £70, holiday £1,200, Chinese £60,
Christmas £800, trainers £120, haircut £50, shirt £95, card bill £200, card bill £20,000,
red bill, red bill, red bill.
Then everything pauses, time stops, my eyes open,
I twitch, I gasp air and I relive that first date with my plastic. Then darkness.
The cost of a human life?
Priceless.
For everything else there was my credit card.

Gavin O'Mally-Richardson
West Sussex

Into The Darkness

The grief and the pain of all the years
The doubts, the pain and the countless tears
Can we place these firmly in Ireland's past
And look to the future with peace at last?

Each person was born an innocent child
In a brutal society young minds were defiled
Blind hatred and bigotry, small children were taught
In the evil-spun web so many were caught.

This sectarian society must take the blame
For they are the people who kindled the flame
The inferno was fanned by misnamed men of God
Who paid no heed at all to 'the Book' or 'the Word'.

We must try to forget and learn to forgive
To make this land fit for all people to live
The shackles are breaking, a joining of hands
And consign to history all marches and all bands.

For what is the use of tribalistic strife
If a child is maimed or there is loss of life?
Let us come to our senses, a new century is here
And walk forward together with no feeling of fear.

We can show to the world just what Ireland can do
A shining example to the Arab and the Jew
For into the darkness there came a white dove
With a message of peace, compassion and love.

Vyna Broom
West Sussex

A Wish

If I was given one wish, it would be for peace on Earth,
It would cover both the poles and surround the planet's girth,
The northern hemisphere and the southern hemisphere,
It would clothe the ground we walk on, and flood the atmosphere.

It would be there for all peoples, of all colours and creeds,
It would permeate each living thing, grow in every seed,
It would flow in every river, it would sail on every sea,
It would sweep across the deserts, the plains, the forests, the trees.

It would scale the highest mountain, lie in the deepest glen,
It would issue from Man's mouth, it would issue from his pen,
It would live in every home, it would live in every soul,
It would mend each broken heart, it would make our world whole.

C MacNaughton
West Sussex

New Orleans Disaster

Putrid water strode on ignorant and peaceful shore,
devouring homes and people's lives, and yet more.
The gods of fate looked down without emotion,
ignoring all the death and vast commotion.

Such tears of rage and sadness marked New Orleans,
its folk, now as flotsam, not human beings.
When the bodies floated in this scouring rage,
America turned another history page.

But yet! Like Phoenix rising from the fire,
when its people had completed pyre on pyre.
In spite of tearful rage, and such bitter pain,
from the wet and boggy sod they will rise again.

A place of great joy and pride will greet the sky,
when a beauty then beholden to Man's eye.
For money shall not bind America's hand,
New Orleans will be the greatest in the land!

Leslie de la Haye
West Sussex

Do You Know

(Dad, we all love and miss you so much, Tony xxxx)

Christmas approaches, the days seem long
I can't sleep at night since you've been gone
It's been five weeks, time's stood still
I can't come to terms with it, I don't think I will

Rain on the window, snow on the floor
My head on the pillow, your life is no more
Was it my fault, did I do something wrong?
If I'd spoken up you might not be gone

These are the thoughts that go through my mind
As I lay in my bed, my head in a bind
You passed so quickly, we don't know why
You passed so quickly, no time for goodbye

What happens now, is it time to grieve
Come to terms and start to believe
Or do I carry on as if nothing took place
Pretend you're still here, imagine your face?

Please answer my questions, please give me a sign
The place you are now, is it better than mine?
Are you watching me now, do you see what I do
But, most of all, do you know I love you?

Anthony O'Sullivan
West Yorkshire

Writing A Poem (1958)

I make up a title and then I am stuck
What to put next, so my pencil I suck.
Then by gazing at stars and scratching my head
I think of the first line, but on being read
It does not sound right, somehow or other,
So I cross it out quickly and think of another.
And then I decide that the title is poor,
For no one can make up a poem I am sure
With a title like that - it just will not do,
So after a moment I cross that out too.
Then the point of my pencil decides it will break,
Which somehow only seems to make
Matters worse than before
And I throw it down useless onto the floor,
And getting up angrily out of my chair
Say with a defiant and resolute air,
'I won't write another, for what d'you think?
I haven't a penknife and I've run out of ink!'

Richard Birch
West Yorkshire

Wordsworth

'I wandered lonely as a cloud'
is what dear Wordsworth said.
And here I aim to prove to you
he was completely off his head!

Wordsworth lived in Cumbria,
land of the wide blue lakes.
And why's there all that water?
Because it rains for goodness sakes!

So consider the master poet
who's writing fills with pride.
'Lonely clouds', my aunt,
he never looked outside!

Kevin Whittington
West Yorkshire

A Love Lost

Gagged and bound from head to toe
Where you are, you'll never know
Dragged for miles from here to there
Strapped to thy electric chair
Specially made for you ya see
Wracked with pain while I sip tea
Beg for mercy, on yer knees
Never mind pathetic pleas
Take the punishment at hand
Mine forever, understand
Bend down double in that box
Wear for me those glass filled sox
Twist until your body rocks
In a headlock you'll remain
Till we see a passing train
Lifeless body on the track
No! Don't have a heart attack
Not just yet, it's nearly here
Not long now, my love, my dear.

Frankie Gaynor-Archer
West Yorkshire

The Card Players

(Taken from the painting by Paul Cezanne)

The game is getting serious,
I wonder who will win,
The stakes are high,
Concentration deep.
A few more puffs on the pipe,
Then perhaps the winning card.

We're getting late for dinner, lad,
What will Mother say?
No bother Dad,
Just carry on,
We'll eat it cold,
The game one of us must win.

Christine Blayney
West Yorkshire

Being Lonely . . .

Being lonely is not nice,
Watching people walking by, not thinking twice.
Of the sight of you there, they don't seem to care,
The whole world's against you and that life's just not fair.

Being lonely can happen in a crowd.
You feel like shouting, 'Hey everybody, I'm here!' really loud.
No one listens or looks to see if you are sad,
Making you more frustrated and indeed, very mad.

Being lonely with emotions you are trying to hide,
Can be so painful when really - you're hurting inside.
Wishing that someone would hear your plight,
Instead of pretending that everything's all right.

Being lonely can be a difficult time
It's nothing bad, it's not even a crime.
Try and put yourself in a lonely person's place,
Give them some loving and put a smile on their face!

Amanda Simpson-Cleghorn
West Yorkshire

Bolton Abbey

A ruined abbey is the backdrop
A most enchanting sight
The scenery is so beautiful
Especially when it's bright

The hills lead to a river
That ripples on its way
There are stepping stones to cross it
Where children love to play

The shades of green are endless
From olive through to lime
Grassy banks, hills and trees
It's so easy to pass time

An old man paints a picture
A couple walk hand in hand
Families enjoying their picnics
Children playing in the sand.

Janet Harrison
West Yorkshire

Nun Wanted

The Angel of Mercy comes
In a white Vauxhall
And tight jeans.
No neat uniform. No smile.
She wears a cape of long black hair.

Her hands are full of
Forms in triplicate,
Wipes, semi-disposable
(Whatever that may mean),
And a carton of plastic gloves
In case she has to touch the patient,
The dying man,
My husband.

She unloads a Mattress Variator
With electrical controls.
It is hung with webbing like an elaborate
Version of a farmyard gate.
A generator sits on the landing
Muttering its message to the hoist
On the seat in the bath
Which unfolds its metal wings as it rises.

I am sidelined, marvelling,
Reading instruction books,
When what I need is a wimpled nun
In a starched apron
With round cheeks and soft hands,
That smell of soap.

Barbara Roberts
West Yorkshire

Far Away

No warning
No note
No outward signs of changed behaviour
Just a desire
A final word,
'I'm going away
Far away.'
She did not go alone
She took with her
Many hopes, many aspirations
She left behind devastation
And the question why?

Kauser Parveen
West Yorkshire

A Lifetime Too Soon

I sit and watch them as they play,
A new game thought of every day.
Piggybacks and blind man's buff,
It seems they've never had enough.
Their energy just never ends,
They dance through every hour God sends.

4 o'clock, it's time for tea,
Their rosy faces lit with glee.
They trundle through, aged two and three,
And fight to sit on Mummy's knee.
Their little hands and dainty feet,
Wide-open-eyed, so keen to eat.

8 o'clock, time for their beds,
A chance to rest their weary heads.

I sit and watch them as they play,
They come to haunt me every day.
Not piggybacks or blind man's buff,
For now it seems they've had enough.
Their energy now at an end,
No more hours dear God will send.

4 o'clock, it's time for tea,
The fire should have taken me!
No little footsteps, face of glee,
No fight to sit on Mummy's knee.
No little hands or dainty feet,
Wide-open eyes with whom to eat.

8 o'clock, was time for their beds,
A lifetime too soon, they laid their heads.

Selena Jayne Marsh
West Yorkshire

Heartland

Limestone scars,
rolling moors,
gentle vales and sheer chalk cliffs.
Quaint stone hamlets,
awesome minsters,
mill scene backdrops and ruined abbeys.
Folk friendly, gruff, determined,
unbowed, humorous.
Home.

Alison Dobson
West Yorkshire

Those Were The Days

Those were the days
When every waking thought
Needed priority for them.
To rise, fill their need
And never act in mutiny.

Those long years -
Providing every want.
Rising day by day and
With ever-increasing exertion
To fulfil the bottomless list
Of expectations.

Those times - when love and duty
Cost all your private dreams.
Yet knowing, still willing,
You went the treadmill journey,
Which always seemed as if it
Would never end.

Days when winsome ways,
Tempers, tears and sunny smiles,
Absorbed, stung and exhilarated,
Trying every emotion.

Came the days of empty rooms,
Memories of pounding feet.
Loud demands, still echoing,
As they would forever,
To be treasured in redundancy
In a parent's heart.

Pauline Boncey
West Yorkshire

Winter's End

Colds and coughs
Lapsing into lassitude
End of season sated

Dying for daffodils
Time for tulips
Hooray for hyacinths

Life lasts
Regularly renews
Harbours hope
Go for it!

Christine Stevens
West Yorkshire

365 Degrees

Winter will again fret me with briny fingers,
Pierce the cotton and chafe my pores,
Sting me on through the swing doors
To where a single, frantic, electric-blue note lingers,
Frozen in snowy hued resonance -
Perfect in its chilled embrace of clarity.

Spring will again solicit me with bejewelled scents,
Lead teasingly down paths of heavy tossed curls -
White-tinged in song - to where broad evenings unfurl
Some capricious, celestial connivance.
And once again, the lady of the lake, quivering in abundance,
Will sanction simply, brazenly, my complicity.

Summer will again seduce me, juice fantasies in flight,
And wrap her waspish, languid warmth around my skin.
The echoes of her laughter, pink and daring,
Will eclipse the shimmering solstice light
And blood-swollen moons,
And will soon blister along horizons to an infinity,

To draw out shadowed evenings, mantled with shivers,
Into tepid free-fall. Can you imagine the dead
At the onset of those winds? As castled leaves thread
Into tangled thickets and nicotine-stained fibres,
Nostrils will flair in air palling in the remnants,
Weeping, sallow . . . pulling the hollow equinox towards me.

Ian Lowery
West Yorkshire

Freedom

Everyone's a prisoner,
We all have chains and thoughts

We all have gods and pray to them,
However we were taught

We all have faith that stays with us,
As long as life will last

We think of past and present times,
The pace of life is fast

One day, I hope, we'll all slow down
And think of others too

Then I know we'll all be blessed
And the world won't stand askew.

Ruth Markinson
West Yorkshire

Peace

What would it be like if there were peace?
In a place undiscovered by man,
In a place uninhabited by woman,
Would there be birds that circled the sky,
Their feathers a thousand colours?
Would there be flowers that danced all around,
Whenever it started to rain?
Would unpolluted rivers,
Sing songs of joy as they flowed
And would creatures with only love in their hearts
Tell stories to all their young children?
There would be no pain, no poverty, no suffering,
There would be peace,
Could there be peace?
A place like this should be treasured forever,
A place like this only exists in our imagination.

Rachel Inhester
West Yorkshire

Life's Beauty

Look around you, see the blue sky
Watch gentle birds fly smoothly by.
Look at bright colours, see flowers and trees,
Wonderful sights one's eye to please.

Look at green fields, rabbits hop by,
Hear traffic noise, a moan, a sigh.
Look at the children playing some game,
Just having fun is really their aim.

Look at the people milling around,
Hoping maybe, a friendly face is found.
Wherever one goes, the world is there,
Yes look, it is everywhere!

Look in your mind, imagine the shore,
Waves and surf rolling for evermore.
Boats a-tossing, as the seas they ride,
Picture gulls screeching as they soar and glide.

Life is there, yes, for everyone to see,
Friends and family, you and *me!*

Pauline Phillimore
West Yorkshire

Journey Home

A veil of mist hung o'er the town
The streets so damp and cold.
No footsteps heard I on the ground
As I was homeward-bound.

The church, a ghostly giant seemed
Rising from out his shroud,
When suddenly a light appeared
It shone there - oh so proud.

I hurried on towards the light
Mist swirled along before me
Never before was such a night
Malice all around me.

Trudging along the rutted road
Hail slashing down once more,
Thro' the mist my home I spy
I'm frozen to the core.

Eva Harper
West Yorkshire

The Air Is Cold

The air is cold,
Brittle and still.
For the trees wave as
Stiff as ice on a winter's day.

As I wait for rainfall,
Puddles start to emerge
From the ashes of the ground.

It's September now,
A blasting beam of sunshine
Fills the air with warmth . . .

And anything could happen.

Sophia Eason (10)
West Yorkshire

Smells

The smell of dusty streets, after pouring rain
The odious smell emerging from an overflowing drain

A smell of many blossoms in the month of May
The smell that always follows, the farmer mowing hay

The smelly breath of a baby feeding from a swollen breast
The smell that comes from wrestlers as the sweat runs down their chest

The musky smell of natives in their jungle home
The smell of burning incense at St Peter's Church in Rome

The smell of purple heather on the moorland heath
The smell that comes from horses with the bit between their teeth.

The lovely smell of roses on the morning dew
The minty smell of sweets that kiddies love to chew

The pungent smell of cheeses in a Dutch market square
The smell of perfumed lacquer sprayed on a woman's hair

The sexual smell of lovers as they tumble on the bed
The smell that comes from battlefields as they bury the rotting dead

The talcum smell of a woman after the morning bath
The smell of circus greasepaint as the clowns make us laugh

All smells would be impossible without the aid of God
He made us all with noses, some large, some small, some odd

Les Luxton
West Yorkshire

Let Me Live!

A moment so still I can't catch my breath
All is laid bare, there's no vale of mistrust
Air closing in, I may smother to death
And all that'll remain is mourning and dust

You seem to forget that I provide life
Look into my heart and see that we're one
All that is, walks on the edge of a knife
To stray would mean the end, nowhere to run.

Abuse my good nature and the result
Not wrath but pain which I will share with you
A past brighter than the future - your fault
But time holds on, you know what you must do.

Heed my warning, this cry for help, this plea
Rescue hope and change, for both you and me.

Louisa Smyllie
West Yorkshire

Tears For Years To Come And Go

The pain you caused us all
Still brings tears to my eyes
Even now two years have gone by.

When I put my head on my pillow
Suddenly the tears begin to flow
It's because I'll always know
Like my heartache, yours won't go
And every victim you make along the way
Will be a constant reminder
Of what you did to me that dreadful day.

And that pain you will always carry inside
Like your shame and guilt, you can never hide
I know of your thoughts of suicide
Regrets for not having any moral pride
Those dark circles around your eyes
We now all see - come as no surprise
You know I'll never be by your side
And you'll remain a broken bride
Even though you put on a brave face
I know when you're all alone at night
You'll feel the pain of your own disgrace
And when those fears begin to flow
I feel sure eventually you'll come to know
They will be for both you and I
And those empty lonely years gone by.

Graham Hare
West Yorkshire

Sunset

God sent me a sunset,
Whose glory filled the skies,
And I stared at it in wonder,
For I couldn't believe my eyes.

Over a clear, blue Heaven,
A line of cloud arched by.
From west to east, a giant stripe
Crossed the evening sky.

Made from a myriad tiny clouds,
It was lit by reddening gold
From the setting sun, which created
A brilliance to behold.

Lorna Lea
West Yorkshire

Who? You, Of Course!

('Empedocles is read after 1900 years' Daily Telegraph, Friday January 29th 1999)

Today the daily papers say
Empedocles survives!
His work - unknown; his life - a blur;
Strasbourg scholars now infer
Papyrus fragments hold the keys
To thoughts not thought since Sophocles.
And Aristotle, too, was quick
To honour him with rhetoric.
Two weighty volumes of his verse -
Philosophy, magic, even worse -
Once lost, again have come to light,
To set his history a-right.

Two thousand years - and somewhat more -
Reveal, to me, a thorough bore!
Whom did he love? That part's obscure;
(Scholars admit they can't be sure).
When my love story scholars view
In a million years, they'll know it's *you!*

Jay Whittam
West Yorkshire

LSD And 2 Es

Ignore the fumes, the tramps and junkies
fight your way through office flunkies
a wholesome city can be found
skulking in the underground
beneath the flies, the grime, the scum
you'll find a city full of fun
of girls and boys and both of course
cos like it or not, for better or worse
girls can be boys and boys can be girls
on the wilder edge of the social whirl
drink and be merry, toss up your cherry
the city won't judge you
the city won't love you
and will always offer a place.

Daryl Leslie
West Yorkshire

My Recipe For Life

I want to do it properly but don't always have the time
In putting pen to paper and writing down my rhyme
I want to be creative, write poems for all to read
Of trials and tribulations, different lives that we all lead.

To some it may seem boring, we're not all made the same
For me it is an outlet, my brain is on a train
We go through many tunnels, some light and some quite dim
I'm looking out of the window, oh no, I'm looking in.

I have escaped my body, I've even lost my mind
But only for this purpose, to let myself unwind
It's like you've got a penpal, although you know you've not
Write down all your feelings, untie those inner knots.

It's sure to make you happy and relaxed throughout the day
So why not try my recipe, prescribed for you my way
Get yourself a pen and paper then sit comfy in a chair
Close your eyes, take a deep breath, breathe out and prepare.

Write down all your worries, clear your mind of all that's in
Then screw them all up tightly and throw them in the bin
Your mind will be a crystal, as clear as one can be
Continue with this recipe, it's poetic justice for me.

Donna Wyles
West Yorkshire

A Happy New Year

While reaching for the stars let first the Earth,
Be soothed by tolerance and harmony,
Among ourselves, proving that we have worth,
To challenge other worlds confidently.

If to alien strangers we are led,
While Earth still has indifference and greed,
With several species still endangered,
This would our credibility impede.

Do we yet dare to strut our stuff above?
Do future generations perhaps fear,
The ones who do not know respect or love,
Yet boldly go from this neglected sphere?

In search of somewhere they may probe and prod,
In that great universe, observed by God.

Kathleen M Scatchard
West Yorkshire

Beamish

Oh come all you folk from far and near
To a land of yesteryear
A pleasant ride by old tramcar
Down to the town it's not too far
There to see ornate bandstand
Set in Victorian park so grand
Then cross the way our thirst to quench
At the Sun Inn on wooden bench,
Down at the station, Stephenson's pride
Stands silent by the platform side
Just waiting for the call
Another train for it to haul
Within the colliery you will find
Instruction on how coal is mined
There's a cheery gang of lads
Hewing coal just like our dads
In pitman's cottage small and neat
The lasses bake a tasty treat
Of scones to eat with cream and jam
Or fresh-baked bread for eggs and ham
Upon the hill you'll find Home Farm
With atmosphere of rustic charm
Cows and pigs, geese and ducks
Open fire and inglenooks
The blacksmith hammers all day long
A monotoned, metallic song
As metal to his will he bends
For farming tools or odds and ends
All in all a carefree day
Awaits you over Beamish way.

Terence Leslie
West Yorkshire

Golden Leaves

Golden leaves pattern the green carpet-lawn
A bright yellow sun dispels the cold, grey mist of dawn.
Golden leaves shimmer on treetops high
Beneath a blue, October sky.
Golden leaves lie upon path and soft, flower bed soil
Busy hands sweep and rake and toil.
Golden leaves tremble on tall robinia trees
Fragile branches bending in the breeze.
Golden leaves fall like golden rain
Pattern the green carpet-lawn, raked in vain.

Anita Cooling
West Yorkshire

Auntie's Road

The road they built through Auntie's house was very long and straight.
They'd drawn it with a ruler, for it did not deviate
From off the straight and narrow, between its start and end:
They could have missed her house with ease, if it had had one bend.

My aunt was in her bedroom when the workmen came to call;
Laying blacktop in the kitchen and a lay-by in the hall.
She should have phoned the council, or written her MP,
Instead she put the kettle on and made them cups of tea.

Now traffic roars beneath her bed throughout the night and day;
When lorries pass along the road, the whole house starts to sway.
They picnic in the lay-by, leaving litter on the stairs;
The kitchen's very draughty and someone's nicked her chairs.

Auntie sits up in her bedroom, drinking endless cups of tea;
Just popping out for teabags and a guide for her TV.
I've never heard her grumble or even make a fuss,
For the road is *most* convenient when she wants to catch a bus!

Tim Harvey
West Yorkshire

Cobbles

On Main Street, Haworth, cobbles fall
In cascade down to Haworth Hall.
These petrous marks of bleaker age
Are weighty notes on earthy page
And ancient 'bytes' of bygone days
That store the ken of different ways.
Their solid shape, shouts out to me:
Persistence in adversity!
What sights have seen, what stories told;
What memories their surface holds -
A death too young, a life lived short,
The breaking of a mother's heart;
For brazen weather roughly beat
Upon the clogged and unshod feet
That strode this road or sat upon
The horse-drawn trap or made to run
Out on the moor, where all laid bare,
To scourging of inclement air.
But where this story first began?
Sisters, Charlotte, Emily, Anne;
Without their face would tourists know
That Haworth village, all aglow,
Was ever less than place of ease
For cups of coffee and cream teas?

Mary C Clarke
West Yorkshire

Running Errands (Fish Shop, 1968)

A crisp, freshly printed, ten shilling note
Out of Mum's purse,
First cut into the weekly housekeeping;
That new ten bob smell.

Mother sends me round
To fetch a family fish and chip tea.
I wait in the queue, hungrily,
It goes down steadily.
Leaning against the comforting, warm fish shop counter,
I ponder, *when I was little, I couldn't see over this*
Now I can.

'New Potatoes' chalked on a board,
It's early summer.
Fish forked out,
But chips not yet ready,
Forcefully frying in beef dripping.
The man, resplendent in
Freshly ironed, crisp white overalls,
Shuts the steel lid and smiles at the next customer.
Not long now.

Newspapers poised tidily to wrap
Piping hot fish and chips
Wrapped with well-practised ease.

A white home-made loaf from the family bakers,
Soft, and still warm,
Wrapped in tissue paper;
I pick at the crust on my way home.

Fish and chips, hot tea,
Bread and butter, mushy peas,
Brown sauce.

Another Monday tea.

John Roberts
West Yorkshire

Bah'tat

Black, the austere rocks
Uninvitingly sharp
Sculptured by nature's
Abandoned quarry
Traumatised.

Moorland sheep weave
Between Sunday morning
Paper rustlers
Alien plastic cups
Raped.

A shiny cobble-stoned path
Disguised as natural
Snakes the summit
Sudden blustery gales
Treacherous.

Documented heritage
Stands testament of time
Wild as Heathcliffe's secrets
Spectacularly
Unforgiving.

Pauline Pickin
West Yorkshire

Yorkshire

I love this county, Yorkshire
With rolling hills and streams
Heather in the valleys
That stretch for miles it seems.

The rugged coast of Whitby
And the outstretching beaches,
With caves and jet,
To all, much it teaches.

The landscape's so picturesque;
I love the countryside,
The grass sways in the breeze,
With golden fields stretching far and wide.

Water trickling from the fountains,
Possessing feature and unity,
Small villages in the surroundings,
All bonded together as a community.

Ramandeep Kaur (17)
West Yorkshire

How Heavenly

How heavenly to catch the sun and feel its warm embrace,
And weave its long and gleaming rays in a rhythmic maypole dance.
To mould my weary body in the softness of the clouds,
Or build artistic landscapes full of minarets and towers.
To leap about on twinkling stars through darkened velvet skies,
And swing upon a crescent moon 'til the sun begins to rise.

How heavenly to glide like rain as it travels down to earth,
To resurrect the arid land and recreate new birth.
To join the romping, rolling streams as they playfully rush down,
From mountain slopes and barren heights to the valleys way below.
To travel on the whirling breeze through far and distant lands,
And whistle melodies like the wind in a heavenly angel band.

What fun to chase the cats and dogs and drive the rain away,
Fill empty pockets with falling stars and hang them up again.
To climb the mountains on the moon and sprinkle them with snow,
And chase the rainbow to its end to find a pot of gold.
If the man in the moon and the smiling sun stretched out their arms to me,
I'd leave all worldly cares behind, and seek eternity.

Angela Bradley
West Yorkshire

Little Egret

I watch you as you pose
Aloof, absorbed and focused,
Patiently waiting
To stab your prey.

Your elegant stance
Among the rocks,
Along the shoreline,
Exudes graceful beauty.

Your snowy plumes
And jet-bead eyes
Belie
Your deadly mission.

In salty pools
At low tide
Spindle legs
Stir no ripple.

Hour by hour
You stand
I stare -
Entranced and silent.

Brenda Artingstall
West Yorkshire

552

The Girl That's Inside Me

(For my mum, a victim of dementia)

The face in the mirror looks back at me, weary,
now grey and pale with the passage of time.
Those eyes are so dull and they see nothing clearly.
It's hard to believe that this face was once mine.
But the face of the girl that is still here inside me is smooth,
and flushed by the glow of the sun.
Her eyes are so bright and sparkle with longing,
no sign of a blemish, a wrinkle or line.

These hands have washed dishes, scrubbed floors, polished tables.
Now rough and painful with veins thick and blue.
They can't turn a page without help from the able.
They could once crotchet finely, now they've nothing to do.
But the hands of the girl that is still here inside me are soft
with nails painted a sharp crimson red.
They play the piano; they're nimble and graceful.
They blow sweetheart kisses, my darling, to you.

These legs will not move now, they can't walk or stand.
They are lifeless and limp from so long in a chair.
It takes two to move me; it's not what I'd planned.
What has happened to me? Well, it just is not fair!
For the legs of the girl that is still here inside me are long
and so shapely wearing stockings with seams.
They are agile and ache to keep up with the music.
They dance all night long with both passion and flare.

She screams, 'Let me out!' That girl that's inside me but
this shell of a body, so feeble and weak,
has trapped her and kept her, a constant reminder,
that inside there's beauty but outside - a freak!

Lesley Elaine Greenwood
West Yorkshire

Where Have You Been?

I've been through Hell!
Just a statement, mere words, but to me more than words could ever tell.

This past year has gone by in a whirl.
So much has happened to me, I cannot begin to tell.
Maybe that's just as well.

Who wants to hear all about sadness and woe?
Many's the time I've wanted to pack a suitcase and go.

But I didn't, I couldn't, faced the music I did.
Keeping my problems and all of the pain so well hid.

Susan Barker
West Yorkshire

You Killed Me Before I Died

My anger is uprooting on the ugly side of me
As I'm thinking of how you dug my bliss
My past bones are dead but my soul is blossoming
Why did you raze me? Where you twinge of my unvenomed rose.

Your voices seeped to slaughter me softly, bit by bit
Although I seethed. To your imaginary I'm six feet under a pit,
But I'm yelling and yelling, 'I'm not, I'm not,' I'm slouching
Right here, cursing and cursing to whom else but you.

Your poisons jerked away my slumber, they made me stiff like ice
Shivered my swallow night and day. What, a poke from a needle? It felt.
Nested myself in it, there was a resemblance between the pain and death
Why did you raze me? So I would salute my survivor I guess.

But still like a seed I matured and now I've found the path
Jettisoning all you did, I rinse my hands and after all, tomorrow never
Dies. To swallow my pride I'll dine with you - 7 o'clock is perfect
Nothing fancy please; it's all we ever eat in Heaven.

Until then I wish you all the best, Dears.

Melissa Muchemwa
West Yorkshire

My Family

One day some years ago
I fell out of the sky
And I saw what I call
My family

My family is not a normal family
They act like the sun to me
They brighten my day
They brighten my life

My family is not a normal family
They are like a treasure to me
They make me smile
They make me laugh

My family is not a normal family
They are like oxygen to me
They keep me fine
They keep me alive

Taranom Movahedi
West Yorkshire

What Price Justification?

Another child dies,
for some, death is the prize,
but we're well *aware*,
of what's going on over there
and that hunger's the real issue,
not *poverty* the thin tissue.

Is the world out on its own,
that the fortunate are to disown,
we with our ideological pursuits,
to only act when it suits?
Man alive, two thousand and five,
here's countries the Earth can't feed,
as we justify a greed,
taking for granted when we need,
a little food and water;
someone's lost their daughter,
down in Niger,
should've been there,
but once again,
who's to care?

Shuttle flies into space,
for the sake of the human race,
billions on a bill,
'bout oil men fight to kill,
a lottery's to gain whilst an infant cries,
whose face is filled with flies,
what's a number on a note,
a cheque somebody wrote,
when a grain of rice can bring,
to a hungry one . . . everything?

Andrew Gruberski
West Yorkshire

The Sloth

The poor old sloth hangs upside down
And never gets a trip to town
He just hangs there eating greenery
Quite 'fed up' with all the scenery.

H H Atkinson
West Yorkshire

A Country Walk

Limping along with wounded knee,
I couldn't see what you could see.
Horses, cows, lambs at play
Farmers baling fields of hay.
Struggling on, but now in pain,
Getting drenched from all this rain.
Whining, moaning, causing a fuss,
I think I should have caught the bus.
No more country walks for me,
Let's get home and have some tea.
Stiff and sore with aching head,
Goodnight all, I'm off to bed.

Tony Beeby
West Yorkshire

A Summer Walk

As I walk along in the summer breeze
The floral blossom makes me sneeze,
The honeysuckle vine climbing up the fence
With sweet jasmine, oh what lovely scents.

Rain gently falling on my wallflower patch
And I feel that tingle in my nose,
With a fragrance so strong,
Which stays so long
Makes me sneeze like nobody knows.

Lavender-blue, the bees like you
Down at the bottom of my garden,
Your pungent aroma takes my breath away
If I give some to my neighbour
I wonder what they will say?

Now it's just getting dusk
As I watch from my cottage door,
And it looks like storm is coming
The frogs will come out,
To sing and to shout
And dance when the rain is drumming.

Summer, summer, how nice are you
With all your glory and your splendour,
This is beautiful, this is treasure
And will stay locked in my heart forever.

Maddie Reade
Wiltshire

Forever Night

What is it like in the darkness
Of night that's a lifetime long?
What is it like to hear a bird
But not watch as it sings its song?
What is it like in December
To touch and to feel black snow?
To sit in the warmth of an open fire
But not see its orange glow?
What is it like to miss the colours
Of all the daylight hours?
A sky of blue, lush fresh green grass
And a patchwork of beautiful flowers?
What is it like as a parent
Unseen, the children grow?
To drop your pennies on the floor
But not see where they go?
Life is a wonderful picture book
With the natural gift of sight.
But what is it like in the darkness
Of life that is one long night?

Kathleen Allen
Wiltshire

Suicidal Serendipity

Floating to the flowers of choice
A wandering mind has the beauty of fright
Landing on the petals of dreams
An untamed imagination knows boundaries aren't right

Dancing with unlimited joy
The destruction button is always in reach
Flying with unlimited sky
The fear of not coming down is almost complete

Sailing in a circular sea
On what you can stand you can slaughter
Finding an island unfound before
While the others get drunk by the water

Levitated by invisible air
Wings of thought beat down without food
The body is cold
The body needs warmth
The mind is perpetually nude.

John Wiseman
Wiltshire

Can You Remember?

Can you remember the things that we did together?
How the energy between us was so high
Those walks in the parks and cuddles on benches
Where we talked and laughed and we cried
The closeness between us was so powerful
We said that nothing would get in our way
There was so much love going on between us
But you had to leave me so you pulled away
Do you remember the passion between us?
As we held each other so tenderly
The words of love that you whispered
And how we realised we were meant to be
Can you remember how we walked through the trees?
And marvelled at the colours all around
How you slipped your hand often in mine
Then laid down with me on the soft ground
You told me that I was so beautiful
The most wonderful person you'd met
I still am all those things that you told me
But now I'm the person you want to forget
Can you remember how I looked at you?
Drew you into my heart with my eyes
You told me that I was truly amazing
We were so close we didn't need to try
You said that you'd love me forever
But your love didn't last it passed by
What is it that's happened between us?
You won't talk to me and tell me why
You said you'd do anything for me
My love for you was so strong
I always had you on a pedestal
But it seems that I got you all wrong.

Margaret Ward
Wiltshire

Our Time

Alive today,
From there to here,
All Earth's days lead to us,
Through all of space we travelled,
Back and back to the big bang,
That was when our time began.

Raymond Barber
Wiltshire

Tree Frog

Tree frog scaled a giant tree, searching for the higher ground
He moves up with a lightning pace, refused to make himself look down.
Tree frog finds a hanging branch and clings to it as best he can
He knows that it is getting late yet hoping to explore the land.
Up ahead he sees the storm, brewed over on a raging sea
Tomorrow he'll continue on and make the most of what is free.
Tropic wind came blowing in and blew away the leaves of green
The bark of tree is standing firm, its vegetation flies upstream.
Down below the ground has sunk, the wild flowers sadly drown,
But tree frog isn't worried none, his sticky limbs have pinned him down.

The downpour thrashed the edgings of the cliff side …
Unfortunate beings thrown into the riptide …
The surface gave away and made a landslide …
Until finally …

Storm has passed and moves along, the island is a fallout zone
Tree frog opens up his eyes, the time has come to get alone.
Tree frog spots a bird of prey and shelters in the undergrowth
The coast is clear as is the air, he frog-marched on and jumped down low.

He jumps each tree, admires his surroundings …
Makes a mental note of all his findings …
Finds a home beneath the ivy twining …
Arriving finally.

Martyn Leroy
Wiltshire

Mum

Your concern
Is our comfort,
Your duty
Our care;
Your hand
Is our guidance,
Willing us there.

Your forgiveness
Our humbling,
Your praise
Builds our pride;
your love
is our being;
your life
is our guide.

Susan Turner
Wiltshire

Dreams

I am lying here
On my bed
A long way from home
I am dreaming of my family.

I am dreaming of the good times,
We have shared as one whole family,
I may not be who you think I am,
I am me and no one can change that.

I am dreaming of the old times,
I remember Katy as a baby,
I loved her then and I love her now.

I may not be who you think I am,
I am me and no one can change that.

I remember you Mum and Dad,
I may be far away,
But I am still with you in spirit,
I will never forget you,
No matter what happens in the future.

I may not be who you think I am,
I am me and no one can change that.

No matter who I am,
I am still the same,
Deep down inside of myself,
Though I may not be the same
Person you know on the outside.

Sarah Langridge
Wiltshire

Our Homeland

Our homeland, of England, is divided into counties,
Each making contribution to its unique, rustic charm.
The artist at his easel, the stitchers, knitters,
Potters and sculptors and the foods from the farm.
The author, the poet writing gifts for posterity,
Blacksmiths, gamekeepers, thatchers and architects,
Wardens of the forest, where the cavemen once stood.
This England with its history, her soldiers, their bravery,
Puts pride in the heart of each woman, each man.
May her land remain fertile, her waters flow clear,
And may God ever look kindly on this land we hold dear.

Pamela Carder
Wiltshire

Over The Hill?

Late in bed
Sleepy head
Walking stick
Generally 'thick'?

Can't do this
Hit and miss
Can't touch toes
Red-veined nose?

Needs a shawl
To cover all
Her honesty
And modesty?

Not at all!
She's on 'the ball'
Can dance and flirt
And wear a skirt!

Not late in bed
Has a clear head,
She's slightly lame
But very game.

To clean her home
Use brush and comb,
To dress her hair -
Choose what to wear.

And give the time
To read a rhyme
To children small -
Or play football!

Kathleen C White
Wiltshire

Transition

Autumn breeze whispers change
Leaves rustle, wait for rain
Fruit rotting into earth
Gather wood beside the hearth
Evenings cooler, morning dew
Skies are russet, pinky blue
Grass is lush, toadstool pale
Rainbow shows above hay bale
End of summer not too soon
Transition after harvest moon.

Deborah Hall
Wiltshire

If I Had My Way

If I had my way, I'd like our Earth to be,
A planet worthy of hosting the beauty that we see.
A world that's full of humans, determined to ensure,
A fairer deal, a better life, for the sick, oppressed and poor.

Each element of life on Earth was crafted with such care.
To each of us the chance was given to claim our rightful share.
But there are those upon this Earth taking far more than they need.
Driven by the human bug of selfish, envious greed.

So hence we have a planet, divided, sliced in two.
In Africa its tenants starve under a blistering sky of blue.
While the people of other continents profit from their toil,
They rest in luxurious comfort and thus the planet spoil.

I'd like to lift the world up high and shake it with great force,
So that everything is jumbled and the Earth can change its course.
To head for a world that's tolerant, where love is held so dear,
Where hate and hunger are banished along with pain and fear.

Alison Adams
Wiltshire

November The Fifth

There's dancing in the square tonight
Singing in the street,
While rockets race towards the sky
Where stars collide
But fail to hide, their brief celestial flight.

Bonfires blaze, children laugh,
In memory of old Guy.
Angelic faces, young and bright;
Stunned by such an awesome sight.
Gloved fingers wrapped round cheesy dips,
There's jacket spuds and ketchupped lips.
The straw-stuffed body burning fast
Reminder of a turbulent past.
Remember, remember, till this time next year
We shall be older, but Guy will be here.
Ageless, resurrected!

Ann Wardlaw
Wiltshire

Nan

I've written a poem all about my nan
She always laughs, I'm her number one fan
I go and see her Tuesdays and Mondays
I'm telling you this, they are always fun days
She sits on the settee and watches the telly,
She's got four grandchildren, me, Laura, Mark and Kelly,
When you arrive, her house is all cosy,
She's always happy, her cheeks red rosy.

Daniel Golby
Wiltshire

Niger

Mamsai was the mother
Of a family of six,
Living in starving Niger
She really was in a fix.

There was no food to be had,
No meals for two days,
How could she feed her family?
Not any hope could she raise.

Umbe, her husband,
Went out to have a look
To see if there was anything
That his wife could cook.

A rat ran over his foot,
In a second he had it fast,
Here was an opportunity
To eat food at last.

The family was delighted
When he brought home the meal,
They anticipated the repast
Their stomach pains would heal.

So they boiled the rat
And cut it into six,
They joyfully ate the food,
Their hunger they had fixed.

How would we fare
Who have three meals a day,
To carve up a rat for six,
And be joyful all the way?

Rita Hardiman
Worcestershire

Malvern

In thinking of Malvern, I picture the hills,
The majesty, the beauty, the history,
In summer - breathtaking, in winter - exciting!
While - low clouds, shroud them in mystery!
But Malvern has much more to offer,
Age-old churches, a castle, a priory,
Winding lanes, common land, wandering sheep,
All, well worth a date in your diary!
Quaint old-time villages, meandering streams,
A spa town in its days of glory,
Surrounded with history, all in the past,
Each place, with its own, oft told, story.
Something for everyone, young or old.
It's 'ancient and modern' - entwined,
Bringing the future, with new styled homes,
Yet - conservation, still underlined!
Steep, hilly roads, patches of woods,
Trees - with a story to tell,
New supermarkets, to steal the scene,
A great library, colleges, a pure, well!
The priory, has features, from days of yore,
The hills - by-laws, unto themselves!
Ancient markets, antique shops, from the past,
New shops, new things on their shelves!
It's a real mixture of old and new,
With a population to match!
It's called Malvern, in Worcestershire,
In case - my *drift* you failed to catch!

E M Eagle
Worcestershire

Remember A Laugh

What is a barrel of laughs?
Is it something you find in a pub?
Or is it the thing you get from your friends
When you go dancing one night in a club?

You can never tell where you'll find them
They can get you at your most unawares
But it's always good to have one
To ease your mind of your worries and cares.

So next time that you're feeling down
Remember a joke, or event
The time that you had a laugh with friends
Is a time in your life well spent.

Tina Garrington
Worcestershire

It's A Dog's Life

My dad takes me for lovely long walks,
I've been on my first today,
Down to the park, it's smashing
I can race around and play.

But it looks like they're going shopping again,
Oh why can't they ever take me?
If I sit in my bed with pathetic sad eyes
A change of heart I may see.

In supermarket I'd be OK,
Midst tinned stuff, and fruit I'd be fine,
I'm partial to a bit of cooked veg
Mum puts in my dinner sometimes.

In the butcher's I'm sure I'd be welcome,
Like a birthday that would be,
To give me a pat, and a cuddle
And a big juicy bone all for me.

But when notice says *no dogs allowed,*
I suppose that must include me,
So it's off for another long walk, with my dad
Back home to Mum's grub for my tea.

Dorothy M Mitchell
Worcestershire

The Lost Hobby

For twenty years my feet have trod the rich
Brown earth of Devon, by the Torridge edge,
And every spring the Hobby brought his pledge
To stay and call and fly o'er forests which
Have grown, been culled, and grown again once more,
And in their darkness and their surging height
My friend has nested, dusk and morning light,
And chased the swallows as they swerve and soar;
But not this year; no more the urgent call,
The sweeping circle high above the trees,
The prayer of thanks - from me - for pleasure gained,
The yearly bounty from my friend obtained,
Seen far into the sky in sun and breeze -
I know not where was borne his final pall
But here the quiet diminishes us all.

John Peaston
Worcestershire

On Tresco Isle

On Tresco Isle where summer seawinds blow,
clear anchored waters merge green into blue,
and coloured blossoms in all sweetness grow.

On beaches, silver shells when tides are low,
and shining silken sands sweep out of view,
on Tresco Isle where summer seawinds blow.

Grand hedges rise in fields carved long ago,
while pretty songbirds chorus long and true
and coloured blossoms in all sweetness grow.

Grey guardian rocks are watching ebb and flow
of painted boats and sails of varied hue,
on Tresco Isle where summer seawinds blow.

Eternal spirits call and time is slow.
In dreamtime gardens Gaia wakes anew
and coloured blossoms in all sweetness grow.

Awash with liquid gold the sunsets glow
and stars spill onto waves as moons wax new,
on Tresco Isle where summer seawinds blow
and coloured blossoms in all sweetness grow.

Helen Dalgleish
Worcestershire

The Calling

You do everything
You are the right in all my wrongs
I cannot be without you
You made my song
You wrote the words
Held on for so long
Nothing could take you away
The raging storm
Could not drag you from today
Holding tight, to love
To simplicity
To love me whole
In an unique yet possible way.

Bryony Freeman
Worcestershire

Anchor Books Information

We hope you have enjoyed reading this book - and that you will continue to enjoy it in the coming years.

If you like reading and writing poetry drop us a line, or give us a call, and we'll send you a free information pack.

Alternatively if you would like to order further copies of this book or any of our other titles, then please give us a call or visit our website at www.forwardpress.co.uk

anchorbooks

Anchor Books Information
Remus House
Coltsfoot Drive
Peterborough
PE2 9JX

Tel: 01733 898102